# ABSOLUTELY EVERYTHING YOU NEED TO KNOW

# LEGO®

# ABSOLUTELY EVERYTHING YOU NEED TO KNOW

Written by
**SIMON HUGO**

# CONTENTS

# CHAPTER ONE

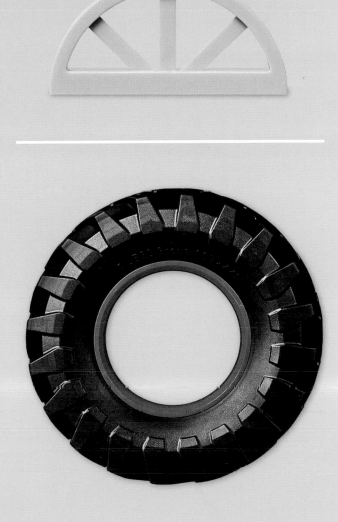

# BRICKS AND PIECES

# BEFORE THE BRICK

In the years before LEGO® bricks, the LEGO Group made a wide selection of toys, first crafted from wood, and then from plastic.

## WOW!

The wooden LEGO Tractor from 1949 may look basic, but it has functional front-wheel steering, just like a LEGO® Technic set.

## FACT STACK

The LEGO Group founder, Ole Kirk Kristiansen, crafted his first wooden toys in 1932.

The first playthings to be sold bearing the LEGO brand name were produced in 1934.

Wooden LEGO toys of the 1930s included the first-ever LEGO cars and trains.

The LEGO Group made its first plastic toys in 1947, alongside its range of wooden items.

## REALLY?!

When a craze for wooden yo-yos ended, the LEGO Group turned its leftover stock into colourful wheels for other toys!

## TOP 5

**Pull-along wooden LEGO toys**

**1** **Duck** opens and closes his beak.

**2** **Clumsy Hans** bobs up and down.

**3** **Monkey** rocks back and forth.

**4** **Dog** turns his head and wags his tail.

**5** **Chickens** peck the ground in turn.

**Q** | Are there any wooden LEGO bricks?

**A** | No – but there were wooden LEGO blocks. From 1946, stackable cubes were made for early learners. They were painted with brightly coloured letters and numbers.

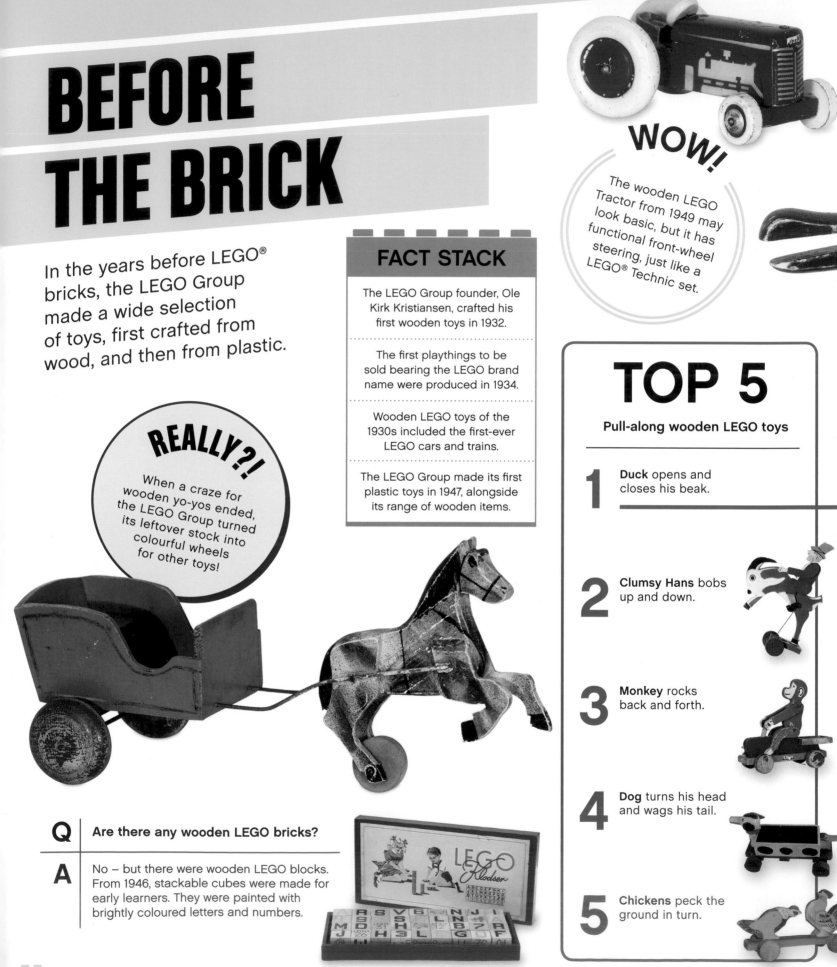

# AWESOME!

One of the first sets to feature plastic playing pieces, Monypoli was a 1948 board game with squares that spelled out the word "LEGO".

## 28

Wooden toys were listed in Ole Kirk Kristiansen's first product catalogue in 1932, including a fire truck, a race car and an aeroplane.

## Brick History

One of the most popular early LEGO toys, 1935's wooden LEGO Duck was recreated as a modern, brick-built LEGO set in 2011 and given to LEGO Group employees as a Christmas gift.

## BRICK CHALLENGE

Choose your favourite from the toys shown here, then make a 21st-century version using your LEGO bricks.

## IT'S A SIGN!

As a mark of quality and authenticity, most wooden LEGO toys were labelled with a sticker showing an early LEGO logo and proudly proclaiming: "BILLUND DENMARK".

## SANDBOX GAME

The first LEGO construction toy was Kirk's Kuglebane ("Kirk's Ball Track", also known as "Kirk's Sand Game"). Released in 1935, it comprised small wooden blocks that could be arranged in a sandbox to make a track for a metal ball.

## PLASTIC PLAYTIME

Some of the first plastic LEGO toys included a baby's rattle shaped like a fish and a sailor figure that could slide down a rope.

# GET WITH THE SYSTEM

Conceived in 1955, the simple but innovative idea that every plastic LEGO element should be part of a wider "System" is still at the heart of LEGO building today.

## Brick History

In 1954, Godtfred Kirk Christiansen came up with the idea for the LEGO System in Play when the chief buyer for a major Danish department store complained that the toy industry had "no system of any kind"!

## FACT STACK

Since 1955, the majority of LEGO sets have been part of the LEGO System in Play.

The LEGO System in Play means that LEGO sets never become obsolete.

The LEGO System in Play is divided into different "themes" that are all compatible.

Modern LEGO System themes include LEGO® NINJAGO®, LEGO® City and LEGO® Friends.

## WOW!

Lots of prototype pieces were made to perfect the "clutch power" that fastens LEGO bricks together without making them too hard to pull apart.

## 915,103,765

The number of ways that six classic 2x4 LEGO bricks of the same colour can be combined.

Today's 2x4 LEGO bricks have exactly the same measurements as the ones made in the 1950s. They will fit perfectly with any brick from the past 60 years.

## KEY DATES

### 1949

The company's first plastic bricks are sold as "Automatic Binding Bricks". They have studs on top, but no tubes underneath, and slits on two sides.

### 1953
Automatic Binding Bricks are officially renamed "LEGO Bricks" ("LEGO Mursten" in Danish). The LEGO name is moulded onto each stud for the first time.

### 1955

The LEGO System in Play launches with the LEGO Town Plan: 28 LEGO brick building sets plus eight vehicles, all designed to be used together.

### 1957

Tubes are built into the underside of LEGO bricks so that they clutch securely to the studs on top of the one below. The new bricks go on sale in 1958.

### 1958
Stud-and-tube interlocking is one of several brick-building systems covered by the LEGO brick patent, awarded on January 28.

**1**

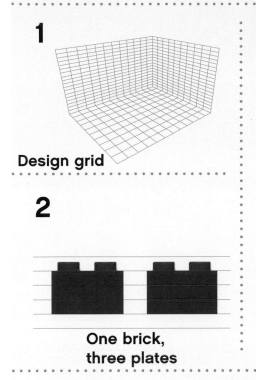

Design grid

**2**

One brick,
three plates

**3**

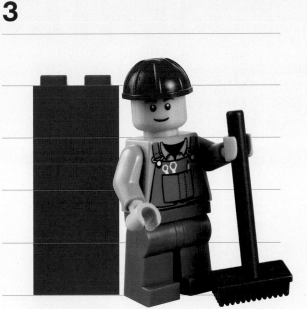

Four bricks

## ON THE GRID

1 To ensure all elements
fit in the LEGO System in
Play, new LEGO parts are
designed according to
a three-dimensional grid.

2 Making sure all LEGO
elements align within the
grid increases the potential
for parts to serve more than
one function – in future sets
or simply in creative play.

3 Even specialised pieces
such as minifigures and
accessories must conform
to the grid. This ensures
they can connect with
other pieces in as many
ways as possible.

## BRICK CHALLENGE

There are 24 ways to combine
two 2x4 LEGO bricks. See if
you can find them all!

**Q** What are LEGO bricks made from?

**A** Until 1963, LEGO bricks were
made from cellulose acetate.
Since then, they have been
made from a different type of
plastic – acrylonitrile butadiene
styrene (ABS) – which is more
durable and colourfast.

## WOW!

When a LEGO
Technic pin is inserted
into a LEGO Technic
hole, it makes a sound
that LEGO employees
refer to as a
"rewarding click"!

## REALLY?!

In 2009, there
were thought to be 62
LEGO bricks for every
person in the world.
Today, the estimate
stands at 102!

## Piece particulars

Some LEGO elements are
named after the
designer that made
them. The Erling brick is
one of them, named
after LEGO Designer
Erling Dideriksen who
invented this element
in 1979.

## MAKING PLANS

Before LEGO "themes" as we know
them today, Town Plan sets were
the first LEGO products to combine
small, brick-built models into an
ever-growing urban scene.

# ELEMENT ESSENTIALS

Right from the early days of LEGO sets, there have been especially useful LEGO elements to help you build in various different ways. Many of those are still around today. Here are 25 bricks and pieces that really put the fun in fundamentals.

**Start here!**

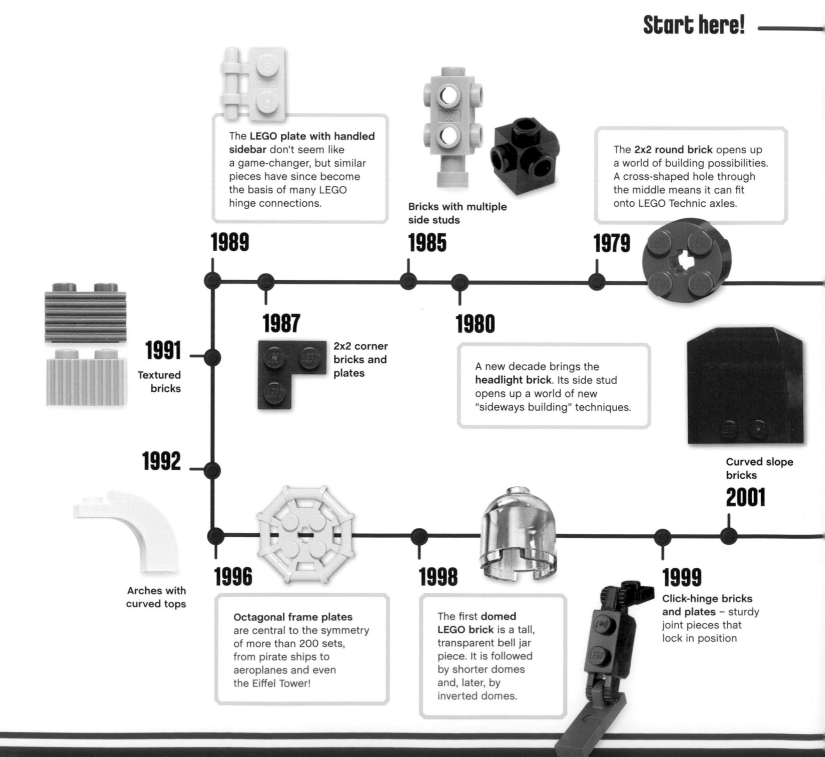

The **LEGO plate with handled sidebar** don't seem like a game-changer, but similar pieces have since become the basis of many LEGO hinge connections.

Bricks with multiple side studs

The **2x2 round brick** opens up a world of building possibilities. A cross-shaped hole through the middle means it can fit onto LEGO Technic axles.

**1989**

**1985**

**1979**

**1987**

**1980**

2x2 corner bricks and plates

**1991**

Textured bricks

A new decade brings the **headlight brick**. Its side stud opens up a world of new "sideways building" techniques.

Curved slope bricks

**2001**

**1992**

**1996**

**1998**

**1999**

Arches with curved tops

Octagonal frame plates are central to the symmetry of more than 200 sets, from pirate ships to aeroplanes and even the Eiffel Tower!

The first **domed LEGO brick** is a tall, transparent bell jar piece. It is followed by shorter domes and, later, by inverted domes.

Click-hinge bricks and plates – sturdy joint pieces that lock in position

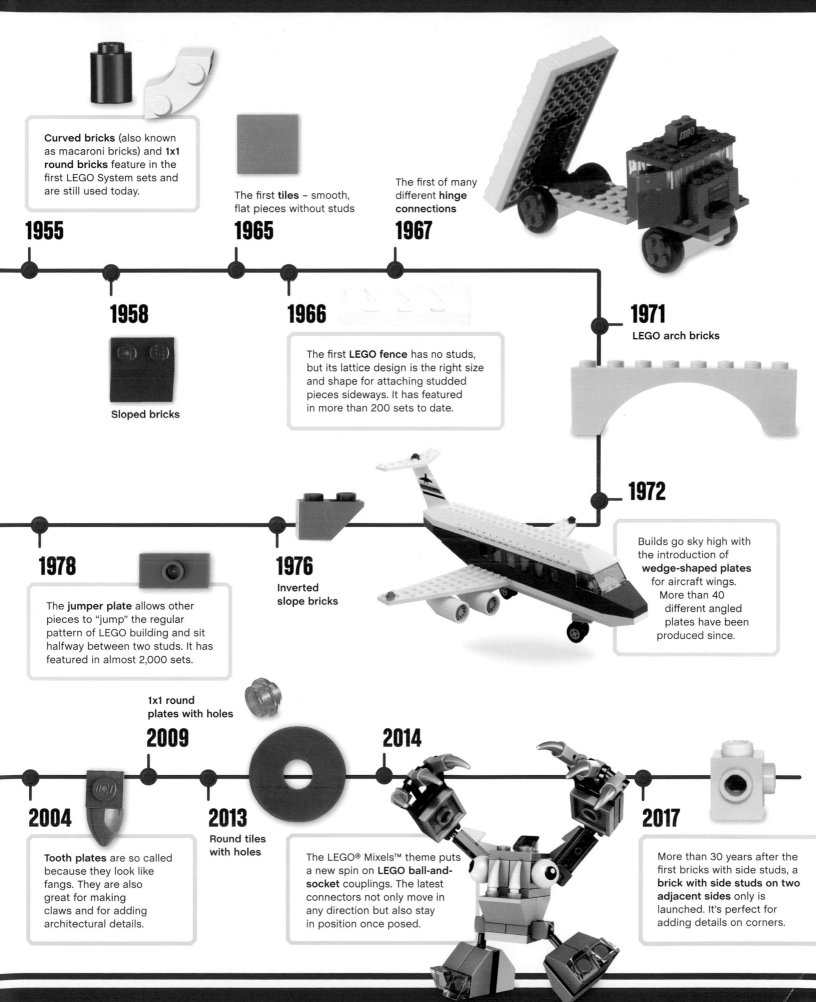

**Curved bricks** (also known as macaroni bricks) and **1x1 round bricks** feature in the first LEGO System sets and are still used today.

**1955**

The first **tiles** – smooth, flat pieces without studs

**1965**

The first of many different **hinge connections**

**1967**

**1958**

Sloped bricks

**1966**

The first **LEGO fence** has no studs, but its lattice design is the right size and shape for attaching studded pieces sideways. It has featured in more than 200 sets to date.

**1971**

LEGO arch bricks

**1972**

Builds go sky high with the introduction of **wedge-shaped plates** for aircraft wings. More than 40 different angled plates have been produced since.

**1978**

The **jumper plate** allows other pieces to "jump" the regular pattern of LEGO building and sit halfway between two studs. It has featured in almost 2,000 sets.

**1976**

Inverted slope bricks

1x1 round plates with holes

**2009**

**2014**

**2004**

**Tooth plates** are so called because they look like fangs. They are also great for making claws and for adding architectural details.

**2013**

Round tiles with holes

The LEGO® Mixels™ theme puts a new spin on **LEGO ball-and-socket** couplings. The latest connectors not only move in any direction but also stay in position once posed.

**2017**

More than 30 years after the first bricks with side studs, a **brick with side studs on two adjacent sides** only is launched. It's perfect for adding details on corners.

## TALLEST TYRE

The LEGO® Technic CLAAS XERION 5000 TRAC VC tractor (set 42054) has tyres that measure a whopping 4.21in (107mm) in diameter.

# REINVENTING THE WHEEL

One good turn deserves another, and there's always a new LEGO wheel rolling into view! Here are the top tyres and weirdest wheels...

**AWESOME!** The most wheels on an individual vehicle (not including trains and trucks with trailers) is 14 on the LEGO City Cargo Plane (set 7734) from 2008.

# TOP 5

**Wheels that make the LEGO world go round**

1 Steering wheel (1978)

2 Cartwheel (1985)

3 Ship's wheel (1985)

4 Fancy carriage wheel (2014)

5 Wheelchair wheel (2016)

## HEAVIEST TYRE

The heaviest LEGO tyres were made for the LEGO Technic Power Puller (set 8457). Each 6oz (170g) tyre weighs more than 150 standard LEGO City car tyres.

**WOW!** LEGO City Tyre Escape (set 60126) features one large tyre but no wheels. It is used as a boat by an escaping crook!

# 730,000,000+

Number of LEGO tyres produced in 2016, making the LEGO Group one of the world's biggest tyre manufacturers.

## SMALLEST LEGO WHEEL

Skateboard axle, with a diameter of 0.3in (80mm)

*SMALL BUT MIGHTY!*

## WEIRDEST WHEEL

The wheel on the LEGO® *Star Wars*™ Hailfire Droid (set 4481) turns within a LEGO Technic frame instead of on a central axle. It is also the biggest LEGO wheel ever made, at more than 8.3in (210mm) in diameter.

## FACT STACK

The first LEGO System wheels were launched in April 1962.

The first wheels came in a set of four and were red with light grey rubber tires.

By 1968, LEGO tyres came in two sizes and were all black.

Today, there are more than 300 LEGO wheel and tyre variants.

## Brick History

The first LEGO wheel designed to run on a rail track was released in 1966. It was also the first to be powered by a motor in Motorised Train Set (set 113).

**Q** Are modern LEGO tyres always black?

**A** Not quite always. A rare exception is a set of four white tyres included in the LEGO® *Spongebob Squarepants*™ Bikini Bottom Express (set 3830) in 2008.

POST    POST    HAMBURG  BASEL  GENOVA

# THE LEGO® COLOUR CHART

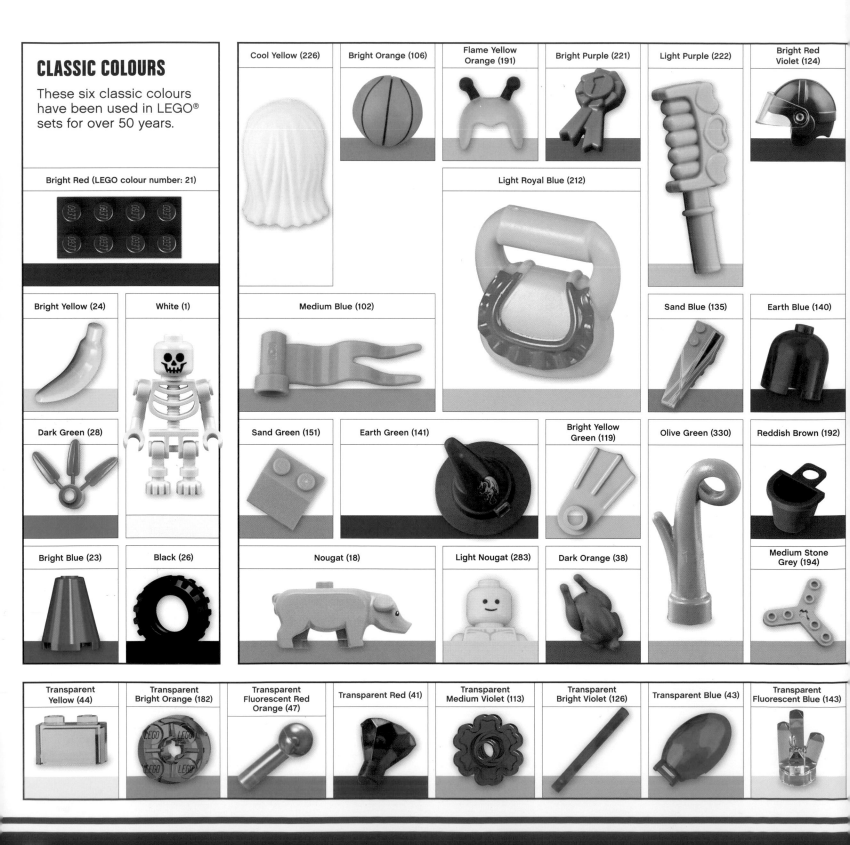

## CLASSIC COLOURS

These six classic colours have been used in LEGO® sets for over 50 years.

**Bright Red (LEGO colour number: 21)**

**Bright Yellow (24)**

**White (1)**

**Dark Green (28)**

**Bright Blue (23)**

**Black (26)**

**Cool Yellow (226)**

**Bright Orange (106)**

**Flame Yellow Orange (191)**

**Bright Purple (221)**

**Light Purple (222)**

**Bright Red Violet (124)**

**Light Royal Blue (212)**

**Medium Blue (102)**

**Sand Blue (135)**

**Earth Blue (140)**

**Sand Green (151)**

**Earth Green (141)**

**Bright Yellow Green (119)**

**Olive Green (330)**

**Reddish Brown (192)**

**Nougat (18)**

**Light Nougat (283)**

**Dark Orange (38)**

**Medium Stone Grey (194)**

**Transparent Yellow (44)**

**Transparent Bright Orange (182)**

**Transparent Fluorescent Red Orange (47)**

**Transparent Red (41)**

**Transparent Medium Violet (113)**

**Transparent Bright Violet (126)**

**Transparent Blue (43)**

**Transparent Fluorescent Blue (143)**

LEGO elements have been made in more than 150 shades since the 1950s. Some colours have come and gone, including solid neons and shades with glitter. This rainbow of colour covers hues that are currently in production.

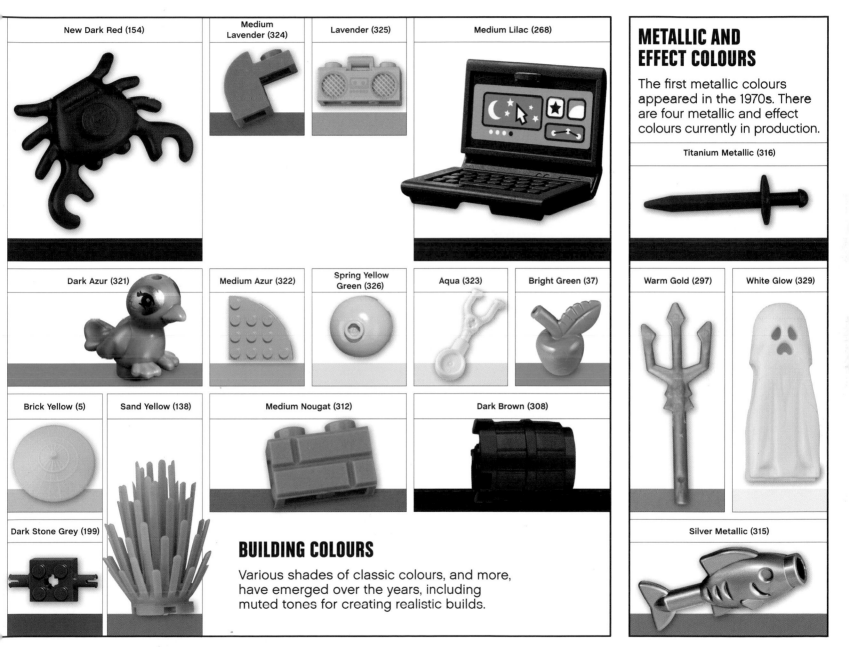

New Dark Red (154)

Medium Lavender (324)

Lavender (325)

Medium Lilac (268)

Dark Azur (321)

Medium Azur (322)

Spring Yellow Green (326)

Aqua (323)

Bright Green (37)

Brick Yellow (5)

Sand Yellow (138)

Medium Nougat (312)

Dark Brown (308)

Dark Stone Grey (199)

## METALLIC AND EFFECT COLOURS

The first metallic colours appeared in the 1970s. There are four metallic and effect colours currently in production.

Titanium Metallic (316)

Warm Gold (297)

White Glow (329)

Silver Metallic (315)

## BUILDING COLOURS

Various shades of classic colours, and more, have emerged over the years, including muted tones for creating realistic builds.

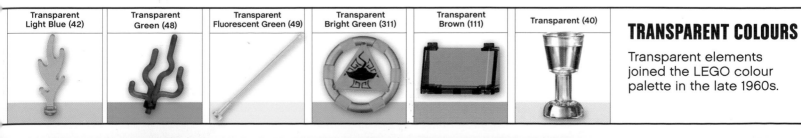

Transparent Light Blue (42)

Transparent Green (48)

Transparent Fluorescent Green (49)

Transparent Bright Green (311)

Transparent Brown (111)

Transparent (40)

## TRANSPARENT COLOURS

Transparent elements joined the LEGO colour palette in the late 1960s.

# THE PATH TO POWER

Lots of electrical innovations have brought light, sound and movement to LEGO sets over the years, culminating in today's "Power Functions".

New "Code Pilot" technology emerges in **LEGO Technic Barcode Multi-Set** (set 8479). Scanning special barcodes controls the speed, sound and actions of this motorised tipper truck.

**Start here!**

The **LEGO® MINDSTORMS® sets** appear. They use infrared technology to send instructions from your home computer to "smart bricks" built into a range of robots.

**1998**

**1998**

**1997**

With instructions for building five powered cars, **Radio Control Racer** (set 5600) is the first set to come with a wireless remote-control unit.

The LEGO® Studios theme launches with a **digital camera** built like a large LEGO element. The camera can be fixed into place for making stop-motion LEGO movies.

The LEGO® Space UFO **Interstellar Starfighter** (set 6979) is one of the only sets to feature fibre-optic cables, which light up with an eerie alien glow.

**2000**

**2002**

The compact **LEGO Technic Speed Computer** (set 5206) appears, allowing you to measure the speed, travel time and distance covered by your vehicle builds.

Send any **LEGO® Spybotics** set on an undercover mission and it will follow your programmed instructions, using light and touch sensors to find its way.

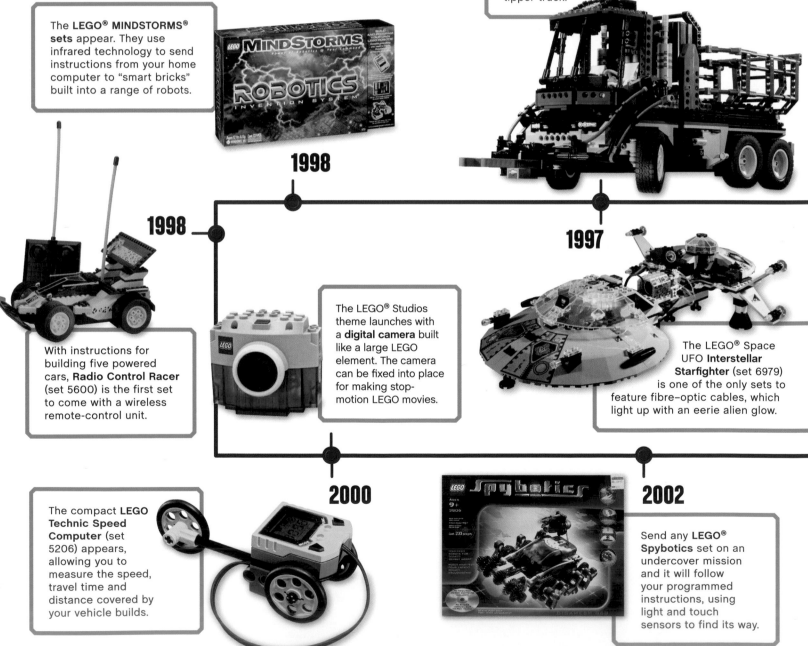

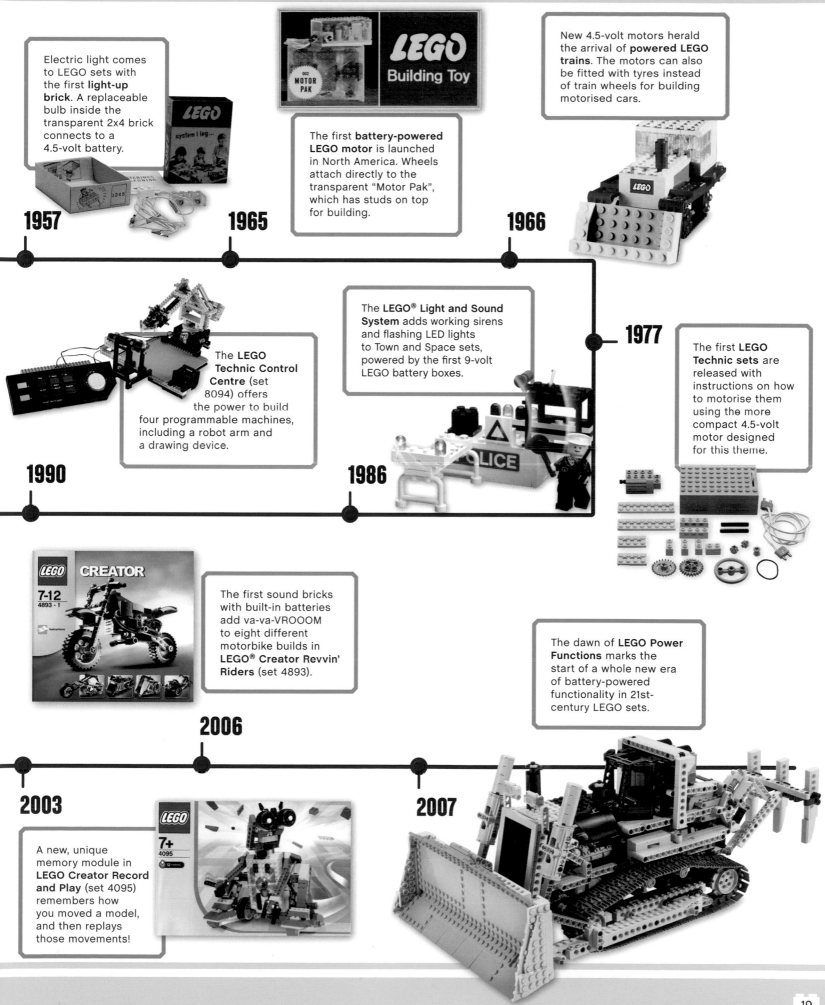

Electric light comes to LEGO sets with the first **light-up brick**. A replaceable bulb inside the transparent 2x4 brick connects to a 4.5-volt battery.

**1957**

**1965**

The first **battery-powered LEGO motor** is launched in North America. Wheels attach directly to the transparent "Motor Pak", which has studs on top for building.

LEGO Building Toy

New 4.5-volt motors herald the arrival of **powered LEGO trains**. The motors can also be fitted with tyres instead of train wheels for building motorised cars.

**1966**

The **LEGO® Light and Sound System** adds working sirens and flashing LED lights to Town and Space sets, powered by the first 9-volt LEGO battery boxes.

**1977**

The first **LEGO Technic sets** are released with instructions on how to motorise them using the more compact 4.5-volt motor designed for this theme.

The **LEGO Technic Control Centre** (set 8094) offers the power to build four programmable machines, including a robot arm and a drawing device.

**1990**

**1986**

The first sound bricks with built-in batteries add va-va-VROOOM to eight different motorbike builds in **LEGO® Creator Revvin' Riders** (set 4893).

CREATOR
7-12
4893 - 1

The dawn of **LEGO Power Functions** marks the start of a whole new era of battery-powered functionality in 21st-century LEGO sets.

**2006**

**2003**

A new, unique memory module in **LEGO Creator Record and Play** (set 4095) remembers how you moved a model, and then replays those movements!

7+
4095

**2007**

# THE ELECTRIC COMPANY

## Piece particulars

The LEGO City Coast Guard Helicopter and Life Raft (set 7738) from 2008 features a small Power Functions winch that winds up without a battery.

Since 2007, the LEGO Group has used "Power Functions" motors and other special elements to animate and illuminate sets in ways never seen before.

## Brick statistics

### Grand Carousel (set 10196)

**3,263 pieces**
Including a Power Functions motor

**13.8in (35cm) high**
And 15in (38cm) across

**8 LEGO Technic camshafts**
Make the ride rise and fall as it turns

**6 AA (1.5V) batteries**
Hidden beneath ride operator's platform

**1 sound brick**
Plays music as the carousel turns

**Q** Can Power Functions be added to any LEGO set?

**A** Anything is possible with a little imagination! But to get you started, a few sets come with instructions for adding Power Functions, such as the LEGO® Mars Mission MT-61 Crystal Reaper (set 7645) from 2008.

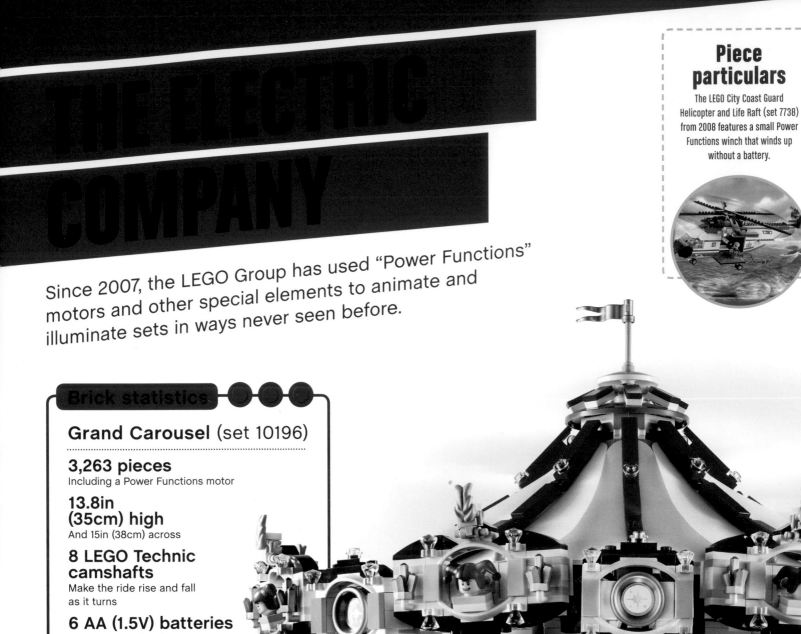

# AWESOME!

The 2007 LEGO Creator Monster Dino (set 4958) can walk, wield its claws, bare its fangs and ROAR!

## TOP 5

**Sets with special light bricks**

**1** Winter Toy Shop (set 10199)

**2** Fiery Legend (set 6751)

**3** Rescue Robot (set 5764)

**4** UFO Abduction (set 7052)

**5** Lighthouse Point (set 31051)

## 20,000

Number of unique number plates created for the limited-run LEGO Technic Power Functions 4x4 Crawler Exclusive Edition (set 41999) in 2013.

EK 00001
of 20000

## FACT STACK

Most LEGO Power Functions motors are just six studs long and three studs wide.

More than 20 LEGO Technic sets have featured Power Functions motors since 2007.

A Power Functions motor with built-in steering features in just two 2009 LEGO Racers sets.

Since 2010, all LEGO City Trains have run on special Power Functions motors.

THIS RIDE HAS REAL HORSE POWER!

## WOW!

The 2010 LEGO Technic Motorised Excavator (set 8043) uses four Power Functions motors – for driving, turning, digging and lifting.

## Brick History

In 2008, a limited edition Wind Turbine (set 4999) was produced in partnership with Danish renewable energy firm Vestas. The set included a Power Functions motor to make its rotors spin.

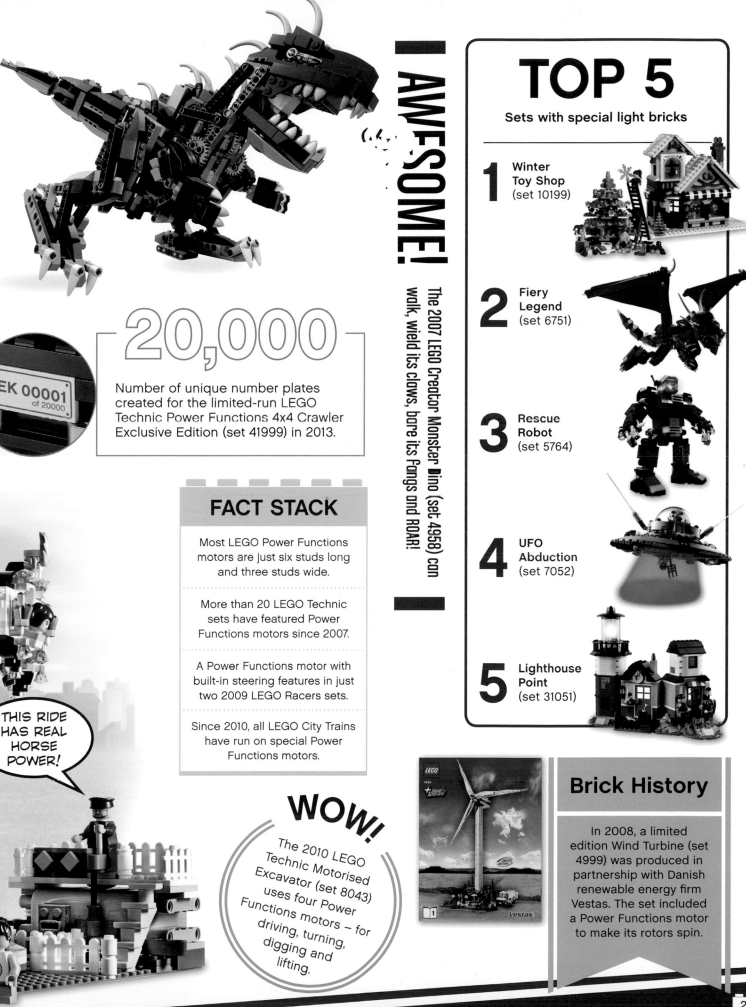

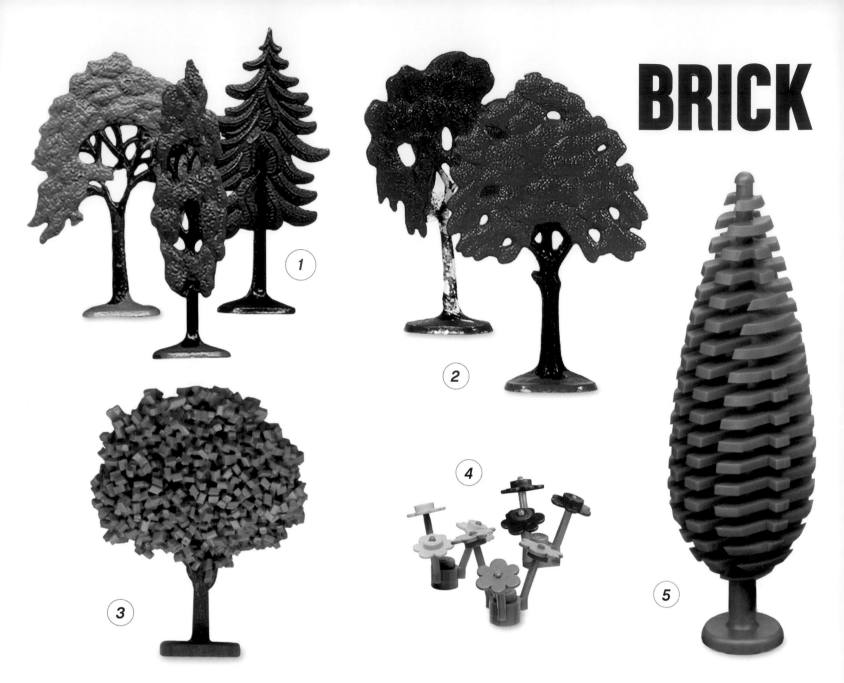

# Notable plants and flowers of the LEGO world

1    **Trees and Bushes (set 230).**
     Rare; these trees were designed
     to add greenery to the LEGO
     Town Plan theme of the 1950s,
     but could not be built onto
     other elements.

2    **Trees and Bushes (set 490).** Rare;
     in the mid 1960s, LEGO trees
     were redesigned with bases
     that could be built onto other

elements, but retained their
detailed, real-world look.

3    **Fruit tree from Trees and Signs
     (set 990).** Rare; most LEGO
     elements are made from tiny
     granules of ABS plastic that are
     heated and shaped in a mould.
     For this 1970s LEGO tree, those
     granules were only partially
     melted to create a unique look.

4    **Flowers.** Widespread; the most
     abundant and diverse flora in
     the LEGO biosphere, LEGO
     flowers bloom most commonly
     in red, but also in blue, yellow,
     white and four shades of pink.

5    **Cypress tree.** Rare; dating back
     to the time of the first LEGO®
     Castle sets, this tree was found in
     just a handful of sets in the 1980s.

# BOTANY

6 **Sea grass.** Widespread; frequently found in underwater habitats, but also seen on mountains, in parks and on islands.

7 **Pine tree.** Widespread; the most common LEGO tree appears in over 100 sets. A hardy evergreen, it is also found snow-capped in two discontinued wintry sets.

8 **Palm tree.** Widespread; originally limited to tropical areas frequented by LEGO® Pirates, a variety with shorter leaves (pictured) has since been found in Heartlake City, home of LEGO® Friends.

9 **Leafy vine**. Restricted; recently discovered by LEGO® botanists, this flexible vine has been established in Heartlake City.

10 **Fruit tree.** Relict; once a familiar sight in LEGO Town and LEGO City, this fruit tree was last seen in 2010. A scarce lime variety was found in one Creator set in 2013.

11 **Prickly bush.** Widespread; this adaptable shrub has been noted in at least 120 locations, mostly in green but also in tan, dark tan and red.

## KEY DATES

### 1977
Also known as Expert Builder Sets, the first Technical Set models include a forklift truck, a tractor and a helicopter.

### 1984
The LEGO Technic theme name appears on boxes for the first time, and the first pneumatic sets use compressed air pumps to power machine functions.

### 1990
The battery-powered Control Centre (set 8094) brings basic programming functionality to LEGO Technic sets for the first time.

### 1999
A forerunner of LEGO BIONICLE, the LEGO Technic Slizer subtheme (known as Throwbots in North America) stars disc-throwing alien robots!

### 2007
Remote-controlled Power Functions add new electronic features to larger LEGO Technic sets. Motorised Bulldozer (set 8275) was the first, and won the Nuremberg Innovation Award.

### 2017
Celebrating 40 years of LEGO Technic, this vehicle can be built using pieces from three LEGO Technic sets (42057, 42061 and 42063), with instructions available at LEGO.com.

**Q** Why do most LEGO Technic beams have an odd number of holes when most LEGO bricks have an even number of studs?

**A** Because any beam with an odd number of holes will always have a connecting point right in the middle – and combining two such beams still allows for even-numbered lengths.

## Brick History

In 1996, the first LEGO Technic studless beam appeared in Space Shuttle (set 8480). Today, studless beams have largely replaced brick-style beams in LEGO Technic sets.

## LOOK CLOSER

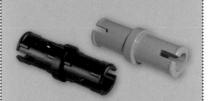

Not all LEGO Technic pins are created equal! Black and blue pins have extra ridges so that they make a tighter connection than grey and tan-coloured ones.

## WOW!
The LEGO Technic *Star Wars* Destroyer Droid (set 8002) uses rubber bands to spring into attack mode when you roll it along!

## AWESOME!
More than a dozen LEGO Technic sets feature pullback motors so they can speed into action without needing batteries.

## BRICK CHALLENGE

Use the LEGO Technic gears in your collection to add movement to a set from another theme.

### Brick statistics

**90+ LEGO Technic cars**
From go-karts to F1 racers

**50+ construction vehicles**
Diggers, cranes, dozers and more

**40+ trucks and tractors**
One of which turns into a robot!

**35+ motorcycles**
Including trikes and ATVs

**30+ aeroplanes and helicopters**
Plus a single space shuttle

**IT'S A SIGN!** Every LEGO Technic set released in 2017 comes with a special printed beam celebrating the theme's 40th anniversary.

## FACT STACK

The first LEGO gears came out in 1965. They are not compatible with LEGO Technic elements.

There are more than 20 types of LEGO Technic gear, counting rack and pinion elements.

LEGO® BIONICLE® elements were originally designed as part of the LEGO Technic theme.

Today, many large LEGO sets rely on LEGO Technic beams and connectors at their cores.

**40** Teeth on the largest LEGO Technic gearwheel.

### Piece particulars

Since 1991, flexible rods have added curves to LEGO Technic sets - sometimes for functional reasons, and sometimes just to look cool!

## TOP 5

Essential LEGO Technic elements

**1** **Beams** form the "skeleton" of any LEGO Technic vehicle.

**2** **Pins** connect beams and other parts at any angle.

**3** **Axles** slot through beams to connect moving parts.

**4** **Gears** are wheels with teeth that turn on axles.

**5** **Bushes** space out elements and hold axles in place.

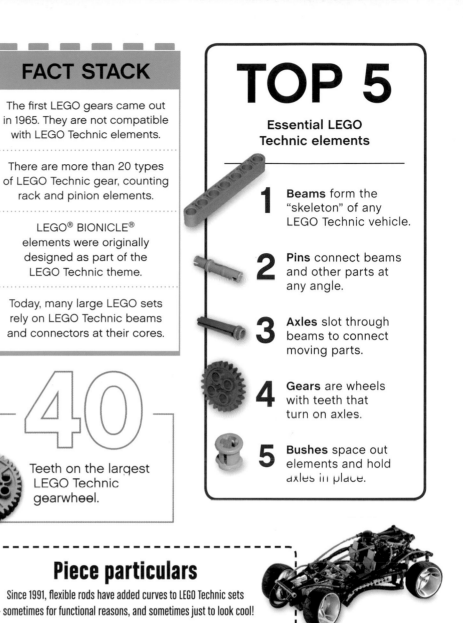

# LET'S GET TECHNICAL

Over the past 40 years, budding engineers have been using LEGO Technic elements to build bigger, more complex models full of moving parts and working mechanisms.

# LEGO® HOMEMAKING

## Doors

## Windows

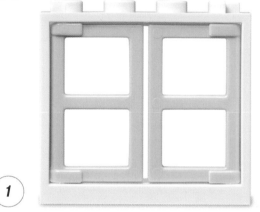

1 **Door with four panes.** This iconic shape was introduced in 1978 and updated in 2008.

2 **Arched door.** This rounded door shape emerged in 2001 for the launch of the LEGO® *Harry Potter*™ theme.

3 **Door with six panes.** This right-handed door appeared in over 20 sets from 1983. A left-handed version came with one 1984 set: Cargo Centre (set 6391).

4 **Door with stud handle.** This door builds into a corner at an angle. It often appears in LEGO® Creative loose-brick boxes, to help fans build their own homes.

1 **Classic.** Technically three pieces (two panes and a frame), this is the most common LEGO window shape.

2 **Lattice.** This old-world-style window has been made in 15 colours. It can even be found in pink.

3 **Panel.** A clear panel clicks into this simple window frame. Some sets come with coloured panes or stickers on the panel.

4 **Fanlight.** This curved window was inspired by classical-style architecture. It appeared in LEGO sets from 2015.

# Fences

**1**    ***Picket fence.*** It is no surprise that white is the most common colour for this piece.

**2**    ***Bar railing.*** This fence piece has a colourful history: it appeared as a pink dance bar in 1996 and in sand green in 2015.

**3**    ***Spindled fence.*** In 2003, this fence with four top studs replaced a version with two studs – one on each end.

**4**    ***Lattice fence.*** A true classic, the 1x4x1 fence panel has been in production since 1966.

**5**    ***Ornamental fence.*** This decorative piece was first found in the fantastical world of LEGO® Elves in 2015.

# Finishing touches

**1**    ***Cupboard.*** These simple cupboards have provided storage for minifigures for more than 30 years.

**2**    ***Drawer.*** Featuring the same basic box element as the cupboard, drawers also help to keep LEGO homes tidy.

**3**    ***Mixer tap.*** This decorative tap has added style to kitchens and bathrooms since 2002.

**4**    ***Mailbox.*** These hinged elements can also be found in sets as fridges, ovens or even as part of a grandfather clock.

# PLENTY OF PIECES

There are several ways to define the biggest LEGO set, but the most common way is to count the number of pieces a set contains. These LEGO behemoths are the five most piece-heavy sets ever.

## 1

### 5,922 PIECES
### TAJ MAHAL

| | |
|---|---|
| SET NUMBER | 10189 |
| YEAR RELEASED | 2008 |
| HEIGHT | 16in (41cm) |
| WIDTH | 20in (51cm) |

## 3

**4,634 PIECES**
**LEGO® GHOSTBUSTERS™: FIREHOUSE HEADQUARTERS**

| | |
|---|---|
| **SET NUMBER** | 75827 |
| **YEAR RELEASED** | 2016 |
| **HEIGHT** | 14in (36cm) |
| **LENGTH** | 14in (36cm) |

## 2

**5,197 PIECES**
**ULTIMATE COLLECTOR'S**
*MILLENNIUM FALCON*

| | |
|---|---|
| **SET NUMBER** | 10179 |
| **YEAR RELEASED** | 2007 |
| **WIDTH** | 12in (32cm) |
| **LENGTH** | 33in (84cm) |

## 4

**4,295 PIECES**
**TOWER BRIDGE**

| | |
|---|---|
| **SET NUMBER** | 10214 |
| **YEAR RELEASED** | 2013 |
| **HEIGHT** | 17in (43cm) |
| **LENGTH** | 40in (102cm) |

## 5

**4,163 PIECES**
**BIG BEN**

| | |
|---|---|
| **SET NUMBER** | 10253 |
| **YEAR RELEASED** | 2016 |
| **HEIGHT** | 23in (60cm) |
| **LENGTH** | 17in (43cm) |

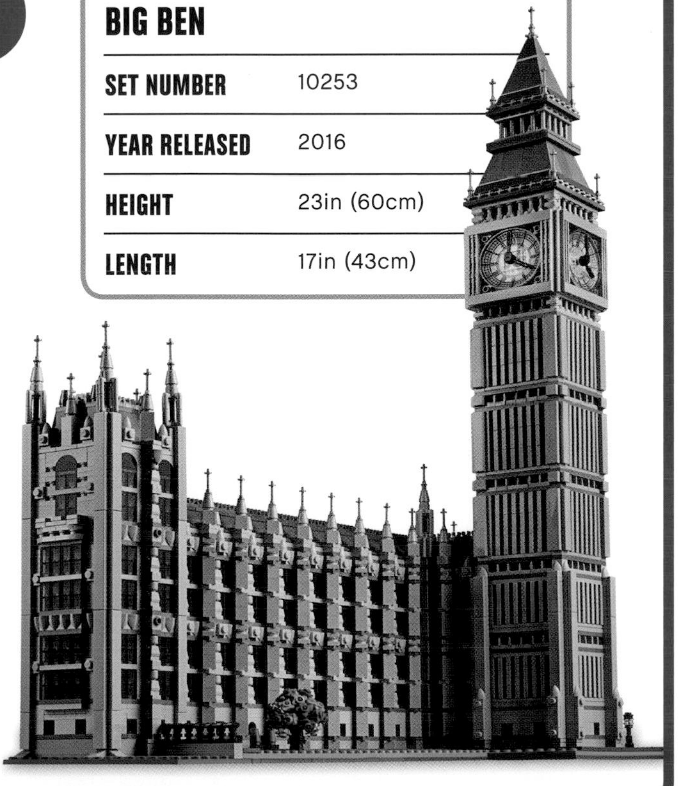

## Fun and games

**1**   *Teddy Bear.* Since accompanying Sleepyhead from the LEGO® Minifigures line to bed in 2012, the Teddy Bear has brought comfort to minifigures in many sets.

**2**   *Paintball gun.* The Paintballer's gun is a unique piece, moulded especially for him in LEGO Minifigures Series 10.

## Sports

**3**   *Ski poles.* These ski poles are most commonly found in white, but they were also made in pearl gold to top the turrets of the LEGO Big Ben set (set 21013) in 2016.

**4**   *Barbell weights.* The weights of this barbell accessory are used by minifigures in training, but is also used as a LEGO vehicle hubcap.

## Music

**5**   *Acoustic guitar.* In 2016, the Serenader was the first minifigure to play an acoustic guitar. His maraca-playing bandmate also debuted his instrument.

**6**   *Violin case.* There is a violin case LEGO accessory but no violin! The Gangster carries the case around – who knows what he keeps inside it!

## Tools of the trade

**7**   *Plunger.* Only two minifigures carry plungers: Groundskeeper Willie from *The Simpsons* LEGO Minifigures series and the Plumber, who has his hands full servicing other LEGO homes.

**8**   *Paint roller.* The paint roller piece can be fitted to any 1x1 round brick to change the paint colour. The Decorator first used this with a light blue piece in 2013.

# ASSORTED

# ACCESSORIES

## Aids to sight

9      ***Magnifying glass.*** The transparent lens of the magnifying glass actually works, enhancing the sight of minifigures and builders alike.

10      ***Binoculars.*** One of the most common LEGO accessories, binoculars appear in over 300 sets. The Lifeguard is the only minifigure to hold them in red.

## Tech

11      ***Laptop.*** There is only one model of laptop available to minifigures, in three colours – black, dark bluish grey and dark purple. There are nine different stickers for laptop screens.

12      ***Camera.*** This black camera is usually found capturing the adventures of minifigures. The only red version can be found in THE LEGO® BATMAN MOVIE Arkham Asylum (set 70912), released in 2017.

## Printed material

13      ***Newspaper.*** Whether it's the *Zombie Times Braaains!* cookery column or *City Financial News* piece on stud growth, minifigures can keep up to date with the latest LEGO news items with printed newspaper tile pieces.

14      ***Map.*** Minifigures can navigate their way to treasure or the town hall with the variety of printed map pieces that are available in the LEGO world.

## Miscellaneous

15      ***Short bone.*** Bones are popular among the canine LEGO population and a few minifigures have taken a shine to them, too. The Cave Woman and LEGO NINJAGO villain Lord Garmadon wear them as hair pieces.

16      ***Coins.*** Until 2011, LEGO currency came in 10, 20, 30 and 40 pieces. In sets produced after this they were in 1, 2, 5 and 10 pieces.

# NICE PART USE

Finding a familiar piece and then using it in an unexpected way is called nice part use, or "NPU", by some LEGO fans. These NPUs prove there is never just one use for any LEGO element!

The Alien Mothership (set 7065) from 2011's LEGO Space Alien Conquest theme uses eight pieces of **railway track** to create its saucer shape.

Torts (set 41520) from 2014's LEGO® Mixels™ range has **starfish** for hands, a **roof piece** for a nose and **wheel arches** for eyebrows.

A piece of **caterpillar track** becomes a perilous twisting bridge in LEGO® NINJAGO® Lava Falls (set 70753) from 2015.

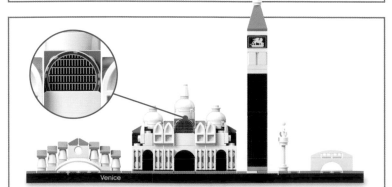

In 2016's LEGO® Architecture Skyline of Venice (set 21026), a printed round tile more often used as a lowly **air vent** becomes the huge, semi-circular window of St Mark's Basilica.

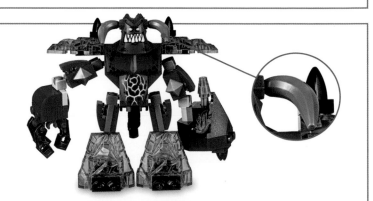

Some fairly bruised-looking **banana pieces** make horns for Burnzie the Lava Monster in the 2016 LEGO® NEXO KNIGHTS™ set Axl's Tower Carrier (set 70322).

A **flag piece** makes an unlikely appearance in the bathroom of LEGO Friends Summer Riding Camp (set 3185) – as a toilet seat cover!

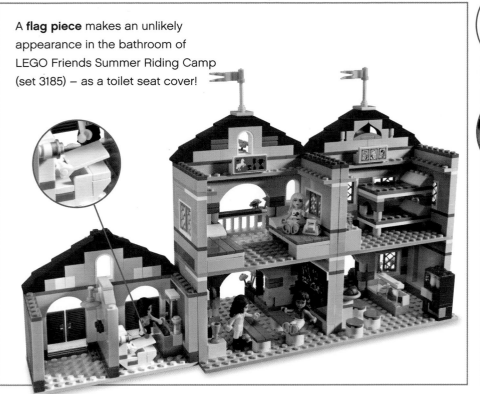

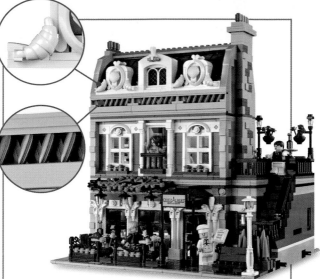

**Croissants** make a tasty architectural detail above a row of **feather pieces** in 2014's Parisian Restaurant (set 10243) from the LEGO® Creator Expert Modular Buildings theme.

The LEGO Creator Expert Big Ben (set 10253) from 2016 uses **minifigure tools** for clock hands, **microfigures** designed for the LEGO® Games theme as statues and **skeleton legs** as railings.

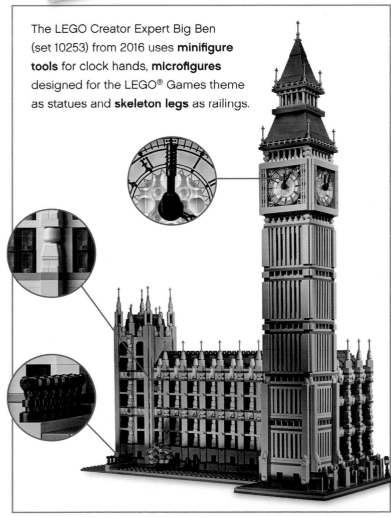

Assembly Square (set 10255) from 2017's LEGO Creator Expert Modular Buildings range has a roof made out of LEGO Technic **excavator buckets**.

# CHAPTER TWO

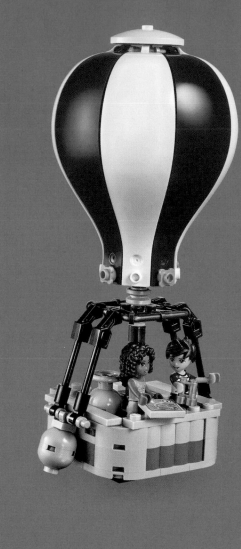

# BUILDING WORLDS

# STARTING BLOCKS

LEGO® DUPLO® is a world of big building pieces for small hands. Since 1969, it has inspired generations of preschoolers to learn more about their environment through colourful, creative play.

## FIRST LEGO DUPLO ANIMAL

A dog in DUPLO Camping (set 536) in 1977

# 98,765,432,110

The biggest number you can build by moving around the numbered blocks in the DUPLO Number Train (set 10558).

**IT'S A SIGN!** duplo

The friendly DUPLO rabbit logo was launched in 1979. In 1985, a fabric version of the rabbit was released – you could store your bricks inside it!

WE'RE HERE FOR ALL YOUR PET EMERGENCIES.

# AWESOME!

In Batman Adventure (set 10599), Batman, Superman and Wonder Woman team up to rescue a cat from a river!

# LOOK CLOSER

The 1980 set School and Bus (set 2645) has a clock with moving hands, a blackboard with interchangeable pictures and a ringing bell.

## Studs in scale

### LEGO brick
Standard LEGO bricks are compatible with DUPLO bricks, but only when built on top of DUPLO bricks.

### LEGO DUPLO brick
The name DUPLO comes from the Latin word for "double", because the dimensions of DUPLO bricks are twice the size of standard LEGO bricks.

## Top 5

DUPLO worlds

1. Farm
2. Airport
3. Dino
4. Castle
5. Pirates

## REALLY?!

The first-ever LEGO toilet appeared in 1986, in the DUPLO set Bathroom (set 2754).

**Q** When did the LEGO DUPLO Zoo close?

**A** The Zoo theme was a firm favourite from 1990, but DUPLO animals have been released into the wild since 2009. They now appear in sets based on their natural environments, such as the Savannah, the Arctic and the Jungle.

## Brick History

The first DUPLO figures, released in 1977, had block-shaped bodies with no arms or legs, and heads that turned but were not detachable.

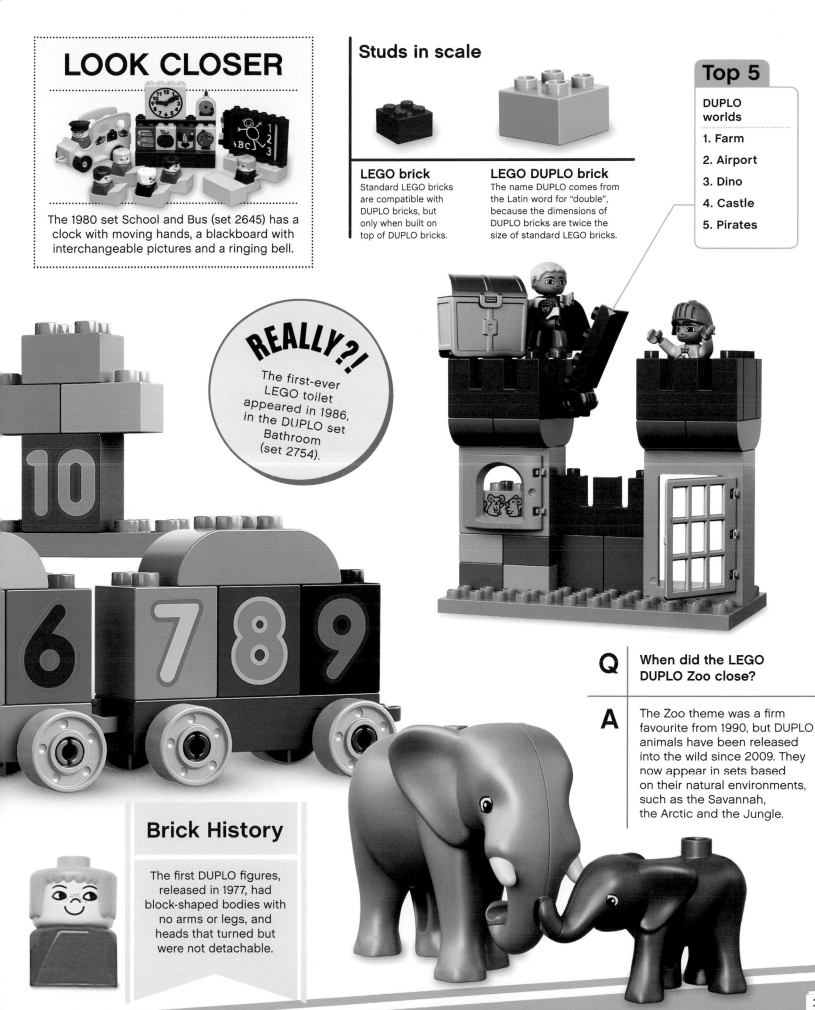

# THE SIGHTS OF LEGO® CITY

There's lots to see and do in LEGO® City. To help visitors get the most out of their stay, this street plan shows some of the most well-known places around.

## CITY MUSEUM

Jewels, swords and paintings such as *Minifigure with a Pearl Earring* are just some of the sights to see (and for LEGO burglars to steal!) at this museum (set 60008).

## USEFUL INFORMATION

**GETTING AROUND**
LEGO City is easily accessible with its range of buses, trams, trains, planes and ferries.

**DINING**
There are endless dining options in LEGO City. Even the street vendors are smartly dressed chefs.

**MAIL**
The first LEGO Post Office (set 6362) opened in LEGO Town in 1982, and today mailboxes can be found across LEGO City.

**BANKING**
Cash can be withdrawn from the LEGO City Bank via ATM, or by stealing the safe with a bulldozer.

## CITY PARK

Popular with dog walkers and cyclists, the Fun in the Park set (set 60134) is fully wheelchair-accessible and includes a picnic area.

## WATERFRONT

See huge cranes and container ships at LEGO City Harbour (set 4645, pictured), then go surfing or sailing at the beachside marina (set 4644).

## SPACEPORT

LEGO City has an extensive space programme, so time your visit to take in a spectacular shuttle launch at the Spaceport (set 60080).

## CITY SQUARE

Take the tram to the heart of the city and seek out the perfect souvenir at the two-story LEGO Store in City Square (set 60097).

I WILL PROTECT YOU, FROGS.

## TOWN SQUARE

Stop off at the bustling Town Square (set 60026) to admire this unusual statue of a knight surrounded by frogs.

## PRISON ISLAND

This offshore jail (set 60130) can be seen from the harbour, so keep an eye out for daring escapes by balloon!

POLICE

# CALL THE COPS

The LEGO City police department keeps crooks at bay and kids at play. Happily, there's no height requirement to join!

## TOP 5

### Crook-catching police vehicles

**1** Helicopters

**2** Motorcycles

**3** Boats

**4** Airplanes

**5** Patrol cars

## Brick History

The first LEGO products to feature police elements were the Town Plan sets way back in 1955, which came with static traffic police.

**01**

**POLICE**

**HA60128**

# AWESOME!

1985's Mobile Police Truck (set 6450) was the first LEGO police vehicle to have flashing lights and a siren.

# LOOK CLOSER

The Traffic Cop in the LEGO® Minifigures line can issue a parking ticket, and the signature on it is that of a real-life LEGO designer!

## KEY DATES

### 1973
The first police minifigure was also the first LEGO minifigure ever. He went on patrol with a stick-on uniform and a police car he couldn't fit into!

### 1980
The first female LEGO police officer came in a special set for schools. She had white hair that matched her open-topped patrol car.

### 1993
LEGO police officers got new-look uniforms as part of the LEGO Town Rescue theme, and featured individual face designs for the first time.

### 2012
The LEGO Forest Police sets saw officers in sun hats and tan-coloured uniforms, dodging huge bears while riding dirt bikes in the woods.

## REALLY?!

There were no LEGO crooks until 1993 and no LEGO handcuffs until 2008. What were the LEGO police doing for 20 years?!

*CHASE BY NAME, CHASE BY NATURE!*

### CHASE ON THE CASE

Of all the LEGO police officers to appear in sets since 1978, the only one to be given an official name is Chase McCain, heroic star of the LEGO® City *Undercover* video games.

## LOOK CLOSER

In Police Headquarters (set 7744), a bored crook has scrawled graffiti on the prison cell walls!

## MOST WANTED

Have you seen any of these infamous LEGO crooks? Some of them have been causing trouble for the LEGO City police for years!

*FUNNY HOW WE'RE ALL THE SAME HEIGHT.*

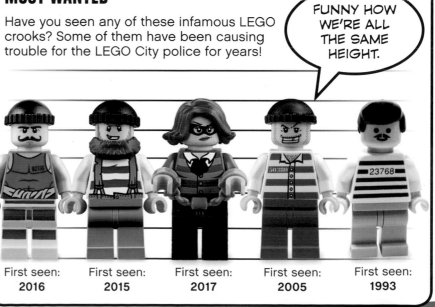

| First seen: | First seen: | First seen: | First seen: | First seen: |
|---|---|---|---|---|
| 2016 | 2015 | 2017 | 2005 | 1993 |

**IT'S A SIGN!** LEGO City police officers can be identified by the gold badges on their uniforms. These sometimes feature a star with four brick-style studs.

# WHAT'S COOKING?

Even LEGO minifigures get hungry! Luckily, there are many LEGO restaurants with all kinds of foods on the menu.

## Brick History

The food on offer in 1990's Breezeway Café (set 6376) and Pizza To Go (set 6350) proved so popular the sets were re-released in 2002 as LEGO® Legends sets.

## CAFÉ CULTURE

Café Corner (set 10182), was the first-ever LEGO® Modular Building in 2007. It is a great place for minifigures to grab a snack and watch the world go by.

## TOP 5

**Abundant fruit and vegetables in the LEGO world**

**1** **Apple**, appears in more than 110 sets.

**2** **Carrot**, appears in more than 95 sets.

**3** **Turkey drumstick**, appears in more than 85 sets.

**4** **Cherries**, appears in more than 80 sets.

**5** **Banana**, appears in more than 75 sets.

**Q** | Can I order pizza by the slice in LEGO City?

**A** | Of course! The Pizza Van (set 60150) was the first set to offer individual pizza slices, but you can also order a whole pizza if you are hungry enough...

## WOW!

The LEGO® Friends theme was the first to use a decorated minifigure head as a pineapple in LEGO sets!

## Piece particulars

LEGO ice cream comes in 11 different flavours. Vanilla must be the most popular - white ice-cream scoops have appeared in 31 sets.

42

**IT'S A SIGN!**

This takeaway coffee cup, seen in THE LEGO® MOVIE™ and with Larry the Barista (set 71004), features the logo of The Coffee Chain, Brickburg's most expensive coffee shop.

## KEY DATES

### 1979
The first LEGO Snack Bar (set 675) opens in LEGO Town, serving ice cream, coffee and more.

### 1980
LEGO Town citizens snack on fish and chips for the first time in LEGO Town Square Castle Scene (set 1592). The Dutch version of this set serves "soup und wurst"!

### 1983
A Hamburger Stand (set 6683) arrives in LEGO Town, serving burgers in the form of stacked 1x1 tiles!

### 1990
LEGO Town gets its first sit-down restaurant with the romantic-looking Italian eatery Breezeway Café (set 6376).

**REALLY?!**

LEGO chefs come in all shapes and sizes! There's even a robot chef named Chef Éclair, who appears in LEGO® NEXO KNIGHTS™ sets.

ANYONE FANCY A BYTE?

### Piece particulars
LEGO minifigures have been enjoying hot-dog sausages since 1998, but they didn't get a bun to go with them until 2016!

## LOOK CLOSER

The LEGO pizza slice is topped with green peppers, mushrooms and olives. Yum!

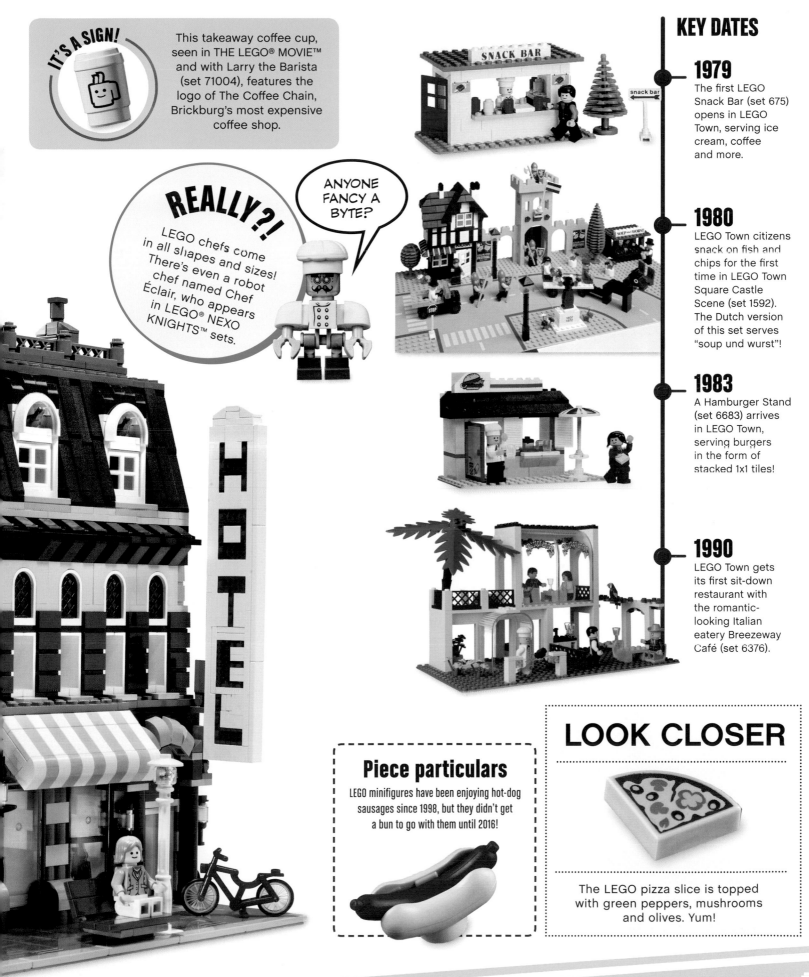

# ISLAND LIFE

**2,028**

The number of pieces in Temple of Airjitzu (set 70751), the largest LEGO® NINJAGO® set.

Welcome to Ninjago Island. The world of NINJAGO sets is one of powerful (LEGO) elements, varying landscapes and battles between the forces of good and evil.

## Piece particulars

The LEGO NINJAGO theme introduced a new LEGO element – an A-shaped plate – which has since become a builder favourite due to its versatility.

## FACT STACK

The ninja and Master Wu protect Ninjago Island from evil forces.

The main elements of Ninjago Island are Fire, Ice, Earth, Lightning and Water.

Ninjago Island and its neighbouring country, Dark Island, form a yin-yang shape.

The capital of Ninjago Island is the hi-tech, high-rise Ninjago City.

## AWESOME!

When their home was lost in a battle, the ninja moved into a wooden sailing ship called *Destiny's Bounty*. It can fly as well as float.

**1** **Spinning katana swords** from Spinjitzu Dojo (set 2504).

**2** **Mace ball** from Mountain Shrine (set 2254).

**3** **Axe head spinner** from Mountain Shrine (set 2254).

**4** **Serpentine sword post** from Ninja Training (set 30082).

**5** **Spear target** from Ninja Training Outpost (set 2516).

**Q** Who created Ninjago Island?

**A** The first Spinjitzu Master created Ninjago Island by combining the four Golden Weapons. He wanted it to be a peaceful land of light, but he learned that light cannot exist without darkness. He became the island's first protector, guarding it against dark forces – just like the ninja do today.

## WOW!

There are 14 realms, or dimensions, that are parallel to the Ninjago dimension. There used to be 16 before two were destroyed.

I'M ON TOP OF THIS... ROOF!

## Piece particulars

Flexible garage door panels create the distinctive curve on the roof of this smugglers' market, part of the Temple of Airjitzu (set 70751).

## REALLY?!

The huge spider-like design on Garmadon's Dark Fortress is more than a terrifying architectural feature – it can jump off to attack unsuspecting ninja!

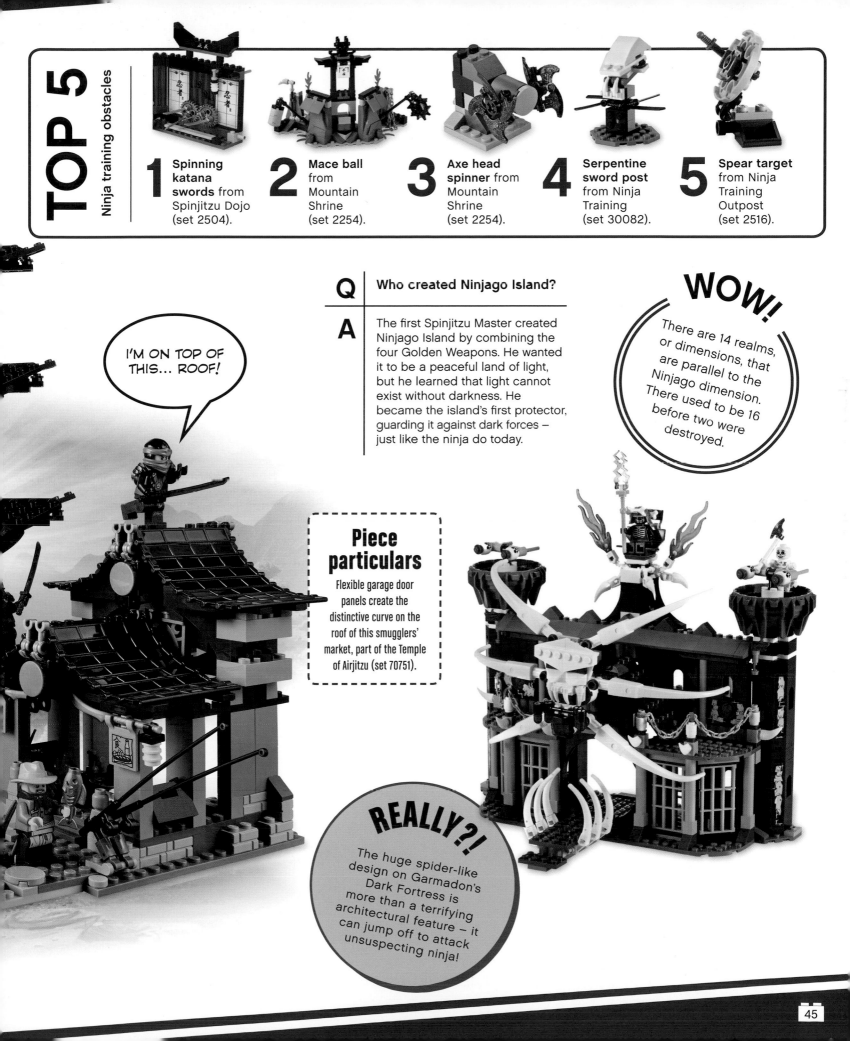

# OUT OF THIS WORLD

The LEGO® Space theme blasted into orbit in the 1970s. Since then it has rocketed beyond our solar system to discover ice planets, space bugs and more!

**WOW!**

Robotic space bugs from the planet Zotax brought a whole new buzz to LEGO Space in the 1998 Insectoids subtheme.

## TOP 5

### Astronaut space bases

**1** Command Center (set 926), 1979

SPACE BASE 1979 TO SPACE BASE 1988. OVER.

**2** Space Supply Center (set 6930), 1983

**3** Message Intercept Base (set 6987), 1988

**4** Space Station Zenon (set 1793), 1995

**5** Space Police Central (set 5985), 2010

## AWESOME!

In 2007, the LEGO® Mars Mission subtheme used hand pumps to launch Martian figures through the base's transport tubes.

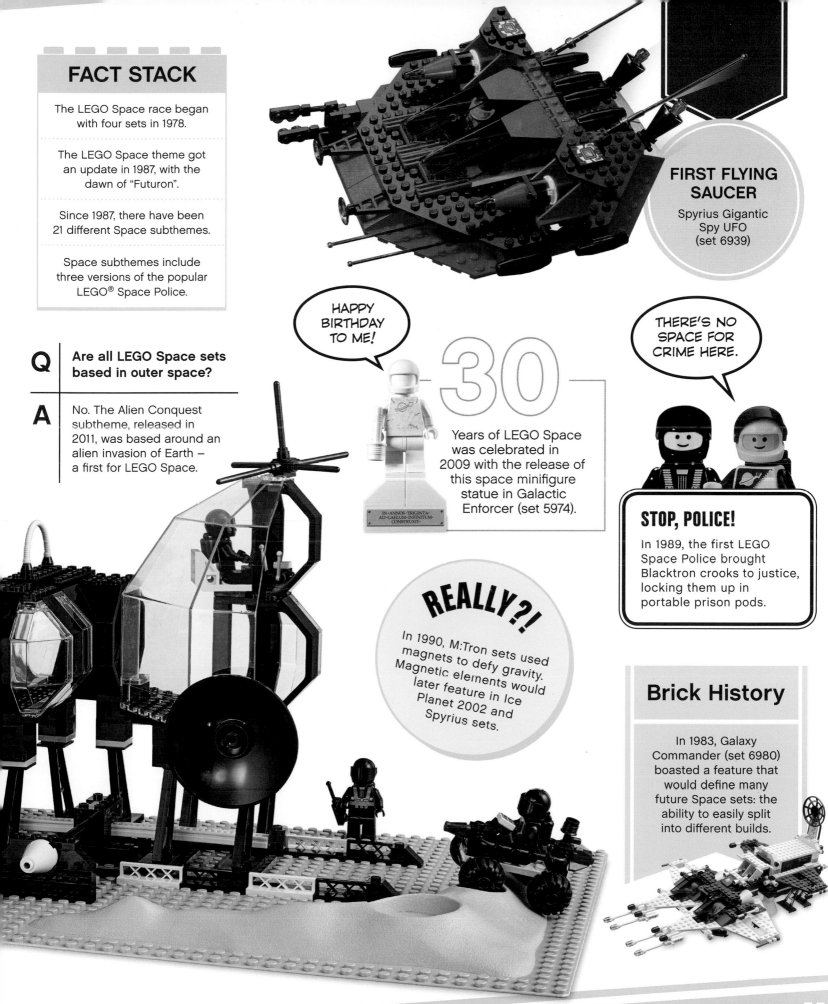

## FACT STACK

The LEGO Space race began with four sets in 1978.

The LEGO Space theme got an update in 1987, with the dawn of "Futuron".

Since 1987, there have been 21 different Space subthemes.

Space subthemes include three versions of the popular LEGO® Space Police.

**Q** | **Are all LEGO Space sets based in outer space?**

**A** | No. The Alien Conquest subtheme, released in 2011, was based around an alien invasion of Earth – a first for LEGO Space.

### FIRST FLYING SAUCER
Spyrius Gigantic Spy UFO (set 6939)

HAPPY BIRTHDAY TO ME!

THERE'S NO SPACE FOR CRIME HERE.

30 Years of LEGO Space was celebrated in 2009 with the release of this space minifigure statue in Galactic Enforcer (set 5974).

IN·ANNOS·TRIGINTA· AD·CAELUM·INFINITUM· CONSTRUXIT·

## STOP, POLICE!

In 1989, the first LEGO Space Police brought Blacktron crooks to justice, locking them up in portable prison pods.

## REALLY?!

In 1990, M:Tron sets used magnets to defy gravity. Magnetic elements would later feature in Ice Planet 2002 and Spyrius sets.

## Brick History

In 1983, Galaxy Commander (set 6980) boasted a feature that would define many future Space sets: the ability to easily split into different builds.

# MAKING HISTORY

Few eras in history are as fondly remembered and action-packed as the bygone age of LEGO® Castle, which included more than just LEGO castles!

## JOINED-UP JOUST

The huge gatehouse in 2012's Kingdoms Joust (set 10223) is shaped so that two identical sets can be arranged back to back, creating an even more impressive building.

## 14

Number of LEGO Castle sets that feature fire-breathing dragons!

## IT'S A SIGN!

The huge shield in 2005's King's Siege Tower (set 8875) is one of the largest LEGO Castle elements. It includes a built-in LEGO brick, so you can add your own details to it.

## REALLY?!

More than a decade before LEGO® NINJAGO®, 1990s LEGO Castle sets, such as Treasure Transport (set 6033), featured the very first LEGO ninja!

48

# AWESOME!

The biggest-ever LEGO Castle set is not a castle at all, but the 1,601-piece Medieval Market Village (set 10193) from 2009.

## CHEQUERED HISTORY

Four LEGO Castle chess sets have been released since 2005, pitching knight against dragon, king against skeleton queen, dwarf against troll, and jester against wizard!

## Brick History

In 2001, two much-loved 1980s sets, Guarded Inn (set 6067) and Black Falcon's Fortress (set 6074), were reissued as "LEGO Legends" sets for a whole new generation to enjoy.

## LOOK CLOSER

In 1988, LEGO Castle horses wore decorative barding for the first time. From 2005, they sometimes wore armoured headgear, too.

## TOP 5

### Pieces first found in LEGO Castle sets

**1** Flags (1984)

**2** Rocks (1992)

**3** Flames (1993)

**4** Bats (1997)

**5** Cows (2009)

## WOW!

In 1984, the LEGO Castle Catapult (set 6030) made use of LEGO® Technic parts to become the first missile-launching LEGO set!

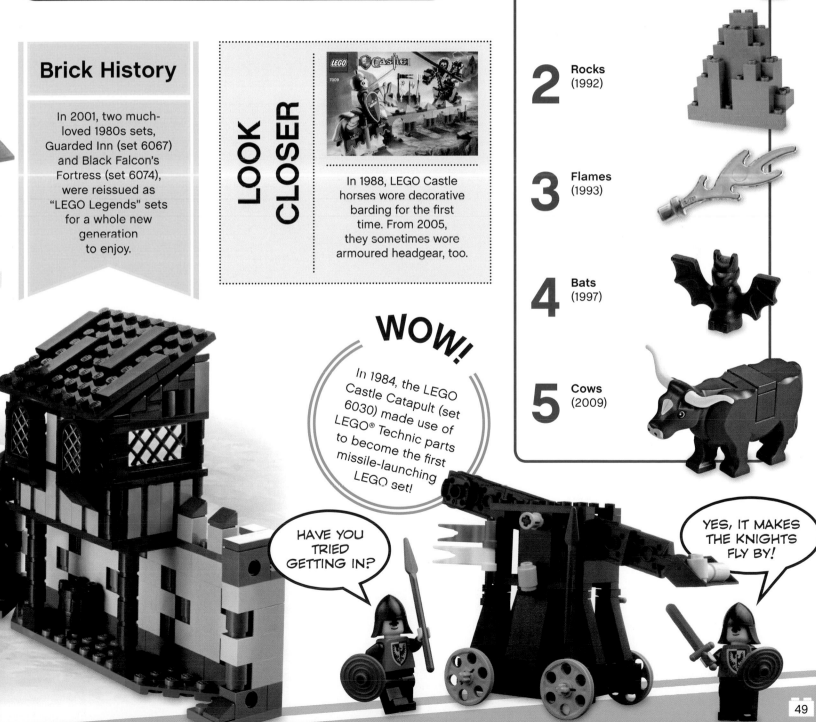

HAVE YOU TRIED GETTING IN?

YES, IT MAKES THE KNIGHTS FLY BY!

# CAPTURING THE CASTLES

In the Middle Ages, it took decades to build a decent castle. Since 1978, there have been scores of LEGO Castle sets that can be built within hours!

New large wall panel pieces made for quicker castle building, and allowed for printed stonework details in sets such as **King's Castle** (set 6080).

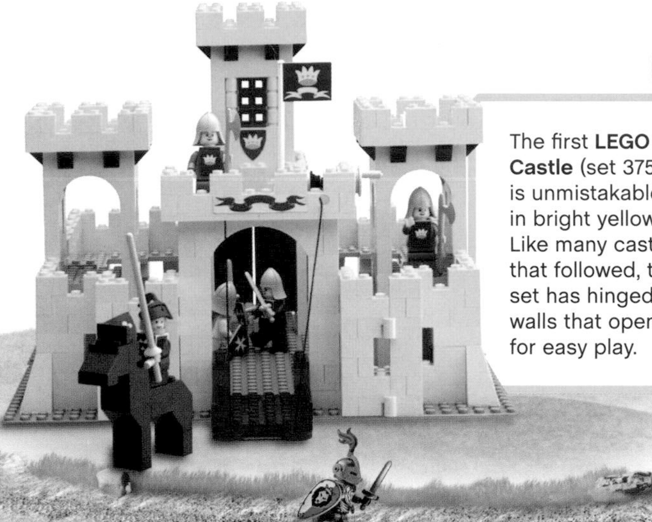

**1984**

**1978**

The first **LEGO Castle** (set 375) is unmistakable in bright yellow. Like many castles that followed, this set has hinged walls that open for easy play.

**2009**

The only LEGO Castle stronghold not to be controlled by knights, **Trolls' Mountain Fortress** (set 7097) has the Crown King guarded by enormous trolls.

**2007**

**King's Castle Siege** (set 7094) blended classic LEGO Castle looks with modern play features such as catapults, a collapsing wall and a spinning bridge.

The first castle to be built on an elevated baseplate, **King's Mountain Fortress** (set 6081) is also home to one of the first-ever LEGO ghosts!

**1990**

**Fire Breathing Fortress** (set 6082) earned its name with a brick-built dragon's head over the doors and an actual LEGO dragon lurking inside!

**1993**

Built on a uniquely shaped elevated baseplate, **King Leo's Castle** (set 6098) has sections that swap over for a swift redesign.

**2000**

LEGO Castle took a trip to Feudal Japan to come up with a castle unlike any other: the four-storey **Flying Ninja Fortress** (set 6093)!

**1998**

**2013**

The biggest enclosed LEGO castle to date, **King's Castle** (set 70404) can combine with The Gatehouse Raid (set 70402) to make it even bigger!

# AHOY MATEY!

Avast ye landlubbers – be on the lookout, there be LEGO® Pirates about! For nearly 30 years this scurvy crew have been causing trouble across the seven seas.

## FACT STACK

The LEGO Pirates theme was launched in 1989.

The LEGO Group has released close to 80 different LEGO Pirates sets.

There have been 10 LEGO Pirates galleon sets, representing various different fighting factions.

Unsurprisingly, more than 35 LEGO Pirates sets feature a treasure chest.

WHY ARE PIRATES CALLED PIRATES?

THEY JUST AARRR!

REDBEARD BY NAME...

## LOOK CLOSER

Captain Redbeard and his crew, released in 1989, were the first minifigures to have extra facial details along with the classic LEGO smile.

# KEY DATES

**1989**
The Bluecoat Imperial Soldiers are the first group to lose their valuable treasure to the Pirates.

**1992**
Next to try and guard their treasure against becoming pirate plunder are the Redcoat Imperial Guard.

**1996**
The Imperial Armada set out to hunt LEGO Pirates, but end up being looted instead!

**2009**
Having no respect for a new Imperial uniform, the Pirates begin stealing from Redcoat Imperials again.

**2010**
While travelling with Redcoat Imperials, the Governor's Daughter has to protect her treasure from the Pirates.

**2015**
The return of the classic Bluecoat Imperials provides updated but familiar faces to steal trom.

## IMPERIAL STRONGHOLD

Governor's Fort Sabre (set 6276) is home to the Pirates' arch-enemies, the Imperial Soldiers. This popular 1989 set features a fort, a dock and a jail where captured Pirates are imprisoned.

## WOW!

Captain Redbeard's pet monkey is called Spinoza. This little rascal has been causing trouble since the very beginning of the LEGO Pirates theme.

## Brick History

A group of Islanders, led by King Kahuka, appeared in six LEGO Pirates sets in 1994 and one 2001 set. They did battle with both the Pirates and the Imperial Soldiers to protect their island home.

## Piece particulars

LEGO Pirates was the first LEGO theme to feature a musket, historical flintlock pistol and cannons.

**IT'S A SIGN!**

Four different versions of the LEGO Pirates' Jolly Roger have appeared in more than 40 sets. In real life, the flag has been seen since as long ago as 1687.

# LEGO® *STAR WARS*™ WORLDS

*The LEGO® Star Wars™ theme launched in 1999 to tie in with the release of Star Wars: Episode I The Phantom Menace. From the beginning, the theme featured sets based around the classic trilogy of Star Wars films as well as the prequels. To date, there have been more than 475 LEGO Star Wars sets. There have been sets based on all nine big-screen movies, as well as three TV shows. LEGO Star Wars is now the longest-running licensed LEGO theme and will celebrate its 20th anniversary in 2019...*

## BIGGEST LEGO *STAR WARS* SET

Ultimate Collector's *Millennium Falcon* (set 10179)

## PLENTY OF PLANETS

Miniature versions of planets from the LEGO *Star Wars* universe were released in 2012 and 2013. The series also included a mini Death Star and an asteroid field.

**Q**  What was the first LEGO lightsaber duel?

**A**  Lightsaber Duel (set 7101), released in 1999, replicated the fierce battle between Qui-Gon Jinn and Darth Maul on Tatooine.

## Brick History

Among the first LEGO *Star Wars* sets to be released in 1999 was the X-Wing Fighter (set 7140).

## WOW!

The planet of Tatooine has the most sets based around it. There are 35 sets that have its sandy surface as their setting.

## LOOK CLOSER

X-Wing Fighter (set 4502) from 2004 includes a version of Yoda's hut while he is in hiding on Dagobah. A secret compartment under Yoda's bed lets him store his lightsaber safely.

# AWESOME!

In 2012, LEGO minifigure paramedics stopped wearing white and suited up in bright red gear with reflective silver safety stripes.

## REALLY?!

The slightly scary operating room in 2006's LEGO City Hospital (set 7892) includes a robot claw hand, a buzz saw and a chain saw!

## MEDICAL SCHOOL

The largest LEGO hospital is a special set for schools from 1993. The 522-piece LEGO Dacta Hospital (set 9364) has four beds, an operating theatre and a gym.

## Piece particulars

Minifigure gurneys with hinged wheel pieces appeared in more than 30 sets between 1985 and 2011, when they were replaced by stretchers without wheels.

## IT'S A SIGN!

Stickers in 1978's Hospital (set 231) include weighing scales, surgical gear, observation charts and a chart for eye tests.

## 12

Windows in 1987's light-filled LEGO Town Emergency Treatment Centre (set 6380) – but no door!

# TOP 5

Air ambulances

1 **Red Cross Helicopter** (set 626), 1978

2 **Med-Star Rescue Plane** (set 6356), 1988

3 **Rescue Helicopter** (set 7903), 2006

4 **Helicopter Rescue** (set 4429), 2012

5 **Ambulance Plane** (set 60116), 2016

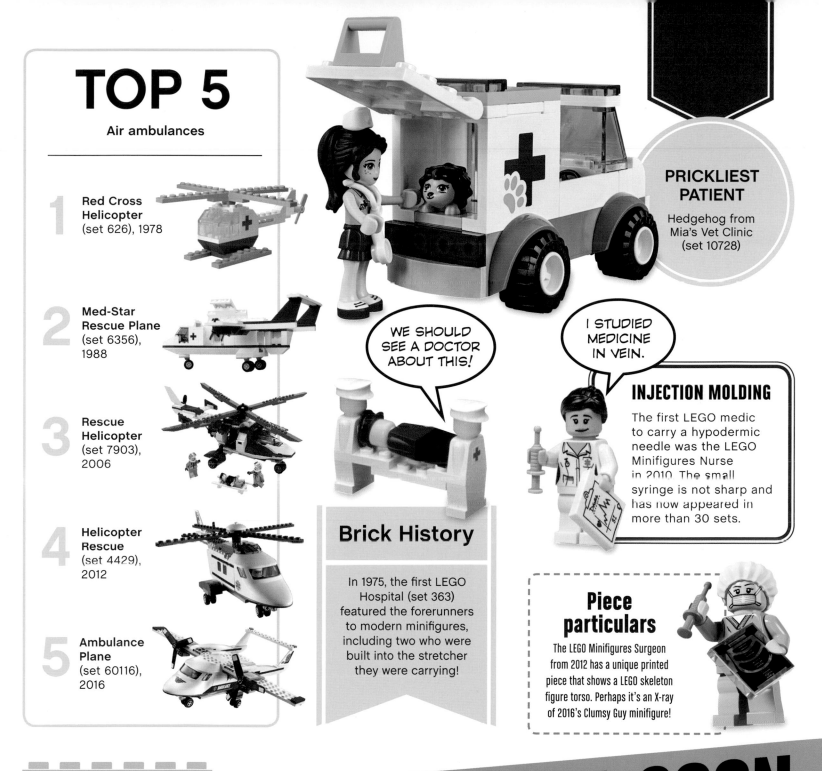

## PRICKLIEST PATIENT

Hedgehog from Mia's Vet Clinic (set 10728)

*WE SHOULD SEE A DOCTOR ABOUT THIS!*

*I STUDIED MEDICINE IN VEIN.*

## INJECTION MOLDING

The first LEGO medic to carry a hypodermic needle was the LEGO Minifigures Nurse in 2010. The small syringe is not sharp and has now appeared in more than 30 sets.

## Brick History

In 1975, the first LEGO Hospital (set 363) featured the forerunners to modern minifigures, including two who were built into the stretcher they were carrying!

## Piece particulars

The LEGO Minifigures Surgeon from 2012 has a unique printed piece that shows a LEGO skeleton figure torso. Perhaps it's an X-ray of 2016's Clumsy Guy minifigure!

## FACT STACK

Minifigure medics debuted in Ambulance (set 606) and Red Cross Car (set 623) in 1978.

The first minifigure hospital was LEGO Town's Paramedic Unit (set 6364) in 1980.

Hospitals, ambulances and doctors have appeared in LEGO® FABULAND and DUPLO sets.

# GET WELL SOON

In the action-packed worlds of LEGO Town and LEGO City, it's good to know there's always a minifigure medic on call, and an ambulance is never far away!

# BEHIND THE MASKS

Originally constructed from LEGO® Technic elements, the BIONICLE® theme features some of the LEGO Group's most exciting and complex storylines.

## The BIONICLE Dictionary

**Matoran:** The most populous species in the BIONICLE universe. Each Matoran corresponds to an element but cannot control its power.

**Toa:** Heroes who protect the Matoran and the Great Spirit Mata Nui by using their elemental power to fight for good.

**Turaga:** Former Toa who gave up their powers to become "elders" and lead the Matoran.

**Kanohi:** Masks worn by the Matoran and Toa that give them power.

**Makuta Teridax:** The evil leader of the Brotherhood of Makuta, who put the Great Spirit into a coma and attempted to enslave the Matoran.

**Q** Are BIONICLE sets always made from LEGO Technic pieces?

**A** No. A special line using a mix of standard bricks and LEGO Technic elements was released between 2005 and 2007, totalling 12 sets. A new figure-building system was also introduced for sets after 2014.

## Brick History

Early BIONICLE characters lived on the surface of the island of Mata Nui. In 2004, Toa Metru sets began to explore the hi-tech city of Metru Nui, deep beneath Mata Nui.

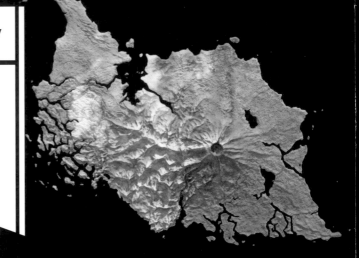

## THE TOA

The first six full-sized BIONICLE heroes to be introduced in 2001 belonged to the Toa tribe. New versions of the six were released in 2015.

**KOPAKA**
Toa of Ice

**GALI**
Toa of Water

**POHATU**
Toa of Stone

# TOP 5
## Fearsome foes of the Toa

The spider–like **Visorak**.

**Bohrok:** swarming mecha–insects.

**Rahkshi:** living suits of armour.

**Umarak the Hunter:** a dark, ancient being.

The thieving and cruel **Piraka**.

# AWESOME!

The six original Toa Mata were re-released in 2016, in a larger size with collectible golden masks.

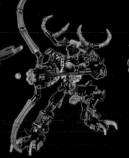

## Brick statistics

### BIONICLE media

**54 comics**
Also collected as graphic novels

**43 books**
Including stories and guides

**6 video games**
Plus two mobile games

**4 DVD movies**
Starting with the *Mask of Light* in 2003

**1 Netflix series**
LEGO BIONICLE: *The Journey to One*

## WOW!

The Battle of Metru Nui (set 8759) from 2005, is an 856-piece fortress playset – and the biggest set in the LEGO BIONICLE theme.

# 311

Number of LEGO BIONICLE sets released between 2001 and 2016.

## REALLY?!

There are over 150 different Kanohi masks, which are worn by most beings in the BIONICLE universe.

**ONUA**

Toa of Earth

**LEWA**

Toa of Air

**TAHU**

Toa of Fire

# HOME IS WHERE HEARTLAKE IS

**Q** What can you do at Heartlake City's Fun Park?

**A** There's a roller coaster, Ferris wheel, arcade, space ride, hot-dog van and bumper cars! Five sets released in 2016 combine to create a world of amusements.

Launched in 2012, LEGO® Friends was a big hit from day one. The theme follows the busy lives of five friends in and around their exciting hometown, Heartlake City.

## FACT STACK

The five LEGO Friends stars are Stephanie, Olivia, Emma, Mia and Andrea.

LEGO Friends was the first theme to use mini-dolls, which are larger and more realistic than minifigures.

More than 800 children and their families helped the LEGO Group get the theme just right.

To date, more than 150 LEGO Friends sets have been released.

## REALLY?!

Of all the LEGO Friends girls, busy bee Stephanie is in the most sets, appearing in more than 30. She does like to be involved in everything!

## LOOK CLOSER

The departure board in Heartlake City Airport represents the home country of each designer working on the LEGO Friends team!

BILLUND 09:00
NEW YORK 10:30
BERLIN 11:15
MADRID 12:30
LONDON 15:00
PARIS 15:45
GLASGOW 17:10
PORTO 18:30
OSLO 20:45

## CRUISING AROUND TOWN

There are all kinds of ways to get around Heartlake City! Here are some of the more unusual modes of transport.

Heartlake Hot Air Balloon (set 41097)

**Pop Star Tour Bus** (set 41106)

Dolphin Cruiser (set 41015)

**Puppy Parade** (set 41301)

# AWESOME!

There are more than 200 different mini-dolls in the LEGO Friends world, including Alicia, Ben, Chloe, David, Ella and James (pictured).

## SCREEN STARS

LEGO Friends made its movie debut on Netflix and had its first direct-to-DVD movie in 2016.

## WOW!

In 2013, just a year after its release, LEGO Friends became a "core" theme, giving it a place among the LEGO greats, such as LEGO City and LEGO Space.

## 6

New colours were introduced to the LEGO palette in LEGO Friends sets: Dark Azur, Medium Azur, Aqua, Spring Yellow Green, Lavender and Medium Lavender.

## TOP 5

Cutest LEGO Friends pets

**1** Toffee the pug

**2** Jazz the bunny

**3** Maxie the cat

**4** Fame the foal

**5** Kiki the parrot

## ENJOY YOUR STAY

Heartlake Grand Hotel (set 41101) is the biggest place in town! This 1,552-piece, three-storey hotel is modular, meaning its rooms can be arranged in multiple ways.

# BUILDING SIGHTS

Thanks to LEGO® Architecture and other advanced building themes, you can now enjoy the world's most impressive buildings from the comfort of your own home.

LET ME LIGHT YOUR WAY AROUND THESE FAMOUS SIGHTS.

33IN (84CM)

## STATUE OF LIBERTY, USA

In 2000, a LEGO Sculptures set used 2,847 sand green pieces to depict a 33in (84cm) high Statue of Liberty (set 3450).

## THE WHITE HOUSE, USA

The LEGO Architecture White House (set 21006) from 2010 uses a transparent minifigure head piece as the large lantern that hangs from the north portico of the official residence of the President of the United States.

The White House

9IN (22CM)

15IN (39CM)

## BURJ KHALIFA, UAE

Based on the world's tallest building, the 2016 Burj Khalifa (set 21031) is also the tallest set in the LEGO Architecture range, at more than 15in (39cm) high. It is the second LEGO set of this Dubai landmark.

Burj Khalifa

## EIFFEL TOWER, FRANCE

The LEGO Architecture Eiffel Tower (set 21019, pictured) from 2014 stands an impressive 12in (30cm) high. However, that's nothing next to the 42in (108cm) LEGO Advanced Models Eiffel Tower (set 10181) released in 2007.

**12IN (30CM)**

## SUNGNYEMUN, SOUTH KOREA

After Sungnyemun burned down in 2008, craftsmen dressed in period costume rebuilt the ancient gateway. Luckily, no dress code is required to build the LEGO Architecture version (set 21016) from 2012.

**4.2IN (10.7CM)**

## LEANING TOWER OF PISA, ITALY

The real Leaning Tower of Pisa tilts because of soft soil and shallow foundations. Its LEGO Architecture equivalent (set 21015) from 2013 is angled using carefully hidden hinges built into the base of the model.

**10.1IN (25.9CM)**

## LONDON SKYLINE, UK

LEGO Creator Expert models of Tower Bridge (set 10214) and Big Ben (set 10253) are among the biggest LEGO sets ever made. But this 2017 LEGO Architecture Skyline of London (set 21034, pictured) depicts them both with just a handful of pieces!

**5IN (15CM)**

London

**11IN (28CM)**

# FIRE POWER

Though the first LEGO flame piece wasn't introduced until 1993, LEGO fire service sets have been around since the 1950s and are still burning brightly today.

## WOW!

Ladder pieces have appeared in 20 fire-themed sets since 1981. They are designed to slot together to create long, telescopic rescue ladders.

## TOP 5
### Burning builds

**1** Abandoned building (set 60003)

**2** Speedboat (set 60005)

**3** Hot-dog stand (set 60110)

**4** TV satellite tower (set 60111)

**5** Lighthouse (set 60109)

## REALLY?!

There have been lots of LEGO fire helicopters, but just one LEGO City Fire Plane (set 4209) for dropping water bombs onto forest fires.

## FACT STACK

The first LEGO Fire Station (set 1308) was part of the Town Plan sets in 1957.

Fifteen different fire stations have served LEGO Town and LEGO City since 1978.

The largest LEGO fire truck is a 1,035-piece LEGO Technic vehicle (set 8289) from 2006.

The smallest fire truck is a nine-piece toy in Winter Holiday Train (set 10254) from 2016.

NOW WHAT DID I COME UP HERE FOR?

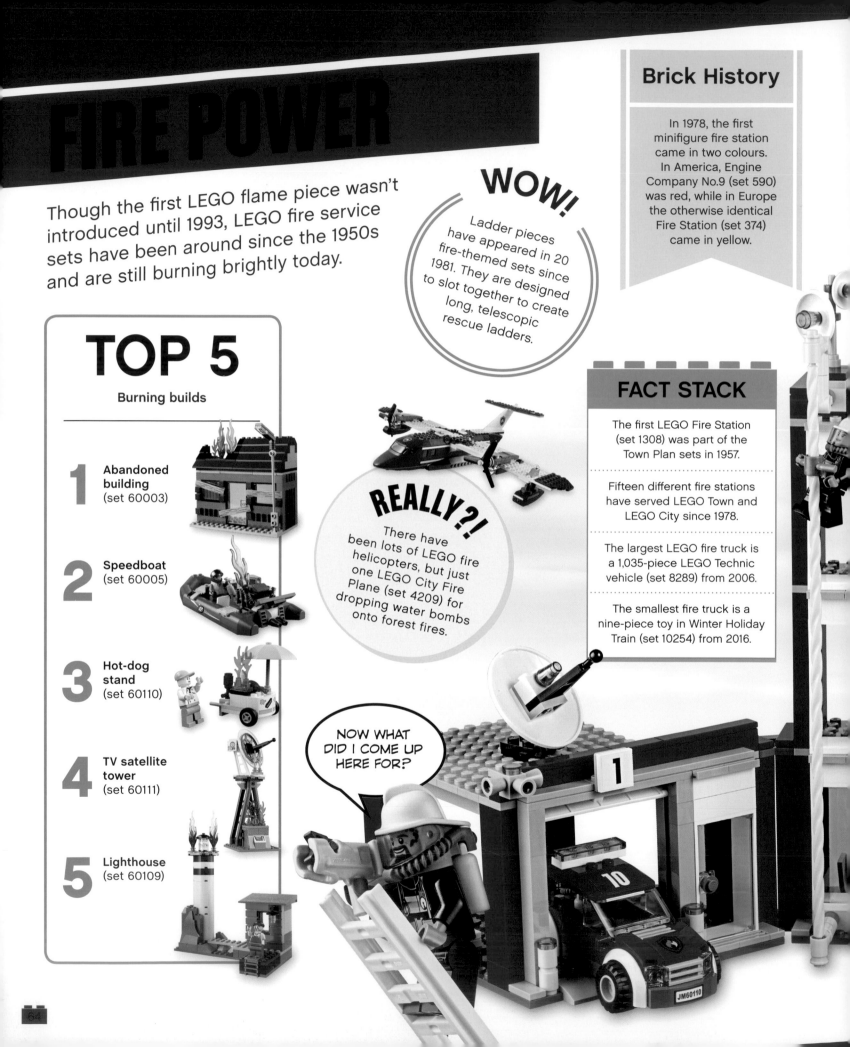

# AWESOME!

Three LEGO City Fire sets from 2016 feature stud-shooting hose pieces for firing "water" at the towering flames.

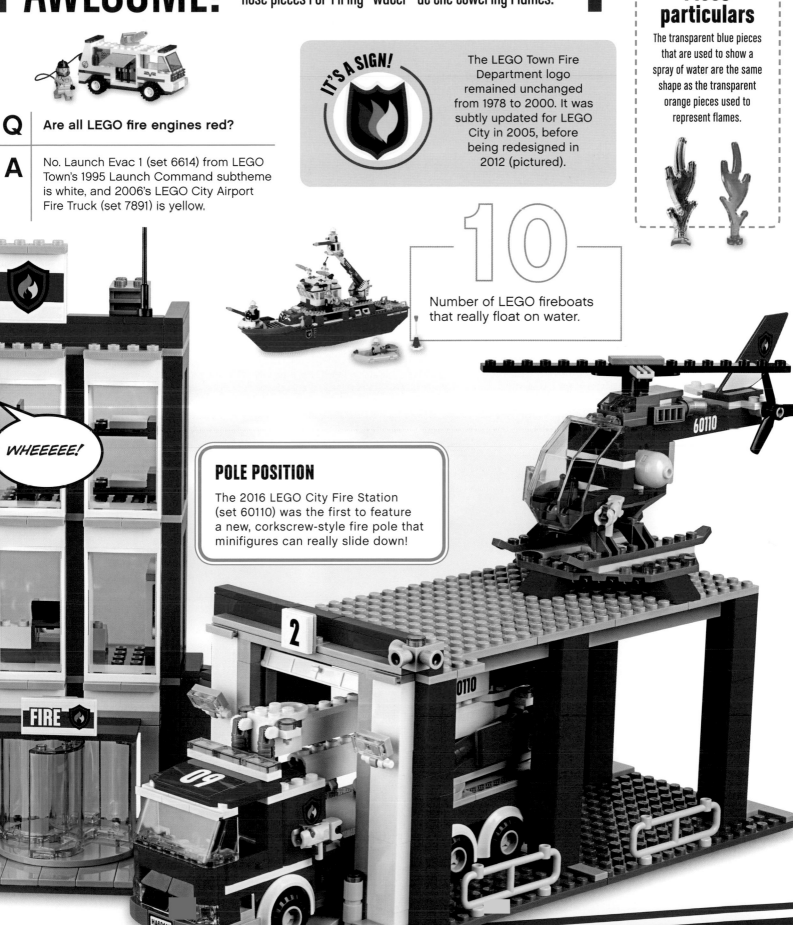

**Q** Are all LEGO fire engines red?

**A** No. Launch Evac 1 (set 6614) from LEGO Town's 1995 Launch Command subtheme is white, and 2006's LEGO City Airport Fire Truck (set 7891) is yellow.

## IT'S A SIGN!

The LEGO Town Fire Department logo remained unchanged from 1978 to 2000. It was subtly updated for LEGO City in 2005, before being redesigned in 2012 (pictured).

## Piece particulars

The transparent blue pieces that are used to show a spray of water are the same shape as the transparent orange pieces used to represent flames.

**10**
Number of LEGO fireboats that really float on water.

WHEEEEE!

## POLE POSITION

The 2016 LEGO City Fire Station (set 60110) was the first to feature a new, corkscrew-style fire pole that minifigures can really slide down!

60110

2

FIRE

09

# TOP 5

LEGO coast-guard
rescue stations

**1** LEGOLAND
Town Coastal
Rescue Base
(set 6387),
1989

**2** LEGO Town
Hurricane
Harbour (set
6338), 1995

**3** LEGO World
City Coast
Watch HQ
(set 7047),
2003

**4** LEGO City
Coast
Guard Platform
(set 4210),
2008

**5** LEGO City
Coast
Guard Head
Quarters
(set 60167),
2017

## Piece particulars

Life got easier for the LEGO
coast guard in 1990 with the
invention of the first minifigure
lifejacket. Ring-shaped lifebuoys
followed in 1999.

## IT'S A SIGN!

The LEGO Town Coast
Guard HQ (set 6435)
from 1999 comes with
red and green flags
to show when it is
safe to swim – and
a printed sign to
explain the system!

## Brick History

In 1998, the LEGO Town
Res-Q team provided
coast-guard and other
emergency response
services in vehicles
such as the Res-Q
Cruiser (set 6473).

**5**

Different emblems have
been emblazoned on
LEGO coast-guard
ships since 1991.

BE CAREFUL
OUT THERE,
BUDDY.

# AWESOME!

In 2013, the LEGO City coast guard got a new look, a new logo and its first proper Coast Guard Plane (set 60015).

## MOST DARING LAUNCH

Water Scooter, launched from Heavy Duty Rescue Helicopter (set 60166)

## A TALE OF TWO COAST GUARDS

In 1976, Coast Guard Station (set 369) was released in Europe with yellow vehicles and featureless figures. In 1978, a near-identical set came out in the US – but now with white vehicles and some of the very first minifigures.

## REALLY?!

LEGO City Coast Guard Patrol (set 60014) from 2013 features more grisly grey sharks than any other LEGO set.

## LOOK CLOSER

The LEGO Minifigures line got its first Lifeguard in 2010. Going by the initials on her swimsuit, she may just share a name with former LEGO Design Master Gitte Thorsen!

## FACT STACK

Before LEGO Town got its own coast guard, it had 1985's Rescue-I Helicopter (set 6697).

C26 Sea Cutter (set 4022) from 1996 was the first coast-guard ship to really float on water.

A coast-guard station forms part of the 1996 LEGO Town set Wave Jump Racers (set 6334).

HEY, I THOUGHT YOU WERE COMING TOO?

# TO THE RESCUE

When LEGO Town and City minifigures stray too far from shore, the LEGO coast guard are ready to make a splash as they race to the scene.

# HOME SWEET HOME

Who wouldn't want to live in a LEGO house? There's an endless range to choose from, and you never need to move when you can just rebuild!

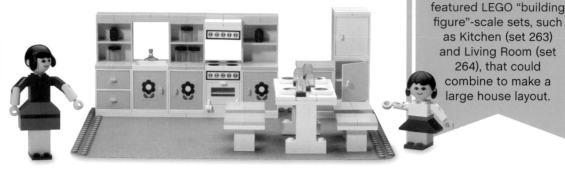

## FACT STACK

The LEGO Town Plan sets of the 1950s featured small homes built with about 20 bricks each.

In the 1960s and 1970s, sets such as House with Car (set 346) depicted realistic homes.

An Unexpected Gathering (set 79003) from 2012 recreates Bilbo Baggins' home from *The Hobbit*™.

The huge LEGO® *Simpsons*™ House (set 71006) from 2014 has seven rooms and a garage!

### MOVING HOME

In 1973, the same stylish house was released as Swiss Villa (set 540) in the USA, Villa Mallorca in Denmark and Italian Villa (set 356) in the rest of Europe.

## REALLY?!

In some LEGO catalogues, Lionel Lion's Lodge (set 3678) from the 1982 FABULAND range was known as "The Story of the Noisy Neighbours"!

HAS ANYONE GOT ABOUT FIFTY EARPLUGS?

## BRICK CHALLENGE

Look at your own home with LEGO builders' eyes and think about how you could recreate it with your collection of bricks.

# AWESOME!

Livi's Pop Star House (set 41135) from the LEGO Friends theme comes with several rare printed pieces, including a gold disc and two sushi rolls.

## TOP 5
### LEGO Town vacation villas

**1** Summer Cottage (set 6365), 1981

**2** Holiday Home (set 6374), 1983

**3** Weekend Home (set 6370), 1985

**4** Vacation House (set 1472), 1987

**5** Poolside Paradise (set 6416), 1992

# AWESOME!

The LEGO® Monster Fighters Haunted House (set 10228) from 2012 has zombie heads built into the brickwork!

## WOW!

Ole Kirk's House is where the LEGO Group began in 1932. In 2012, LEGO Group employees received a model of it (set 4000007) as a Christmas gift.

## SWEETEST RETREAT

Gingerbread House (set 40139)

I'M THE HEAD OF THIS HOUSEHOLD!

## LOOK CLOSER

A light brick in the fireplace of Winter Village Cottage (set 10229) fills the whole house with a warming glow throughout the winter months.

# JOINED-UP THINKING

In 2007, the first LEGO Modular Buildings brought new levels of detail to a minifigure-scale world. Since then, this desirable neighbourhood has kept on growing, as each new building slots seamlessly onto the last.

## WOW!

A LEGO fan clearly lives in 2017's Assembly Square (set 10255). One room contains micro-scale models of LEGO sets such as the Eiffel Tower.

## REALLY?!

Built into the details of Detective's Office (set 10246) from 2015 are all the clues you need to solve a cookie-smuggling mystery.

**Q** Is Market Street really a Modular Building?

**A** Though the fan-designed Market Street (set 10190) was released as part of the LEGO Factory theme, it was designed to fit the Modular format. Its status was confirmed when it was included in Mini Modulars (set 10230) in 2012.

## Brick History

In 2012, Mini Modulars (set 10230) celebrated five years of the Modular Buildings range. The miniature street scene had 1,356 pieces and depicted every Modular Building released up to that point.

**KEY DATES**

**2007**
Café Corner (set 10182) and Market Street (set 10190, pictured)

**2008**
Green Grocer (set 10185)

**2009**
Fire Brigade (set 10197)

**2010**
Grand Emporium (set 10211)

# LOOK CLOSER

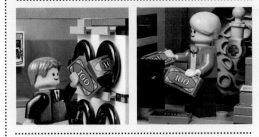

An "out of order" launderette washing machine is actually a back way into the bank vault for a spot of literal money laundering in 2016's Brick Bank (set 10251).

## 1891

The build date commemorated on the Town Hall (set number 10224) is also the year that LEGO Group founder Ole Kirk Kristiansen was born.

## Piece particulars

There is at least one white street lamp in every Modular Building to date. LEGO Set Designer Jamie Berard promised to keep using the piece to save it from being retired!

## FACT STACK

Modular Buildings have storeys that separate easily for access to the detailed interiors, like in Detective's Office (set 10246, pictured).

Each Modular Building can be quickly built on to any other using LEGO Technic pins.

LEGO Modular Buildings are the only modern sets to use the classic smiling minifigure face.

Since 2013, LEGO Modular Buildings have been part of the Creator Expert theme.

The "sunburst" sign over the door of Café Corner (set 10182) is made by fanning out minifigure skis on a curving tube.

## AWESOME!

**2011**
Pet Shop
(set 10218)

**2012**
Town Hall
(set 10224)

**2013**
Palace Cinema
(set 10232)

**2014**
Parisian
Restaurant
(set 10243)

**2015**
Detective's
Office
(set 10246)

**2016**
Brick Bank
(set 10251)

**2017**
Assembly Square
(set 10255)

# DIVE IN!

LEGO themes went into space and back in time before they ventured underwater. But when they finally took the plunge, these subaquatic worlds really made a splash!

## FACT STACK

The first underwater-themed sets featured the LEGO Town Divers in 1987.

In the 1990s, a futuristic deep-sea theme known as "Sea-Tron" was planned but not released.

The 1997 LEGO Town Divers set Shark Attack (set 6599) was originally released without any sharks!

Every LEGO City Deep Sea Explorers set featured at least one piece of treasure to find.

## SUCKERS!

LEGO® Aquazone Hydronauts craft could pick things up using limpet-like suction-cups. These special pieces have never appeared in any other theme.

## WOW!

The 1997 LEGO Town set Deep Sea Bounty (set 6559) features a brick-built whale skeleton. Its tail is made from an airplane piece.

**DEEP, MAN.**

## 12

Brand-new, brightly coloured printed pieces were created for The Beatles' Yellow Submarine (set 21306).

## TOP 5
### LEGO® Atlantis deep-sea dwellers

**1** Squid Warrior (set 8061)

**2** Barracuda Guardian (set 7985)

**3** Hammerhead Warrior (set 7984)

**4** Lobster Guardian (set 7985)

**5** Manta Warrior (set 8073)

**IT'S A SIGN!**

The LEGO® Aquazone Aquasharks styled their ships with scary stick-on eyes and teeth – plus a surprisingly smiley shark logo!

THIS PLACE IS A REAL DIVE.

# KEY DATES

## 1995
The first LEGO Aquazone sets pitch brave, crystal-hunting Aquanauts against the Aquasharks in the first underwater LEGO theme.

## 1997
A new wave of Aquazone sets introduces the Aquaraiders – mineral hunters who are not afraid to smash up the seabed!

## 1998
Heroic Hank Hydro leads the Hydronauts into battle against the Stingrays in the third and final era of LEGO Aquazone.

## 2007
Almost sharing its name with an Aquazone faction, Aqua Raiders is a new theme in which treasure hunters tackle scary sea monsters!

## 2010
LEGO Atlantis explorers set out to find the fabled lost city of Atlantis, meeting many strange creatures along the way.

**Q** What is the biggest underwater-themed LEGO set?

**A** Portal of Atlantis (set 8078) from the LEGO Atlantis theme has 1,007 pieces, including two brick-built sharks and special treasure keys to unlock the portal!

# Piece particulars
Crystal pieces were created especially for the LEGO Aquazone theme in 1995, and have since appeared in more than 150 sets.

**REALLY?!**
An unfortunate diver can be seen inside the squid in 2007's LEGO® Aqua Raiders Aquabase Invasion (set 7775). His skeleton still has its diving mask on!

# SOMETHING OLD, SOMETHING NEW

The LEGO® NEXO KNIGHTS™ world is a place where advanced digital technology sits side-by-side with knights and monsters straight out of the medieval era.

## Brick statistics

### Jestro's Volcano Lair
(set 70323)

**1,186 pieces**
One of the biggest LEGO NEXO KNIGHTS sets

**8 minifigures**
Plus two Scurrier figures

**6 NEXO Powers**
Included on scannable shields

**4 animals**
Look out for a rat, chicken, spider and frog

**3 spell books**
Including the scary Book of Monsters

**Q** | How do you become a knight?

**A** | Apprentices enroll at the Knights' Academy, a prestigious school where Merlok 2.0 teaches the next generation about combat, NEXO Powers and the Knight's Code.

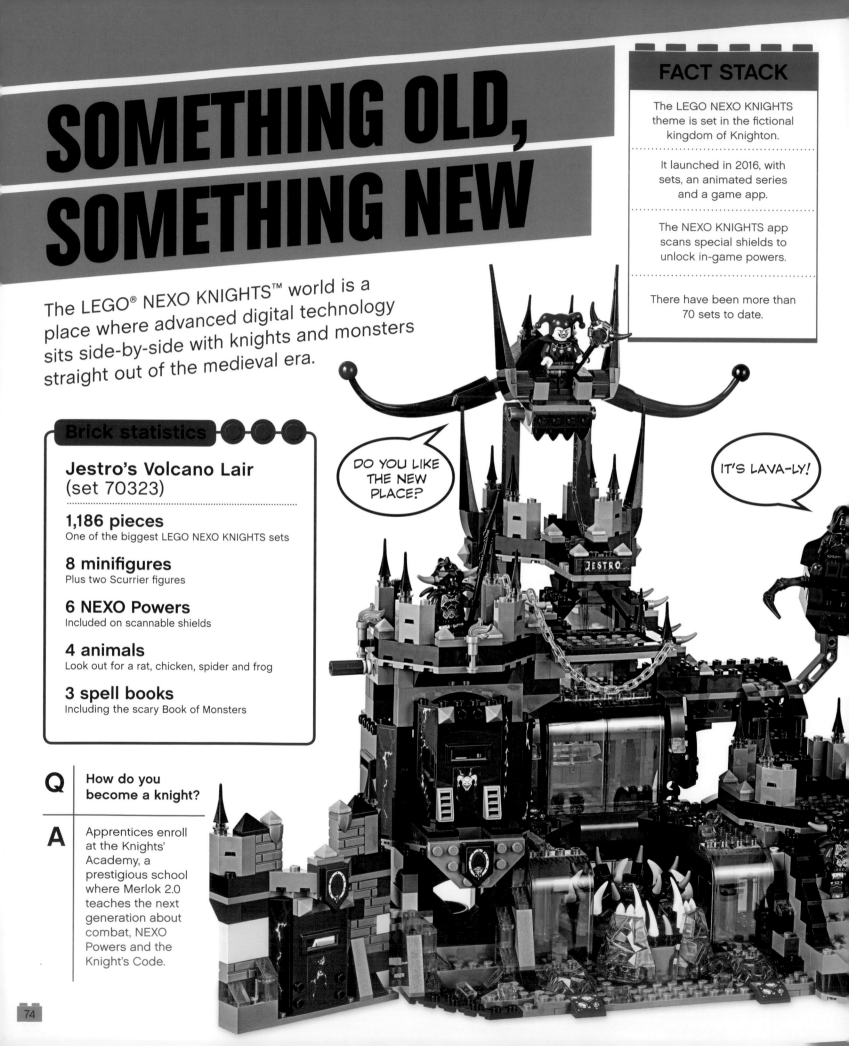

DO YOU LIKE THE NEW PLACE?

IT'S LAVA-LY!

# NEXOgraphy of Knighton

The **Lava Lands** are a bleak volcanic wilderness full of dangerous monsters.

Knighton's capital city is called **Knightonia**, which is designed around the royal castle.

**Diggington** is a charming rural town in the northern Hill Country.

**Auremville** in the mountainous west is renowned for its riches.

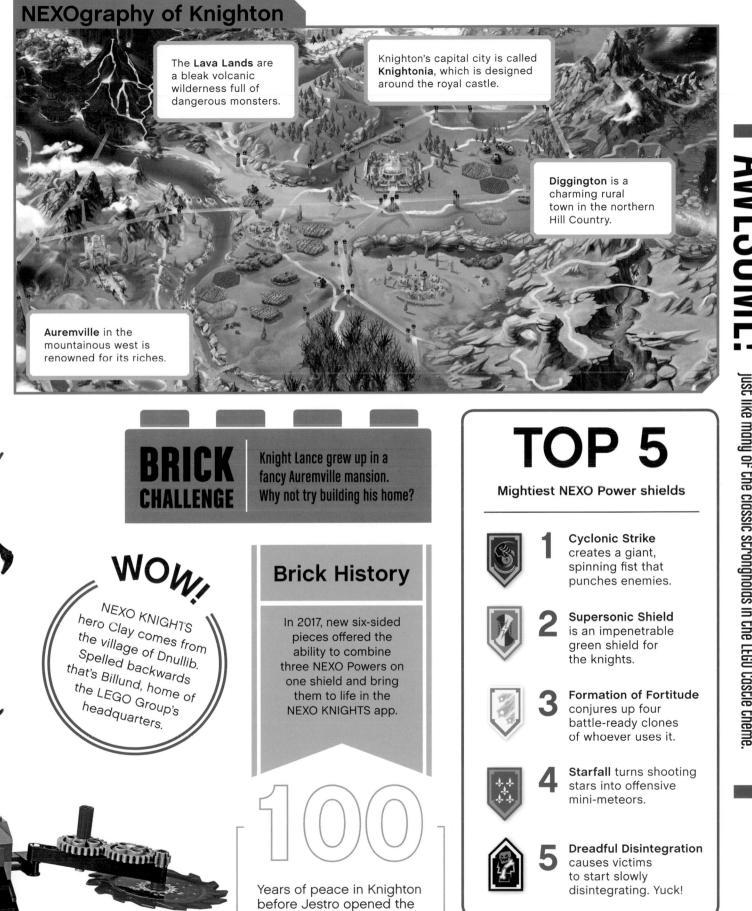

## AWESOME!

King Halbert's huge Knighton Castle (set 70357) swings open on hinges, just like many of the classic strongholds in the LEGO Castle theme.

## BRICK CHALLENGE

Knight Lance grew up in a fancy Auremville mansion. Why not try building his home?

## WOW!

NEXO KNIGHTS hero Clay comes from the village of Dnullib. Spelled backwards that's Billund, home of the LEGO Group's headquarters.

## Brick History

In 2017, new six-sided pieces offered the ability to combine three NEXO Powers on one shield and bring them to life in the NEXO KNIGHTS app.

## 100

Years of peace in Knighton before Jestro opened the Book of Monsters!

## TOP 5

### Mightiest NEXO Power shields

**1 Cyclonic Strike** creates a giant, spinning fist that punches enemies.

**2 Supersonic Shield** is an impenetrable green shield for the knights.

**3 Formation of Fortitude** conjures up four battle-ready clones of whoever uses it.

**4 Starfall** turns shooting stars into offensive mini-meteors.

**5 Dreadful Disintegration** causes victims to start slowly disintegrating. Yuck!

# WORLD CRAFTING

Combining virtual construction game *Minecraft* with real-world LEGO bricks was always going to build into something special. In 2013, the exciting LEGO® *Minecraft*™ theme was spawned!

## FACT STACK

LEGO *Minecraft* started out as an idea on the LEGO CUUSOO (now LEGO Ideas) website.

It took just 48 hours for LEGO *Minecraft* to win 10,000 votes from LEGO CUUSOO users!

LEGO *Minecraft* Micro World (set 21102) was released as a LEGO CUUSOO set in 2012.

A fully fledged theme called LEGO *Minecraft* followed Micro World into stores in 2013.

## 1,600
Pieces in the largest LEGO *Minecraft* set, The Village (set 21128), from 2016.

# AWESOME!
The first four LEGO *Minecraft* sets came in cube-shaped boxes that looked like *Minecraft* building blocks.

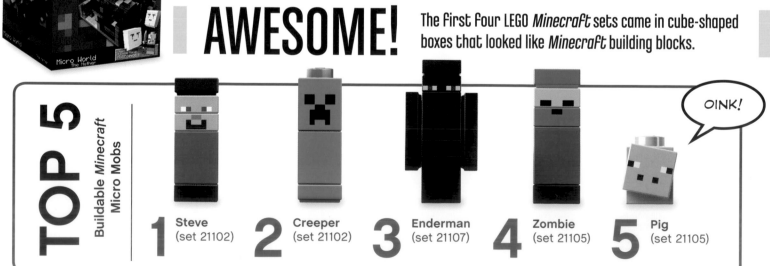

## TOP 5
### Buildable Minecraft Micro Mobs

**1** Steve (set 21102)

**2** Creeper (set 21102)

**3** Enderman (set 21107)

**4** Zombie (set 21105)

**5** Pig (set 21105)

OINK!

## BIGGEST BOSS

The Ender Dragon (set 21117)

## Piece particulars

Minifigures in the LEGO *Minecraft* universe have unique cube-shaped heads that are 1.5 studs wide. These pieces have no studs on top, so their 2 studs-wide helmets clutch at the sides instead.

## REALLY?!

*Minecraft* sets use so many 2x2 jumper plates that the LEGO Group had to make a new mould to keep up with demand.

# WE ARE THE MOBS

"Mob" is the *Minecraft* name for any creature that is mobile. LEGO *Minecraft* features all six of the main Mob categories found in the game itself.

Sheep and Pigs are friendly **Passive Mobs**.

Cave Spiders are **Neutral Mobs** that attack if provoked.

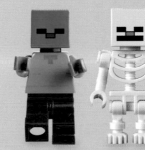

Watch out for **Hostile Mobs**, such as Zombies and Skeletons.

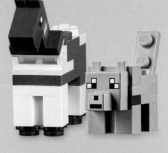

You can befriend **Tameable Mobs**, such as Horses and Wolves.

**Utility Mobs**, such as Iron Golems, can fight off Hostile Mobs.

Beware **Boss Mobs**, such as Withers, which are huge and very hostile!

# LOOK CLOSER

*Minecraft* Mobs multiply by spawning. To see spawning in action, turn the round brick in The Dungeon (set 21119) and watch the baby Zombie move inside the cage-like spawner.

## MICRO MANAGING

Each LEGO *Minecraft* Micro World set is made up of four modular sections that can be rearranged and mixed together to make a bigger *Minecraft* world.

# A SET FOR

## JANUARY

In the Chinese zodiac, 2017 is the Year of the Rooster. This little cockerel (set 40234) was released in time to mark the Chinese New Year on 28th January 2017.

## FEBRUARY

No valentine could resist this brick-built Rose (set 852786). It's as fresh today as it was on its release in 2010.

Valentine's Day Dinner (set 40120) includes this gold-colored ring – or is it a bracelet? – for one lucky minifigure to wear.

## MARCH & APRIL

A cuddly bunny with a bag of DUPLO bricks (set 852217) marked Easter in 2008. In 2016, a brick-built Easter Chick (set 40202) proved just as cute, if not so cuddly!

## SEPTEMBER

Fall Scene (set 40057) features tree trunks that can be decorated with autumnal colours. Any fallen leaves are swept up by minifigures!

## OCTOBER

This Halloween Bat (set 40090) is one of several LEGO sets released over the years to mark Halloween.

## NOVEMBER

Several LEGO sets have marked US Thanksgiving, including a turkey (set 40011), a pilgrim (set 40204), and this turkey dressed as a pilgrim (set 40091)!

# ALL SEASONS

## MAY

The LEGO Group has marked *Star Wars* Day on 4th May with several exclusive sets, including Escape the Space Slug (set 6176782) in 2016.

## JULY

US Flag (set 10042) from 2003 is one of two small stars-and-stripes builds released to mark US Independence Day, which is celebrated on 4th July.

## AUGUST

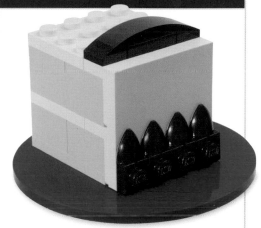

The LEGO Group's birthday is in August, and this slice of Birthday Cake (set 40048) helped it to celebrate in 2012.

## DECEMBER

In 2009, the LEGO Holiday Countdown Candle (set 852741) was released. It features 24 numbered bricks – one to be removed each day in the lead-up to Christmas.

The first Christmas set was Santa and Sleigh (set 246) in 1977. Other brick-built Santas followed, including this Santa on Skis (set 1128) from 1999.

Since 2009, winter-themed Creator sets have combined to make a snow-capped village featuring a toy shop, bakery, market, train and even Santa's Workshop (set 10245, pictured).

# A TRIP TO MINILAND

From California to Malaysia, the heart of each and every LEGOLAND® park is its MINILAND, a remarkable LEGO brick recreation of landmarks from around the world.

**Q** Do the models in MINILAND move?

**A** Yes. Every year, the MINILAND vehicles at LEGOLAND Billund travel a distance equivalent to almost three trips around the world!

## AWESOME!

Built at 1:50 scale, the Allianz Arena soccer stadium in LEGOLAND Deutschland features more than one million bricks and 30,000 minifigure spectators.

Miles (300km) of underground cable are used to power MINILAND's moving parts at LEGOLAND Windsor.

## WORLD'S TALLEST LEGO BUILDING

Burj Khalifa at LEGOLAND Dubai, measuring 55ft (17m)

## BRICK CHALLENGE

It takes around 40 bricks to build a MINILAND figure. Can you make a model of yourself in MINILAND scale?

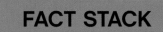

## FACT STACK

The first MINILAND was "Lilleby" (Little Town), at LEGOLAND Billund in 1968.

So far, more than 20 million LEGO bricks have been used to make MINILAND in Billund.

LEGO *Star Wars* scenes have formed part of the MINILAND world since 2011.

The MINILAND at LEGOLAND Dubai is inside a giant, see-through, air-conditioned dome.

## TIPPING THE SCALE

Most MINILAND buildings are built at a scale between 1:20 and 1:40. In other words, they are between 20 and 40 times smaller than the real thing.

## WOW!

In March 2017, a LEGO Star Wars Star Destroyer measuring 16ft (4.8m) was unveiled at MINILAND in LEGOLAND California.

## LOOK CLOSER

A MINILAND ship at LEGOLAND Florida has the registry number 0937. Look at those numbers upside down and they spell out "LEGO".

# A TRIP TO MINILAND

## CONTINUED

## REALLY?!

Gardeners at LEGOLAND Billund plant around 100,000 flowers and bulbs every year to make sure MINILAND is always in bloom.

# FANTASY FOREST

The LEGO® Elves theme launched in March 2015, with a TV special on the *Disney* Channel to introduce its magical characters and the forest world of Elvendale.

## Top 5

### Elvendale's largest sets

**1. Ragana's Magic Shadow Castle** (set 41180), 1,014 pieces

**2. Queen Dragon's Rescue** (set 41179), 833 pieces

**3. Skyra's Mysterious Sky Castle** (set 41078), 808 pieces

**4. Breakout from the Goblin King's Fortress** (set 41188), 695 pieces

**5. The Secret Market Place** (set 41176), 691 pieces

## WOW!

The Dragons of Elvendale are linked to the elements water, fire, earth and wind, just like the Elves. The Queen dragon, Elandra, uses a different one: love!

## Piece particulars

The 1x4x2 ornamental fence piece was introduced in the LEGO Elves theme and has since popped up in other sets, including The *Disney* Castle (set 71040).

Ragana's Magic Shadow Castle

Queen Dragon's Rescue

Skyra's Mysterious Sky Castle

# MAGICAL CREATURES

Elvendale is home to many enchanting animals, from owls and foxes to chameleons and pegasi.

Flamy the fox

Delphia the dolphin

Hidee the chameleon

Golden Glow the pegasus

Nascha the owl

Lil' Blu the baby bear

## REALLY?!

In the LEGO Elves TV show, whenever fire elf Azari gets embarrassed, her ears turn white!

## LOOK CLOSER

All of Elvendale's animals have a unique pattern printed on them, giving each a mystical look, just like the Elves.

**Q** | Is Elvendale a dangerous place?

**A** | It can be when the goblins are around! They use plant traps and catapults to make trouble for the elves.

YUM.

YUM!

# AWESOME!

Each baby dragon hatches from a two-part dragon egg created especially for the LEGO Elves theme.

Breakout from the Goblin King's Fortress

The Secret Market Place

# AT THE MOVIES

As well as making its own engrossing worlds, the LEGO Group has often teamed up with filmmakers to create play themes based on big-screen favourites.

## LEGO® GHOSTBUSTERS™

Since 2014, there have been LEGO sets based on both the 1985 and 2016 *Ghostbusters* movies. With its 4,634 pieces, **LEGO *Ghostbusters* Firehouse Headquarters** (set 75827) was the largest LEGO set released in 2016.

THAT SIGN ISN'T VERY WELCOMING.

SHE'S BEHIND YOU. BOO!

## LEGO® HARRY POTTER™

The longest running licensed theme after LEGO *Star Wars*, LEGO *Harry Potter* ran from 2001 to 2012, with a break in 2008–2009. Its dozens of sets included a detailed depiction of magical **Diagon Alley** (set 10217).

THIS IS ORC-WARD.

THAT IS NOT A WIZARD IDEA, SARUMAN.

## LEGO® *THE LORD OF THE RINGS*™

LEGO *The Lord of the Rings* and LEGO *The Hobbit* launched in 2012, recreating Middle-earth in minifigure scale. The largest set from either theme was the 28in (73cm) tall **Tower of Orthanc** (set 10237).

# CHAPTER THREE

# CARS, PLANES, SHIPS AND TRAINS

# STREET CARS

There are more than 700 vehicles in LEGO® Town and LEGO City, of which these are just a few. Every one is the starting point for an endless number of adventures.

The Town **Horse Trailer** (set 6359) offers two modes of transport in one set.

**1986**

**1988**   **Blizzard Blazer** (set 6524)

HEY YOU, STOP HORSING AROUND!

**1978**

This open-top **Police Car** (set 621) is one of the first Town cars to hit the road.

GO!

**1982**   Mail Truck (set 6651)

POLICE

**2009**   Tractor (set 7634)

**2010**

This VIP stretch vehicle is part of **Helicopter and Limousine** (set 3222).

AG60102

IT'S USUALLY ME HOLDING UP THE TRAFFIC.

143 CITY

143 CITY

HA60026

**2013**

This eight-seater City bus stops off at **Town Square** (set 60026).

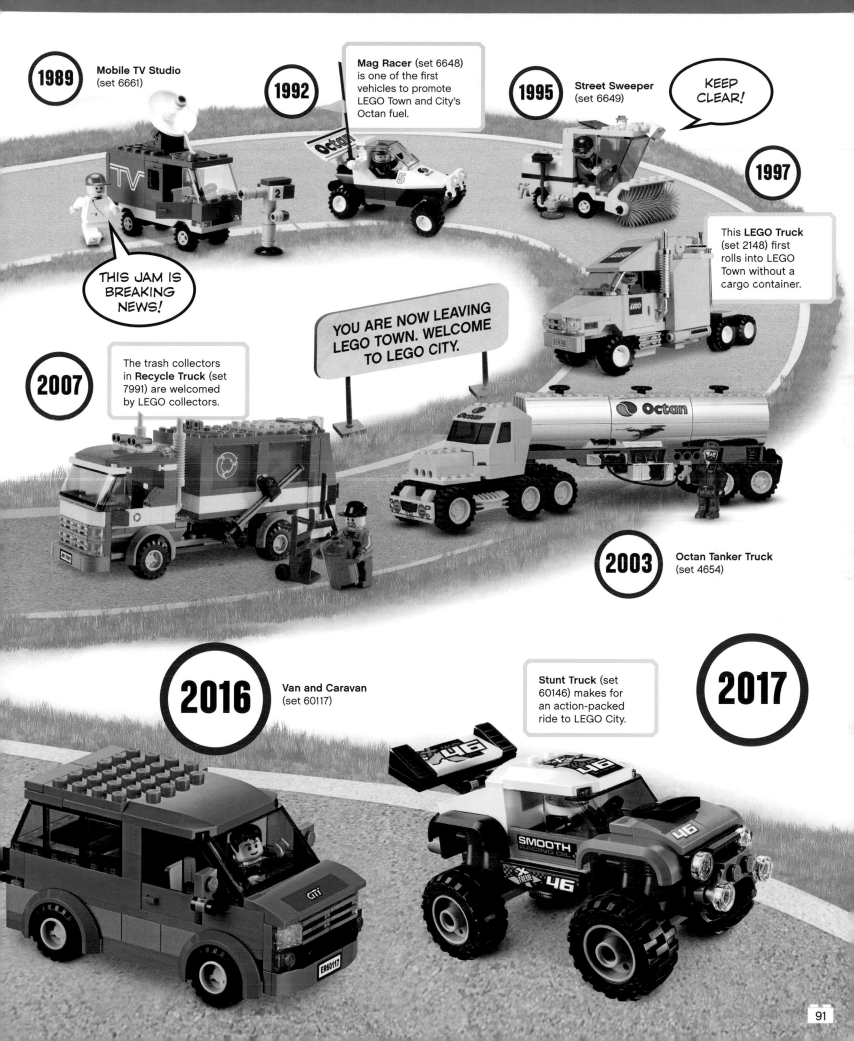

**1989** Mobile TV Studio (set 6661)

THIS JAM IS BREAKING NEWS!

**1992** Mag Racer (set 6648) is one of the first vehicles to promote LEGO Town and City's Octan fuel.

**1995** Street Sweeper (set 6649)

KEEP CLEAR!

**1997** This LEGO Truck (set 2148) first rolls into LEGO Town without a cargo container.

YOU ARE NOW LEAVING LEGO TOWN. WELCOME TO LEGO CITY.

**2007** The trash collectors in Recycle Truck (set 7991) are welcomed by LEGO collectors.

**2003** Octan Tanker Truck (set 4654)

**2016** Van and Caravan (set 60117)

Stunt Truck (set 60146) makes for an action-packed ride to LEGO City.

**2017**

# CAN YOU DIG IT?

LEGO fans love to build and rebuild, so it's no surprise that there are dozens of sets based on real-life construction and demolition vehicles!

## FACT STACK

In 1964, the 64-piece Building Crane (set 804) was the first construction-themed vehicle.

Minifigure construction crews got to work in 1978, driving two diggers into LEGO Town.

There have been more than 40 construction-themed LEGO® Technic vehicles since 1979.

LEGO® DUPLO vehicles with a construction theme include the *Bob the Builder* range.

**I GET PAID FOR DOZING ON THE JOB!**

## WOW!

The huge LEGO City Heavy Loader (set 7900) from 2006 carries an entire bridge that can be built into your LEGO City street system.

## Piece particulars

The LEGO City Dozer (set 7685) from 2009 is one of only two sets to feature jet engine turbines but no jet engine housings.

## Brick History

In 2012, the LEGO City Mining subtheme featured several diggers and tippers. A special mining logo distinguishes these from similar construction vehicles.

**IT'S A MINER DIFFERENCE!**

## 21.6

Inches (55cm) is the full extent of the aptly named LEGO City XXL Mobile Crane (set 7249) from 2005.

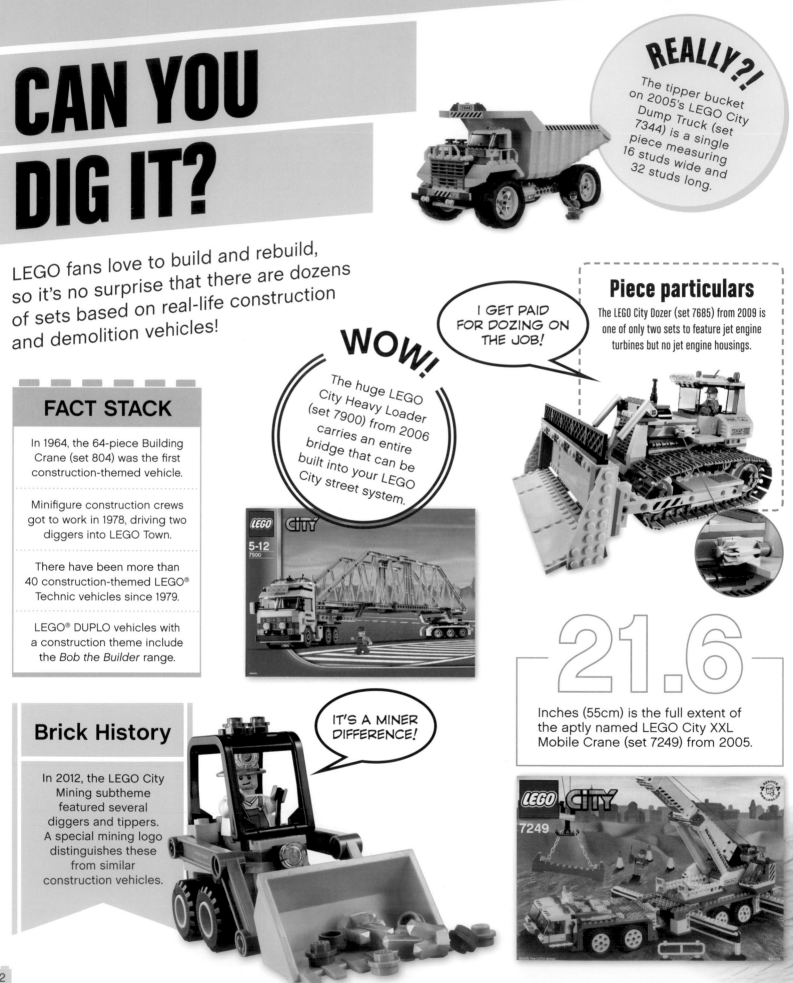

# AWESOME!

The crane in 2010's LEGO City Level Crossing (set 7936) has two sets of wheels – one for roads and one for train tracks.

## Brick statistics

### 28 diggers and loaders
In the LEGO Town and City themes

### 25 dumpers, tippers and dozers
Across all of LEGO Town and City

### 7 mobile cranes and wreckers
In Town and City construction sets

### 3 cement mixers
1 in LEGO Town, 2 in LEGO City

### 1 Construct-o-Mech
Only in the world of THE LEGO® MOVIE™!

**Q** Are all LEGO construction vehicles yellow?

**A** Not all! There was a blue LEGO Town Tractor (set 6504) in 1988 and an orange digger in LEGO City Juniors Road Work Truck (set 10683) in 2015.

## IT'S A SIGN!

The familiar symbol of a worker with a shovel has featured in many LEGO sets, and even got a "Minifigures at Work" makeover!

# TOP 5

**Building-site special pieces**

**1** Excavator scoop (1971)

**2** Spring-loaded grabber (1974)

**3** Tipper bucket (1974)

**4** Cement mixer drum cone (1985)

**5** Wrecking ball (2015)

10T

# BUILT FOR SPEED

If you've ever wanted to own a supercar, these LEGO racing sets can make your dreams come true. Many of them are based on real-life cars.

## FACT STACK

The first LEGO racing set was Car with Trailer and Racer (set 650) in 1972.

The first minifigure racing driver came in the Race Car set (set 6609) in 1980.

More than 200 LEGO Racers sets came out from 2001 to 2013.

There have been three video games featuring LEGO racing cars.

## REALLY?!

The LEGO Power Racers Tow Trasher (set 8140) from 2007 is designed to fall apart – purely for dramatic effect!

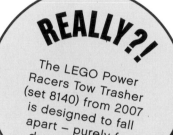

## LOOK CLOSER

The Tiny Turbos subtheme of LEGO® Racers features fun, fast cars made with the fewest pieces possible. They are still packed with details, though – as the tiny stickered logos on this Rally Sprinter (set 8120) show!

The wheels on LEGO Speed Champions cars have realistic interchangeable hubcaps, not seen in any other theme.

# AWESOME!

## REAL RACING

Since 2015, the LEGO® Speed Champions theme has recreated real-life racecars at minifigure scale, with impressively realistic results. Here are some of the sets released so far.

Ford Mustang GT
(set 75871)

Porsche 918 Spyder
(set 75910)

# KEY DATES

## 1998
Radio Control Racer
(set 5600) becomes the first
radio-control LEGO vehicle.
It comes with instructions
for five different racecars.

## 2001
LEGO Racers sets screech
into stores. They feature
small cars with speed-
demon driver pieces made
especially for the theme.

## 2002
Racers step up a gear
with larger sets, remote-control
units, pullback motors and
drivers with minifigure heads
on one-piece bodies.

## 2005
LEGO Power Racers mixes
ramps, launchers, motors,
fly-apart features and spinning
obstacles to create an array
of exciting stunt vehicles.

## 2010
LEGO World Racers
pitches minifigure team
the X-treme Daredevils
against the Backyard
Blasters in racecars,
race bikes, race boats
and race snowmobiles!

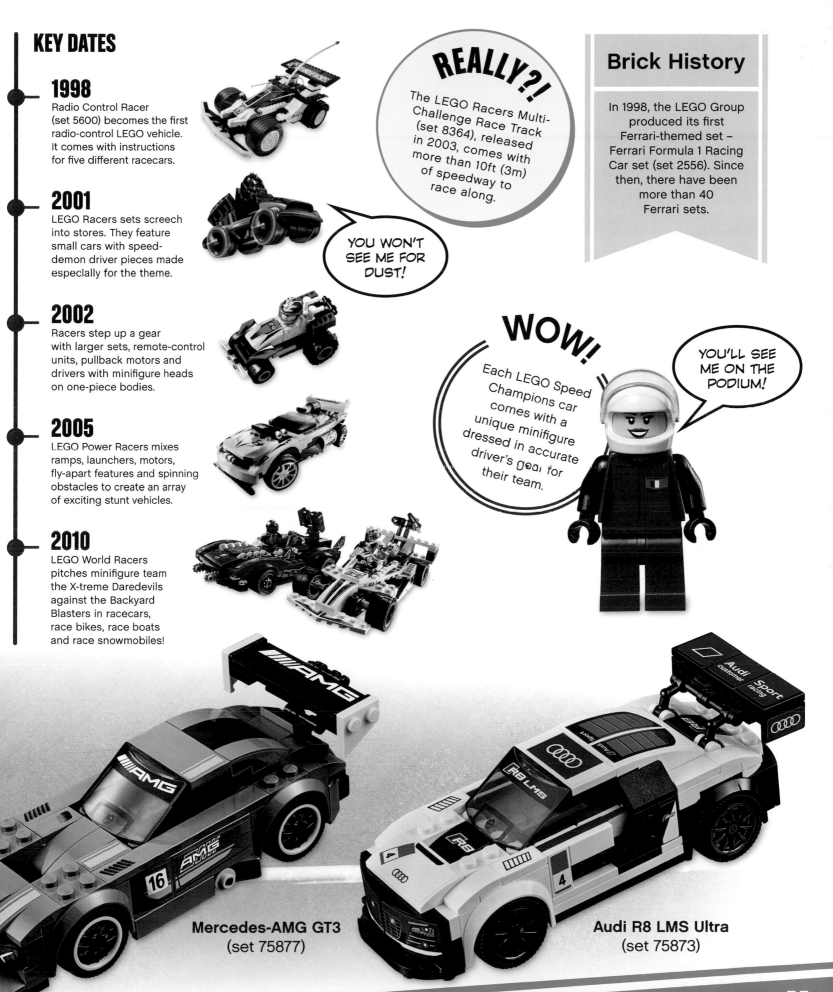

## REALLY?!
The LEGO Racers Multi-
Challenge Race Track
(set 8364), released
in 2003, comes with
more than 10ft (3m)
of speedway to
race along.

YOU WON'T
SEE ME FOR
DUST!

## WOW!
Each LEGO Speed
Champions car
comes with a
unique minifigure
dressed in accurate
driver's gear for
their team.

YOU'LL SEE
ME ON THE
PODIUM!

## Brick History

In 1998, the LEGO Group
produced its first
Ferrari-themed set –
Ferrari Formula 1 Racing
Car set (set 2556). Since
then, there have been
more than 40
Ferrari sets.

Mercedes-AMG GT3
(set 75877)

Audi R8 LMS Ultra
(set 75873)

## GOING OFF-ROAD

LEGO Town Amazon
Crossing (set 6490)

LEGO Town Arctic
Ice Surfer
(set 6579)

LEGO City Jungle
Mobile Lab
(set 60160)

LEGO® Technic
Arctic Rescue Unit
(set 8660)

LEGO® Friends
Jungle Bridge
Rescue
(set 41036)

LEGO City Arctic Outpost
(set 60035)

ARCTIC-3

### FORESTS
### AND JUNGLE

Whether exploring
the Amazon
Jungle or the
fictional forests
of Heartlake City,
these vehicles all
have large, sturdy
wheels – perfect
for navigating
dense foliage.

### SNOW AND ICE

LEGO Town and City
have had an Arctic
outpost since 2000.
Vehicles have
adapted for the cold
conditions, with
strong wheels, sails
and skis to cope
with slippery terrain.

Not all LEGO vehicles are meant to stick to streets! For every cool city car, there's a mighty off-roader ready to tackle some tougher terrain.

**LEGO® Creator Desert Racers**
(set 31040)

## BEACH AND DESERT

Heavy-tred tyres get to grips with desert sand dunes on these four-wheel drive cars. The LEGO® Friends beach scooter has just three wheels, but still tackles sand with ease.

**LEGO Technic Desert Racer**
(set 42027)

**LEGO City Volcano Crawler**
(set 60122)

EVERY LIFEGUARD NEEDS A RESCUE PUG!

**LEGO Friends Mia's Beach Scooter**
(set 41306)

**LEGO Model Team Big Foot 4x4**
(set 5561)

**LEGO City The Mine**
(set 4204)

DIGGING THROUGH MINES? I KNOW THE DRILL.

## ROCKS AND MOUNTAINS

Equipped with drills and jackhammers, these specialist LEGO vehicles are ready for a bumpy ride over rocks, in mines or on red-hot lava.

# HEROIC RIDES AND VILLAINOUS VEHICLES

In the battle between LEGO® DC Comics Super Heroes and their criminal counterparts, victory depends on what vehicle you drive! Here are some of the best and the baddest.

## AWESOME!

Wonder Woman's Invisible Jet is made using almost all transparent pieces.

> THE CONTROLS ARE HARD TO READ.

### IT'S A SIGN!

The symbol on Green Lantern's spaceship (set 76025) is shaped like a green lamp: the insignia of intergalactic peacekeeping group the Green Lantern Corps.

## FACT STACK

The first LEGO DC Universe Super Heroes sets came out in 2012.

In 2014, the theme became LEGO DC Comics Super Heroes.

Heroes in the theme can call on almost 40 different modes of transport.

Bad guys are at the controls of more than 20 different vehicles.

## TOP 5
Mighty micros sets

**1** **Catwoman's** Catmobile has ears and a tail!

**2** **The Flash** drives a lightning-fast red racer.

**3** **Killer Moth's** car gets ahead by a nose!

**4** **Superman's** supercar flies along with outstretched arms.

**Q** Riddle me this: what's long, thin, fast and green?

**A** A runner bean! Or the Riddler's Dragster from Batman: The Riddler Chase (set 76012).

# LOOK CLOSER

The front of Brainiac's flying saucer, Brainiac Attack (set 76040), is a scary skull face!

SMILE FOR THE ROLLER!

BANG BANG

## Brick History

Two-Face was the first villain to get his own getaway car, in Batmobile and the Two-Face Chase (set 6864, released 2012). Like him, it had two very different sides!

**5** **Bizarro's** car is Superman's built backwards!

# REALLY?!

In Batman: The Penguin Face Off (set 76010), the bird-brained Penguin gets around in a giant rubber duck!

IT'S BATH TIME, BATMAN!

# BAT-VEHICLES

With a Batcave full of crime-fighting cars and other hi-tech transport, Batman is always on the move in the LEGO® Batman and LEGO DC Super Heroes themes.

**REALLY?!**

Robin's Scuba Jet (set 7885) is the only set in the LEGO Batman theme not to feature Batman.

## FACT STACK

The first LEGO Bat-vehicles hit the streets in 2006, in the LEGO Batman theme.

In 2012, LEGO Batman became part of the DC Super Heroes theme.

To date, there have been more than 40 LEGO Bat-vehicles.

There are 10 different LEGO Batmobiles, all of them black!

## TOP 5

Batmobiles

**1** The first Batmobile from **2006** has a massive missile in the bonnet.

**2** This **2014** Batmobile looks like a Formula 1 racing car.

**3** The Batmobile from **2015** has a classic 1930s hot rod vibe.

**4** Released in **2016**, this Batmobile is straight out of the 1960s!

**5** This **2016** Batmobile is compact but heavily armoured.

# AWESOME!

There have been two LEGO Bat-Tanks. The latest (in set 76055) has a front section that folds upright to make a huge battering ram!

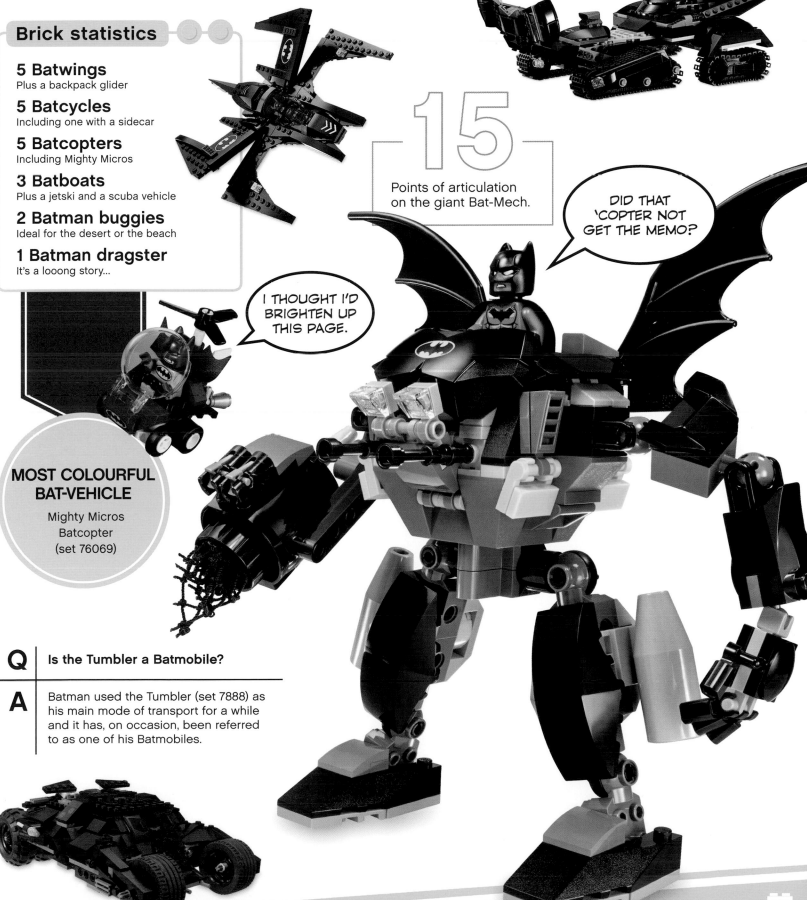

## Brick statistics

**5 Batwings**
Plus a backpack glider

**5 Batcycles**
Including one with a sidecar

**5 Batcopters**
Including Mighty Micros

**3 Batboats**
Plus a jetski and a scuba vehicle

**2 Batman buggies**
Ideal for the desert or the beach

**1 Batman dragster**
It's a looong story...

**15**
Points of articulation on the giant Bat-Mech.

DID THAT 'COPTER NOT GET THE MEMO?

I THOUGHT I'D BRIGHTEN UP THIS PAGE.

### MOST COLOURFUL BAT-VEHICLE

Mighty Micros Batcopter (set 76069)

**Q** | Is the Tumbler a Batmobile?

**A** | Batman used the Tumbler (set 7888) as his main mode of transport for a while and it has, on occasion, been referred to as one of his Batmobiles.

## Famous four-wheelers from film and TV

1 **The Patty Wagon.**
Of all the zany vehicles in the
LEGO® *Spongebob Squarepants*™
theme, this burger on wheels from
Krusty Krab Adventures (set 3833)
has to be the craziest.

2 **The Mystery Machine (set 75902).**
This *Scooby-Doo* van has space for
mystery-solving tools including a
camera, noticeboards, computers
– and a giant sandwich for
Shaggy and Scooby to share!

3 **Ecto-1 (set 75828).**
This set from the 2016 movie
*Ghostbusters* has room inside
for all four ghoul-catching heroes.
It is based on a 1980 Cadillac
Hearse Wagon.

# CARS

4    **The DeLorean Time Machine (set 21103).** This time-travelling car comes with instructions to turn it into the three versions seen in all three *Back to the Future* movies.

5    **The Simpsons' family car.** This car from *The Simpsons* has a large sunroof to make room for Marge Simpson's hair! It fits in the garage of The Simpson's House (set 71006).

6    **The Weasley's Ford Anglia.** The Weasley's flying family car appeared in two LEGO® *Harry Potter*™ sets: Escape from Privet Drive (set 4728) and Hogwarts Express (set 4841).

# BIG AND BOLD

Some of the biggest LEGO vehicles look like they should be built for display rather than play purposes, but these impressive models all offer hours of building fun and plenty of interactive detail.

## FACT STACK

In the 1970s, LEGO® Hobby Set vehicles were among the first designed for play *and* display.

.................................................

The LEGO® Model Team range was the home of large-scale vehicles in the 1980s and 1990s.

.................................................

Today, the most challenging vehicles to build are part of the LEGO® Creator Expert theme.

## LARGE-SCALE RAIL

Part of the 1970s Hobby Set range, Thatcher Perkins Locomotive (set 396) is the only LEGO train engine larger than minifigure (or DUPLO figure) scale.

SOPWITH

BIO226

## WOW!

The 2012 Sopwith Camel (set 10226) doesn't just look amazing – it also has working wing and tail flaps, controlled by a joystick in the cockpit.

# ▌AWESOME!

The 1978 model ship *USS Constellation* (set 398) is so fondly remembered that it was re-released in 2003 (set 10021), complete with retro packaging.

A surf scene in the homely interior of Volkswagen T1 Camper Van (set 10220) includes the initials of the set's designer, John-Henry Harris!

## Brick History

In 2003, Wright Flyer (set 10124) was released to mark the 100th anniversary of the first real-world powered aeroplane. It has 670 pieces in just five colours.

### Piece particulars

The car door handles on the MINI Cooper (set 10242) from 2014 are more usually used as minifigure ice skates!

## 27

Inches (69cm) – the wingspan of the Boeing 787 Dreamliner (set 10177), the largest of any LEGO aircraft.

## REALLY?!

The biggest set in the advanced LEGO Model Team range, Giant Truck (set 5571) has 1,757 pieces – including a cat for a bonnet ornament!

# STEPPING UP A GEAR

As well as looking incredible, the biggest LEGO Technic vehicles are marvels of miniature engineering – and they keep on getting bigger with each passing year! Here are the biggest LEGO Technic vehicles ever.

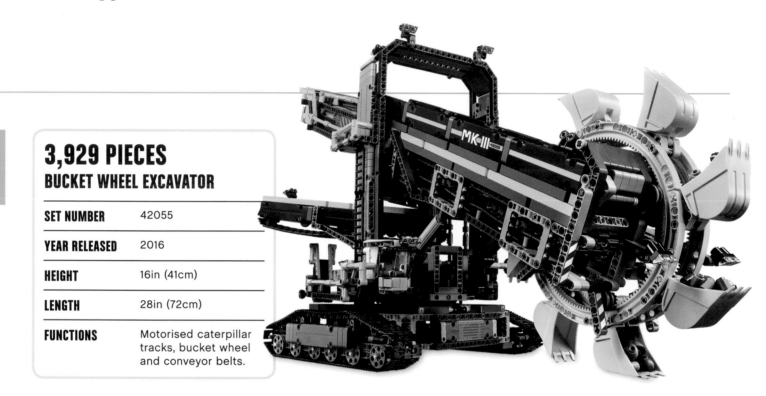

## 1

### 3,929 PIECES
**BUCKET WHEEL EXCAVATOR**

| | |
|---|---|
| **SET NUMBER** | 42055 |
| **YEAR RELEASED** | 2016 |
| **HEIGHT** | 16in (41cm) |
| **LENGTH** | 28in (72cm) |
| **FUNCTIONS** | Motorised caterpillar tracks, bucket wheel and conveyor belts. |

## 2

### 2,793 PIECES
**MERCEDES-BENZ AROCS 3245**

| | |
|---|---|
| **SET NUMBER** | 42043 |
| **YEAR RELEASED** | 2015 |
| **HEIGHT** | 22in (57cm) max. |
| **LENGTH** | 29in (75cm) |
| **FUNCTIONS** | Motorised outriggers, crane arm, grabber and tipper body. |

# 3

## 2,704 PIECES
### PORSCHE 911 GT3 RS

| SET NUMBER | 42056 |
|---|---|
| YEAR RELEASED | 2016 |
| HEIGHT | 6in (17cm) |
| LENGTH | 22in (57cm) |
| FUNCTIONS | Working gearbox and steering, suspension and adjustable spoiler. |

# 5

## 2,048 PIECES
### MERCEDES-BENZ UNIMOG U 400

| SET NUMBER | 8110 |
|---|---|
| YEAR RELEASED | 2011 |
| HEIGHT | 12in (30cm) |
| LENGTH | 19in (48cm) |
| FUNCTIONS | Motorised winch and pneumatic crane with working grabber. |

# 4

## 2,606 PIECES
### MOBILE CRANE MK II

| SET NUMBER | 42009 |
|---|---|
| YEAR RELEASED | 2013 |
| HEIGHT | 30in (77cm) max. |
| LENGTH | 23in (59cm) |
| FUNCTIONS | Motorised outriggers, extendable crane arm and winch. |

# STATION TO STATION

LEGO passenger trains have been getting LEGO citizens to where they need to go since... before there were LEGO citizens! Some are superfast, while others belong to the age of steam.

**Brick History**

In 1976, Western Train (set 726) was the first to carry passengers, in the form of three cowboy figures and a brick-built horse.

**IT'S A SIGN!**

DB
7715

In the 1980s, most LEGO trains came with sticker sheets featuring the logos of different national rail operators, so you could customise your train according to your country!

**WOW!**

Designed for use with the 1991 Metroliner (set 4558), Club Car (set 4547) from 1993 is the only double-decker LEGO Trains set.

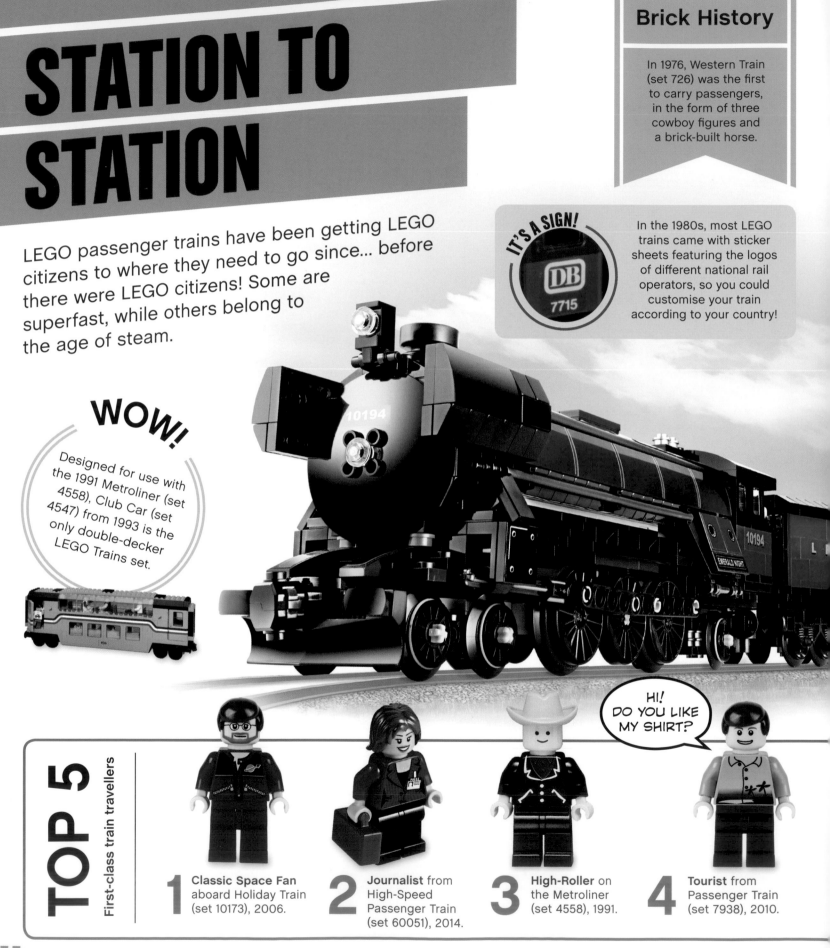

10194

10194

EMERALD NIGHT

HI! DO YOU LIKE MY SHIRT?

## TOP 5
### First-class train travellers

**1** **Classic Space Fan** aboard Holiday Train (set 10173), 2006.

**2** **Journalist** from High-Speed Passenger Train (set 60051), 2014.

**3** **High-Roller** on the Metroliner (set 4558), 1991.

**4** **Tourist** from Passenger Train (set 7938), 2010.

# AWESOME!

The LEGOLAND® Train (set 4000014) is a very rare replica of a ride at LEGOLAND Billund. It was given away to a few lucky fans in 2014.

The LEGOLAND® Train

## FACT STACK

The LEGO Group first produced a wooden locomotive in 1932, with wagons sold separately.

The first LEGO System Train (set 323) was a 1964 push-along vehicle with no rails.

LEGO Trains without a power source are designed so that one can be added easily.

To date, there have been more than 25 passenger trains in a variety of LEGO themes.

## DREAM DESIGNS

When 2009's awesome Emerald Night (set 10194) was being designed, the LEGO Group flew 10 fan builders to its head office in Denmark, then got them to describe their dream LEGO train.

## REALLY?!

Passengers could drive their cars onto 1999's futuristic Railway Express (set 4561) before heading to the onboard pizza restaurant!

## Piece particulars

The large grey switches that controlled 12-volt trains in the 1980s could also remotely operate lights, signals, points, level crossings and even wagon separation.

IT'S WHY I'M WEARING SHADES.

**5** **Definitely Not a Spy** on the High-Speed Train (set 4511), 2003.

**7** Speeds to choose from with 2014's superfast High-Speed Passenger Train (set 60051).

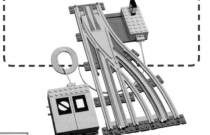

## KEY DATES

### 1966
The first powered LEGO train features a 4.5-volt battery pack and special train wheels, and runs on new blue track pieces.

### 1969
Mains-powered LEGO trains driven by a 12-volt conductor rail and the first powered rail-switching points are introduced in Europe.

### 1980
A new look for LEGO Trains includes realistic grey tracks and a revamped 12-volt system offering a wealth of remote-control functions.

### 1991
A single 9-volt mains-powered system replaces both 4.5-volt battery power and 12-volt mains power as the standard for LEGO Trains.

### 2006
The LEGO Trains theme is integrated into LEGO City, and a new infrared remote-control system powered by rechargeable batteries is launched.

### 2010
The first of several LEGO City trains designed specifically for use with a battery-operated LEGO Power Functions motor is released.

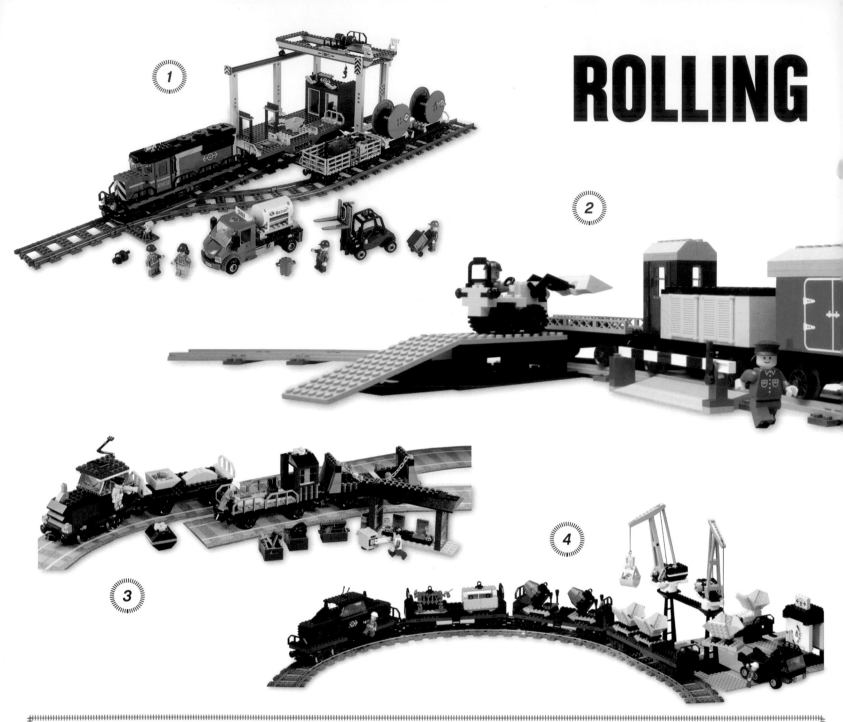

# ROLLING

① ② ③ ④

## Special cargo transported by train

*Elephants* on LEGO DUPLO My First Train (set 3770), 2005.

*Lots of toys* aboard Holiday Train (set 10173), 2006.

*Christmas trees* inside Winter Holiday Train (set 10254, pictured), 2016.

*Gold bars* on the Cargo Train (set 4512), 2003.

*LEGO sets* aboard the Cargo Train (set 7939), 2010.

*Helicopters* on the Heavy-Haul Train (set 60098), 2015.

# STOCK

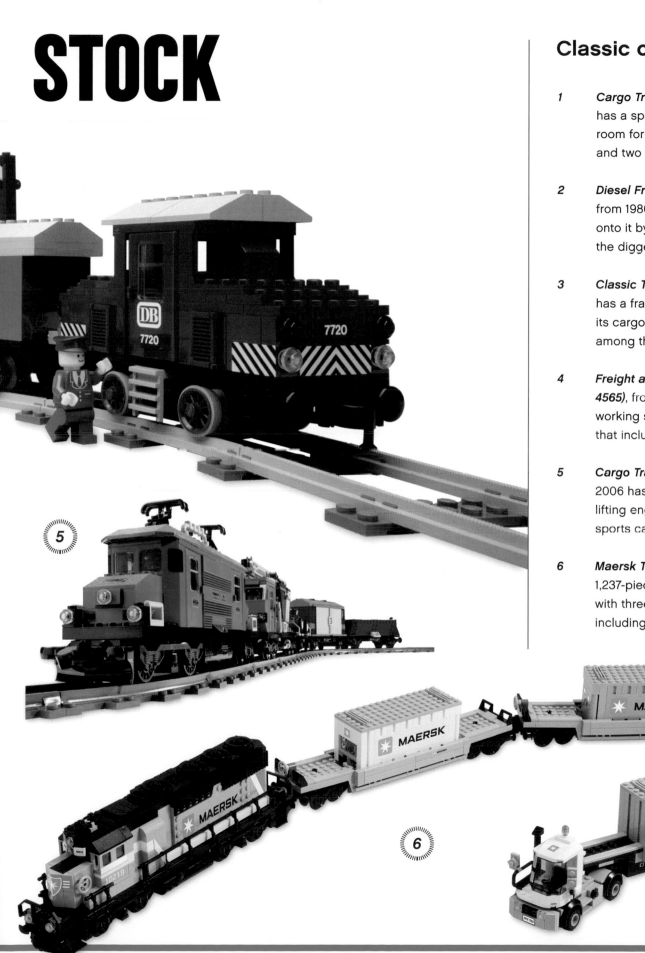

## Classic cargo trains

1    *Cargo Train (set 60052)*, from 2014 has a spacious cattle truck, plus room for a fuel tank, a forklift and two giant cable drums!

2    *Diesel Freight Train Set (set 7720)*, from 1980 carries cargo loaded onto it by a digger – as well as the digger itself!

3    *Classic Train (set 3225)*, from 1998 has a fragile crate of glasses amid its cargo, and a $100 note hidden among the mail!

4    *Freight and Crane Railway (set 4565)*, from 1996 comes with a working scale for weighing cargo that includes two cement mixers!

5    *Cargo Train Deluxe (set 7898)*, from 2006 has an onboard crane for lifting engines, oil drums and even sports cars on its flatbed wagons!

6    *Maersk Train (set 10219)*. This 1,237-piece train from 2011 is loaded with three huge cargo containers, including one refrigerator container.

# SET SAIL!

There are enough LEGO boats and ships to fill an ocean – well, at least a couple of bathtubs! Some of them float, while others are designed to look sunken.

The 2015 LEGO City Deep Sea Exploration Vessel (set 60095) comes with a shipwreck that collapses when you pull a hidden lever!

**2,741**

Number of pieces in the biggest LEGO ship: MetalBeard's Sea Cow (set 70810) from THE LEGO® MOVIE™.

## FACT STACK

In 1966, Master Mechanic Set (set 003) featured a moving, motorised Viking ship!

The first ship to be piloted by a minifigure was Police Boat (set 709) in 1978.

LEGO DUPLO ships include a glow-in-the-dark Pirate Ship (set 7881) from 2006!

There have been more than 60 boats in LEGO City, and 50 in the LEGO Pirates theme.

## REALLY?!

Some LEGO vessels can float using special watertight hull pieces. The first was Tugboat (set 310), released in 1973.

## WOW!

In 2005, two LEGO® Vikings sets featured longboats coming under attack from a dragon and a giant sea serpent!

**Q** When was the first LEGO Pirates ship launched?

**A** Black Seas Barracuda (set 6285) first set sail in 1989. It made such a splash that it was re-released as a LEGO Legends set (set 10040) in 2002.

## OCEANS APART

The LEGO Technic Ocean Explorer (set 42064) from 2017 has a whopping 1,327 pieces. The LEGO Creator Ocean Explorer (set 31045) from 2016 packs all its details into just 213!

# AWESOME!

# TOP 5

## Fanta-sea ships

**1** LEGO Castle Troll Warship (set 7048)

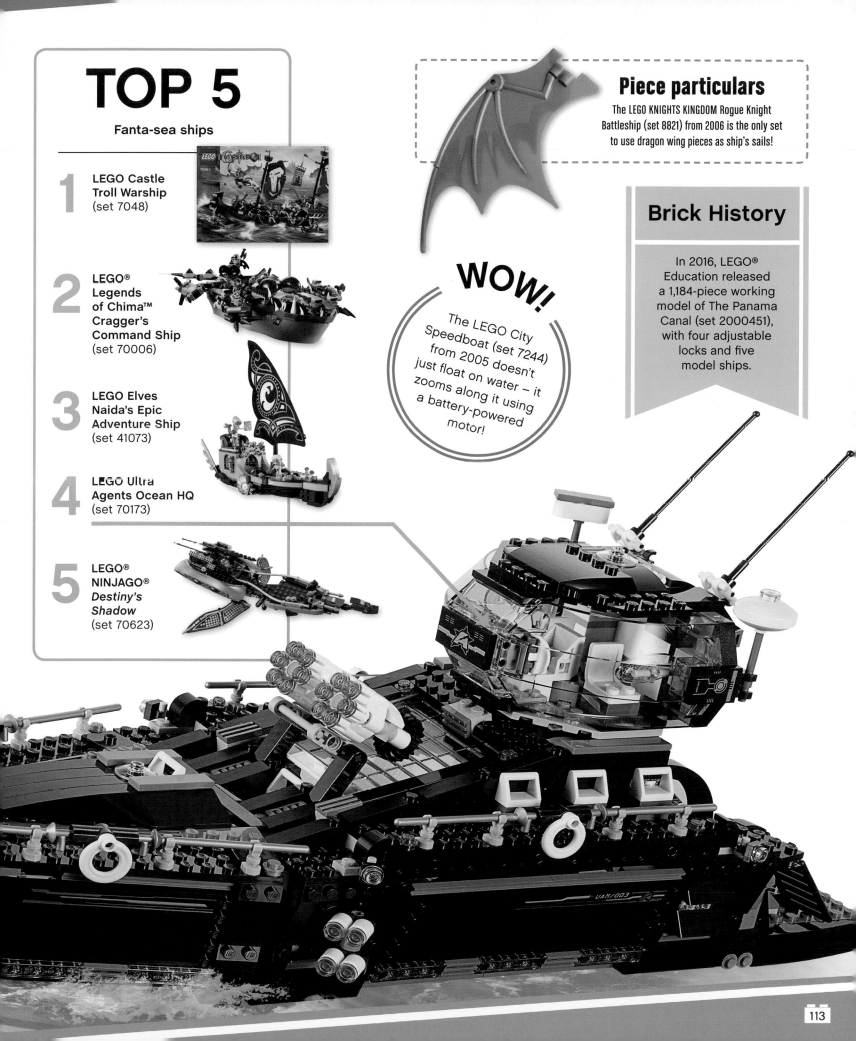

**2** LEGO® Legends of Chima™ Cragger's Command Ship (set 70006)

**3** LEGO Elves Naida's Epic Adventure Ship (set 41073)

**4** LEGO Ultra Agents Ocean HQ (set 70173)

**5** LEGO® NINJAGO® *Destiny's Shadow* (set 70623)

## Piece particulars

The LEGO KNIGHTS KINGDOM Rogue Knight Battleship (set 8821) from 2006 is the only set to use dragon wing pieces as ship's sails!

## WOW!

The LEGO City Speedboat (set 7244) from 2005 doesn't just float on water – it zooms along it using a battery-powered motor!

## Brick History

In 2016, LEGO® Education released a 1,184-piece working model of The Panama Canal (set 2000451), with four adjustable locks and five model ships.

# UP, UP AND AWAY

These amazing aeroplanes and high-flying helicopters are packed so full of play features, it's a wonder they ever get off the ground!

LEGO Coast Guard Station 575

## PLANE PACKAGING

LEGO® DUPLO® Airplane (set 5504) was released in 2005. It comprises 30 standard DUPLO bricks stored within a special aeroplane-shaped container.

## Brick History

The historic first flight by a minifigure was made by the helicopter pilot in the Coast Guard Station (set 575), a US-only set from 1978.

## LOOK CLOSER

The goods being transported by plane in 2013's Cargo Terminal (set 60022) include two brick-sized LEGO sets – including the LEGO City Cement Mixer (set 60018) from the same year!

**Q** Why is there a set with a spaceship on top of a plane?

**A** Until 2012, real-world jumbo jets were used to transport space shuttles in the US. This was the inspiration for the 1995 LEGO Town set Shuttle Transcon 2 (set 6544).

## TOP 5
### Heavy-duty helicopters

**1** Light & Sound Rescue Helicopter (set 6482)

**2** Fire Helicopter (set 7206)

**3** T-rex Hunter (set 5886)

**4** Arctic Helicrane (set 60034)

**5** Volcano Heavy-Lift Helicopter (set 60125)

## FACT STACK

The first LEGO aircraft was the 79-piece Aeroplanes (set 311), which flew into stores in 1961.

More than 100 LEGO Town sets and 80 LEGO City sets feature planes or helicopters.

The biggest LEGO aircraft is the LEGO Technic Cargo Plane (set 42025) from 2014.

There were two planes in the LEGO® FABULAND theme. Both of them were flown by birds!

## WOW!

The biplane in the LEGO City Airport Air Show (set 60103) from 2016 has a platform on top for a daredevil wing-walker!

I WISH I'D GONE BUSINESS CLASS.

## REALLY?!

One of the strangest LEGO City planes is Cargo Heliplane (set 60021) from 2013. As its name suggests, it is half helicopter, half aeroplane.

## 5

Pieces used to make each aeroplane in 2014's Billund Airport (set 4000016).

## SKY-HIGH SALES

Several aircraft sets have been made specially for sale on airlines. Holiday Jet (set 4032) from 2003 came with different logo decorations depending on which airline you were travelling with.

LC 7893

## IT'S A SIGN!

In a change from the airline logos of LEGO Town, LEGO City Airlines uses a stylised bird as its logo.

## Piece particulars

The 54-stud-wide wing plate first used in Passenger Plane (set 7893) from 2006 is one of the largest LEGO pieces ever produced!

MY BUSINESS IS REALLY TAKING OFF!

# THE SKY'S

## High-flying vehicles from across the LEGO world

1   **Creative Ambush (set 70812).**
    This 2014 aeroplane from THE
    LEGO® MOVIE™ started out as a
    kebab stand – but was rebuilt in
    the battle against Lord Business!

2   **Witch's Windship (set 6037).**
    She may have a broomstick,
    but this LEGO Castle minifigure
    witch prefers to fly using dragon
    power in this 1997 set!

3   **King Crominus' Rescue (set 70227).**
    Cragger's Fire Helicroctor comes
    from a LEGO Legends of Chima
    set released in 2015. It's ideal if you
    need to be somewhere in a snap!

4   **Aaron Fox's Aero-Striker V2 (set
    70320).** Battling Ash Attackers in
    the LEGO® NEXO KNIGHTS™ world,
    this crossbow-shaped set shot
    into being in 2016.

5   **Flying Time Vessel (set 6493).**
    Part pirate ship, part aeroplane
    and possibly even part dragon,
    the LEGO® Time Cruisers' craft
    would look strange in any era,
    but was released in 1996.

6   **Expedition Balloon (set 5956).**
    This LEGO® Adventurers vessel,
    from 1999, is the only set to ever
    feature this immense airship piece.

# THE LIMIT

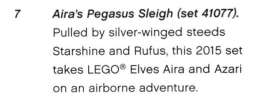

6

7

8

THE TRAFFIC UP
HERE IS
TERRIBLE.

**7    Aira's Pegasus Sleigh (set 41077).**
Pulled by silver-winged steeds
Starshine and Rufus, this 2015 set
takes LEGO® Elves Aira and Azari
on an airborne adventure.

**8    Aero Nomad (set 7415).**
Brave LEGO Adventurers use
this hot-air balloon to make
their way up Mount Everest
in this 2003 set.

# NINJA, GO!

**Q** What is the biggest LEGO NINJAGO vehicle set?

**A** Final Flight of Destiny's Bounty (set 70738) has 1,253 pieces. The flying ship in the set measures 23in (59cm) long.

Ninja skills can only get you so far. The ninja need some fast vehicles to get around the vast world of NINJAGO sets in—and so do their enemies!

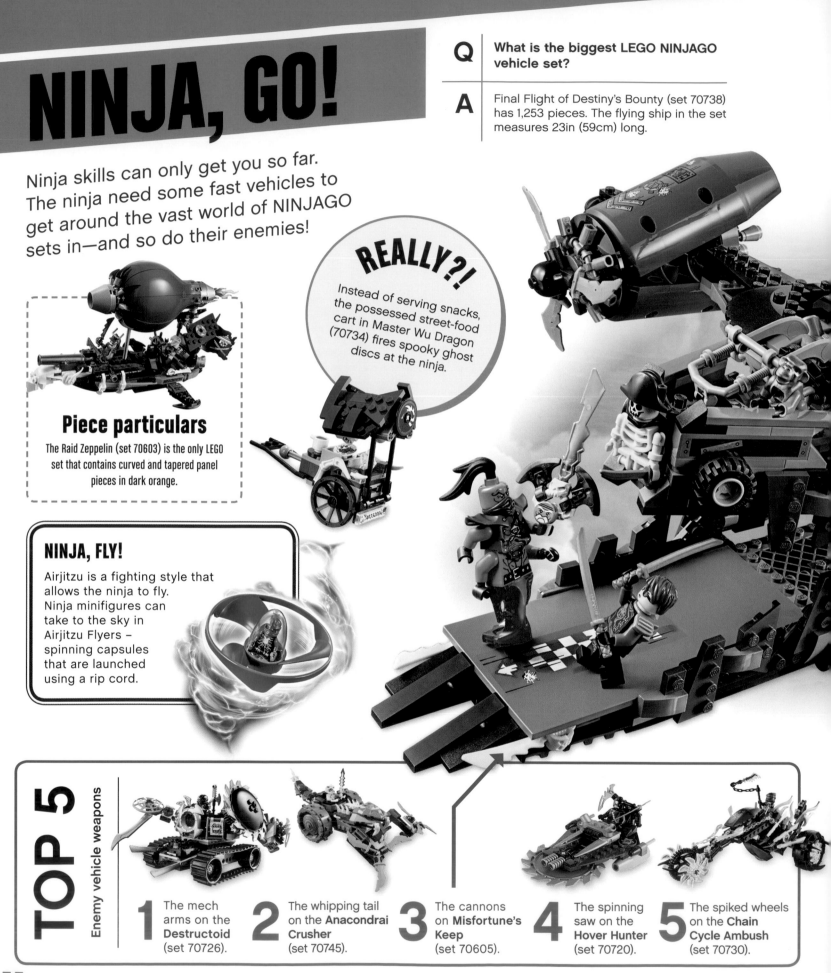

## REALLY?!

Instead of serving snacks, the possessed street-food cart in Master Wu Dragon (70734) fires spooky ghost discs at the ninja.

## Piece particulars

The Raid Zeppelin (set 70603) is the only LEGO set that contains curved and tapered panel pieces in dark orange.

## NINJA, FLY!

Airjitzu is a fighting style that allows the ninja to fly. Ninja minifigures can take to the sky in Airjitzu Flyers – spinning capsules that are launched using a rip cord.

## TOP 5
### Enemy vehicle weapons

**1** The mech arms on the **Destructoid** (set 70726).

**2** The whipping tail on the **Anacondrai Crusher** (set 70745).

**3** The cannons on **Misfortune's Keep** (set 70605).

**4** The spinning saw on the **Hover Hunter** (set 70720).

**5** The spiked wheels on the **Chain Cycle Ambush** (set 70730).

THESE NUTS
ARE HARD
TO CRACK!

## NUTTIEST PROJECTILE

Coconuts on
Tiger Widow Island
(set 70604)

## WOW!

The ninja's Ultra Stealth Raider (set 70595) from 2016 can split into four separate vehicles to take on Master Chen's Chenosaurus mech!

## IT'S A SIGN!

The ninja often put symbols on their vehicles to show their elemental powers – such as this fiery face on Kai's Blade Cycle (set 9441).

## LOOK CLOSER

The Blacksmith's Workshop in the Temple of Airjitzu (set 70751) has a glider tucked away in the attic, just in case!

## REALLY?!

The throne in Garmadon's Dark Fortress (set 2505) doubles as a flying machine so he can make a quick getaway if it looks like the ninja might defeat him... again.

# BIG STEPS FOR MECHS

Mechs have walked the LEGO world for many years. Mechanical suits manned by minifigures, these innovative machines are always receiving upgrades and getting bigger with every step.

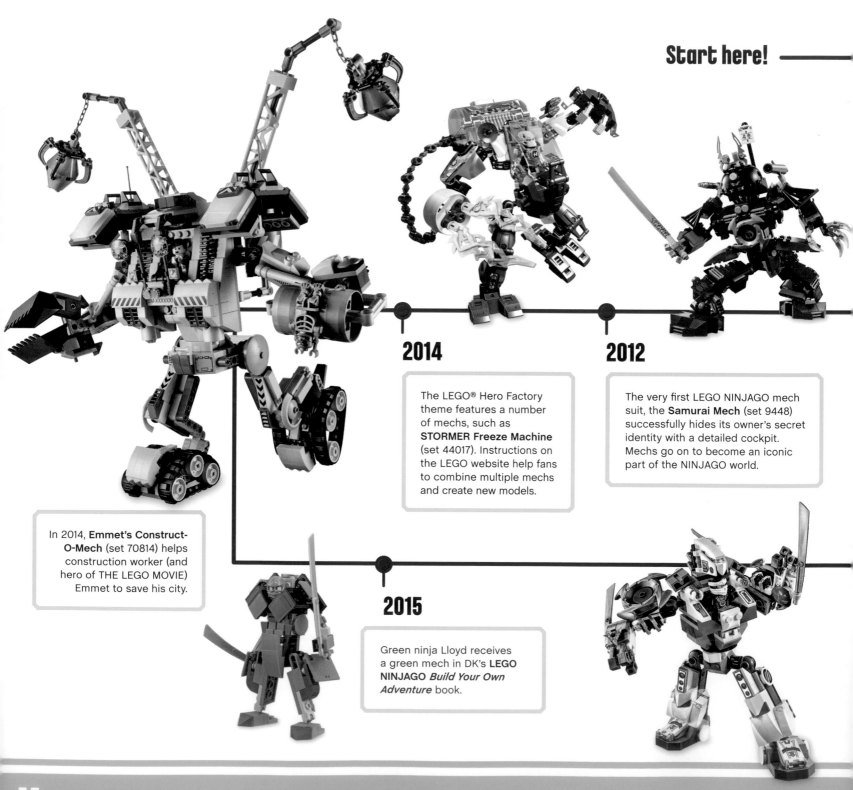

**Start here!**

## 2014

The LEGO® Hero Factory theme features a number of mechs, such as **STORMER Freeze Machine** (set 44017). Instructions on the LEGO website help fans to combine multiple mechs and create new models.

## 2012

The very first LEGO NINJAGO mech suit, the **Samurai Mech** (set 9448) successfully hides its owner's secret identity with a detailed cockpit. Mechs go on to become an iconic part of the NINJAGO world.

In 2014, **Emmet's Construct-O-Mech** (set 70814) helps construction worker (and hero of THE LEGO MOVIE) Emmet to save his city.

## 2015

Green ninja Lloyd receives a green mech in DK's **LEGO NINJAGO** *Build Your Own Adventure* book.

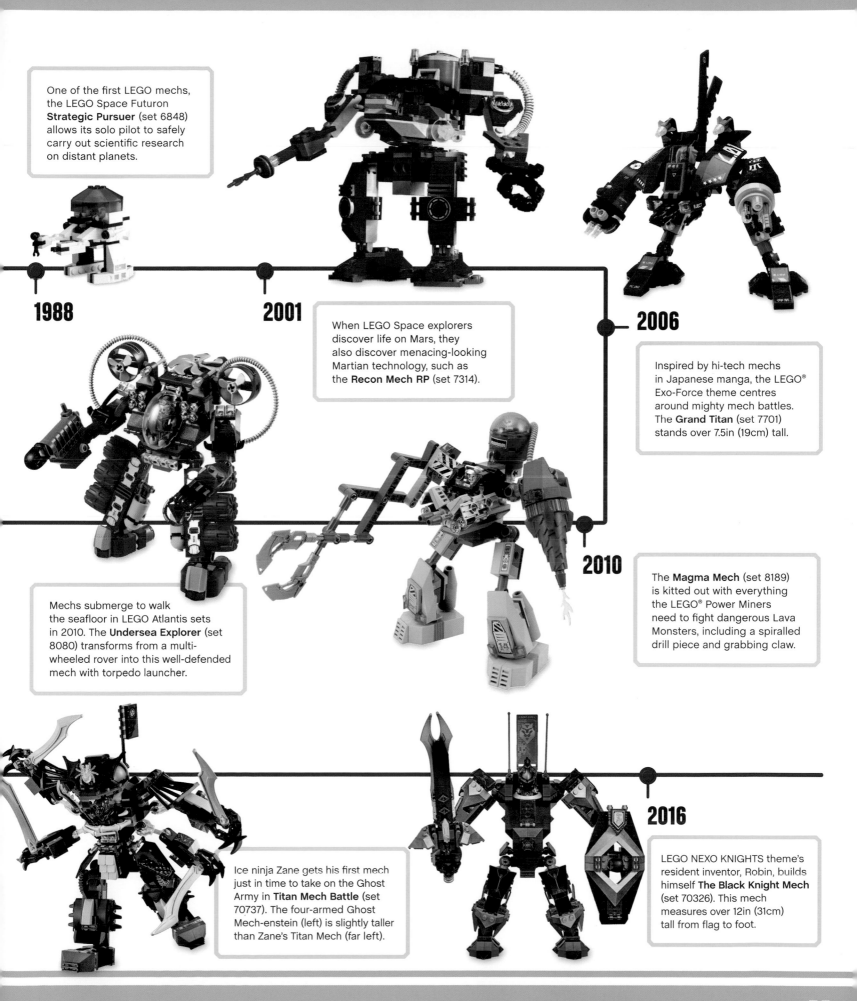

One of the first LEGO mechs, the LEGO Space Futuron **Strategic Pursuer** (set 6848) allows its solo pilot to safely carry out scientific research on distant planets.

**1988**

**2001**

When LEGO Space explorers discover life on Mars, they also discover menacing-looking Martian technology, such as the **Recon Mech RP** (set 7314).

**2006**

Inspired by hi-tech mechs in Japanese manga, the LEGO® Exo-Force theme centres around mighty mech battles. The **Grand Titan** (set 7701) stands over 7.5in (19cm) tall.

Mechs submerge to walk the seafloor in LEGO Atlantis sets in 2010. The **Undersea Explorer** (set 8080) transforms from a multi-wheeled rover into this well-defended mech with torpedo launcher.

**2010**

The **Magma Mech** (set 8189) is kitted out with everything the LEGO® Power Miners need to fight dangerous Lava Monsters, including a spiralled drill piece and grabbing claw.

Ice ninja Zane gets his first mech just in time to take on the Ghost Army in **Titan Mech Battle** (set 70737). The four-armed Ghost Mech-enstein (left) is slightly taller than Zane's Titan Mech (far left).

**2016**

LEGO NEXO KNIGHTS theme's resident inventor, Robin, builds himself **The Black Knight Mech** (set 70326). This mech measures over 12in (31cm) tall from flag to foot.

# KNIGHTS ON THE MOVE

When it comes to protecting their homeland from a villain named Jestro and his monsters, a sword and shield aren't always enough. Both the NEXO KNIGHTS team and their enemies have fleets of vehicles.

## Piece particulars

The NEXO KNIGHTS theme introduced a new pointed windshield piece, which features on many of the theme's vehicles.

## IT'S A SIGN!

The shield on Axl's Tower Carrier (set 70322) is a scannable, rock-throwing NEXO Power.

**Q** Do the NEXO KNIGHTS heroes ride horses?

**A** Not just horses, but robot horses! Lance's Mecha Horse (set 70312) from 2016 is a huge robo-steed that can turn into a motorbike.

## HEROES' HQ

The Fortrex (set 70317) is the NEXO KNIGHTS heroes' mobile base – a castle and a battle wagon all in one!

## FIRST LEGO CASTLE ON WHEELS

The Fortrex (set 70317)

# AWESOME!

You may have heard of horsepower, but what about lava power? Jestro's Evil Mobile (set 70316) is a two-wheeled ride pulled along by a hulking lava giant named Sparkks.

## TOP 5
### Mega mean machines

**1** **General Magmar's Siege Machine of Doom (set 70321)** rumbles along on six wheels or rises up to become a seige tower.

**2** **Jestro's Headquarters (set 70352)** features colossal rocky wheels and a detachable stone boat.

**3** **Jestro's Evil Mobile (set 70316)** has jaws that open and close as the vehicle moves.

**4** **Beast Master's Chaos Chariot (set 70314)** is pulled along by two giant, snapping Globlins.

**5** **Ruina's Lock & Roller (set 70349)** has a jail cell that opens when you push the Forbidden Power shield.

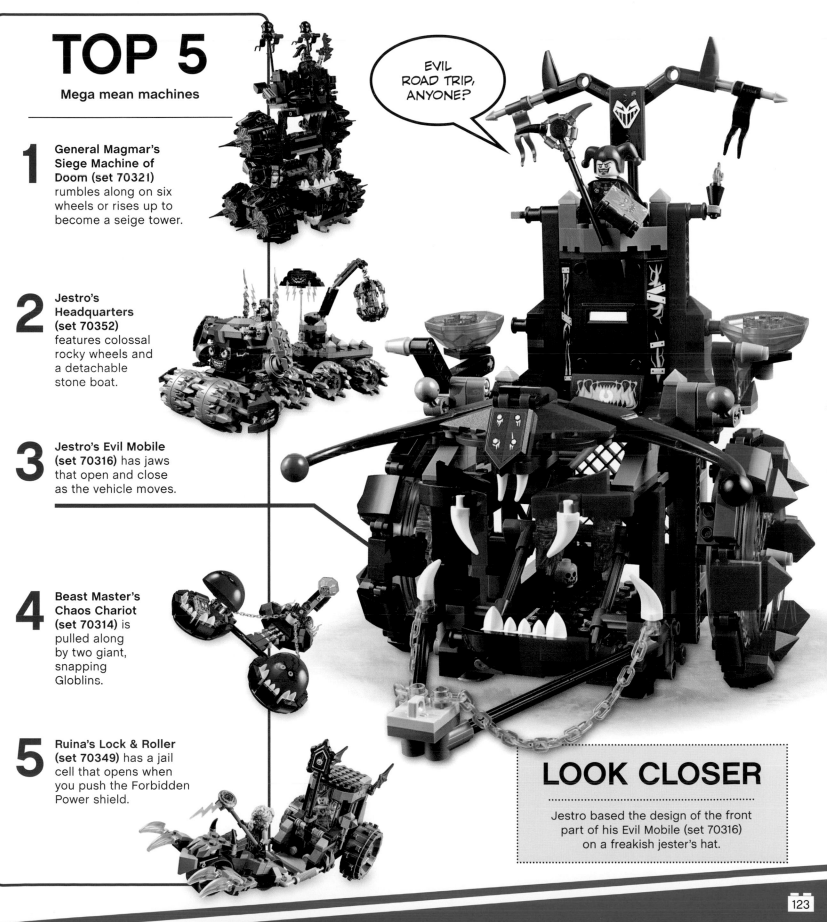

EVIL ROAD TRIP, ANYONE?

## LOOK CLOSER

Jestro based the design of the front part of his Evil Mobile (set 70316) on a freakish jester's hat.

# TO THE MOON AND BACK

While the LEGO Space theme explored the realms of science-fiction, many other LEGO sets have explored real-world space exploration – even way back before the first real-life Moon landing in 1969!

## FACT STACK

The first outer space LEGO set was a 115-piece rocket in 1964.

LEGO Town joined the space race in 1990, with the addition of its first space shuttle.

More than 40 LEGO sets have had a real-world space theme.

## KEY DATES

### 1973
Rocket Base (set 358) features a realistic rocket and command centre, a year after NASA's last manned Moon mission.

### 1995
LEGO Town rivals NASA with its very own space programme, in the subtheme Launch Command.

### 2003
The LEGO Group partners with Discovery Channel for six space sets, including a Lunar Lander (set 10029) with two Apollo astronauts.

### 2015
LEGO City gets a brand-new spaceport, plus a Training Jet Transporter (set 60079) for future shuttle pilots!

124

## MARTIAN LEGO PIECES

To help compare colours picked up by their cameras in Martian daylight, NASA fitted red, blue and yellow "LEGO plates" to its Mars rovers in 2003. The plates looked like real LEGO pieces, but they were made out of metal to survive in space.

The LEGO NASA Mars Science Laboratory Curiosity Rover (set 21104) was designed by real-life NASA engineer Stephen Pakbaz.

### LARGEST LEGO IDEAS SET

Apollo 11 Saturn V Rocket (set 21309) at 39in (1m) tall

The astronaut in 1999's Space Simulation Station (set 6455) is undergoing G-force training in this spinning set!

I HOPE I DON'T HAVE HELMET HAIR.

## Brick History

In 1975, Space Module with Astronauts (set 367) replicated a Moon landing with three brick-built spacemen, whose helmets could be swapped for faces.

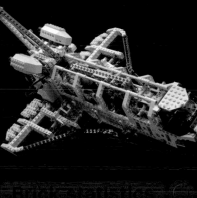

**Brick statistics**

## LEGO Technic Space Shuttle (set 8480)

**1,366 pieces**
Including a 9-volt motor

**6 fibre-optic cables**
For lighting the engine exhausts

**2 motorised bay doors**
Built with angled beam pieces – new in 1996!

**1 working crane arm**
For launching the on-board satellite

# AWESOME!

# 5,304,140

Miles (8,536,186km) travelled by a LEGO model of the space shuttle *Discovery* in 2010, while on board the real NASA space shuttle *Discovery*.

**Stardefender 200**
(set 6932)

# A HISTORY OF THE FUTURE

LEGO Space has changed a lot over the years, but one thing ties all the eras together, and that's spaceships, spaceships, SPACESHIPS!

## 1980s

New-look white exploration vessels continue to research the universe, while Space Police are on patrol for notorious Blacktron craft.

**Galactic Peace Keeper** (set 6886)

## 1990s

Flying saucers and alien insects are just some of the strange sights to be spotted deeper into space.

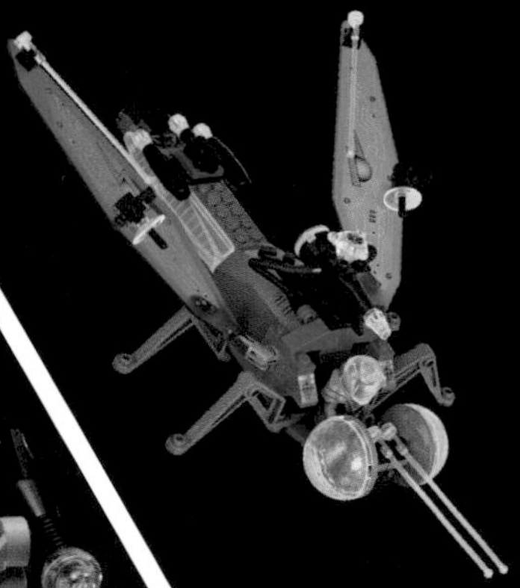

**Xenon X-Craft**
(set 6872)

**Space Transporter**
(set 924)

**Insectoid Sonic Stinger** (set 6907)

**Space Dart I**
(set 6824)

## 1970s

The first LEGO astronauts blast off in blue and grey ships that don't stray too far from scientific fact.

**Space Scooter**
(set 885)

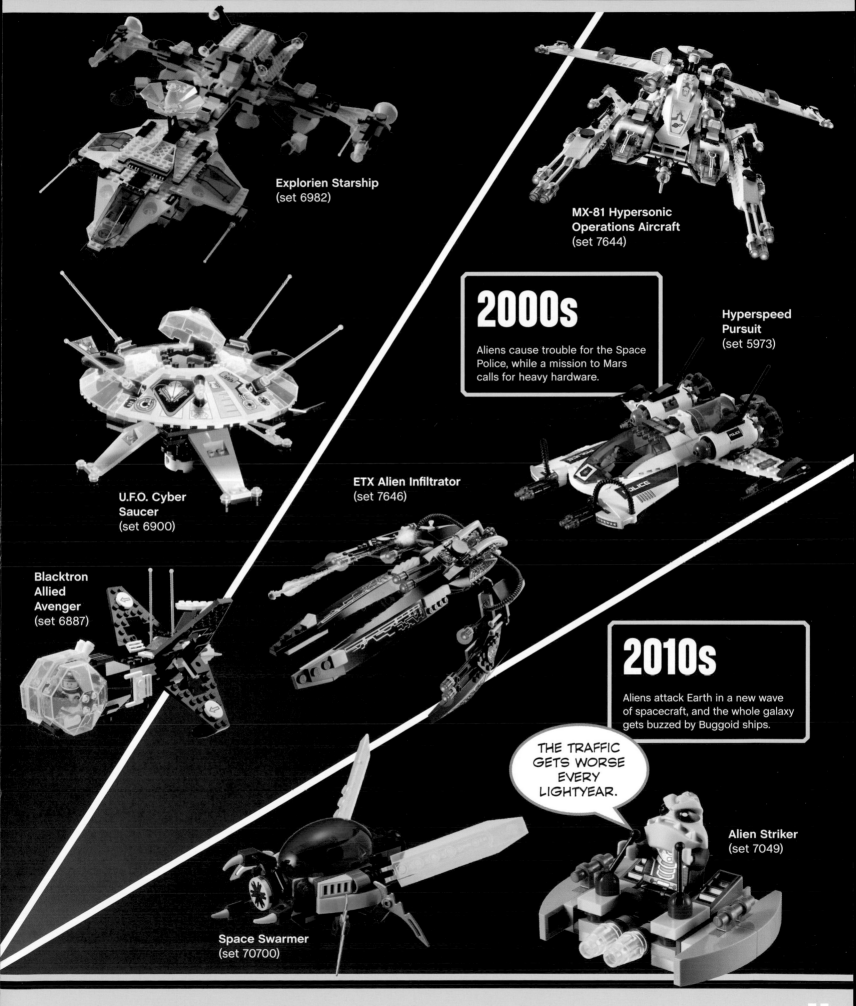

Explorien Starship
(set 6982)

MX-81 Hypersonic
Operations Aircraft
(set 7644)

## 2000s

Aliens cause trouble for the Space Police, while a mission to Mars calls for heavy hardware.

Hyperspeed Pursuit
(set 5973)

U.F.O. Cyber Saucer
(set 6900)

ETX Alien Infiltrator
(set 7646)

Blacktron Allied Avenger
(set 6887)

## 2010s

Aliens attack Earth in a new wave of spacecraft, and the whole galaxy gets buzzed by Buggoid ships.

THE TRAFFIC GETS WORSE EVERY LIGHTYEAR.

Alien Striker
(set 7049)

Space Swarmer
(set 70700)

# PARKING SPACE

With 1,012 pieces, the aptly named Galactic Titan (set 70709) is the biggest LEGO Space set ever. It has huge caterpillar tracks for going into battle with... huge alien caterpillars!

Spaceships aren't the only way to get around the galaxy! With the help of wheels and walkers, LEGO astronauts have charted strange new worlds in these tough land-based vehicles.

I'M THE TREADED GALACTIC TITAN!

I'M WHEELY AWESOME.

## FACT STACK

Moon buggies featured in all four of the first LEGO Space sets in 1978.

More than 100 LEGO Space sets feature wheels.

Mono Jet (set 7310) is the only LEGO Space vehicle to run on only one wheel.

## 12

Wheels on the giant Roboforce Robomaster (set 2154) from 1997.

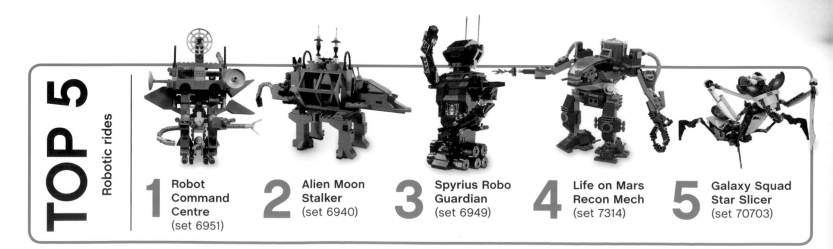

## TOP 5
### Robotic rides

**1** Robot Command Centre (set 6951)

**2** Alien Moon Stalker (set 6940)

**3** Spyrius Robo Guardian (set 6949)

**4** Life on Mars Recon Mech (set 7314)

**5** Galaxy Squad Star Slicer (set 70703)

## AWESOME!

The centrepiece of the Space subtheme Futuron was the battery-powered Monorail Transport System (set 6990), which had more than 10ft (3m) of "Space Trak".

START THE SPACE ENGINES!

## Brick statistics

### Solar Power Transporter (set 6952)

**6 large wheels**
Fit sideways under cockpits during flight

**4 astronauts**
And one friendly droid fit in the vehicle

**2 cockpits**
Detachable from the front and back

**2 space engines**
Attach to cockpits to make spaceships

**1 control room**
Stands freely on fold-down struts

### LOST IN SPACE

This six-wheeled satellite-launcher was designed in the 1980s but never released. A single prototype box is kept securely in the LEGO Group archives.

# GET ME TO A GALAXY FAR, FAR AWAY!

The LEGO® *Star Wars*™ theme has been flying high for nearly 20 years, and these are just some of the spaceships that have taken it to new heights.

## 386

Black pieces in Krennic's Imperial Shuttle (set 75156).

## FACT STACK

The first LEGO *Star Wars* spaceships launched in 1999.

More than 150 LEGO *Star Wars* spaceships have been released to date.

Almost 100 sets are based on ships from the *Star Wars* movies.

More than 50 ships are inspired by *Star Wars* TV shows and games.

## Piece particulars

Not all LEGO *Star Wars* flying machines are futuristic! Wicket the Ewok flies a glider made with fishing rod pieces in The Battle of Endor (set 8038).

## Brick statistics

### 18 TIE fighters
Released at minifigure scale, including TIE variants

### 7 X-wing fighters
At minifigure scale, including Poe Dameron's X-wing

### 5 *Millennium Falcons*
At minifigure scale, including one Ultimate Collector's set

### 3 Imperial Shuttles
At minifigure scale, including one Ultimate Collector's set

## GETTING FROM A TO Y

Lots of *Star Wars* ships are named for their resemblance to letters, and every single one has been spelled out in LEGO bricks.

**B IS FOR...**
B-Wing (set 75050)

**A IS FOR...**
A-Wing (set 75175)

**U IS FOR...**
U-Wing (set 75155)

**1** *Slave I* (set 7144), 2000

**2** Jango Fett's *Slave I* (set 7153), 2002

**3** *Slave I* (set 6209), 2006

**4** Mini *Slave I* (*Star Wars* Celebration V Exclusive), 2012

**5** Ultimate Collector's Series *Slave I* (set 75060), 2015

# AWESOME!

The LEGO *Star Wars Rebels* Wookiee Gunship (set 75084) from 2015 was the first Wookiee spaceship and the first set to feature rapid-fire stud shooters.

Imperial measures

4in (10cm)

## WOW!

Count Dooku's Solar Sailer (set 7752) from LEGO *Star Wars: The Clone Wars* has sails that spread out like flower petals to soak up solar rays.

## REALLY?!

Luke Skywalker's X-Wing Fighter (set 4502) from 2004 comes covered in Dagobah swamp gunk.

37in (94cm)

**Imperial Star Destroyer Ultimate Collector's version**
(set 10030)
3,104 pieces, 37in (94cm) long

**Imperial Star Destroyer Microfighter version**
(set 75033)
97 pieces, 4in (10cm) long

## X IS FOR...
X-Wing (set 75149)

## Y IS FOR...
Y-Wing (set 9495)

## V IS FOR...
V-Wing (set 75039)

# GROUND WARS

The LEGO *Star Wars* saga stretches across more than just space. In worlds of sand, snow, forest and fire, ingenious ground vehicles are required to get around.

## FACT STACK

The LEGO *Star Wars* theme hit the ground in 1999 with 13 sets.

All but two of the first sets featured some kind of ground transport.

2014's Sandcrawler (set 75059) is the largest LEGO *Star Wars* ground vehicle.

Gungan Sub (sets 7161 and 9499) is the theme's only submarine.

## REALLY?!

TIE fighters aren't only found in the sky! The TIE Crawler (set 7664) from 2007 runs on caterpillar tracks.

**Q** I need a speeder bike for my trip to Endor but I don't like brown. Can you help me?

**A** Certainly! As well as brown, speeder bikes are also available in red, white and green.

## WAY TO GO!

There are almost as many ways to get around a planet as there are planets to get around! All you need to do is pick a mode of propulsion…

## TRACK POWER

Half tank, half droid, the Corporate Alliance Tank Droid (set 75015) crawls along on a single caterpillar track.

## LEG POWER

Captain Rex's AT-TE (set 75157) from LEGO *Star Wars Rebels* has been modified from a walking weapon to a home.

## Brick History

In 2007, a Motorised Walking AT-AT (set 10178) strode onto the scene. It could be set to walk forwards or backwards at the flick of a switch.

## BABY STEPS

Since 2014, LEGO *Star Wars* Microfighters have depicted classic *Star Wars* craft such as the AT-DP (set 75130), using just a handful of pieces each.

### BEST UNICYCLIST

General Grievous on his Wheel Bike (set 75040)

# WOW!

Republic Dropship with AT-OT Walker (set 10195) is an airship and walker all in one. It is the biggest LEGO *Star Wars: The Clone Wars* set, with 1,758 pieces.

## 15

Pieces used to make Luke's landspeeder in the 2014 LEGO *Star Wars* Advent Calendar.

## WHEEL POWER

The 10-wheeled Clone Turbo Tank (set 8098) has more wheels than any other LEGO *Star Wars* vehicle, plus working suspension.

*I APPEAR TO BE GOING THE WRONG WAY.*

## POD POWER

Anakin Skywalker's homemade Podracer (set 7962) is nearly all engine, with just a small seat for a pilot pulled along behind.

# ULTRA COOL SETS

Unbelievably Complex Spaceships? Utterly Convincing Sculptures? In the LEGO *Star Wars* theme, UCS stands for Ultimate Collector's Series. These are some of the most advanced LEGO sets in the galaxy!

**TIE Interceptor**
(set 7181)

**Start here!**

## 2008

The UCS **General Grievous** (set 10186) is made primarily from LEGO Technic pieces. It features an opening chest plate that reveals the villain's cyborg innards.

## 2007

The Ultimate Collector's Series *Millennium Falcon* (set 10179) is the first UCS set to come with minifigures, as the range begins to include more play features.

The Ultimate Collector's Series **R2-D2** (set 10225) has 2,127 pieces and is more than 200 times bigger than a minifigure-scale Artoo!

## 2012

## 2010

**Imperial Shuttle** (set 10212), not only includes five minifigures, it is also the first UCS set to be built at the same scale as its pilots and passengers.

**X-Wing Fighter**
(set 7191)

Looming 17in (43cm) tall, the UCS **Darth Maul Bust** (set 10018) is almost as large as life – and just as scary.
## 2001

## 2000

The Ultimate Collector's Series launches with a 703-piece **TIE Interceptor** (set 7181) and a 1,304-piece **X-Wing Fighter** (set 7191).

## 2002

The first-ever set to have more than 3,000 pieces, the huge UCS **Imperial Star Destroyer** (set 10030) also comes with a tiny Rebel blockade runner.

## 2005

The UCS **Death Star II** from *Return of the Jedi* (set 10143) is both the first LEGO Death Star and the largest, with a circumference of 60in (152cm).

## 2014

With more play features than ever, the **UCS Sandcrawler** (set 75059) features working cranes and steering, eight opening sections, seven minifigures and six droids.

## 2016

The latest version of the **Death Star** (set 75159) features details that take the piece count to more than 4,000.

# THE WORLD'S BIGGEST LEGO® VEHICLE: X-WING STARFIGHTER

On May 23, 2013, the LEGO Group unveiled a life-sized LEGO Star Wars X-Wing starfighter in New York's Times Square.

## Brick statistics

### 5,335,200 bricks
Weighing 45,980lbs (20,865kg)

### 32 LEGO master builders
Worked on it in the LEGO Model Shop
in Kladno, Czech Republic

### 43ft (13.1m) long
With a 44ft (13.4m) wingspan

### 42 times bigger
Than the X-Wing Starfighter set (set 9493)
on which it is based

### 17,336 hours to build
That's about four months!

# FANTASTIC VOYAGERS

There's more to LEGO vehicles than City cars and spaceships – just ask the drivers of these fantasy dream machines!

AND YOU THOUGHT I WAS EXTINCT!

**Q** Why does Maula's Ice Mammoth Stomper (set 70145) have propellers on its sides?

**A** Because this LEGO Legends of Chima set is actually two vehicles in one: a huge, woolly mammoth-like walker and a smaller, folding flyer that wraps across its back!

## Brick statistics

### LEGO EXO-FORCE Mobile Devastator (set 8108)

**1,009 parts**
Including four giant, bright green wheels

**23.5in (60cm) long**
And 13.5in (34cm) tall

**10 robot warriors on board**
Including robot leader Meca One

**2 detachable robot scout ships**
Connected to the elevating battle tower

**1 hero stands in its way**
In his Blazing Falcon battle machine!

NO MEDALS! CAN'T YOU SEE I'M UNDERCOVER?

**MOST INAPPROPRIATELY NAMED VEHICLE**
LEGO Ultra Agents Stealth Patrol (set 70169)

# AWESOME!

In a world of hay carts and horses, Troll Battle Wheel (set 7041) is the most way-out weapon LEGO Castle has ever seen!

**WOW!**
When battling the LEGO® Alpha Team, evil Ogel's Scorpion Orb Launcher (set 4774) can stand up on its mighty stinger to attack!

## LOOK CLOSER

The printed face on the front of the LEGO® Monster Fighters Ghost Train (set 9467) looks even scarier when you see it glowing in the dark!

## BRICK CHALLENGE

Think of the wackiest way to get around, then build it with your LEGO bricks!

**6**
Legs on the creepy-crawly LEGO® BIONICLE Toa Terrain Crawler (set 8927).

# CHAPTER FOUR

# MINIFIGURES, MONSTERS AND MORE

# SMALL BEGINNINGS

In 1978, the first minifigures added new character to the worlds of LEGO sets. Their insistent smiles and ingenious design made them an instant hit.

## Brick History

In 1975, the forerunner of the minifigure debuted in sets. These early figures were made from three pieces (plus a hat). They had no faces, and only the suggestion of arms and legs.

## FACT STACK

Out of the LEGO colours available in 1978, yellow was chosen for minifigures as it was considered the best choice to represent all skin tones.

The fundamental minifigure form has not changed since it was perfected in 1978.

The unique design of the LEGO minifigure was first protected by a patent in Denmark in 1977.

Since 2000, the distinctive minifigure shape has been recognised as a trademark.

I LIKE YOUR HAIR.

I LIKE *YOUR* HAIR!

## REALLY ?!

Until 1983, there were only two minifigure haircuts: pigtails and side parting. There have been more than 200 styles since.

## TOP 5

**Early minifigure tools still in use today**

**1** Axe (1978)

**2** Sword (1978)

**3** Shovel (1978)

**4** Radio (1979)

**5** Spanner (1979)

## TORSO COUTURE

The first minifigures had plain torsos that could be decorated with stickers. Printed torsos were introduced later in 1978, starting with a Train Conductor.

**40**

Minifigure variants were released in 1978. Today there are more than 8,000!

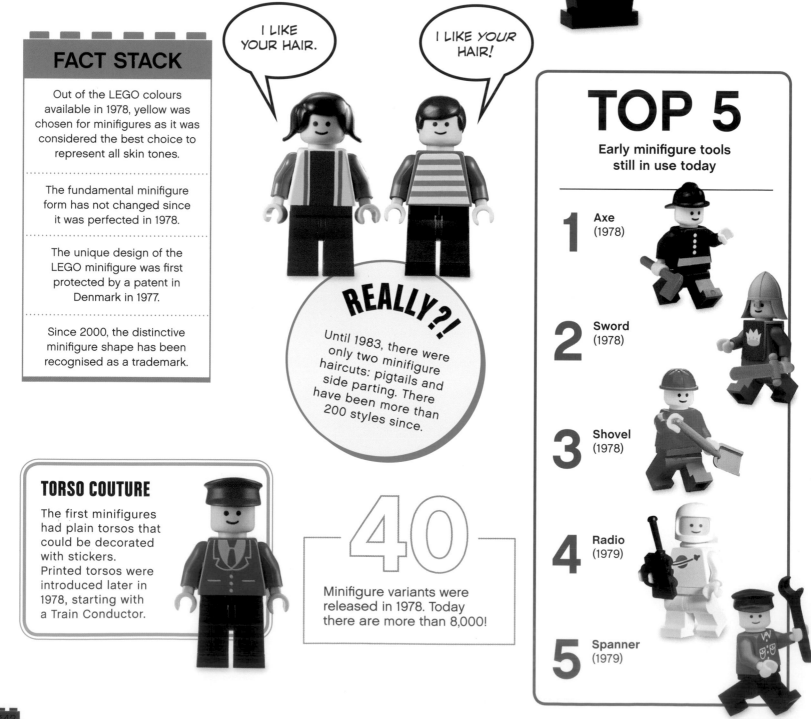

**Q** What are LEGO minifigures made from?

**A** Just like LEGO bricks, minifigures are made from a tough plastic compound called acrylonitrile butadiene styrene, known as ABS for short.

# WOW!

A team of LEGO designers, led by Jens Nygård Knudsen, made 50 different minifigure prototypes from plastic and tin before arriving at the final design.

# LOOK CLOSER

675    SNACK BAR    LEGO    snack bar ►

The boxes of several 1979 sets show minifigures wearing a hair piece that was never released. The final element was more intricately shaped to suggest ears.

## ONE OF THE FIRST-EVER MINIFIGURES

Policeman (1978)

I'M ALWAYS FIRST ON THE SCENE!

## MAYBE BABIES

As well as appearing as adults in LEGOLAND® sets, some of the first minifigures were cast as infants in larger scale LEGO Homemaker sets, alongside tall "building figures".

# THE MAKING OF A MINIFIGURE

## THE DESIGN PROCESS

It can take a whole year to design and make a minifigure! From coming up with new ideas to testing the finished product, every step is vital to make each minifigure the best it can be…

### 1 MAKING A START

The LEGO Group has a dedicated design team for minifigures. Its members work closely with set designers to help each model tell its story with the right collection of characters.

### 2 FIGURING IT OUT

The design team starts by brainstorming ideas, making rough sketches by hand and doing research – for example, visiting a fire station if they are designing firefighters.

WHAT ABOUT MY PANTS?

### 3 PICTURING THE PIECES

Next, graphic designers work on a blank minifigure template to refine and develop the initial sketches, choosing colours for different body parts, and adding more detail to facial features and clothing.

### 4 MINIFIGURE MODELLING

If a design calls for a new hair piece, accessory or body part, an element designer sculpts an extra-large version out of clay, or makes a virtual 3-D computer model. This allows the sculptor to create the finer details for each piece.

## MINIFIGURE, OR NOT?

Many LEGO themes feature minifigure characters, but not every character in those themes is a minifigure! Characters made from non-standard parts are known as "creature figures" and come in lots of different shapes and sizes.

This **policeman** is a minifigure because he has all the standard minifigure parts: torso, arms, legs and a head.

This **skeleton** is classed as a creature figure, not a minifigure, because it does not have a standard torso or any standard limbs.

This **Scurrier** is also classed as a creature figure because it does not have any standard minifigure parts at all!

The classic minifigure form has not changed since 1978, but the details and decorations that make each one special still offer plenty of scope for new ideas.

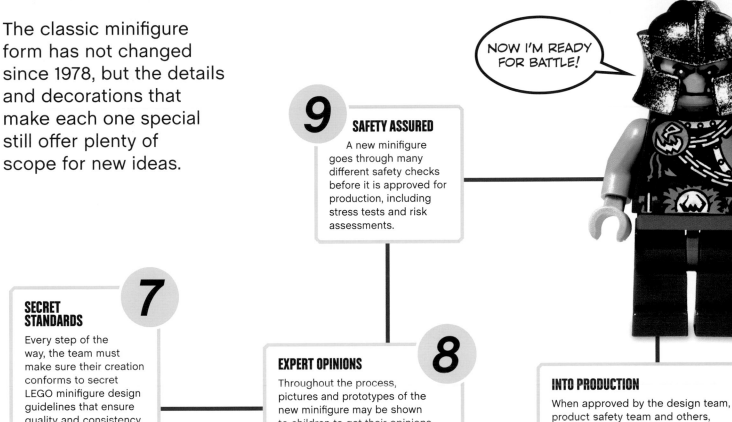

NOW I'M READY FOR BATTLE!

## 9 SAFETY ASSURED

A new minifigure goes through many different safety checks before it is approved for production, including stress tests and risk assessments.

## 7 SECRET STANDARDS

Every step of the way, the team must make sure their creation conforms to secret LEGO minifigure design guidelines that ensure quality and consistency across the whole LEGO range.

TOP SECRET

## 8 EXPERT OPINIONS

Throughout the process, pictures and prototypes of the new minifigure may be shown to children to get their opinions on its design and playability.

## 10 INTO PRODUCTION

When approved by the design team, product safety team and others, the minifigure can finally be sent to the factory for production.

## 6 THE BIG PICTURE

Next, a small number of prototype pieces are made at actual size. Stickers showing the graphics are added, and all elements of the design are reviewed as a complete package.

## 5 UPLOADING...

When a clay sculpt (known as a maquette) is finished, it is scanned into a computer and adjusted to make sure its dimensions fit perfectly with existing LEGO elements.

## MAKING FACES

Though modern minifigures have many different faces, their features all conform to strict design rules. This means they can be easily identified and all of them can wear the same hats, helmets, masks and hair pieces.

Most minifigures have black eyes, but some non-human characters have coloured eyes.

Most minifigure children are designed with bigger than average eyes and freckles to distinguish them from adults.

Minifigures with scared or unhappy faces usually have a happy face printed on the other side of their head.

# 9,610,000,000

Approximate distance from the Earth to the Moon, measured in minifigures.

## Brick History

In 2008, all five colours of the classic space minifigure were reissued to celebrate 30 years of minifigures. All wore modern helmets, but without visors.

## FACT STACK

In 1978, the first LEGO space minifigures wore either red or white outfits.

Yellow spacesuits appeared in 1979 then blue and black in 1984.

Black spacesuits are the rarest, appearing in fewer than 10 sets.

The most recent sets feature astronauts in red, blue, green and orange.

## KEY DATES

### 1987
The LEGO® Futuron space minifigures are the first to get helmets with transparent visors.

### 1992
The first LEGO Space minifigures to have special face prints appear in Space Police sets.

### 1993
Ice Planet 2002 sets are the first to distinguish between male and female astronauts.

### 2011
Space minifigures get double-sided face prints so they can look alarmed in Alien Conquest sets!

# AWESOME!

In 2003, pictures of two "Astrobot" minifigures, Biff and Sandy, were sent to Mars on real spaceships.

## BROKEN BENNY

Benny from the THE LEGO® MOVIE™ was based on the original blue Space minifigure from 1984. His helmet was designed to look like it was broken due to it being played with a great deal, for that authentic toybox vibe!

## IT'S A SIGN!

The classic LEGO Space logo is still in use after almost 40 years.

## BRICK CHALLENGE

Try building a LEGO planet for your astronaut minifigures to explore, like this inspirational model.

# FLYING COLOURS

Red alert! And yellow! And blue! In 1978, these explorers made a giant leap for LEGO minifigures. Boldly going where no bricks had gone before, they were the first to venture into LEGOLAND Space. They have remained beloved figures for lightyears since.

# MINIFIGURES THROUGH THE AGES

LEGO® Minifigures have taken inspiration from historical (and prehistorical) humans from as early as 10,000 BCE. These characters range from cavemen to modern starlets and scientists.

**Start here!**

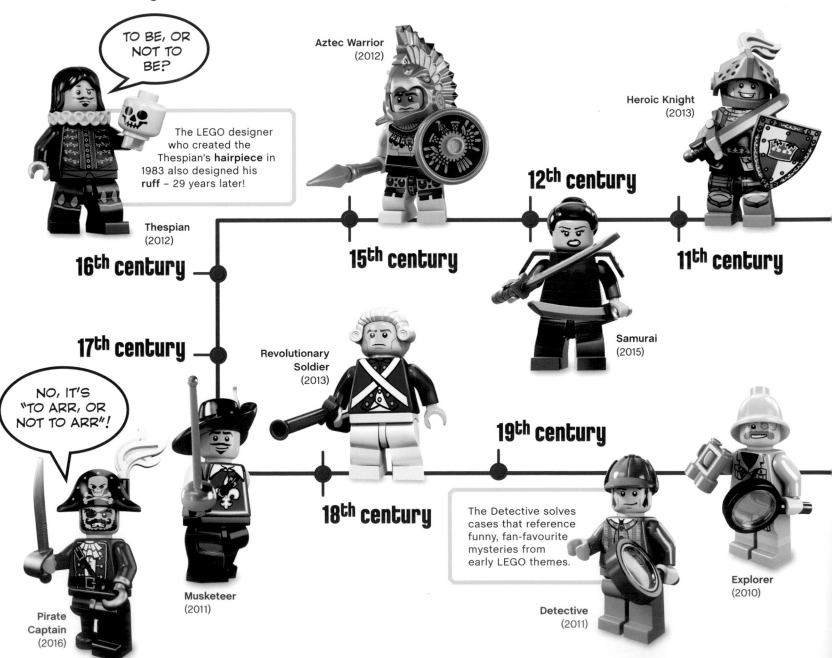

TO BE, OR NOT TO BE?

The LEGO designer who created the Thespian's **hairpiece** in 1983 also designed his **ruff** – 29 years later!

**Thespian**
(2012)

**Aztec Warrior**
(2012)

**Heroic Knight**
(2013)

**12th century**

**16th century**

**15th century**

**11th century**

**Samurai**
(2015)

**17th century**

**Revolutionary Soldier**
(2013)

NO, IT'S "TO ARR, OR NOT TO ARR"!

**19th century**

**18th century**

The Detective solves cases that reference funny, fan-favourite mysteries from early LEGO themes.

**Pirate Captain**
(2016)

**Musketeer**
(2011)

**Detective**
(2011)

**Explorer**
(2010)

UG?

Caveman
(2010)

NO HUGS UNTIL YOU'VE SHAVED.

Cave Woman
(2011)

c.10,000 BCE

Spartan Warrior
(2010)

c.500-400 BCE

Pharaoh
(2010)

The Pharaoh's **snake-topped staff** was designed especially for this regal minifigure.

c.300-100 BCE

Egyptian Queen
(2011)

The Viking Woman's **horns** were intended as a one-off piece, but they have become a versatile element. It is a good job they are detachable, as historians believe Vikings didn't actually have horned helmets!

Viking Woman
(2012)

5th century

9th-10th century

ET TU, BRUTE?

c.50 BCE-4th century

WHO ARE YOU CALLING A BRUTE?

Hun Warrior
(2014)

Roman Emperor
(2013)

Roman Commander
(2013)

Disco Diva
(2015)

20th century

Hollywood Starlet
(2013)

I CAN SEE THROUGH TIME!

Scientist (2013)

21st century

The fashion-forward Hippie is the first minifigure ever to don **tie-dye clothes**, an iconic element of 1960s style.

Hippie
(2012)

Wildlife Photographer
(2016)

# WE COME IN PIECES!

In the LEGO Space universe, aliens and robots come in many shapes and sizes. Some are peaceful, but others are preparing for battle!

**IT'S A SIGN!**

The cyborg Space Villain from the LEGO Minifigures line wears a green "B" symbol, first used by Blacktron crooks in 1991's LEGO Space sets.

## MEET THE MARTIANS

In 2001, LEGO® Life on Mars sets mixed astronauts with brand-new Martian figures. These friendly aliens featured new parts and colours and were named after real stars and constellations.

MY NAME IS VEGA.

**Q** Who was the first alien minifigure?

**A** Alpha Draconis and his fellow U.F.O. aliens made first contact in 1996. They wore unique, out-of-this-world helmets, with scary printed faces underneath.

**Top 5**

**Cosmic citizen collectibles**

1. **Space Alien**
(Series 3, 2011)

2. **Classic Alien**
(Series 6, 2012)

3. **Alien Trooper**
(Series 13, 2015)

4. **Alien Villainess**
(Series 8, 2011)

5. **Alien Avenger**
(Series 9, 2013)

**Space Alien**          **Classic Alien**

## FACT STACK

The first LEGO Space droids were brick-built helpers in 1985 sets.

A 1986 set was called Alien Moon Stalker, but it did not include any aliens.

It was 1996 before LEGO aliens were identified in LEGO Space U.F.O. sets.

Unusually for LEGO sets, the U.F.O. subtheme featured no human characters at all.

### REALLY?!

The spooky Space Skulls starred in a 2008 LEGO® Factory set, piloting giant, skull-shaped spaceships!

### SMALLEST ALIEN

One-eyed Clinger from Alien Conquest sets

## Brick History

The first minifigure designed to represent a robot was the Spyrius Droid from 1994. He was also the first minifigure to have printed legs.

# 245633

The prisoner number of escaped alien crook Jawson, who was on the loose in LEGO Space Police sets during 2010.

**Alien Trooper**

**Alien Villainess**

**Alien Avenger**

# THE MAGIC OF MINIFIGURES

Every minifigure has a touch of magic, but these wizards, enchanters, witches and wish-granters have a little bit more than most.

## Brick History

In 2012, the LEGO® *The Lord of the Rings*™ and *The Hobbit*™ themes launched, reimagining magical characters such as Gandalf the Grey in minifigure form.

## REALLY?!

In the LEGO® NINJAGO® world, magical, wish-granting beings known as djinn inhabit a parallel realm called... Djinjago!

## MYTHS AND LEG-ENDS

The magical, mystical Faun from the LEGO Minifigures theme has a special leg piece used in no other set. Though his goat-like limbs are slim, his hooves still fit onto LEGO studs.

**Q** | Can you still get LEGO *Harry Potter* sets?

**A** | Though the LEGO® *Harry Potter*™ theme came to an end in 2011, minifigure versions of Harry, Hermione and Lord Voldemort are still having magical adventures in the LEGO® DIMENSIONS™ theme.

## BRICK CHALLENGE

Build a LEGO box with a hidden compartment to make a disappearing minifigure magic trick!

## PICK A POTTER

There are many different minifigure versions of Harry Potter, yet each one shares the same familiar lightning-bolt scar!

GOATEE BEARD?
I'VE GOT A GOATY
*EVERYTHING!*

## TOP 5

**LEGO Minifigures conjurors**

1 **Fairy**
(Series 8, 2012)

2 **Leprechaun**
(Series 6, 2012)

3 **Wizard**
(Series 12, 2014)

4 **Genie Girl**
(Series 12, 2014)

5 **Wacky Witch**
(Series 14, 2015)

8

Different wizards have appeared in LEGO Castle sets since 1995.

## WOW!

Amset-Ra is the Pharaoh at the heart of 2011's Pharaoh's Quest theme. His six magical treasures are guarded by enchanted warriors such as Flying Mummies.

# MINIFIGURE FIRSTS

These pioneers have all earned their place in history by taking LEGO minifigures into new areas of innovation, fashion and play!

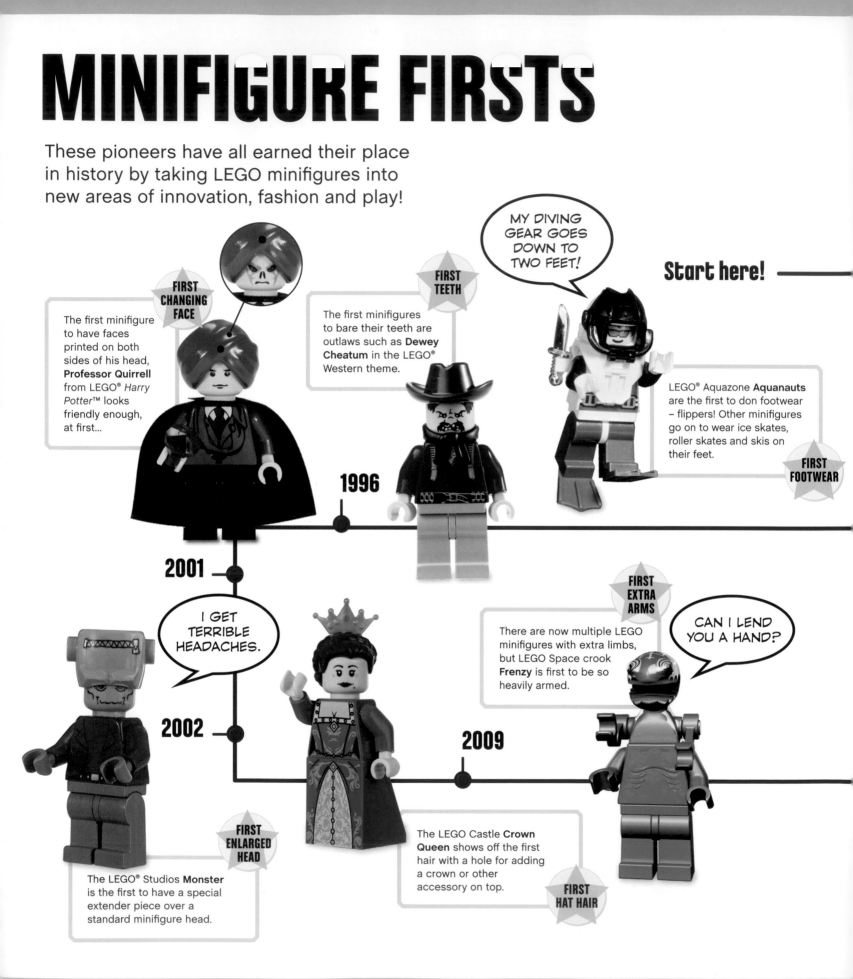

**FIRST CHANGING FACE**

The first minifigure to have faces printed on both sides of his head, **Professor Quirrell** from LEGO® *Harry Potter*™ looks friendly enough, at first...

**FIRST TEETH**

The first minifigures to bare their teeth are outlaws such as **Dewey Cheatum** in the LEGO® Western theme.

MY DIVING GEAR GOES DOWN TO TWO FEET!

**Start here!**

LEGO® Aquazone **Aquanauts** are the first to don footwear – flippers! Other minifigures go on to wear ice skates, roller skates and skis on their feet.

**FIRST FOOTWEAR**

1996

2001

I GET TERRIBLE HEADACHES.

**FIRST EXTRA ARMS**

There are now multiple LEGO minifigures with extra limbs, but LEGO Space crook **Frenzy** is first to be so heavily armed.

CAN I LEND YOU A HAND?

2002

**FIRST ENLARGED HEAD**

The LEGO® Studios **Monster** is the first to have a special extender piece over a standard minifigure head.

2009

The LEGO Castle **Crown Queen** shows off the first hair with a hole for adding a crown or other accessory on top.

**FIRST HAT HAIR**

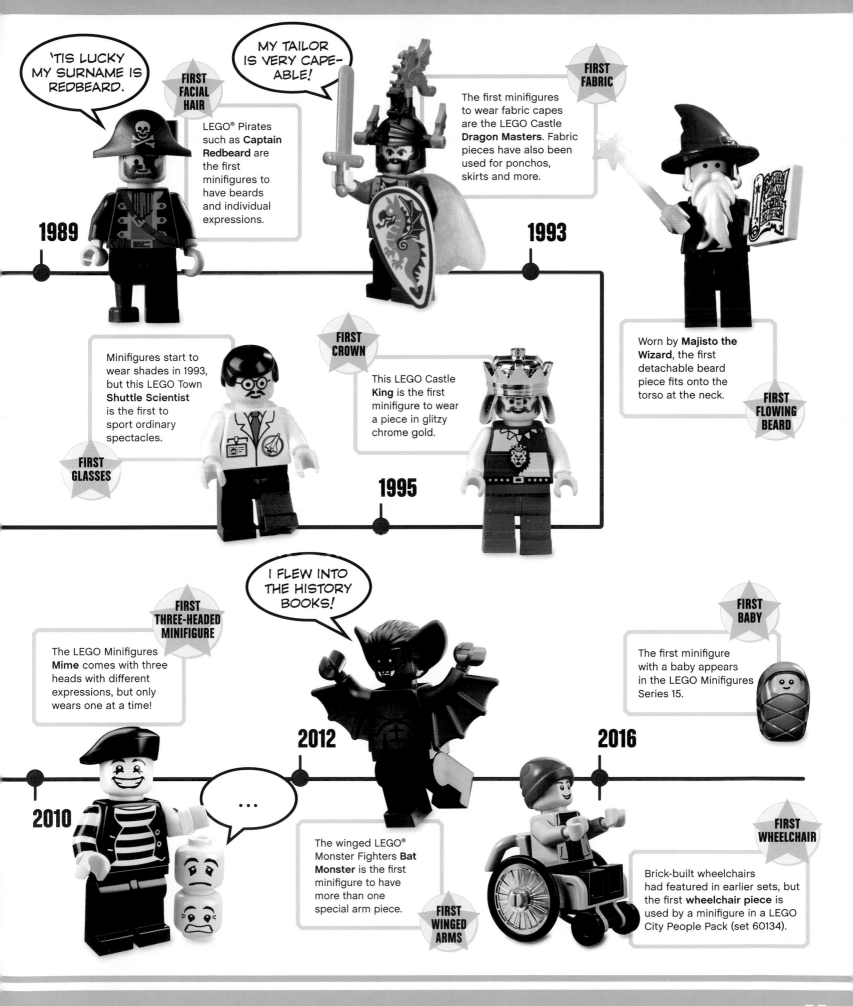

'TIS LUCKY MY SURNAME IS REDBEARD.

**FIRST FACIAL HAIR**

LEGO® Pirates such as **Captain Redbeard** are the first minifigures to have beards and individual expressions.

MY TAILOR IS VERY CAPE-ABLE!

**FIRST FABRIC**

The first minifigures to wear fabric capes are the LEGO Castle **Dragon Masters**. Fabric pieces have also been used for ponchos, skirts and more.

**1989**

**1993**

Minifigures start to wear shades in 1993, but this LEGO Town **Shuttle Scientist** is the first to sport ordinary spectacles.

**FIRST GLASSES**

**FIRST CROWN**

This LEGO Castle **King** is the first minifigure to wear a piece in glitzy chrome gold.

**1995**

Worn by **Majisto the Wizard**, the first detachable beard piece fits onto the torso at the neck.

**FIRST FLOWING BEARD**

**FIRST THREE-HEADED MINIFIGURE**

The LEGO Minifigures **Mime** comes with three heads with different expressions, but only wears one at a time!

I FLEW INTO THE HISTORY BOOKS!

...

**2010**

**2012**

The winged LEGO® Monster Fighters **Bat Monster** is the first minifigure to have more than one special arm piece.

**FIRST WINGED ARMS**

**FIRST BABY**

The first minifigure with a baby appears in the LEGO Minifigures Series 15.

**2016**

Brick-built wheelchairs had featured in earlier sets, but the first **wheelchair piece** is used by a minifigure in a LEGO City People Pack (set 60134).

**FIRST WHEELCHAIR**

# THE WILD BUNCH

These LEGO characters are no ordinary creatures. In their play themes, animals talk, wear clothes and have amazing adventures!

**Eagles**
Other tribes of birds include the Ravens and the Vultures.

## FACT STACK

The first LEGO® DUPLO® animal figures were a dog and a cat, found in several 1970s sets.

Unikitty from THE LEGO® MOVIE™ is a rare example of a brick-built animal character.

Licensed themes with animal characters include Mickey Mouse and Winnie the Pooh.

Two wolf-headed Anubis Warriors appear in 2011's Pharaoh's Quest theme.

## 27

Pieces used to build Spinlyn the Spider from LEGO® Legends of Chima™, making her the biggest minifigure ever!

**Saber-toothed Tigers**
One of two tribe species extinct in the real world, along with Mammoths.

**Phoenixes**
The only Legends of Chima tribe to be based on a mythical creature.

## FANTASTIC BEASTS

For centuries, explorers have searched for mythical animals. If they just checked out the LEGO Minifigures line, they would find a Minotaur, a Yeti and the unmistakable tracks of a "Square Foot"!

THIS SUIT CAME WITH A LARGE BILL!

| TOP 5 Collectible critter costumes | | | | |
|---|---|---|---|---|
| 1 Lizard Man (Series 5, 2011) | 2 Bunny Suit Guy (Series 7, 2012) | 3 Bumblebee Girl (Series 10, 2013) | 4 Shark Suit Guy (Series 15, 2016) | 5 Penguin Suit Guy (Series 16, 2016) |

## THE TRIBES OF CHIMA

Animals from 21 tribes appeared in LEGO Chima sets between 2013 and 2015, including…

### Lions
One of 14 mammal tribes, alongside Wolves, Beavers, Bears and Bats.

### Crocodiles
The only other cold-blooded tribes are the Scorpions and Spiders.

### Brick History

In 2016, six LEGO sets based on *The Angry Birds Movie* were packed full of plummeting piggy figures, plus brand new bird pieces to send barrelling towards them.

# AWESOME!

In 2013 and 2014, LEGO® Teenage Mutant Ninja Turtles sets featured minifigure turtles, plus rat, dog, fish and alligator figures.

# FAB FRIENDS

The animal characters of LEGO® FABULAND® were the first LEGO figures to have individual names and stories. Between 1979 and 1989, more than 40 characters appeared in almost 100 sets, including…

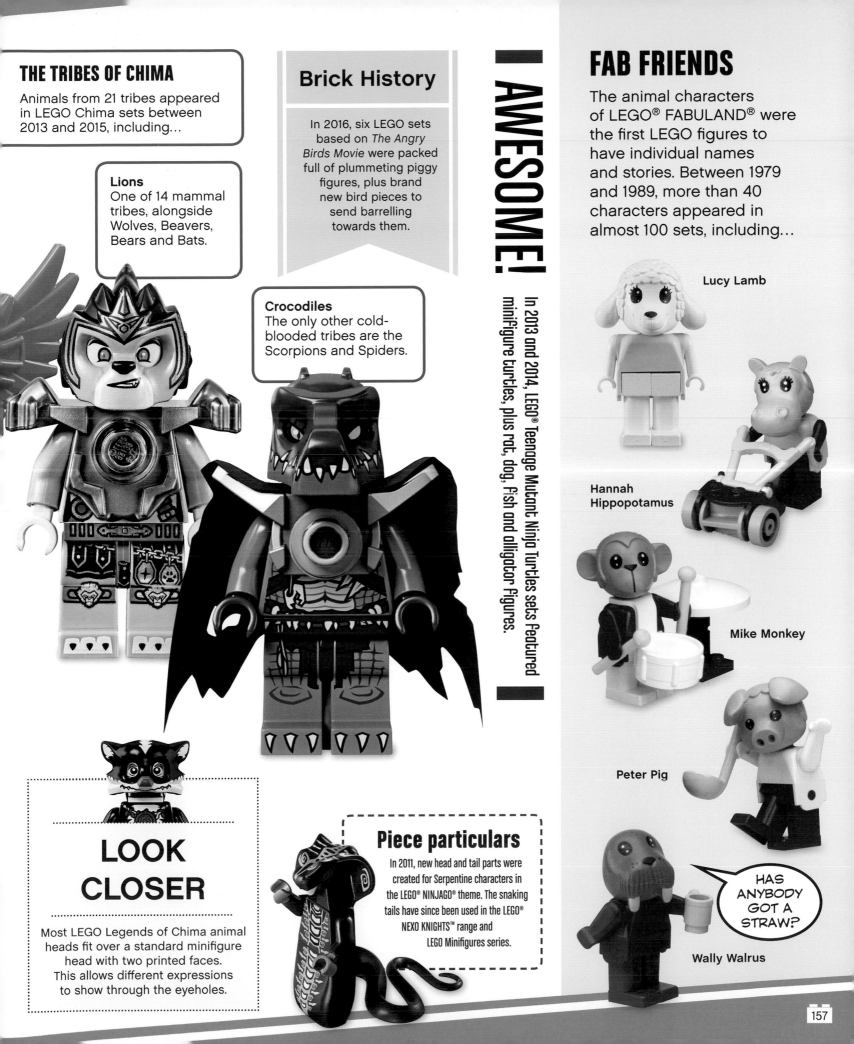

Lucy Lamb

Hannah Hippopotamus

Mike Monkey

Peter Pig

HAS ANYBODY GOT A STRAW?

Wally Walrus

# LOOK CLOSER

Most LEGO Legends of Chima animal heads fit over a standard minifigure head with two printed faces. This allows different expressions to show through the eyeholes.

### Piece particulars

In 2011, new head and tail parts were created for Serpentine characters in the LEGO® NINJAGO® theme. The snaking tails have since been used in the LEGO® NEXO KNIGHTS™ range and LEGO Minifigures series.

# Sea creatures

**1**   **LEGO shark** *(Squalus legodtus)*. Grey sharks were widespread in the era of LEGO Pirates and can still be seen in LEGO City harbour. White sharks have also been spotted off LEGO Town.

**2**   **LEGO fish** *(Piscis legodtus)*. The most common variety of LEGO fish is silver-scaled, and ranges as far as the LEGO® *Star Wars*™ universe. Look out for orange and green species, too.

**3**   **LEGO octopus** *(Octopus legodtus)*. Black and red varieties of LEGO octopus have been spotted by LEGO Pirates and others, but only the LEGO® Agents have identified a glow-in-the-dark one!

**4**   **LEGO crab** *(Carcinus legodtus)*. Red crabs are local to LEGO® BELVILLE™, but light orange examples range across LEGO City, Heartlake City, Ninjago Island and elsewhere.

**5**   **LEGO crocodile** *(Crocodylus legodtus)*. First discovered by LEGO Pirates, crocodiles have also been spotted by LEGO® Adventurers in the jungle, and explorers in the LEGO Town Outback.

# Mammals

**6**   **LEGO horse** *(Equus legodtus)*. The horse is one of the most widespread LEGO species. Since 2012, a more athletic breed – given to rearing – has become the dominant variety.

**7**   **LEGO cat** *(Felis legodta)*. LEGO cats are most popular as pets in LEGO BELVILLE, but can also be seen alongside LEGO witches and being rescued from trees by LEGO City firefighters.

**8**   **LEGO dog** *(Canis legodtus)*. Huskies, Chihuahuas, Dalmatians and terriers are just some of the LEGO dog breeds to be seen in LEGO City or further afield with LEGO minifigure owners.

# ANIMALS

**9**    **LEGO bear (*Ursus legodtus*).** LEGO Town Arctic explorers were the first to encounter polar bears, while the LEGO City Forest Police have regular run-ins with mighty brown bears.

**10**    **LEGO monkey (*Simius legodtus*).** Abundant in the era of LEGO Pirates, a small number of LEGO monkeys also go about their business in LEGO Town and LEGO BELVILLE.

**11**    **LEGO elephant (*Elefantus legodtus*).** Only the LEGO Adventurers have encountered LEGO elephants. Though very rare, they are also very large, so if there is one to be seen, you won't miss it!

**12**    **LEGO farm animals (*Domesticus legodtus*).** LEGO goats, pigs, chickens and cows were all reared in the LEGO Castle era, with pigs and cows still a familiar sight in certain areas of LEGO City.

## Creepy crawlies

**13**    **LEGO frog (*Rana legodta*).** Frogs abound in a variety of LEGO environments, from the era of LEGO Castle to modern Heartlake City. They have even made the giant leap into LEGO Space!

**14**    **LEGO snake (*Serpens legodtus*).** The common LEGO snake spans many habitats and is most often coloured red. Its fanged cousin comes in many colours and is largely restricted to Ninjago Island.

**15**    **LEGO spider (*Aranea legodta*).** More than 10 different colours of spider have been seen across a range of LEGO habitats, including glow-in-the-dark specimens found by LEGO Monster Fighters.

**16**    **LEGO scorpion (*Scorpio legodtus*).** Most often encountered by LEGO Adventurers, scorpions are also found on Ninjago Island. Rare, brightly coloured varieties have been recorded further afield.

# FASHION STATEMENTS

LEGO characters always dress to impress in a range of outfits, from the stylish to the outlandish. Here are some of their best and boldest fashion choices.

**MOST LAID-BACK MINIFIGURE**

The Dad from Ferris Wheel (set 10247)

## 2,642

The number of sets that black trousers have been found in since they first appeared in 1978, making them the most popular trousers for minifigures.

*MY CAPE IS A LITTLE STIFF.*

### Piece particulars

The first LEGO capes were plastic pieces which mostly appeared on knight, king and maiden minifigures from 1984 until 2003.

## LOOK CLOSER

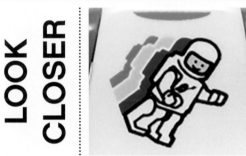

Some minifigures wear clothes that hark back to earlier LEGO eras. This funky top showing a classic LEGO astronaut appears in 14 sets.

# AWESOME!

"Where Are My Pants?" Guy from THE LEGO MOVIE Minifigures range is more famous for the clothes he doesn't wear than the ones he does!

## TOP 5
### LEGO Minifigures in traditional costumes

**1** Bagpiper (Series 7, 2012)

**2** Flamenco Dancer (Series 6, 2012)

**3** Hula Dancer (Series 3, 2011)

**4** Lederhosen Guy (Series 8, 2012)

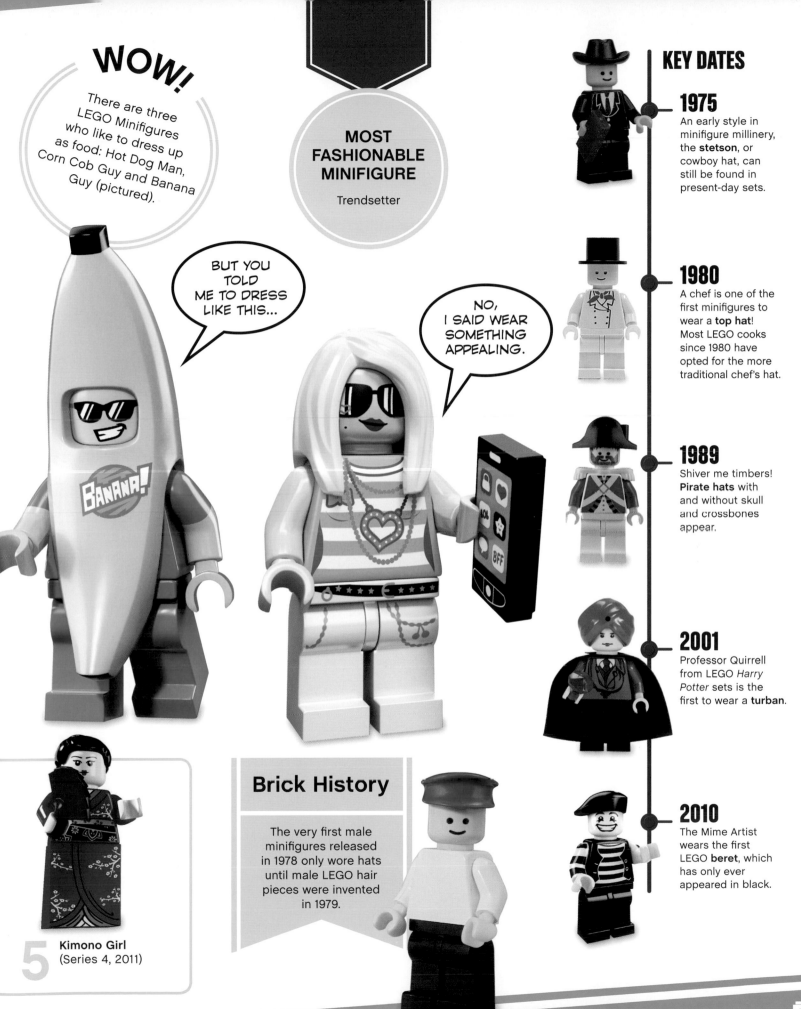

## WOW!

There are three LEGO Minifigures who like to dress up as food: Hot Dog Man, Corn Cob Guy and Banana Guy (pictured).

## MOST FASHIONABLE MINIFIGURE

Trendsetter

BUT YOU TOLD ME TO DRESS LIKE THIS...

NO, I SAID WEAR SOMETHING APPEALING.

**5** Kimono Girl
(Series 4, 2011)

## Brick History

The very first male minifigures released in 1978 only wore hats until male LEGO hair pieces were invented in 1979.

## KEY DATES

### 1975
An early style in minifigure millinery, the **stetson**, or cowboy hat, can still be found in present-day sets.

### 1980
A chef is one of the first minifigures to wear a **top hat**! Most LEGO cooks since 1980 have opted for the more traditional chef's hat.

### 1989
Shiver me timbers! **Pirate hats** with and without skull and crossbones appear.

### 2001
Professor Quirrell from LEGO *Harry Potter* sets is the first to wear a **turban**.

### 2010
The Mime Artist wears the first LEGO **beret**, which has only ever appeared in black.

# A GALAXY OF STARS

From Han and Luke to Finn and Rey, the heroes of the *Star Wars* saga are some of the world's most iconic characters. They are all instantly recognisable as LEGO minifigures, too.

## MOST UNDERDRESSED MINIFIGURE

Luke Skywalker (Bacta Tank variant, set 7879)

## FACT STACK

In 2002, Yoda was the first LEGO minifigure to have short legs.

All new parts were needed to create the R2-D2 figure in 1999.

Jar Jar Binks was the first minifigure to have a specially shaped head mould.

There are 35 different minifigure versions of Luke Skywalker.

## ROYAL EXCLUSIVE

Padmé Amidala wears her full Queen of Naboo regalia in Gungan Sub (set 9499). Her circular skirt has never been used in any other set.

*I'VE GOT A GOOD FEELING ABOUT YOU, KID!*

**50** Approximate age difference in years between Young and Old Han Solo.

## IT'S A SIGN!

Graffiti artist Sabine Wren from *Star Wars Rebels* wears a starbird icon of her own design. A similar emblem later becomes the symbol of the Rebel Alliance.

## AWESOME!

Rowan, Zander and Kordi Freemaker are the first LEGO *Star Wars* minifigures to get their own TV show – LEGO *Star Wars: The Freemaker Adventures.*

## TOP 5

Strange species of the LEGO *Star Wars* world with specially crafted heads

**1** Mon Calamari (Admiral Ackbar)

**2** Ithorian (Jedi Master)

**3** Twi'lek (Hera Syndulla)

**4** Ewok (Wicket)

**5** Um... (Maz Kanata)

## Brick History

From 1999 to 2004, most LEGO *Star Wars* minifigures had yellow hands and faces. The first to have a realistic skin tone was Lando Calrissian in 2003.

**REALLY?!**

In Jabba's Sail Barge (set 75020) R2-D2 is built with an extra piece to turn him into a serving tray!

**Q** | What is the rarest LEGO minifigure?

**A** | That is probably the solid silver C-3PO made to celebrate the 30th anniversary of *Star Wars* in 2007. Only one was ever made, along with five in solid gold.

LOOKS LIKE WE'RE NO LONGER THE NEW GUYS.

Finn

Rey

## KEY DATES

### 1999
The first LEGO® *Star Wars*™ sets include Qui-Gon Jinn, Luke Skywalker, Obi-Wan "Ben" Kenobi, Padmé Amidala and other heroes.

### 2008
Sets based on animated TV series *Star Wars: The Clone Wars* follow the adventures of Obi-Wan Kenobi, Anakın Skywalker and Ahsoka Tano.

### 2014
A new animated series, *Star Wars Rebels*, spawns LEGO *Star Wars* sets featuring young Ezra Bridger and the crew of the *Ghost*.

### 2015
Finn and Rey meet old friends Han, Chewie and Leia as the first LEGO *Star Wars: The Force Awakens* sets are released.

### 2016
Jyn Erso and a ragtag band of new minifigures try to steal the Death Star plans in LEGO *Star Wars: Rogue One* sets.

# A HIVE OF FUN AND VILLAINY

Sometimes it's fun to play the bad guy... These minifigure meanies make the LEGO *Star Wars* universe a more exciting place to visit!

## FACT STACK

The first LEGO Sith Lord was Darth Maul back in 1999.

Stormtroopers didn't show up in any sets until 2001.

The Jabba the Hutt figure is LEGO *Star Wars*' largest villain.

Jabba's nephew, Rotta the Huttlet, is one of the smallest figures.

## Brick History

Since 2011, special minifigures have been given away to mark *Star Wars* Day on 4th May. The 2014 minifigure was the mysterious Darth Revan.

ROGER, ROGER, ROGER, ROGER, ROGER, ROGER, ROGER...

## 147

Battle droid figures found in 54 different LEGO sets.

## Brick statistics

**10,000 limited-edition white Boba Fetts**
Based on *Star Wars* concept art and given away in 2010

**6 Boba variants with printed faces**
Hidden beneath printed visors

**5 Boba variants with plain black heads**
Visible through helmets with cutaway visors

**2 young Bobas**
As seen in *Episode II: Attack of the Clones*

**1 solid bronze Boba**
Awarded to a US competition winner in 2010

## AWESOME!

Shiny Captain Phasma is the first minifigure to have a silver blaster. She also has a unique, red-trimmed cape.

**Q** Which LEGO set has the most minifigures?

**A** With 14 Imperials and nine rebels (plus two astromech droids), the 2016 Death Star (set 75159) has more minifigures than any other LEGO set!

I FEEL YOUR PRESENTS.

**MOST FESTIVE SITH LORD**

Santa Darth Vader (set 75056)

## WOW!

The General Grievous figure is made from eight special pieces, none of which is used to make any other character.

### IT'S A SIGN!

Get close (but not too close!) to Jabba the Hutt and you'll see the symbol of the Desilijic crime family tattooed on his right arm.

### EVIL EYES

Minifigures in sets based on the animated *Star Wars: The Clone Wars* TV show have cartoon-style facial features. This Chancellor Palpatine has striking eyes – no doubt focused on becoming Emperor.

## TOP 5
### Stylish super troopers

**1** Stormtrooper with Orange Pauldron (2012)

**2** Red Sith Trooper (2013)

**3** Shadow Trooper (2015)

**4** Imperial Shock Trooper (2016)

**5** Shore Trooper (2016)

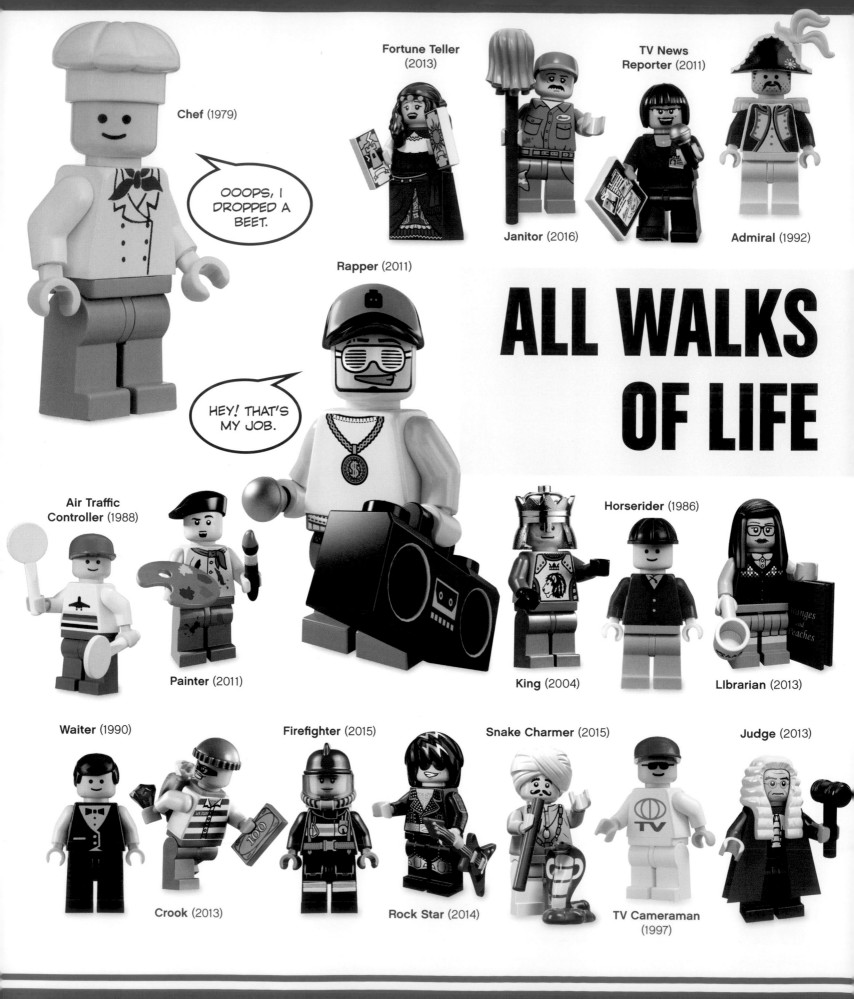

Chef (1979)

OOOPS, I DROPPED A BEET.

Fortune Teller (2013)

Janitor (2016)

TV News Reporter (2011)

Admiral (1992)

Rapper (2011)

HEY! THAT'S MY JOB.

# ALL WALKS OF LIFE

Air Traffic Controller (1988)

Painter (2011)

Horserider (1986)

King (2004)

Librarian (2013)

Waiter (1990)

Crook (2013)

Firefighter (2015)

Rock Star (2014)

Snake Charmer (2015)

TV Cameraman (1997)

Judge (2013)

DJ (2012)

Coast Guard (1999)

Sheriff (1996)

Farmer (2009)

Paleontologist (2015)

Evil Mastermind (2001)

They may be small, but no job is too big for these LEGO minifigures. From kings to crooks, they've got every vacancy filled!

Demolition Worker (2015)

Zookeeper (2011)

Scientist (1999)

Ninja (2010)

Jester (2008)

Football Referee (1998)

Wrestler (2010)

Angler (2017)

Stunt Pilot (1993)

WHY WALK WHEN YOU CAN DANCE?

Clown (2010)

Diver (1998)

Carpenter (2015)

LEGO Store Worker (2015)

Barber (2015)

Ballerina (2016)

# WE ARE NINJA

Since LEGO® NINJAGO® sets launched in 2011, a team of brave warriors has taken on skeletons, snakes, spooks, Sky Pirates and more!

## LOOK CLOSER

Ever since Zane merged his own mind with the operating system of the android P.I.X.A.L., his visual display has featured the letters "PXL" written backwards.

**Master Wu**

DON'T LOOK NOW BUT THE OTHER PAGE IS FULL OF TERRIBLE VILLAINS.

## 1,210

Megawatts generated by Jay when he uses his full electrical power.

**Zane**   **Jay**   **Lloyd**

**Cole**   **Kai**   **Nya**

## REALLY?!

Before he was an ninja, Lloyd wanted to be a villain. It seemed the obvious choice for the son of evil Lord Garmadon!

## Brick History

Kai and Nya's mum and dad were the Elemental Masters of Water and Fire. Nya followed in their mum's footsteps to become the new Master of Water.

## AWESOME!

Cole was able to walk through walls when Morro the evil Wind Master turned him into a living ghost.

# TOP 5

Careers of Ninjago villains before they turned bad

**1** Lord Garmadon: peaceful teacher.

**2** OverBorg: brilliant inventor.

**3** Master Chen: noodle-bar owner.

**4** Morro: apprentice ninja.

**5** Nadakhan: pirate (OK, still bad).

## Brick History

The Overlord is the oldest villain in the Ninjago world. He was created at the same time as the island itself, and then banished beneath the sea.

**IT'S A SIGN!**

Nadakhan and his Sky Pirates all wear this scary skull-and-crossed-swords symbol.

**General Kozu**

**TALLEST LEGO MINIFIGURE**

General Kozu (set 70504)

**Overlord**

**Nadakhan**

**Master Chen**

**Morro**

**Skulkin**

**Lord Garmadon**

**Pythor**

| Q | Why did Pythor change colour? |
|---|---|
| A | Pythor used to be purple, but he was bleached white by the stomach acid of a monster that swallowed him. Ugh! |

**Overborg**

## Prehistoric LEGO beasts

1   **DUPLO *dinosaurs*.** The first LEGO dinosaurs lived in LEGO DUPLO sets from the late 1990s. More preschool than prehistoric, these creatures had more chance of getting chewed themselves than of biting anyone else!

2   ***Dino Island.*** In 2000, the LEGO Adventurers took a trip to Dino Island, where Johnny Thunder and his fellow explorers discovered the blocky footprints of tyrannosaurs, triceratops and stegosauruses.

3   ***Adaptable dinos.*** In 2001, a dedicated LEGO® Dinosaurs theme featured four-in-one dino models such as the aquatic lizard Mosasaurus (set 6721), which could be rebuilt as an iguanodon, a postosuchus and a dimetrodon.

# FOR DINOS

4 **Double Trouble.** The Dino Attack and Dino 2010 themes were launched in 2005, in the US and Europe respectively. The sets had some differences, but shared the same rampaging raptors and a T-rex with light-up eyes.

5 **LEGO** *Dino.* In 2012, the daring Dino Defence team battled prehistoric beasts in the LEGO® Dino theme. Their quarry included new designs for flying pteranodons, plus a new coelophysis dino with stripes.

6 **LEGO® Jurassic World™.** A colourfully crested Dilophosaurus and an impressive Indominus rex were among the new discoveries when a band of brave minifigures took a trip to LEGO *Jurassic World* in 2015.

# CREATURE FEATURE

Some LEGO animals come fully formed, but these brick beasts are all built to be wild!

## Brick History

In 2014, the LEGO Group gave employees a gift set of brick birds native to the UK, China, the USA, Singapore and Denmark, to celebrate having offices in all those countries.

## FACT STACK

One of the first LEGO brick-built animals came in Cowboy & Pony (set 806) in 1964.

The first LEGO Castle knights rode brick-built horses in two 1970s sets.

Fearsome Legend Beasts were among the brick-built creatures in LEGO Legends of Chima.

LEGO® Elves sets feature brick-built dragons similar to the ones in LEGO NINJAGO theme.

## WOW!

LEGO® Creator sets such as Red Animals (set 31032) from 2015 can be made into three different animals – in this case a dragon, a snake and a scorpion.

## REALLY?!

Feed the hungry parrot in LEGO Creator Rainforest Animals (set 31031) from 2015 and his food literally passes right through him!

## TOP 5
### LEGO NINJAGO dragons

**1** The **Fusion Dragon** has the powers of both its riders – Fire ninja Kai and Water ninja Nya.

**2** The ghostly **Morro Dragon** was the first NINJAGO dragon to have fabric wings.

**3** The **Green NRG Dragon** soars through the sky with a wingspan of 22in (57cm).

**4** Lloyd's **Golden Dragon** has a moulded head piece, like all NINJAGO dragons released before 2014.

## THE ONLY LEGO® TECHNIC ANIMAL

Control Centre II Dinosaur (set 8485)

## Piece particulars

Deep Sea Predators (set 4506) from 2004 used rare glow-in-the-dark pieces to make fearsome fish teeth and spooky squid bits!

**WOW!**

Far from prehistoric, the 2008 LEGO Creator Stegosaurus (set 4998) contains a light-up brick to create glowing eyes.

## AWESOME!

In 2010 and 2011, LEGO® Atlantis sets pitted minifigure divers against brick-built sea creatures, including an angry angler fish!

## MINI BEASTS

Every month, LEGO stores around the world hold Mini Model Builds, where fans can make and keep a free LEGO model. In 2017, the builds included unusual animals like narwhals and platypuses.

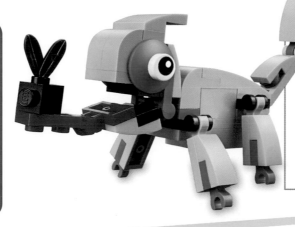

**2**

Number of pieces needed to make a LEGO fly – like the one on the tongue of this LEGO Creator Chameleon (set 30477) from 2017!

**5**

The mighty four-headed **Ultra Dragon** is four Elemental Dragons combined into one force!

# CHARACTER BUILDING

LEGO figures don't have to be mini! From purely brick-built characters to articulated action figures, there are many ways to build a big personality.

## FACT STACK

The first brick-built characters could not be posed and had no jointed or moving parts.

Today's buildable characters use parts other than bricks to allow for realistic movement.

Modern buildable figures are designed to be as robust in play as normal action figures.

There have been more buildable models of Santa Claus than any other character!

HO! HO! HO!

## Piece particulars

LEGO ball-and-socket joints were introduced in 1970 for connections such as vehicle tow bars. Most buildable figures are made with newer ball-and-socket friction joints, which connect more tightly for poseability.

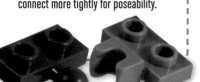

### REALLY?!

Looking good enough to eat, Birthday Buddy (set 40226) is a brick-built cupcake character released in 2016.

## FRESH FACES

In 1974, the first LEGO figures with printed faces and articulated arms were released. Now known as "maxifigures" by fans, they had torsos and legs built from standard bricks, and appeared in more than 30 sets.

**Q** | What is the Character and Creature Building System (CCBS)?

**A** | CCBS is the LEGO Group's name for a figure-building system that was introduced in 2011. It features jointed "skeleton" parts and snap-on "shell" pieces that can create large, articulated characters and creatures.

# TOP 5

**Cool parts used in LEGO Mixels**

1 **Volectro** has hair made out of a bush.

2 **Slumbo** has minifigure helmets for eyelids.

3 **Turg** has a tail piece for a tongue.

4 **Forx** has banana pieces for eyebrows.

5 **Dribbal** has a crystal piece as his... Ugh!

## BRICK CHALLENGE

Build a model of yourself out of LEGO bricks. Can you make it move using joints or hinge pieces?

### 1999

The LEGO Technic Slizer subtheme (also known as Throwbots) introduces buildable figures articulated using large ball-and-socket friction connectors.

### 2001

The first BIONICLE buildable figures blend LEGO Technic articulation with unique, characterful mask pieces and a detailed storyline.

### 2011

LEGO® Hero Factory introduces a new buildable figure system, still based on ball-and-socket joints, but easier to build and stronger in play.

### 2015

After a four-year break, LEGO® BIONICLE® returns to stores with sturdy new figures based on the LEGO Hero Factory building system.

HAS ANYONE GOT A TISSUE?

**13**

Points of articulation on Burnzie from LEGO NEXO KNIGHTS Axl's Tower Carrier (set 70322).

**ODDEST BRICK-BUILT CHARACTERS**

Clowns (set 321)

## Brick History

In 1963, the US-only Doll Set (set 905) included more than 200 pieces for building a pirate captain, ballet dancers, a musician, a coachman and more.

**WOW!**

Characters that exist as minifigures and large buildable figures include Batman, Buzz Lightyear, Spongebob Squarepants and Laval from LEGO Legends of Chima.

# GO SPORTS!

In a world where croissants are the size of your arm, LEGO minifigures need to stay in shape. Luckily for them, there's a healthy array of sport-themed sets.

I CHEER WHEN THERE'S A GHOUL!

## REALLY?!

The LEGO Minifigures theme has featured three different cheerleaders, with the latest being a Zombie Cheerleader.

# 7

Cyclist minifigures in 2000's Telekom Race Cyclists and Winners' Podium (set 1199) – but only one winner in a yellow jersey!

## Brick History

In 2016, the German football team were turned into a LEGO Minifigures series. Fifteen players came with footballs, while manager Joachim Löw came with a unique tactics board.

## BUILT ON ICE

Between 2003 and 2004, LEGO® Sports Hockey sets featured minifigures, small figures built from LEGO Technic elements and larger, BIONICLE style figures with powerful puck-hitting mechanisms!

# AWESOME!

In 2003, LEGO Sports Gravity Games featured daredevil skateboarder and snowboarder minifigures who could be sent speeding down special ramp pieces.

I BETTER GET THIS SHOT NOW EVERYONE IS WATCHING.

YOU CAN DO IT, CHAMP!

## Piece particulars

The Boxer from 2011 was the first minifigure not to have at least one standard hand piece. His gloves attach straight onto his arms!

**COMES-WITH-AN-ACTUAL-MEDAL WINNER**

Swimming Champion

**WOW!**

In 2000, LEGO® Football (also known as LEGO Soccer) used tilting, turning minifigure bases so that players could aim and kick.

**IT'S A SIGN!**

In 2001, Women's Team (set 3416) featured six female football players, plus stickers to kit them out in American, Canadian, Brazilian or Mexican shirts.

## TOP 5
Collectible competitors

**1** Downhil Skier (Series 8, 2012)

**2** Sumo Wrestler (Series 3, 2011)

**3** Tennis Ace (Series 7, 2012)

**4** Roller Derby Girl (Series 9, 2013)

**5** Fencer (Series 13, 2015)

## Top 5

**Most brick-chilling collectibles**

1. **Banshee** (series 14, 2015)
2. **Zombie Businessman** (series 14, 2015)
3. **Spectre** (series 14, 2015)
4. **Medusa** (series 10, 2013)
5. **Fly Monster** (series 14, 2015)

**Banshee**

**Zombie Businessman**

**IT'S A SIGN!**

The Zombie Pirate Captain's hat has an even creepier skull-and-crossbones design than regular LEGO pirates.

**ZOMBIE TIMES**

**BRAAAIN**

**Spectre**

**Fly Monster**

# 13

Number of sets released in the LEGO® Monster Fighters theme in 2012.

## Brick History

LEGO vampires first appeared in LEGO® Studios sets in 2002. Since then, more vampires have emerged from the shadows in LEGO Minifigures, LEGO® Games and LEGO Monster Fighters sets.

## Piece particulars

The LEGO Minifigures Monster from 2011 has a special head extension, stitched up to keep his brain in place. This spooky part has been used in different creepy colours for Monster Rocker (pictured) and Monster Butler minifigures.

**Q** What do LEGO monsters do in their spare time?

**A** They chill! The Monster Butler in 2012's Haunted House (set 10228) likes to dance to music. His mummy friends got him into rapping.

## ARRGH!

White head pieces with spooky skull designs appear in more than 70 sets – and not always with bodies to rest on!

## LOOK CLOSER

The Werewolf minifigure wears the same shirt as the Lumberjack. One unlucky night in the woods and the poor Lumberjack was transformed, howling at the Moon!

## BOO!

In 1990, the ghost shroud was the first glow-in-the-dark LEGO element. Glowing ghosts have since appeared in 16 scary sets.

# MINI MONSTERS

Did you know that the LEGO world has a darker side? These ghouls and monsters make LEGO sets go bump in the night and will get your teeth chattering!

## Special scale LEGO figures

1   **DUPLO** *dolls.* Four large LEGO DUPLO dolls with realistic proportions and fabric clothes were released in 2001. Standing about 18 bricks high, each doll came with its own, much smaller, doll toy that was slightly larger than a LEGO minifigure.

2   **SCALA** *dolls.* The largest and most realistic of all LEGO figures, LEGO® SCALA dolls stood more than 6in (15.2cm) tall, wore fabric clothes and had brushable hair. The dolls featured in more than 40 sets between 1997 and 2001.

3   **LEGO Technic** *figures.* The first LEGO Technic figures braved the cold in Arctic-themed sets from 1986. Looking like taller, more athletic minifigures, they appeared in 36 sets in 28 variations – including scary cyborgs!

4   **BELVILLE** *figures.* Twice the height of a minifigure, each BELVILLE figure had 14 points of articulation – more than any other LEGO figure. Launched in 1994, the theme also included baby figures and, later, small fairies without any articulation.

# ALL SHAPES AND SIZES

**5**   **FABULAND** *figures*. More than 20 animal species inhabited the FABULAND world between 1979 and 1989. They all shared the same articulated body shape and included crocodiles, hippos and walruses.

**6**   **DUPLO** *figures*. In 1977, the first LEGO DUPLO figures had chunky single-block bodies and heads that turned but didn't come off. By 1983, some DUPLO figures had moving arms and legs, but still no removable parts for safety reasons.

**7**   *Basic figures.* LEGO Basic figures came in two variations between 1981 and 1991: blue and red. Their hollow bodies meant they could be used as finger puppets, and they were the first LEGO figures to have noses!

# FACTION PACKED

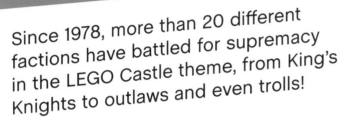

> I WENT GREEN BEFORE IT WAS FASHIONABLE!

Since 1978, more than 20 different factions have battled for supremacy in the LEGO Castle theme, from King's Knights to outlaws and even trolls!

## 14

Knights in 1978's Castle (set 375) – the most minifigures in any 20th-century set.

## HAIR TO THE THRONE

For the first 20 years of LEGO Castle, only four minifigures had hair pieces instead of helmets. The first were nobles in Knight's Joust (set 383) from 1979.

## SHIELDS UP!

LEGO Castle knights have fought with more than 40 different shields since 1978. Here are just a few from over the years.

| Crusaders (1984) | Black Falcons (1984) | Forestmen (1988) | Dragon Knights (1993) | Royal Knights (1995) | Lion Knights (2000) | Shadow Knights (2005) |

# AWESOME!

In 2004, LEGO® KNIGHTS' KINGDOM™ characters could be collected in minifigure form or as big, buildable action figures.

## TOP 5
LEGO Castle fantasy figures

**1** Ghost, in sets from 1990.

**2** Skeleton, in sets from 1995.

**3** Dwarf, in sets from 2007.

**4** Troll, in sets from 2008.

**5** Giant Troll, in sets from 2008.

FOR ONE KNIGHT ONLY!

**WOW!**
A 2016 LEGO.com exclusive (set 5004419) featured a 1980s-style knight and a LEGO knights timeline in a special presentation box.

**MOST BLING KING**
Crown King (set 7078)

**IT'S A SIGN!**
The first LEGO Castle knights from 1978 came with a sheet of stickers to decorate their plain grey tabard and shield pieces.

## Brick History

In 1993, the Dragon Masters became the first minifigures in any theme to have mismatched arms and legs – a style later taken up by LEGO Castle jesters.

Skeleton Warriors (2007)

Troll Warriors (2007)

King's Knights (2013)

I'M A GOOD GUY, REALLY!

**Q** Who are the bad guys in early LEGO Castle sets?

**A** That's entirely up to you! It was not until the 1990s that villainous factions such as the Wolfpack appeared in LEGO Castle sets.

# MODERN KNIGHTS

Meet the minifigure citizens of the NEXO KNIGHTS kingdom; from the heroes that fight to defend it, to the monsters who want to destroy it!

## FACT STACK

Clay Moorington is determined to become the greatest knight ever. His emblem is the falcon.

Aaron Fox is a reckless daredevil and a great archer. His emblem is the fox.

Lance Richmond is a celebrity knight who is not as brave as his fans think! His emblem is the horse.

Axl is big and strong – probably because he eats so much! His emblem is the bull.

Macy Halbert is a princess but her true calling is knighthood! Her emblem is the dragon.

Clay

Aaron

Lance

## IT'S A SIGN!

In Aaron's Stone Destroyer (set 70358), Robot Hoodlum the rebel squirebot wears the same stag emblem as the LEGO Castle Forestmen.

## WHAT'S A BOT?

While the NEXO KNIGHTS heroes are busy saving the realm, lots of everyday jobs in Knighton are done by mechanical bots. Chef Eclair is the King's chefbot, and each knight has a faithful squirebot to help them out.

| Q | Who is the bad guy in the LEGO NEXO KNIGHTS world? |
|---|---|
| A | Jestro, the King's former jester, is the theme's main villain. The Book of Monsters tricked him into turning bad and now he kind of likes it! |

# AWESOME!

Knight-in-training Robin Underwood hasn't graduated from the Knight's Academy yet, but he still goes undercover as the mysterious Black Knight.

## Piece particulars

The Book of Monsters is made up of two pieces that were first introduced in NEXO KNIGHTS sets: a book "plate" and a hinged book cover.

OPEN ME UP, I DARE YA!

## ROYAL RELATIONS

King and Queen Halbert are the kindly rulers of Knighton. Macy is their daughter. She has more in common with her courageous mum than her easily frightened father!

Axl

Macy

## LAVA MONSTERS

| | |
|---|---|
| **MADE FROM** | Molten-hot lava |
| **SKILLS** | Shooting fire, burning knights |
| **LEADER** | General Magmar |
| **RANKS** | Flame Throwers, Scurriers, Globlins |
| **MONSTER FACT** | Lavaria is the Lava army's sneaky spy |

## STONE MONSTERS

| | |
|---|---|
| **MADE FROM** | Super-hard rock |
| **SKILLS** | Crushing things, blasting electricity |
| **LEADER** | General Garg |
| **RANKS** | Stone Stompers, Gargoyles, Bricksters |
| **MONSTER FACT** | They were rocks and statues before lightning brought them to life |

VS.

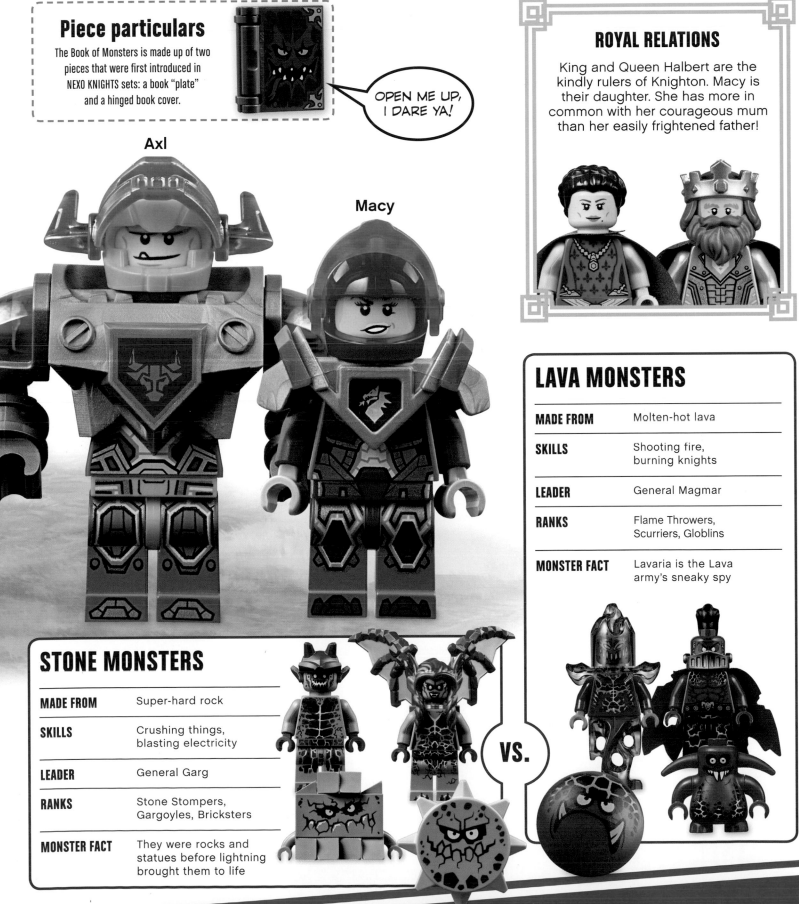

# SMALL BUT MIGHTY

Heroes come in all shapes and sizes, but in the world of LEGO® DC Super Heroes, they are all approximately four bricks high!

**Q** What is LEGO Robin's true identity?

**A** There have been several LEGO Robins, including Tim Drake (also known as "Red Robin"), Dick Grayson and Damian Wayne. But keep that under your cape!

## Brick History

Though the first LEGO DC Super Heroes sets were not released until 2012, exclusive Batman, Superman and Green Lantern minifigures were given away at special events in 2011.

## FACT STACK

There are more than 130 LEGO DC Super Heroes minifigures.

More than 60 minifigures in the theme fight on the side of truth and justice.

The assorted heroes include more than 20 Batman variations.

Superman and other Kryptonians appear in over a dozen sets.

*I'M ROBIN!*

*NO, I'M ROBIN!*

**Tim Drake**

**Dick Grayson**

**Damian Wayne**

*LOOK INTO MY EYES...*

### LITTLE WONDER

There have been four different Wonder Woman minifigures, but only the Mighty Micros version comes with short legs.

**9**

LEGO themes in which Batman appears: LEGO Batman, LEGO BrickHeadz, LEGO DC Super Heroes, LEGO® DIMENSIONS™, LEGO DUPLO, LEGO Juniors, LEGO Minifigures, THE LEGO® BATMAN MOVIE™ and THE LEGO MOVIE!

**❙AWESOME!** Armoured Batman from Clash of the Heroes (set 76044) is the only LEGO DC Super Heroes minifigure with glow-in-the-dark eyes!❙

## TOP 5
### Lesser-known heroes

**1** **Plastic Man**
(set 5004081)

**2** **Beast Boy**
(set 76035)

**3** **Hawkman**
(set 76028)

**4** **Blue Beetle**
(set 76054)

**5** **Katana**
(set 76055)

## LOOK CLOSER

Part of an exclusive 2015 gift cube
(set 5004077), the rare Lightning Lad
minifigure has lightning-bolt eyebrows!

**IT'S A SIGN!**

Superman's "S-Shield"
is actually a Kryptonian
family crest. It is also
worn by his father, Jor-El,
and his cousin, Kara, also
known as Supergirl.

# BUILT TO BE BAD

Super Heroes are nothing without their enemies. This Rogues Gallery causes chaos for the good guys in LEGO DC Super Heroes sets.

*WHAT A BUNCH OF CLOWNS!*

## LOOK CLOSER

In Batman: Rescue from Rā's al Ghūl (set 76056), anti-hero Talia al Ghūl has carved "B+T" (Batman and Talia) in a heart shape on the wall of a hideout.

**MOST BADLY DRESSED BADDIE**

Trickster

**The Joker**

**The Riddler**

## REALLY?!

Lex Luthor battles Superman in three sets, but only in Heroes of Justice: Sky-High Battle (set 76046) does he have any hair.

*CALL ME "LOCKS LUTHOR"!*

## THE JOKER'S WILD!

The Joker isn't just a minifigure. In 2012, he was one of four LEGO DC Super Heroes Buildable Figures (set 4527), and in 2017 he was one of the first LEGO BrickHeadz models (set 41588).

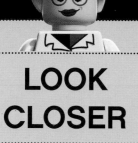

## LOOK CLOSER

Harleen Quinzel might look like a friendly doctor, but under her white coat you can see the red and black outfit of villainous Harley Quinn!

**WOW!**

Green Lantern's alien enemy Sinestro is the only minifigure ever to have a bright purple head!

NO, I'M NOT HOLDING MY BREATH.

### Top 5

LEGO villains based on the 1960s *Batman* TV series

1. The Joker
2. The Riddler
3. The Penguin
4. Mr. Freeze
5. Catwoman

**The Penguin**

**Mr. Freeze**

**Catwoman**

**REALLY?!**

Black Manta is an undersea enemy of Aquaman who seeks to control the oceans using laser-shooting cyborg sharks.

**IT'S A SIGN!**

Batzarro is a mixed-up monster version of Batman, created by Lex Luthor. He wears the Caped Crusader's famous symbol on his chest but, like his Utility Belt, it is upside-down.

Bad guys so big they don't fit into minifigure form: Gorilla Grodd, Killer Croc and Darkseid.

## Stars of the DC Super Hero Girls theme

1  **Harley Quinn.** She might be the class clown, but Harley is also a brilliant brain and an agile gymnast. She pilots a jet plane (set 41231).

2  **Wonder Woman.** She has a Lasso of Truth that stops others from telling lies. This hero also has an invisible bike in Wonder Woman Dorm Room (set 41235).

3  **Supergirl.** Superman's cousin is the most powerful teen on the planet. Instead of a vehicle, she uses her ace flying skills to catch the bad guys.

4  **Batgirl.** She is a tech genius as well as a determined crime-fighter. Batgirl flies a Batjet (set 41230) with net and stud shooters.

5  **Bumblebee.** This hero can fly like a real bee and has electric-blast sting powers. Her Bumblebee Helicopter (set 41234) helps her see off troublemakers.

6  **Poison Ivy.** A biology expert with a passion for plant life, Poison Ivy drives a plant-shooting green motorbike (set 41232).

7  **Lashina.** This young warrior is known for her whip-cracking skills. She drives a tough tank (set 41233).

8  **Super Hero High School.** The girls' school (set 41232) transforms into battle mode when attacked, with a ramp that lowers from the tower and a rooftop shooter.

# POWER!

# CHAPTER FIVE

# BEYOND
# THE BRICK

# FACT STACK

The LEGO Group was founded by master carpenter and joiner Ole Kirk Kristiansen.

Ole Kirk ran the company until 1957, when his son, Godtfred Kirk Christiansen, took over.

In 1979, Ole Kirk's grandson, Kjeld Kirk Kristiansen, was made chief executive officer.

Today, the LEGO Group is jointly owned by Kjeld Kirk and his three children.

## WOW!

Ole Kirk Kristiansen came up with the LEGO name by combining the Danish words "leg godt" meaning "play well".

Ole, Godtfred and Kjeld Kirk Kristiansen together in 1951.

## KEY DATES

**1891**
Ole Kirk Kristiansen is born in Omvrå, in the Blaahøj-Filskov region of Denmark (not far from Billund), on 7th April.

**1903**
Ole Kirk becomes an apprentice carpenter and joiner, learning skills from his brother Kristian Bonde Kristiansen in Give, Denmark.

**1916**
After completing his apprenticeship and military service, Ole Kirk buys a joinery factory in the rural community of Billund.

**1924**
Wood shavings in Ole Kirk's workshop catch fire, causing the workshop and the family home to burn down. Work starts on rebuilding a new house (pictured).

**1932**
A global economic crisis threatens Ole Kirk's rebuilt business. With no other carpentry work available, he begins to make wooden toys.

**1934**
Ole Kirk holds a competition among his employees to name his growing company. He wins it himself by devising the LEGO name!

**Q** | Why are Ole Kirk Kristiansen and Godtfred Kirk Christiansen's surnames spelled differently?

**A** | Both were born "Kristiansen", but it was common to use both spellings interchangeably. Ole Kirk used both versions, but kept "Kristiansen" on his birth certificate, while Godtfred officially changed to the "Ch" spelling in the 1980s.

## IT'S A SIGN!

**DET·BEDSTE·ER·IKKE·FOR·GODT**

When Ole Kirk Kristiansen coined the LEGO Group motto "Only the best is good enough" in 1936, his son Godtfred Kirk Christiansen turned it into a woodcut for the wall of their workshop.

## REALLY?!

In its early days as a wooden toy manufacturer, the LEGO Group also made ladders and ironing boards!

## Brick History

In 1942, fire destroyed the LEGO factory. Though his life's work was lost, Ole Kirk Kristiansen set about building a new factory – the birthplace of the LEGO plastic brick.

# AWESOME!

The house and workshop Ole Kirk Kristiansen built in 1924 still stands in Billund, and has even been made into a LEGO set.

# 10

The number of employees who worked at the LEGO factory in 1939.

## PLASTIC PIONEER

Ole Kirk Kristiansen was among the first to see the potential of plastic toys. An early success was a model tractor in 1952. Though expensive to make, the tractor turned a healthy profit, which helped him to further develop another product: plastic bricks.

# WHERE IT ALL BEGAN

The worldwide success of the LEGO Group can all be traced back to one man in a workshop in Billund, Denmark, where the company still has its headquarters today.

# BRICK BEGINNINGS

LEGO® bricks get to be spaceships, sports cars, castles and more – but there's another amazing journey they all go on first!

**1** LEGO bricks start out as small plastic granules called granulate, each one smaller than a grain of rice. The Billund factory, Kornmarken, can get through 110 tons (100 tonnes) of granulate in a single day.

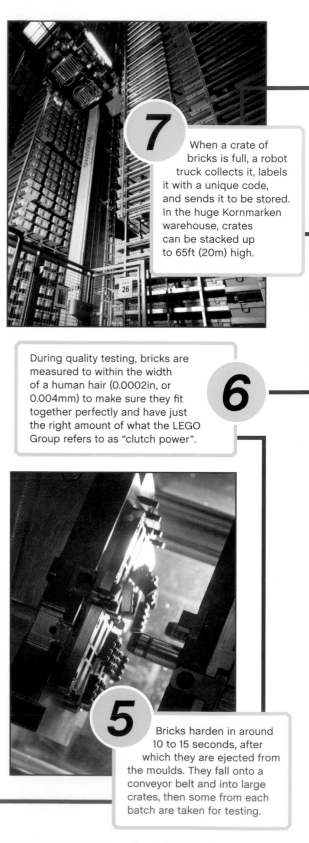

**7** When a crate of bricks is full, a robot truck collects it, labels it with a unique code, and sends it to be stored. In the huge Kornmarken warehouse, crates can be stacked up to 65ft (20m) high.

**2** Powerful vacuum pumps suck the granulate out of huge metal silos and whiz it through pipes into moulding machines. Every factory has many miles of pipes and several hundred moulding machines.

**6** During quality testing, bricks are measured to within the width of a human hair (0.0002in, or 0.004mm) to make sure they fit together perfectly and have just the right amount of what the LEGO Group refers to as "clutch power".

**3** When it reaches the machinery, the granulate is melted into a thick, gooey liquid at temperatures ranging from 446°F to 590°F (230°C to 310°C) – that's up to three times hotter than boiling water.

**4** The liquid plastic is injected into a metal mould and instantly starts to cool. To make sure it forms a perfect brick, it is subjected to pressure of up to 14.5 tons per square inch (2 tonnes per cm$^2$).

**5** Bricks harden in around 10 to 15 seconds, after which they are ejected from the moulds. They fall onto a conveyor belt and into large crates, then some from each batch are taken for testing.

**8**

When a crate is needed, a robot crane knows exactly where it is! It confirms what's inside using the unique label, slides the crate out of the stack and sends it on its way along a conveyor belt.

**15**

Robot cranes load the packaged sets onto pallets for distribution by road and by sea. Bricks that were piles of granulate just a short time ago are now on their way to stores and homes around the world!

**9**

If the bricks in the crate need a printed design on them, such as the vests on these LEGO City Police minifigure torsos, they are sent to the decoration department.

**14**

The plastic bags pass down chutes and are placed in the cardboard display boxes they will be sold in. The boxes are checked and sealed by machine, then sealed into larger boxes for delivery.

**10**

Some parts are put together in the factory, including minifigure legs onto hips and wheels onto tyres. These parts go through their own special assembly machines before they rejoin the main production line.

**13**

High-precision scales weigh the boxes along the route to make sure no pieces are missing. At the end of the conveyor belt, another machine seals the contents of each small box inside a plastic bag.

**11**

After any printing and assembly, all bricks arrive in the packing department. They are loaded into machines that eject the bricks one at a time, or in the numbers needed for a specific set.

**12**

Bricks of different kinds meet for the first time as small boxes pass beneath the packing machines, filling up with the precise selection of parts required as they go along.

# BOX CLEVER

The LEGO Group gives its boxes, bags and tubs the same care and attention that it gives to the LEGO bricks and models inside the packaging.

**Q** Do all LEGO sets come in boxes?

**A** No, not all. There have also been LEGO® BIONICLE® carry canisters, LEGO brick-shaped creative building tubs and LEGO® DUPLO® sets shaped like everything from aeroplanes to animals.

## WOW!

Since June 2014, standard LEGO products have been sold in more environmentally friendly boxes, made from materials certified by the Forest Stewardship Council®.

## REALLY?!

In 2008, Kjeld Kirk Kristiansen reprised his role as a LEGO box star for Town Plan (set 10184), celebrating 50 years of the LEGO brick. By this point, Kjeld Kirk was also the owner of the LEGO Group.

## LOOK CLOSER

Several LEGO set boxes of the 1950s featured LEGO Group founder Ole Kirk Kristiansen's grandchildren, Hanne, Gunhild and Kjeld Kirk, playing with the bricks inside.

## Brick History

Between 1956 and 1959, the front of LEGO Town Plan boxes featured paintings of the sets inside, along with a friendly figure usually known as the LEGO Gnome.

### REALLY?!

From 1957 to 1972, some LEGO sets came in large wooden boxes. They are now collector's items – even when they don't have any LEGO bricks in them!

All modern LEGO sets have a picture of a life-size LEGO brick or minifigure somewhere on the packaging, just in case anyone has never seen a real LEGO brick before!

# 10,004

Number of pieces contained in the biggest-ever LEGO box. The Ultimate Battle For CHIMA contained 25 LEGO® Legends of Chima™ sets and was the grand prize in a 2015 LEGO Club competition.

LEGENDS OF CHIMA™

Ages/edades 9+

The ultimate battle for CHIMA

10004 pcs/ Stck/pzs/db

Building Toy
Konstruktionsspielzeug
Jouet de construction
Juguete para Construir
Brinquedo para Construir
Építőjáték

# I MADE THIS

LEGO Designers put their all into making new sets, so it's no surprise that they sometimes include personal references and nods to their favourite old sets.

***Dizzy heights.*** The nervous-looking minifigure in 2015's LEGO Creator Expert Ferris Wheel (set 10247) is a joke about Set Designer Jamie Berard's reluctance to ride on the real thing!

***Why is she waiting?*** The LEGO Minifigures Diner Waitress from 2013 is based on LEGO Designer Tara Wike, and she wears a name badge to prove it.

***Written in the stars.*** Stickers in 2011's LEGO Space Earth Defence HQ (set 7066) are Set Designer Mark Stafford's tribute to the late Nate Nielsen, a LEGO fan builder known online as "Nnenn".

***On the map.*** The "LEGO Town" map in 2008's 50th anniversary LEGO set, Town Plan (set 10184), actually shows where the LEGO Group was founded in Billund, Denmark.

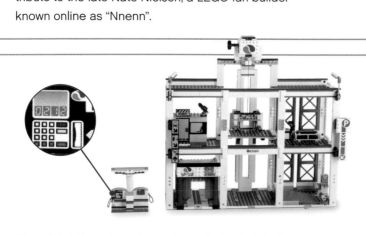

***It's a date!*** The price of gas shown in 2012's City Garage (set 4207) from the LEGO City theme just happens to be the birth date of Designer Samuel Johnson.

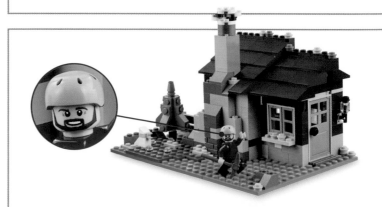

***Smiling selfie.*** The bearded trail biker in the LEGO Creator Mountain Hut (set 31025) from 2014 is a minifigure self-portrait by Set Designer Morten Rauff.

**Face of the farm.** The farmer in 2009's LEGO City Farm subtheme is based on LEGO Designer Chris Bonveen. When Chris himself came to design a new farmer in 2016, he used the opportunity to show how he had aged in real life!

*A familiar face.* Designer Matthew Boyle based the banker's portrait in 2016's LEGO Creator Expert Brick Bank (set 10251) on Chris Bonveen (see left). He reasoned that it was a picture of the minifigure farmer's brother!

*Pet project.* Glurt (set 41519) from 2014's LEGO® Mixels™ range is based on LEGO Set Designer Mark Stafford's dog – only green and much more slimy.

**Family affair.** Set Designer Jamie Berard based a minifigure in 2009's Winter Toy Shop (set 10199) on his mum, and named Chez Albert in 2014's Parisian Restaurant (set 10243) after his dad.

**DUPLO D.O.B.** Senior Designer Mette Grue-Sørensen used number plates to personalise her designs. The cars at 2009's LEGO DUPLO Petrol Station (set 5640) and Busy Garage (set 5641) all have her initials and date of birth on the back.

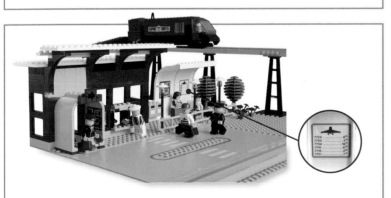

**Train tribute.** The flight numbers listed on the departure board in 1990's LEGO Town Airport Shuttle (set 6399) are, in fact, set numbers of classic 1980s LEGO Trains.

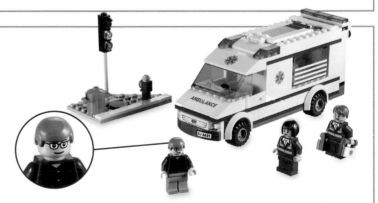

**Model mentor.** Set Designer Samuel Johnson based the look of the cyclist minifigure in 2012's LEGO City Ambulance (set 4431) on his mentor, LEGO Master Model Coach Torben Skov.

# WOW!

At the world's largest LEGO Store in Leicester Square, London, the LEGO Mosaic Maker will turn your photo into a personalised LEGO portrait.

## 250,000

People are expected to visit the new LEGO® House in Billund, Denmark every year.

## TOP 5

Models at the LEGO Store in Leicester Square, London

**1** **LEGO Big Ben** stands over 21ft (6.5m) tall and chimes every hour.

**2** This **LEGO London Underground train** is the biggest model in the store.

## A WORLD OF DISCOVERY

LEGOLAND® Discovery Centres are indoor attractions with rides, building areas, 4-D cinema shows and more. There are Discovery Centres in Germany, Turkey, the UK, China, Japan, Canada and Australia – plus nine in the USA alone.

**Q** What is the LEGO House?

**A** The LEGO House is a new way to discover the LEGO story in the home of the LEGO brick. The three-acre (12,000m²) building in Billund, Denmark is packed full of fun things to see and do, spread across six different interactive zones.

## LOOK CLOSER

The "Keystone" on top of the LEGO House in Billund, Denmark is shaped like a giant 2x4 LEGO brick.

**3** Store mascot, **Lester**, is built from 24,500 bricks.

**4** This **LEGO telephone box** weighs more than 1,500lbs (700kg).

**5** Brickley the **Dragon** took 725 hours to build.

The LEGO Group sometimes makes micro-scale models of its factories, such as Kladno Campus in the Czech Republic, as gifts for staff.

## Brick History

In 1974, the first LEGO factory outside Denmark opened in Switzerland. Today, LEGO bricks are produced in factories in Denmark, Hungary, Mexico, the Czech Republic and China.

### Brick statistics

**The LEGO factory in Jiaxing, China**

**20 football fields**
Would fit inside the 40-acre (165,000m²) factory

**1,200+ employees**
Worked at the factory in 2016

**20,000 solar panels**
Provide green energy for the factory

**400,000 LEGO boxes**
Can be stored in the factory warehouse

## FACT STACK

There are more than 130 LEGO Brand Retail Stores in 10 countries around the world.

LEGO Group HQ is still based in Billund, Denmark, where the company was founded.

Every LEGO office around the world is stocked with bowls of bricks for staff to play with!

People from more than 30 countries work at LEGO HQ in Billund, Denmark.

### REALLY?!

Every year, a few lucky fans get to see inside the LEGO factory in Billund, Denmark, as part of the LEGO Inside Tour.

# COME ON IN

Not all LEGO buildings are made from plastic bricks! There are also the factories, stores, offices and visitor centres found in various locations around the world.

# IT'S A LEGOLAND® WORLD!

The first LEGOLAND® park opened in Billund, Denmark, in 1968. Less than 50 years later, there are now eight LEGOLAND destinations in three continents.

## WOW!

The 4-D movie theatres at LEGOLAND parks can feature live wind, water and smoke effects to bring the action on screen to life!

## FACT STACK

LEGOLAND Billund stands in the town where LEGO bricks were invented.

The heart of every LEGOLAND park is MINILAND, built using millions of bricks.

Each park also includes water rides, rollercoasters, a driving school and a castle.

More LEGOLAND parks are set to open in the future, so keep an eye out for new ones across the globe!

## TOP 5

### LEGOLAND rollercoasters

**1** Polar X-plorer at LEGOLAND Billund
Height: 62ft (18.8m)
Speed: 40mph (65kmph)

**2** The Dragon at LEGOLAND Deutschland and Dubai
Height: 53ft (16m)
Speed: 37mph (60kmph)

**3** LEGO® Technic Rollercoaster at LEGOLAND California
Height: 52ft (15.8m)
Speed: 35mph (56kmph)

**4** Flying School at LEGOLAND Florida
Height: 48ft (14.6m)
Speed: 26mph (42kmph)

**5** The Dragon at LEGOLAND Windsor
Height: 34ft (10.3m)
Speed: 30mph (48kmph)

## LEGOLAND FLORIDA
### United States, opened 2011

Incorporates a botanical garden that has stood on the site since 1936.

## LEGOLAND CALIFORNIA
### United States, opened 1999

Home to the world's first LEGOLAND Water Park.

## THE LEGO GLOBE

The eight LEGOLAND parks are spread around the world, each with something special to see.

## BRICK CHALLENGE

Can you design a new LEGOLAND ride using your own LEGO bricks?

# AWESOME!

Many rooms in LEGOLAND hotels contain a locked safe with LEGO treasures inside – and clues for cracking the code!

## REALLY?!

The original Traffic School cars in LEGOLAND Billund ran from 1968 to 2015 before they needed to be replaced.

## 55,000,000+

Visitors to LEGOLAND Billund since it opened in 1968.

## Brick statistics

### LEGO® NINJAGO® World at LEGOLAND Billund

**727,000 LEGO bricks**
Used to build the attraction in 2016

**400ft (122m) of track**
Winding through LEGO NINJAGO: The Ride

**42ft (13m) across**
Size of the largest 3-D display in the attraction

**30 laser beams**
To dodge in Lloyd's Laser Maze

### LEGOLAND DEUTSCHLAND

Germany, opened 2002

See it all from the 164ft (50m) observation tower.

### LEGOLAND BILLUND

Denmark, opened 1968

The first LEGOLAND has trebled in size since it opened.

### LEGOLAND JAPAN

Japan, opened 2017

A day at this park starts with a LEGO factory tour.

### LEGOLAND WINDSOR

United Kingdom, opened 1996

Built with more than 80 million LEGO bricks.

### LEGOLAND DUBAI

United Arab Emirates, opened 2016

The only LEGOLAND Resort with an indoor MINILAND.

### LEGOLAND MALAYSIA

Malaysia, opened 2012

The first LEGOLAND Resort to open in Asia.

# FAN-TASTIC IDEAS

Thanks to the LEGO® Ideas theme, LEGO fan builders can now see their coolest creations turned into official LEGO sets for everyone to enjoy!

## Brick History

Daniel Siskind was the first LEGO fan to have his idea turned into an official set: the LEGO My Own Creation Blacksmith Shop (set 3739), back in 2002.

## IT'S A SIGN!

No new parts are created for LEGO Ideas sets, but new prints are used to decorate existing pieces – such as the stylish stripes and sevens on 2016's Caterham Seven 620R (set 21307).

## FACT STACK

LEGO Ideas started out as LEGO CUUSOO, a website for LEGO fans in Japan, in 2008.

"Cuusoo" is a Japanese word meaning "imagination" and can also mean "wish".

LEGO CUUSOO launched around the world in 2011 and became LEGO Ideas in 2014.

More than 20,000 fan-designed projects have been submitted to the LEGO Ideas website.

*I'M A BIG LEGO FAN MADE SMALL.*

## STAR NAMES

Fan builder Peter Reid hasn't just designed a LEGO Ideas set – he's been turned into a minifigure! The two astronauts in his Exo Suit (set 21109) from 2014 are called Pete and Yve, after him and his girlfriend, Yvonne Doyle.

Colibri thalassinus

**Q** How do I submit an idea for a new LEGO set?

**A** If you are aged 13 or older, you can create a LEGO Ideas profile, submit your own ideas and support others at ideas.LEGO.com.

## AWESOME!
Fan builder Thomas Poulsom has designed 40 LEGO birds as well as the three that feature in his 2015 LEGO Ideas set, Birds (set 21301).

# WOW!

The LEGO Ideas Maze (set 21305) from 2016 is a mechanical ball game with tip-and-tilt controls. The set comes with ideas for customising the maze design.

## LARGEST LEGO IDEAS SET

Old Fishing Store (set 21309)

# REALLY?!

Andrew Clark, the fan designer behind Doctor Who (set 21304), is the nephew of Paul McGann – the eighth actor to play the Doctor in the BBC sci-fi series.

## ROLE-MODEL MAKING

LEGO fan builder Ellen Kooijman designed 2014's Research Institute (set 21110) to inspire girls to become anything they want to be – including paleontologists, chemists and astronomers.

*Cyanocitta cristata*

*Erithacus rubecula*

# 10,000

The number of supporters a project needs before being considered by the LEGO Review Board as a possible set.

# EVERYTHING IS AWESOME

In 2014, THE LEGO® MOVIE™ proved that everything is AWESOME!!! A sequel to THE LEGO MOVIE is expected to arrive in cinemas early in 2019. Even more AWESOME!!!

**MOST FORGETFUL MINIFIGURE**

Where Are My Pants? Guy

OH, HERE THEY ARE!

## TOP 5

**Classic LEGO set cameos in the movie**

1 **LEGO Pirates Brickbeard's Bounty** (set 6243), 2009

2 **LEGO Castle King's Castle** (set 70404), 2013

3 **LEGO® Friends Sunshine Ranch** (set 41039), 2014

4 **LEGO FABULAND Cathy Cat's Fun Park** (set 3676), 1989

5 **LEGO Vikings Viking Ship Challenges the Midgard Serpent** (set 7018), 2005

**4**

Different versions of the infectious theme song Everything is AWESOME!!! feature on THE LEGO MOVIE soundtrack. AWESOME!!!

**REALLY?!**

Fan-made "brickfilm" *Gorgy Wants a Horse* won a competition to appear in THE LEGO MOVIE. It is in the sequence where everyone unleashes their building potential.

**FACT STACK**

THE LEGO MOVIE hit US cinemas on February 7, 2014, and became one of the biggest animated movies of the year.

Everything you see in THE LEGO MOVIE was built using digital versions of real LEGO bricks.

Animators added scratches, teeth-marks and fingerprints to make the minifigures look like authentic toys.

More than 20 sets were released based on THE LEGO MOVIE including Super Cycle Chase (set 70808, pictured).

# AWESOME!

When the *Millennium Falcon* appears, the voices of C-3PO and Lando Calrissian are provided by the same actors who play those characters in the live-action *Star Wars*™ saga.

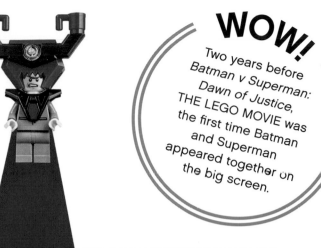

## WOW!

Two years before *Batman v Superman: Dawn of Justice*, THE LEGO MOVIE was the first time Batman and Superman appeared together on the big screen.

## Brick History

Space minifigure Benny was based on one particular character that Chris Miller (one of THE LEGO MOVIE writer/directors) has owned since childhood, right down to his worn-out printing and broken helmet.

## Piece particulars

Lord Business's cape is actually a life-sized businessman's tie! Towards the end of the movie, "the Man Upstairs" can be seen wearing one in the same colour.

SPACESHIP!

YOU SPEAK FRENCH, NOW?

## WHAT'S IN A NAME?

One of the titles considered for THE LEGO MOVIE was "The Piece of Resistance". The phrase, used throughout the film, is a riff on "pièce de résistance", French for "the most important thing"!

# BIG-SCREEN BATMAN

After LEGO® Batman got his big-screen debut in THE LEGO MOVIE, he got to star in his own movie with a supporting cast of heroes and villains.

> I DO ALL MY OWN STUNTS.

## FACT STACK

LEGO Batman appeared in 11 of the first 13 sets released to coincide with THE LEGO® BATMAN MOVIE.

The LEGO Minifigures line that accompanied the movie included 20 minifigures – the first of this size.

Animators built all of the movie locations using virtual LEGO bricks.

They used over 3,000 different piece types to create 75 unique locations.

## Piece particulars

Batman got an upgrade to his Utility Belt for his own movie, with a specially moulded piece that fits between his leg and torso pieces.

**Q** What is even cooler than the Batmobile?

**A** An Ultimate Batmobile! Batman's most ambitious build contains a Batmobile, Bat-Jet, Bat-Tank and Bat-Bike – a vehicle for each member of his new team.

> LET'S GET GROOVIN'!

# AWESOME!
Robin customises a "Reggae Man" Batsuit from the Batcave wardrobe to create his own dazzling Super Hero costume.

## COSTUME CHANGES

Harley Quinn is a master of disguise, so it's no surprise she has many different looks in THE LEGO BATMAN MOVIE, from a tutu-clad rollerskater to a distinguished-looking doctor.

**Tutu Harley**

**Roller Derby Harley**

**Nurse Harley**

**Doctor Quinzel**

## Brick History

Actor Billy Dee Williams played good guy Harvey Dent in the 1989 movie *Batman*, but not his villainous alter ego Two-Face. Williams now appears as the voice of minifigure Two-Face.

# 81

Number of muddy brown 1x1 round plates in Clayface Splat Attack (set 70904).

## REALLY?!

Emmet built his friends a double-decker couch in THE LEGO MOVIE. It reappears on a grimy Gotham City street in THE LEGO BATMAN MOVIE.

## LOOK CLOSER

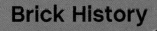

Batman's foe Bane has an unusual decoration on his buggy: a teddy bear! It is a reference to the villains's favourite toy as a child.

## WOW!

The movie's director, Chris McKay, has a Catwoman tattoo on his arm.

## Brick statistics

### Arkham Asylum (set 70912)

**1,628 pieces**
Make up the secure facility set

**236 pages**
In the instruction booklet

**12 minifigures**
Including five inmates

**2 of every food piece**
Double sausages, donuts, watermelon slices and pretzels

**1 basketball hoop**
For recreation time

# SO NINJA!

Everyone's favourite ninja team span into cinemas in 2017, with the release of THE LEGO® NINJAGO MOVIE™. The ninja face new challenges, including life at Ninjago High School!

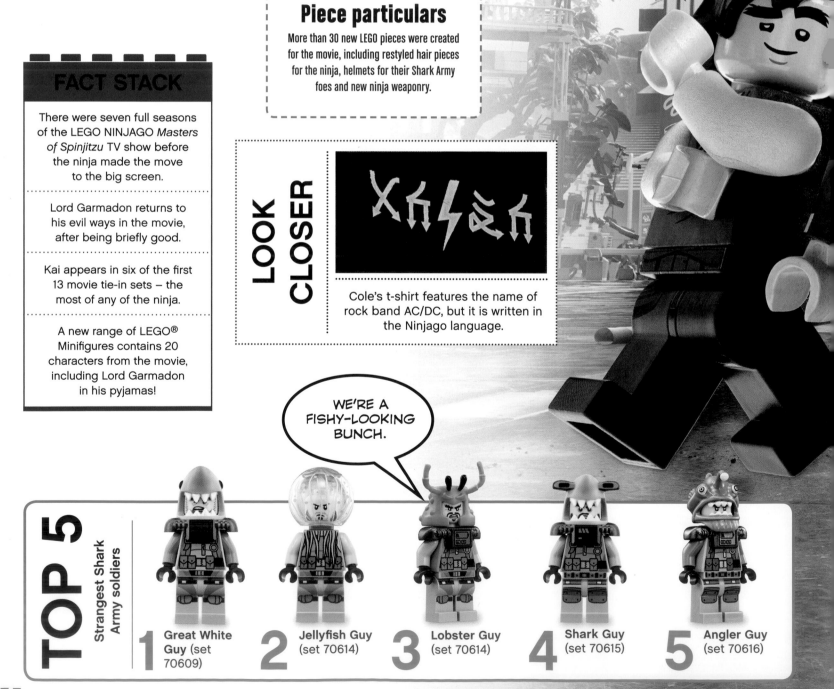

ANYONE WANT TO GO TO THE MOVIES?

## Piece particulars

More than 30 new LEGO pieces were created for the movie, including restyled hair pieces for the ninja, helmets for their Shark Army foes and new ninja weaponry.

## FACT STACK

There were seven full seasons of the LEGO NINJAGO *Masters of Spinjitzu* TV show before the ninja made the move to the big screen.

Lord Garmadon returns to his evil ways in the movie, after being briefly good.

Kai appears in six of the first 13 movie tie-in sets – the most of any of the ninja.

A new range of LEGO® Minifigures contains 20 characters from the movie, including Lord Garmadon in his pyjamas!

## LOOK CLOSER

Cole's t-shirt features the name of rock band AC/DC, but it is written in the Ninjago language.

WE'RE A FISHY-LOOKING BUNCH.

## TOP 5
### Strongest Shark Army soldiers

**1** Great White Guy (set 70609)

**2** Jellyfish Guy (set 70614)

**3** Lobster Guy (set 70614)

**4** Shark Guy (set 70615)

**5** Angler Guy (set 70616)

## WORD ON THE STREET

Signs in Ninjago City are written in the Ninjago language, which was created especially for the movie. The Ninjago language is based on the Roman alphabet, but the symbols can be read left to right, top to bottom, or in clusters.

## REALLY?!

It took animation company Animal Logic a whole year to build Ninjago City, a huge and complex virtual metropolis.

# STARS OF THE SMALL SCREEN

From FABULAND to the Freemakers, NINJAGO ninjas to NEXO KNIGHTS™ heroes, LEGO characters have a long history of coming to life on TV and DVD.

## 1,100,000

US viewers tuned into the finale of LEGO® NEXO KNIGHTS® season one!

**Q** What was the first-ever LEGO TV show?

**A** Way back in 1987, the animals of LEGO FABULAND were made into clay figures for the stop-motion animated series *Edward and Friends*. It starred Edward the Elephant… and his friends!

## TOP 5

**Unmissable LEGO TV and DVD specials**

**1** LEGO *Atlantis: The Movie* (2010)

**2** LEGO® *Star Wars™: The Padawan Menace* (2011)

**3** LEGO *Star Wars: The Empire Strikes Out* (2012)

**4** LEGO® *DC Comics Super Heroes: Batman Be-Leaguered* (2014)

**5** LEGO® *Scooby-Doo™: Knight Time Terror* (2015)

## Brick statistics

### LEGO NINJAGO: *Masters of Spinjitzu*

**74 regular episodes**
Since 2011, divided into seven seasons

**4 pilot episodes**
Introducing the ninja for the first time

**6 mini-episodes**
Set between the pilots and season one

**29 webisodes**
Short bursts of story on LEGO.com

**1 TV special**
The 2016 epic, *Day of the Departed*

**30 hours**
Time it would take to watch it all!

### IT'S A SIGN!

In the 2016 *Disney* XD miniseries LEGO *Star Wars: The Resistance Rises*, BB-8 disguises Poe Dameron's ship by slapping First Order stickers over the Alliance symbols!

## REALLY?!

The 550th episode of *The Simpsons* is a special, digitally animated story, set in a world made entirely from LEGO bricks!

## 2005

LEGO *Star Wars* makes its TV debut in the animated short film LEGO *Star Wars: Revenge of the Brick*, shown on Cartoon Network.

## 2013

*Legends of Chima: The Animated Series* launches alongside the first LEGO Legends of Chima sets. It goes on to run for three seasons.

## 2015

Viewers get their first glimpse of the LEGO NEXO KNIGHTS TV series in December, just before the first sets launch in January 2016.

## 2016

Two new LEGO series launch on the Netflix streaming service – LEGO BIONICLE: *The Journey to One* and LEGO Friends: *The Power of Friendship*.

## MEET THE FREEMAKERS

In 2016, LEGO *Star Wars: The Freemaker Adventures* was the first LEGO *Star Wars* TV series to focus on brand-new characters, rather than familiar faces from the movie saga.

# AWESOME!

LEGO NEXO KNIGHTS viewers can download NEXO Powers straight from the TV screen using the NEXO KNIGHTS app.

**Rowan Freemaker**
A brave young boy who finds out he can use the Force.

**R0-GR**
The Freemakers' battered old battle droid – known as Roger!

**Zander Freemaker**
An ace pilot who flies the family ship, *StarScavenger*.

**Kordi Freemaker**
The brains behind the Freemakers' salvage business.

# BRICKS AND PIXELS

LEGO video games combine timeless LEGO play and familiar minifigures with huge virtual worlds that could never be built in real life.

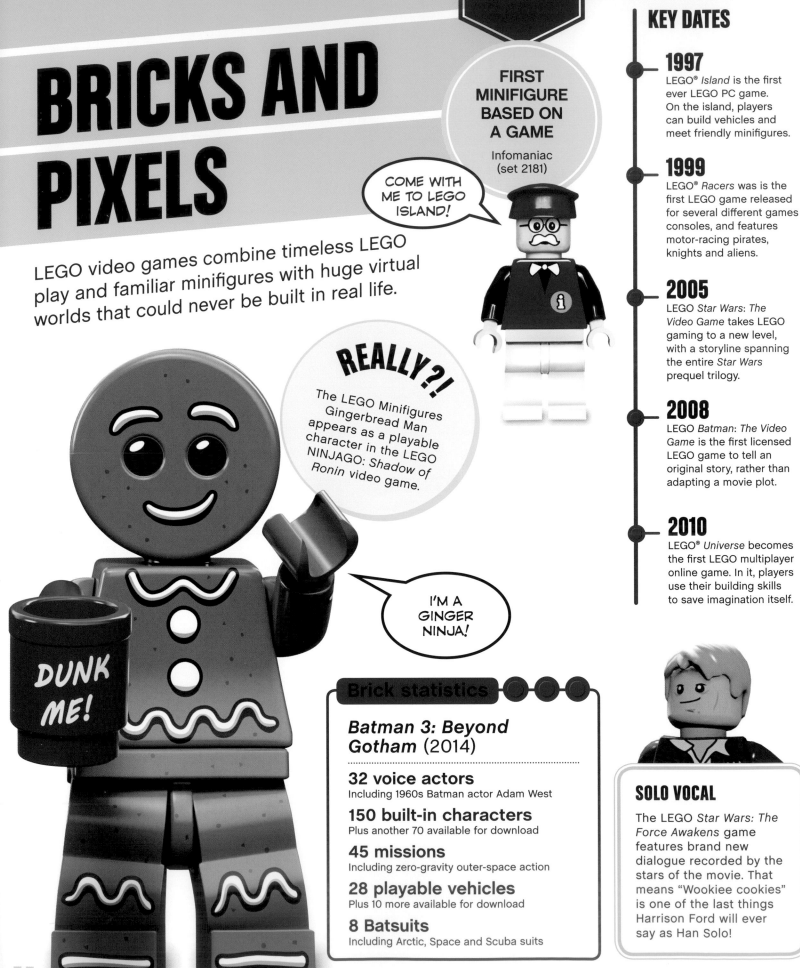

**COME WITH ME TO LEGO ISLAND!**

## FIRST MINIFIGURE BASED ON A GAME
Infomaniac (set 2181)

## REALLY?!
The LEGO Minifigures Gingerbread Man appears as a playable character in the LEGO NINJAGO: Shadow of Ronin video game.

**I'M A GINGER NINJA!**

**DUNK ME!**

## KEY DATES

### 1997
LEGO® *Island* is the first ever LEGO PC game. On the island, players can build vehicles and meet friendly minifigures.

### 1999
LEGO® *Racers* was is the first LEGO game released for several different games consoles, and features motor-racing pirates, knights and aliens.

### 2005
LEGO *Star Wars*: *The Video Game* takes LEGO gaming to a new level, with a storyline spanning the entire *Star Wars* prequel trilogy.

### 2008
LEGO *Batman*: *The Video Game* is the first licensed LEGO game to tell an original story, rather than adapting a movie plot.

### 2010
LEGO® *Universe* becomes the first LEGO multiplayer online game. In it, players use their building skills to save imagination itself.

## Brick statistics

### Batman 3: Beyond Gotham (2014)

**32 voice actors**
Including 1960s Batman actor Adam West

**150 built-in characters**
Plus another 70 available for download

**45 missions**
Including zero-gravity outer-space action

**28 playable vehicles**
Plus 10 more available for download

**8 Batsuits**
Including Arctic, Space and Scuba suits

## SOLO VOCAL

The LEGO *Star Wars*: *The Force Awakens* game features brand new dialogue recorded by the stars of the movie. That means "Wookiee cookies" is one of the last things Harrison Ford will ever say as Han Solo!

# LOOK CLOSER

## UNIVERSE

The "U" in the logo for 2010's LEGO *Universe* game is a minifigure hand viewed from above.

## IT'S A SIGN!

Clicking on this symbol in LEGO® *Worlds* lets you customise your minifigure avatar's head, hair and clothes.

## 200+

Number of cars you can drive in 2013's LEGO® City *Undercover* video game.

## WOW!

Want to see the world from a minifigure's point of view? LEGO *Worlds* includes a first-person play option for doing just that.

## Brick History

THE LEGO MOVIE *Video Game* had the first game environment built entirely from virtual LEGO bricks – making it technically possible to build the game world for real!

## FACT STACK

The first LEGO video game was LEGO® *Fun To Build*, released for the Sega Pico console in 1995.

Other early games included LEGO® *Chess* and city-building simulator, LEGO® *Loco*.

Since 2005, almost 30 LEGO video games have been made by developers TT Games.

There are dozens of LEGO mini-games to play for free on LEGO.com

# AWESOME!

The 2017 "sandbox" game LEGO *Worlds* acts as an infinite LEGO collection that allows players to build anything they can imagine from an endless array of bricks.

# BREAK THE RULES!

LEGO® DIMENSIONS™ is a video game launched in 2015 that brings real minifigures and LEGO sets to life in a digital world.

*PRECIOUS MEDAL.*

## SCARIEST DIMENSIONS DOUBLE ACT

Gollum and Shelob (from *The Lord of the Rings*)

## FACT STACK

LEGO DIMENSIONS is a game for up to two players.

You need a Starter Pack and a compatible games console to play.

Extension Packs let you add more adventures and characters over time.

Some Expansion Packs add battle arenas with four gameplay modes for up to four players.

## Brick History

LEGO DIMENSIONS comes with a Starter Pack that includes a Toy Pad to connect real LEGO minifigures, vehicles and gadgets to the game.

*THEY'RE MY RELATIVE DIMENSIONS!*

## DOCTOR, DOCTOR...

The DIMENSIONS minifigure of the Doctor from *Doctor Who* has only one face, but he can be used to play the game as any one of the character's 13 incarnations!

## REALLY?!

Little is known about the evil LEGO DIMENSIONS villain Lord Vortech. He is so mysterious that no LEGO minifigures have ever been made of him.

**Q** | My Toy Pad is flashing! Why?
---|---
**A** | The LEGO DIMENSIONS Toy Pad lights up, flashes and changes colour to give players clues for solving puzzles, finding items or to point characters in the right direction.

## Piece particulars

The brick-built figure of BMO from the LEGO DIMENSIONS *Adventure Time* Team Pack has blue sausage pieces for arms.

# AWESOME!

In LEGO NINJAGO, Master Wu's Dragon (set 70734) is made from hundreds of pieces. In LEGO DIMENSIONS, the creature is recreated using fewer than 50.

## WOW!

All DIMENSIONS packs includes a vehicle or gadget that can be built in three different ways, to unlock different in-game features.

## REALLY?!

In their first in-game encounter, Batman mistakes Krusty the Clown from *The Simpsons* for his archenemy, the Joker!

## WOW!

LEGO DIMENSIONS is at least the 80th time Sonic the Hedgehog has appeared in a video game – but the first time he has been turned into a minifigure.

# SMART BUILDING

LEGO® MINDSTORMS® blends LEGO building and computer programming to create real-life robots, inspiring endless inventions from young engineers.

## FACT STACK

LEGO MINDSTORMS robots are programmed with easy-to-use, free LEGO software.

Each robot is brought to life using a LEGO MINDSTORMS Intelligent Brick.

Intelligent Bricks act on user instructions sent to them via infrared, Bluetooth or Wi-Fi.

LEGO MINDSTORMS is the best-selling product in the history of the LEGO Group.

## TOP 5

**Robots that can be made with MINDSTORMS EV3 (set 31313)**

**1** The surefooted, bazooka-blasting, blade-spinning **EV3RSTORM**.

**2** The handy, heavy-lifting, grab-and-go **GRIPP3R**.

**3** The slithering, snake-like, superfast **R3PTAR**.

**4** The snapping, shooting, six-legged **SPIK3R**.

**5** The blasting, bashing, go-anywhere **TRACK3R**.

## WOW!

LEGO MINDSTORMS is in the Carnegie Mellon University Robot Hall of Fame, alongside robots such as C-3PO, R2-D2 and WALL-E!

## KEY DATES

### 1984
The LEGO Group partners with the Massachusetts Institute of Technology Media Laboratory to develop educational computer-controlled LEGO sets for schools.

### 1998
The LEGO MINDSTORMS Robotics Invention System (set 9719) introduces the programmable RCX (Robotic Command eXplorer) brick for building working robots!

### 2006
LEGO MINDSTORMS NXT (set 8527) makes LEGO robotics more powerful, but also easier to use, using the NXT Intelligent Brick.

### 2009
LEGO MINDSTORMS NXT 2.0 (set 8547) keeps LEGO robots at the cutting edge with new programming options and extra sensors.

# 3.256

Seconds taken by LEGO MINDSTORMS robot Cubestormer III to solve a Rubik's Cube.

## AWESOME!

You can build a working cuckoo clock by combining LEGO MINDSTORMS EV3 with 2016's LEGO Technic Heavy Lift Helicopter (set 42052).

### REALLY?!

In 2014, 12-year-old Shubham Banerjee used LEGO MINDSTORMS EV3 to build Braigo – the world's lightest, quietest, most cost-effective braille printer!

## BRICK CHALLENGE

On LEGO.com/mindstorms there are more instructions for EV3 robots, including LEGO Technic combination builds. What robotic creation will you come up with?

### Brick statistics

#### LEGO MINDSTORMS EV3 (set 31313)

**357 LEGO Technic elements**
For building robots up to 16 inches (41cm) tall!

**1 EV3 Intelligent Brick**
The control centre of your MINDSTORMS robot

**3 environmental sensors**
Respond to colour, touch and infrared light

**2 large servo motors**
For powerful, precise movement

**1 infrared beacon**
To control your robot remotely

### A LEAGUE OF THEIR OWN

In 2008, the LEGO Group and educational charity FIRST (For Inspiration and Recognition of Science and Technology) launched a LEGO MINDSTORMS competition for school students. Today, the *FIRST* LEGO® League has more than 32,000 school teams worldwide.

## 2013

LEGO MINDSTORMS EV3 (set 31313) takes LEGO programming to the next level, with complete control from your smartphone or tablet.

## 2017

LEGO BOOST (set 17101) brings coding to a younger audience with buildable, programmable characters such as Vernie the Robot and Frankie the Cat.

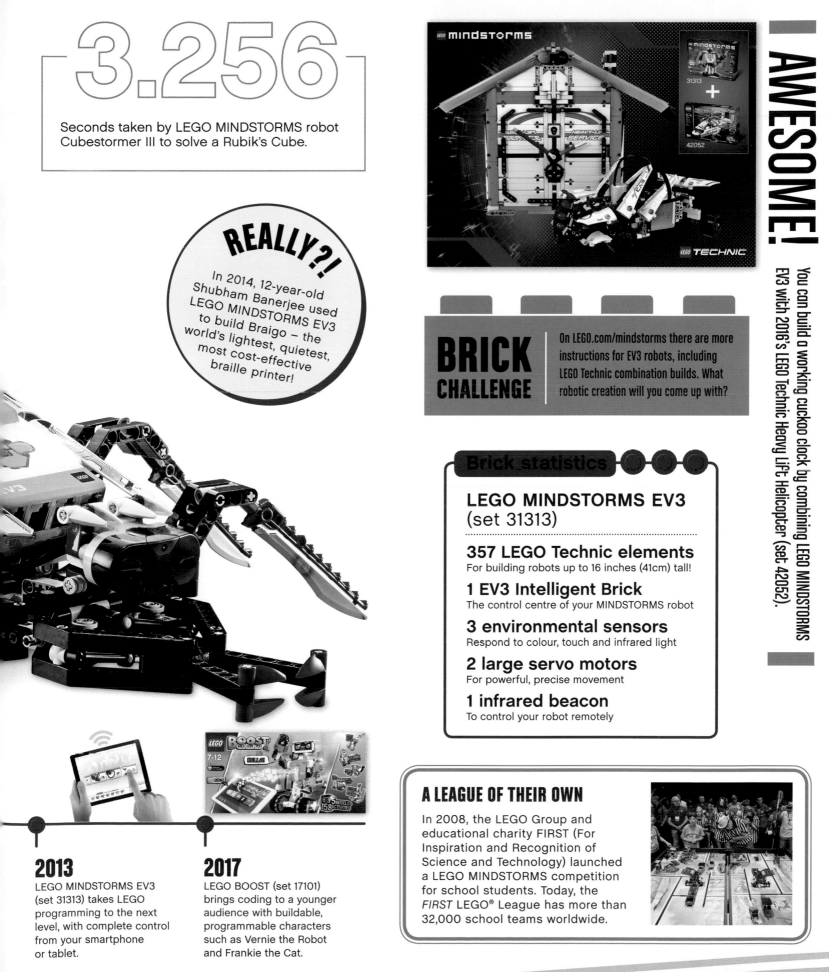

# JOIN THE CLUB!

For years, the official LEGO® Club delighted millions of members around the world, and in 2017 it became LEGO Life, a growing community of fans of all ages.

## FACT STACK

In 2017, the former LEGO Club was rebranded as LEGO Life.

LEGO Life is a free club for LEGO fans in 25 countries around the world.

Members can sign up for a magazine and email updates.

LEGO Life is a free social app full of LEGO videos, building challenges, quizzes and more.

## WOW!

There were more than 30 different versions of the former LEGO *Club* magazine published in 10 different languages around the world.

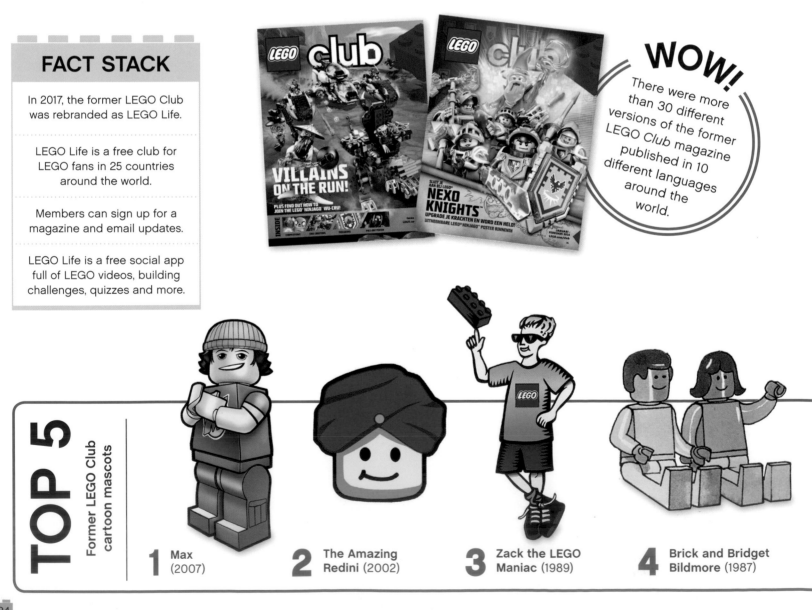

## TOP 5
### Former LEGO Club cartoon mascots

**1** Max (2007)

**2** The Amazing Redini (2002)

**3** Zack the LEGO Maniac (1989)

**4** Brick and Bridget Bildmore (1987)

# AWESOME!

Every issue of LEGO *Life* magazine is packed full of comics, puzzles, building ideas, pictures of reader's very best builds and more.

**Q** Are there LEGO clubs for older builders?

**A** Yes, there are adult fan communities all around the world. The oldest such "LEGO User Group" is De Bouwsteen ("The Building Block") in the Netherlands.

## READ ALL ABOUT IT!

Over the years, the various LEGO Club magazines included *Brick Kicks*, *Bricks 'n Pieces*, LEGO *Mania Magazine* and LEGO *Tech Torque*, which was especially for LEGO Technic fans.

## Piece particulars

In 2010, the former LEGO Club's cartoon mascot, Max, was made into a real minifigure (set 852996), featuring all exclusive parts.

## Brick History

In 1963, Snap, "The fun book for LEGO Club members", launched in the USA. The first official LEGO Club was set up in Canada three years later.

**5** Johnny and Jane LEGO (1963)

## REALLY?!

If every former LEGO Club member joined hands, the line would stretch all the way from the USA to Russia!

# THE ART OF

## Notable LEGO artworks

1 **Paul Hetherington** won the Best in Show award at LEGO fan event BrickCon 2015 for his mechanical "steampunk love story" sculpture, "Unchain My Heart".

2 **Vesa Lehtimäki** uses sets and minifigures from the LEGO *Star Wars* theme to compose photographs full of action, wit and atmosphere.

3 Since 2004, **Nathan Sawaya** has worked as a full-time LEGO artist, and has toured the world with his exhibition "The Art of the Brick".

4 "Dispatchwork" is a collaborative art project devised by **Jan Vormann** in which LEGO bricks are used to fill cracks and voids in damaged walls.

5 In 2012, street artist **Megx** painted a disused rail bridge in Wuppertal, Germany, to look as if it were made from giant LEGO bricks.

6 "The Collectivity Project" is a touring art installation by **Olafur Eliasson.** It invites visitors to rebuild a vast LEGO city according to their own vision.

# BUILDING

**6**

**5**

**7**

**8**

**7** **Mike Doyle** builds elaborate, tumbledown LEGO houses, which he photographs for limited-edition art prints before taking them apart and starting again.

**8** **Sean Kenney** is a professional artist who creates LEGO sculpture. His latest exhibition, "Nature Connects", features more than 100 lifelike LEGO animals and plants.

# TOP 5

LEGO online game categories

**1** **Action games,** such as LEGO NINJAGO *Skybound*.

**2** **Strategy games,** such as LEGO® *Bits and Bricks*.

**3** **Adventure games,** such as LEGO NEXO KNIGHTS *Super Mega Power Panic*.

**4** **Creative games,** such as LEGO Friends *Art Maker*.

**5** **Preschool games,** such as LEGO® Juniors *Fire Truck*.

## REALLY?!

In 2015, the LEGO Facebook page invited fans to build and upload an image of a Kronkiwongi – whatever that is!

## ONE-STOP SHOP

Customers at the LEGO Shop area of LEGO.com can buy everything from huge, hard-to-find LEGO Creator Expert sets to individual elements using the Pick A Brick service.

AREN'T I JUST CONQUIST-ADORABLE!

### FIRST LEGO INSTAGRAM STAR

Conquistador

## CHOOSE LIFE

LEGO Life is a free app for smartphones and tablets that lets you share your best builds, take on building challenges and chat with other fans using special LEGO emojis!

You have to be 13 or older to use most third-party social media sites

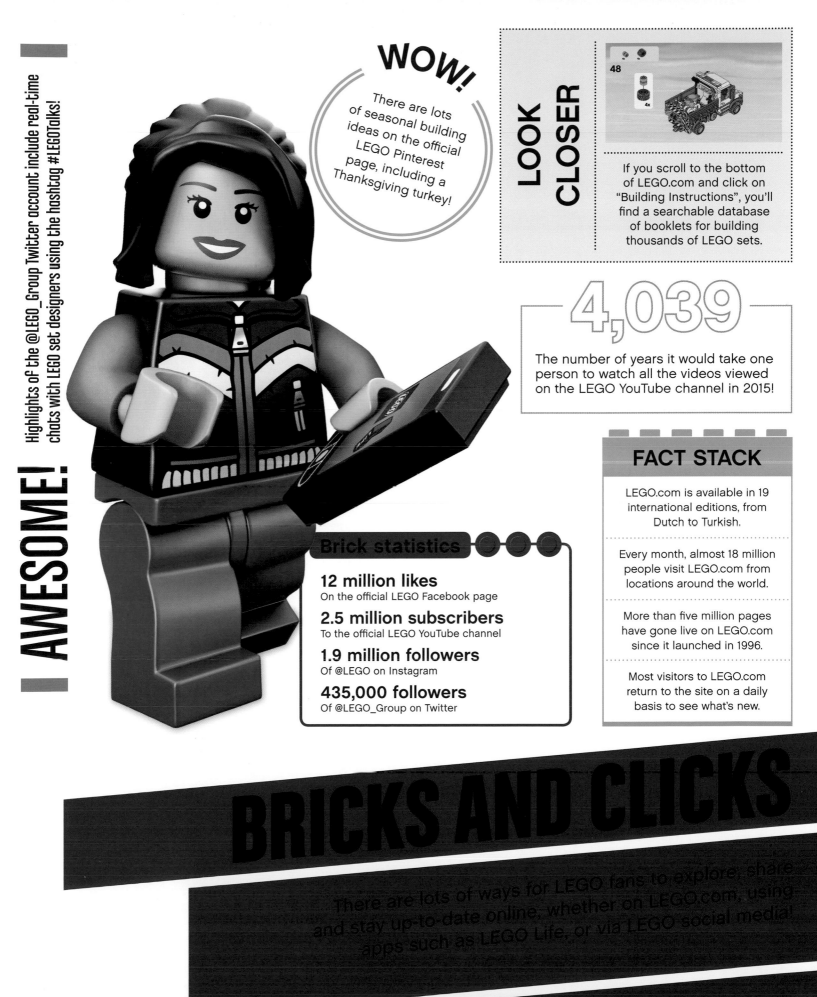

Highlights of the @LEGO_Group Twitter account include real-time chats with LEGO set designers using the hashtag #LEGOTalks!

## WOW!

There are lots of seasonal building ideas on the official LEGO Pinterest page, including a Thanksgiving turkey!

## LOOK CLOSER

48

4x

If you scroll to the bottom of LEGO.com and click on "Building Instructions", you'll find a searchable database of booklets for building thousands of LEGO sets.

## 4,039

The number of years it would take one person to watch all the videos viewed on the LEGO YouTube channel in 2015!

### Brick statistics

**12 million likes**
On the official LEGO Facebook page

**2.5 million subscribers**
To the official LEGO YouTube channel

**1.9 million followers**
Of @LEGO on Instagram

**435,000 followers**
Of @LEGO_Group on Twitter

### FACT STACK

LEGO.com is available in 19 international editions, from Dutch to Turkish.

Every month, almost 18 million people visit LEGO.com from locations around the world.

More than five million pages have gone live on LEGO.com since it launched in 1996.

Most visitors to LEGO.com return to the site on a daily basis to see what's new.

# BRICKS AND CLICKS

There are lots of ways for LEGO fans to explore, share and stay up-to-date online, whether on LEGO.com, using apps such as LEGO Life, or via LEGO social media!

# RECORD-BREAKING BRICKS

There really are no limits when it comes to LEGO building, as these remarkable record setters and smashers all set out to show!

The **longest LEGO brick sculpture** ever made was a 5,179ft (1,579m) millipede built out of 2,901,760 bricks over the course of two months in 2005. Thousands of families contributed to the creepy-crawly at a shopping centre in Italy, in an event organised by Consorzio Esercenti CC.

**LONGEST LEGO SCULPTURE**

**FASTEST BRICK STACK**

The world record for **most LEGO bricks built onto a baseplate in 30 seconds** is currently 127 bricks. The record was set by Kamil Dominowski from Poland at a 2015 LEGO fan event held in the UK. How many bricks can you add to a baseplate in just 30 seconds?

**LARGEST MINIFIGURE DISPLAY**

*AM I TOO LATE TO JOIN?*

In 2008, LEGO Group employees in the UK assembled an army of 35,210 LEGO *Star Wars* clone troopers to create the **largest display of LEGO minifigures** ever seen! The troopers were arranged in just six and a half hours to raise money for UK charity the National Autistic Society.

**LONGEST RAILWAY TRACK**

In May 2013, the record for the world's **longest LEGO railway** was set by Henrik Ludvigsen and more than 80 other LEGO fans in Denmark. It took a battery-powered LEGO train almost four hours to travel the 2.5-mile (4km) route, which was made from more than 93,000 LEGO elements!

The world record for **most assembled LEGO sets in one private collection** was set by Kyle Ugone in 2011. At the time, his array of built sets totalled 1,091 and was kept at his home in Arizona, USA, where it had been accumulating since 1986!

LARGEST LEGO AIRPLANE

The world's **largest LEGO airplane** was shown at the World's largest LEGO show in Krakow, Poland. The model of the US Presidential aircraft, *Air Force One*, measures 36ft (11m) long and 9ft (3m) high and is about 1/6 the size of the real thing.

The world's **largest LEGO house** was assembled in the UK by 1,200 volunteers as part of a BBC TV series. The finished two-storey structure had four life-sized rooms, including a kitchen and a bathroom, and stood 15ft (4.6m) tall.

LARGEST LEGO HOUSE

The LEGO Group broke its own world record for building the **tallest LEGO tower** in 2015! Around 18,000 volunteers contributed to the 114ft (35m) tower in Italy, which comprised more than half a million bricks. The tower took five days to complete, and was built to raise money for an environmental charity.

TALLEST LEGO TOWER

# THE WORLD'S BIGGEST LEGO® SCULPTURE: TOWER BRIDGE

In September 2016, this giant model of London's Tower Bridge was declared the new world-record holder as the world's largest LEGO sculpture.

## Brick statistics

**5,805,846 bricks**
Weighing 45,980lbs (20,865kg)

**28 LEGO builders**
Worked on the project, including LEGO Certified Professional Duncan Titmarsh, founder of the company Bright Bricks

**42ft (13m) high**
And 144ft (44m) wide

**29 times taller**
Than the LEGO Tower Bridge set (10214)

**7 months to build**
And a year to develop from start to finish

# INDEX

# ACKNOWLEDGEMENTS

## The publisher would like to thank the following for their kind permission to reproduce their photographs:

THE LEGO MOVIE, THE LEGO BATMAN MOVIE, and THE LEGO NINJAGO MOVIE © The LEGO Group & Warner Bros Entertainment Inc.
(s17)

Copyright © 2017 DC Comics. All related characters and elements are trademarks of and © DC Comics. Products used courtesy of Warner Bros. Entertainment Inc. and DC Comics.
(s17)

HARRY POTTER ™ & © Warner Bros. Entertainment Inc.
Harry Potter Publishing Rights © JKR
(s17)

THE LORD OF THE RINGS ©2017 New Line Productions, Inc. ™ Middle-earth Enterprises to New Line Productions, Inc.
(s17)

LEGO® Mixels™: CARTOON NETWORK and logo are trademarks of and © 2017 Cartoon Network.
All rights reserved.

Boeing and Boeing logo inclusion approved by Boeing Brand Identity.

Star Wars and Indiana Jones and all characters, names, and all related indicia are trademarks of & © Lucasfilm Entertainment Company Ltd. or Lucasfilm Ltd © 2017.
Used under authorisation. All rights reserved.

SCOOBY-DOO ™ & © Hanna Barbera
(s17)

The Beatles © Apple Corps 2009–2017

NASA and NASA logo Courtesy of NASA

© 2017 Daimler AG

© Allianz 2000–2017

© 2017 Emaar PJSC

THE SIMPSONS™ & © 2017 Twentieth Century Fox Film Corporation. All Rights Reserved.

Nickelodeon's "SpongeBob Squarepants" is used with permission by Nickelodeon. ©2017 Viacom Media Networks. All Rights Reserved. Nickelodeon, all related titles, characters and logos are trademarks owned by Viacom Media Networks, a Division of Viacom International Inc.

© 2017 Mojang AB and Mojang Synergies AB. MINECRAFT is a trademark or registered trademark of Mojang Synergies AB. All images used with permission from Mojang AB.

©1985 Universal City Studios, Inc.

Adventure Time™ & © 2017 Cartoon Network. A Time Warner Company. All Rights Reserved.

© 2017 Porsche Cars

LEGOLAND images © 2017 Merlin Entertainments 2017

The Maersk Group. All rights reserved 2017

© 2017 Ford Motor Company

Ghostbusters™ & © COLUMBIA PICTURES © 2017 SONY PICTURES DIGITAL PRODUCTIONS INC. All rights reserved.

© 2017 AUDI AG. All rights reserved.

© 2017 The LEGO Group. ™ & © DC Comics. THE LEGO MOVIE © The LEGO Group & WBEI. © New Line. ™ & © SZC lic. to WBIE. Doctor Who logo © 2009 & TM BBC. Lic. by BBC WW Ltd. ADVENTURE TIME and all related characters and elements are trademarks of and © Cartoon Network. ™ & © 2016 Twentieth Century Fox Film Corporation. All rights Reserved. ™ & © WBEI. TM, ® & ©2016 Paramount Pictures. All Rights Reserved. © SEGA. All rights reserved. SEGA, the SEGA logo and SONIC THE HEDGEHOG are either registered trademarks or trademarks of SEGA Holdings Co., Ltd. or its affiliates.
All Rights Reserved.

© 2017 Caterham Cars

Sonic Hedgehog™ & © SEGA. SEGA and the SEGA logo are either registered trademarks or trademarks of the SEGA Holdings Co., Ltd or its affiliates. All rights reserved.

BBC, DOCTOR WHO, DALEK, and TARDIS (word marks, logos & devices) are trademarks of the British Broadcasting Corporation and are used under licence.

## Picture library credits:

(Key: a-above; b-below/bottom; c-centre; f-far; l-left; r-right; t-top)

80 Getty Images: AFP Photo / Adrian Dennis (cra). 82–83 Getty Images: MyLoupe / UIG via Getty Images. 136–137 Getty Images: AFP Photo / Emmanuel Dunand. 204 Getty Images: Daniel Leal-Olivas / AFP (tr, tc). 205 Getty Images: Daniel Leal-Olivas / AFP (tc); Freya Ingrid Morales / Bloomberg via Getty Images (cb); Ben Perry (tr); Leon Neal (tl). 226 Getty Images: Giuseppe Ciccia / Pacific Press / LightRocket (cl). 227 Getty Images: AFP Photo / Keld Navntoft (tr). 231 Getty Images: AFP Photo / Giuseppe Cacace (r); Omar Marques / Anadolu Agency (cl). 232–233 Getty Images: Handout / Getty Images Entertainment / Getty Images for Land Rover

## DK would also like to thank the following people for their help in producing this book:

Signe Wiese, Kristian Reimer Hauge, Camilla Pedersen, Jan Ryaa and the many designers at the LEGO Group who contributed additional insider facts for this book • Randi Sørensen, Paul Hansford, Martin Leighton Lindhardt and Heidi K. Jensen at the LEGO Group for their roles in bringing this book to fruition • Joel Baker for the use of his LEGOLAND Florida photography • Jan Vormann, Sean Kenney, Mike Doyle, Megx, Paul Hetherington and Vesa Lehtimäki for allowing us to feature images of their LEGO artworks.

Specially produced for Ted Smart,
Guardian House, Borough Road,
Godalming, Surrey GU7 2AE.

**ISBN 1 85613 031 2**

# CREDITS

**Craft Designs by:** Cheryl Owen, Rosalind Burdett, Annette Claxton,

Suzie Major, Susy Smith and Juliet Bawden

**Editor-in-chief:** Jilly Glassborow

**Designers:** Kathy Gummer, Philip Gorton and Tony Truscott

**Photographers:** Steve Tanner and Terry Dilliway

**Typeset by:** Barbican Print and Marketing Services, London, and The Old Mill, London

**Colour Separation by:** Fotographics Ltd, London – Hong Kong and Scantrans Pte Ltd., Singapore

**Printed in Italy**

# CONTENTS

# PAPER CRAFTS FOR THE HOME

# *INTRODUCTION*

Paper is a remarkably versatile material and rather
underated as a durable and exciting craft medium. It is available
in a wide range of types, from flimsy gossamer tissue to tough, practical
cardboard, from simple gummed squares to exquisite gift wraps. You will probably have
a number of materials already to hand at home; but virtually all the items
mentioned in this book are easy to obtain from stationers, craft shops
and art suppliers, and are relatively inexpensive to buy.

In Section One of *The Art of Paper Crafts* we will show
you how to transform paper and cardboard into a vast array of both
decorative and practical items for the home. We have included original gift
ideas such as pictures, picture frames, lampshades, letter racks, and personalized
stationery. There is also a chapter devoted to children's designs, where
you will find ideas to brighten up kids' bedrooms, as well as
projects which children can undertake themselves. A host of
festive garlands, party pieces, table decorations
and place settings complete the section.

If you look around your home you may be surprised to find how many suitable materials you already have from which to make your designs – materials such as left-over wrapping paper and wallpaper, or cardboard packets and boxes that can be cut up and re-used.

## PAPER

The range of papers available for paper crafts is endless and very inspiring. Apart from plain coloured papers available from art and craft shops, there is a wide variety of handmade papers and exotic gift wraps that will add a touch of sophistication to any design. Textured and flock papers are also available, adding a third dimension to collages.

Crepe paper is a very adaptable material because it stretches and comes in a wide range of colours. When cut against the grain, the cut edge can be gently stretched to give an attractive fluted edge.

Tissue paper and iridescent film, although delicate, can be used to stunning effect on mobiles or as a lining for handmade boxes and bowls. Paper doilies and pictures from greeting cards or magazines are perfect for making gift tags and greeting cards or to decorate boxes.

Brightly coloured gummed paper squares are easy to apply – you simply moisten the back and stick in position. This type of paper is very convenient when working on an intricate design.

## CARDBOARD

Generally, where cardboard is required for a project, you should use thin, lightweight cardboard, roughly the same thickness as that used for cereal packets. Where thick cardboard has been suggested, it should be sturdy enough to crease when bent. Some cardboards have a thin coating on one side which has an attractive shiny, metallic or textured finish. These are particularly good for making party hats and masks. Mounting board can be used for items that will be handled a lot. It is made up of layers of cardboard and comes in many thicknesses.

## CRAFT ACCESSORIES

Even though you may wish to specialize in paper crafts, this shouldn't exclude using a wide range of other materials in conjunction with paper for that extra special effect. It is often the finishing touches that make a handmade item so special, and you will find craft shops are a treasure trove of suitable decorative objects – many of them very reasonably priced. Cotton pulp or polystyrene shapes are lightweight and suitable for decorating in many ways. Similarly, coloured pipecleaners, tiny pom-poms, stick on eyes, beads, sequins and jewellery components all add interest to a design.

Nowadays, there is an exciting range of Victorian scraps that are ideal for paper crafts, plus a wide variety of decorative sticky tapes that help give a professional finish to a project. Giftwrapping ribbons can also be used to great effect. They come in many colours and widths. The wide ribbons can be moistened so that they will stick to themselves and the narrow ribbons will coil attractively when pulled smoothly over the blade of a pair of scissors.

*A wide range of different coloured and textured papers is available from art and craft shops, and the choice can be increased one hundred-fold if you also consider using wrapping paper or wallpaper for your designs. Giftwrapping ribbons, adhesive tapes, pipecleaners and pom-poms also come in a variety of bright colours and help add the finishing touches.*

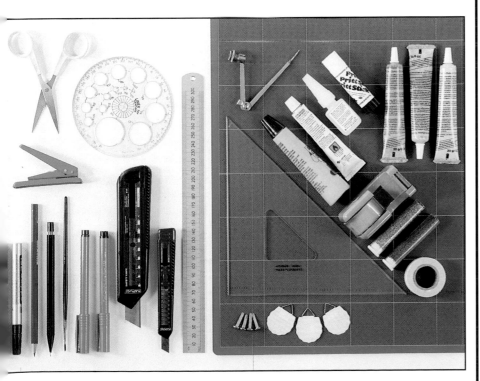

*Here are just some of the things you will find useful when working with paper. They include a cutting mat, set square, steel rule, compass, craft knife and scissors, plus a range of pencils, pens, glues and tapes.*

# EQUIPMENT

You may well find that you already have much of the basic equipment required for working with paper and cardboard at home. For best results, be sure to work on a clean, flat surface and, for safety, be sure not to leave any sharp implements lying around afterwards for children to find.

## PENCILS AND DRAWING AIDS

An HB pencil is the most versatile pencil to use, but a softer lead such as 2B is better for sketching. Always keep pencils sharpened to a fine point so that your drawing is accurate. Be sure to use a ruler for drawing straight lines. A set square should be used for drawing squares and rectangles so that the angles are correct. Draw circles with a compass or, for tiny circles, use a plastic stencil.

## SCISSORS AND KNIVES

A sharp, pointed pair of scissors is essential for working with paper. A small pair is more useful and easier to handle than a large pair. Craft knives give a better finish than scissors when cutting thick cardboard. Replace the blades frequently as they soon become blunt.

Always cut on a cutting mat – use a purpose-made mat or improvise, using a piece of corrugated cardboard. When cutting through thick cardboard, do not cut right through in one go but make several cuts, going deeper each time. Cut straight lines against a steel rule, preferably a safety one to protect your fingers. When cardboard needs to be folded, 'score' the surface lightly with a craft knife, being sure not to cut too deep into the board.

## ADHESIVES AND TAPES

It is important to use the right glue for the job. Read the manufacturer's instructions carefully and test glues on scraps of paper first. When sticking thin papers together, make sure the glue does not seep through the paper. Also take care with printed papers as some glues will smudge the pattern. Use a plastic spreader or strip of cardboard to apply glue evenly over a flat surface.

For a professional finish use spray adhesive. Either put your work on newspaper spread over the work surface or place it inside a box to protect the surrounding area from spray. Spray an even film over the surface and then stick in place. The sprayed paper can be repositioned which is very useful, and any tacky areas can be cleaned up with lighter fuel. Always use an ozone-friendly spray adhesive and work in a well ventilated room.

PVA medium has many purposes. It is a non-toxic, white solution that does not stain, and is quite suitable for children to use. It can be used as a glue and to make papier-mâché. As it dries to a clear, glossy finish, it is also useful as a protective varnish.

Double-sided tape is sticky on both sides and provides a neater, cleaner alternative to glue. Clear sticky tape is very-functional but remember that it does yellow and become brittle with age. An alternative is an opaque tape sometimes called magic or invisible tape which is longer-lasting but does not adhere so well.

Masking tape is a low-tack tape which is handy for holding paper and cardboard in place while you are working, and it does not leave a mark.

Paper and cardboard can be quite tough and durable, so in this chapter we have included a number of clever ideas which make thoughtful and personal gifts for family and friends. Jewellery, personalized stationery and letter racks, pictures and picture frames, are just some of the many attractive items you can create. There is also a stylish lampshade, stunning Chinese lantern and a variety of designs to enhance ordinary trinket boxes. And this chapter also provides a selection of projects showing you how to create little novelty items such as gift cones and bon-bon baskets, ideal for dinner or party guests to take home with them.

Fill this pretty cone with potpourri and allow the scent to waft through your home. Draw a 30cm (12in) diameter semi-circle with a compass on a piece of mottled peach-coloured paper. Cut it out and bend into the cone shape. Cut away a slice so the ends overlap smoothly and glue the overlapped ends together. Leave to dry.

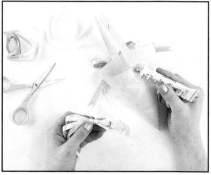

Cut out motifs from a white paper doily and stick to the cone with spray glue. Coat the cone all over with PVA medium. Set aside until the medium has hardened and become clear and then apply two more coats.

Cut a strip of paper 25cm x 1.5cm (10in x ⅝in) for the handle. Glue the ends inside the cone and coat with the PVA medium. Hang the handle over a door handle to dry. Tie ribbons in a bow and glue to the cone below the handle.

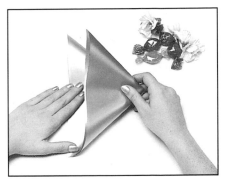

To make one of these pretty baskets you will need a sheet of paper 20cm (8in) square. Fold the square in half diagonally, then diagonally again. Place the triangle with the single fold running vertically. Bring the upper of the two free points up to meet the single point, opening the flap out as you do so to form a square. Crease the folds and repeat on the other side.

Position the newly formed square with the free edges pointing away from you. Fold the top free corner down to meet the opposite corner, then fold it back on itself to the horizontal centre line. Fold the flap in half once more. Repeat on the other side as shown. Turn the top left flap over to the right side, then fold it back on itself so that the corner meets the vertical centre line.

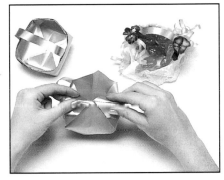

Fold the left hand corner in towards the vertical centre line also. Turn the basket over and repeat on the other side as shown. Open out the shape slightly and fold the top two flaps down inside the basket. Flatten the base. Cut a thin strip of paper for a handle and slip the ends into the slots on each side of the basket rim. Staple in place and decorate the basket with ribbons or lace.

To make this simple gift for the table, fill a paper cone with chocolate drops or jellies for a children's party, or with sugared almonds for grown-ups. All you need is a small square of brightly coloured wrapping paper, a ribbon rosette, and some tissue paper. Simply roll the paper into a cone from corner to corner, taping it into a nice rounded shape.

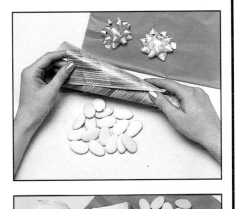

Flatten the cone slightly, positioning the top point in the centre; then fold up the bottom and stick on the ribbon rosette.

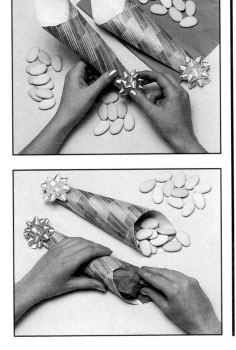

Scrunch up a little bit of tissue paper and slip it inside the cone to hold it in shape, then fill the top with sweets so that they spill out onto the point. You could attach a place card to each cone and use the cones to mark place settings at a large party.

Quilling is the traditional papercraft of making pictures from coiled paper strips. Cut coloured paper strips 4mm (³⁄₁₆in) wide and about 20cm (8in) long. Scratch the end of a strip to soften the paper. Now coil the strip tightly between your thumb and finger. Release the coil so it springs open and glue the end against one side.

The coils can be gently squeezed into various shapes to fit your chosen design. Experiment with forming different shapes such as triangles and teardrops. To make smaller coils, cut shorter paper strips.

Draw a design on the lid of a wooden box and spread paper glue on a section of the lid. Arrange the coils on the glue and then move onto the next section. Fill in the whole design – any gaps around the motif can be filled with coils that match the colour of the box.

Transform ordinary pencils into these smart covered ones with scraps of wrapping paper. Choose round rather than hexagonal-shaped pencils. Cut a strip of wrapping paper wide enough to wrap around the pencil and as long as the pencil. Spray the back heavily with spray glue and wrap around the pencil.

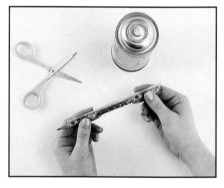

To finish, simply trim away the excess at the end of the pencil with a pair of small scissors.

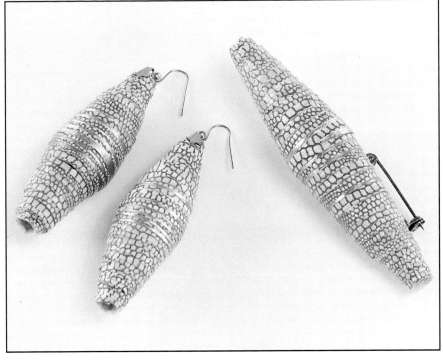

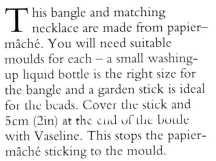

T his bangle and matching necklace are made from papier–mâché. You will need suitable moulds for each – a small washing-up liquid bottle is the right size for the bangle and a garden stick is ideal for the beads. Cover the stick and 5cm (2in) at the end of the bottle with Vaseline. This stops the papier-mâché sticking to the mould.

Tear paper into small strips. Wallpaper lining paper was used for the bangle and newspaper for the necklace. Mix PVA medium (available at art shops) with a little water to thin it. Dip a brush in the solution, pick up a strip with the brush and press it onto the mould. Cover the Vaseline overlapping the strips. Apply four layers and leave to dry.

Build up the layers to about 5mm (¼in) thick and allow to dry overnight. Remove the jewellery, trim the bangle to 3cm (1¼in) wide with a craft knife and cut beads 3cm (1¼in) long. Tear giftwrap into small strips and apply to jewellery with the thinned PVA solution. Apply two coats of PVA medium as varnish. Thread beads onto cord.

N o one will guess that this beautiful jewellery is made of paper. For each earring cut a long triangle of snakeskin-effect paper (available from specialist art shops) 76cm (30in) long with a 6cm (2¼in) wide base and gold giftwrap 75cm (29in) long with a 5cm (2in) wide base. Using PVA medium stick the giftwrap centrally to the wide end of the snakeskin piece.

Spread Vaseline on a length of wood dowel to stop the paper sticking to the wood. Starting at the wide end, roll the triangles tightly around the dowel, brushing with PVA medium as you go. Give the beads a final coat of the medium as a varnish, leave to dry, then gently remove the dowel.

Pierce a hole through the top of each earring and attach a triangle wire. Fix a small jump ring to the triangle wire with a pair of pliers. Attach an earring hook to the ring. The brooch is made in the same way with wider triangles of snakeskin and gold paper. Glue a brooch pin to the back of the brooch. Craft shops sell jewellery components.

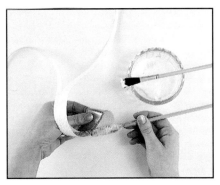

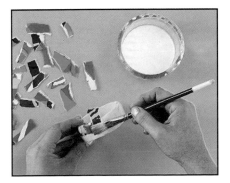

# REGENCY SILHOUETTE

# POT OF ANEMONES

Give your home a period touch with this classic decoration. You can use a clear profile sketch or a photograph as a basis for your picture. Make a tracing of the outline and place it face down on the back of a piece of black paper. Redraw the design to transfer it.

Cut out the motif with a pair of small, sharp scissors and glue the design to white paper. Trim the paper to fit your frame. Place the picture in the frame and glue a small ribbon bow to the top.

This delightful picture will brighten a dreary day. Cut a 3cm (1¼in) diameter circle of black paper; cut a fringe around the edge and a small hole in the centre. Cut a 6cm (2¼in) diameter circle of black tissue paper and wrap it over a small ball of cotton wool (absorbent cotton). Twist the edges together and insert into the hole.

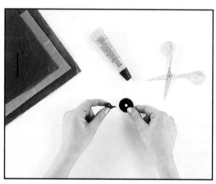

Use the template on page 25 to cut six petals from tissue paper and glue to the twisted end. Make two more flowers. Glue some striped wallpaper to a piece of cardboard and some cream paper over the lower third. From thick brown paper, cut a rectangle 13cm x 10cm (5in x 4in) for the pot and a strip 15cm x 2.5cm (6in x 1in) for the rim.

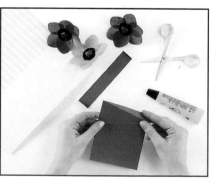

On one long edge of the pot mark 2.5cm (1in) from each end. Draw a line from the marks to the top corners and fold back the ends along the lines. Fold under 5mm (¼in) at the ends of the rim. Glue the folded ends of the pot to the background, slightly bowing the pot outwards. Glue the rim over the top in the same way. Glue flowers in place above the pot.

# PHOTO FINISH

# BORDERLINES

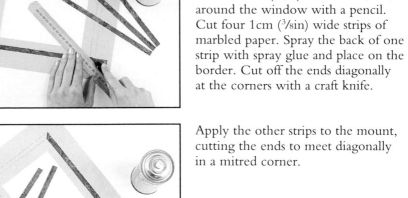

The right mount can really enhance a picture. Buy a plain cardboard mount to fit your picture. Draw a 1cm (³/₈in) wide border around the window with a pencil. Cut four 1cm (³/₈in) wide strips of marbled paper. Spray the back of one strip with spray glue and place on the border. Cut off the ends diagonally at the corners with a craft knife.

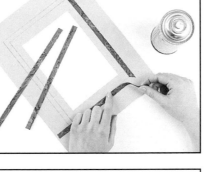
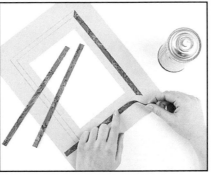

Apply the other strips to the mount, cutting the ends to meet diagonally in a mitred corner.

To make these smart frames, cut two pieces of mounting board 25cm x 19cm (10in x 7¹/₂in). Cut a window 17cm x 11cm (7in x 4¹/₂in) in the centre of one piece. Cut two pieces of giftwrap to cover the frames. Lay the window mount on the wrong side of one piece and cut a window in the giftwrap, leaving a 2cm (³/₄in) margin. Snip to the corners and glue the margins down.

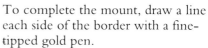

To complete the mount, draw a line each side of the border with a fine-tipped gold pen.

Cover the back of the frame with giftwrap, then cut two 1cm (³/₈in) wide strips of mounting board 18cm (7¹/₄in) long and one 22cm (8¹/₂in) long. Cover with paper and glue to the wrong side of the back just inside three of the edges. Spread glue on the strips and carefully place the front of the frame on top, checking that the outer edges are level.

Cut a rectangle of mounting board 18cm x 6cm (7¹/₄in x 2¹/₄in) for the stand. Score across the stand 5cm (2in) from one end. Cover the stand with giftwrap and glue the scored end to the back with the other end level with either a long or short side depending on whether your photo is in landscape or portrait form. Bend the stand outwards.

— 13 —

Drop two or three colours onto the water and swirl together with the end of a paint brush. Cut plain paper to fit the tray. Wearing rubber gloves, start at one end of the tray and lower the paper onto the surface of the water so it can pick up the pattern. Carefully lift up the paper.

Leave the paper to dry overnight on newspaper. You can remove the paint from the tray by drawing strips of newspaper across the surface of the water.

The marbled paper can be used in many ways. Here, a plain book takes on a sophisticated look when recovered. Cut a rectangle of marbled paper large enough to wrap around the book with a 2.5cm (1in) margin on all sides. Wrap the paper around the book, open the cover and glue the paper inside the opening edges.

Prop up the book so the cover is open at a right angle. Snip the paper each side of the spine and stick the top and bottom margin inside the covers, folding under the corners.

There are many methods for marbling paper but this way needs little equipment. Fill a shallow tray with water. Put spots of enamel paint on the water with a paint brush. If they sink the paint is too thick and needs thinning with a little white spirit. If they disperse into a faint film it is too thin and should be mixed with more paint.

Push the paper at the ends of the spine between the spine and the pages with the points of a pair of scissors. Arrange jewellery stones on the cover and use a strong glue to stick them in place. Cut two pieces of paper to fit inside the covers and glue inside.

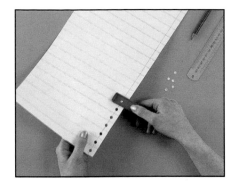

Co-ordinate your home with a pleated lampshade to match the wallpaper. For a 30cm (12in) wide shade cut a strip of wallpaper 130cm x 20cm (51in x 8in). On the wrong side, rule pleat lines across the strip 2cm (¾in) apart then draw a line along the length 1.2cm (½in) from the top. Punch a hole on this line between each pleat line.

Fold the strip in concertina pleats along the pleat lines. On the wrong side, slide each pleat into the punch in turn and make half a hole on the fold on the line. These holes will rest on the top section of the frame when the lampshade is finished.

Overlap the ends of the lampshade and thread ribbon through the holes in the middle of each pleat. Draw up the pleats and slip the lampshade over the frame, resting the notches on top of the frame. Pull the ribbon ends to tighten the top and tie in a decorative bow.

F̲ill this pretty basket with tiny sweet eggs to delight a child at Easter. Using the templates on page 25 cut out two sides and a base in pale blue cardboard and the grass in green gummed paper. Lightly score the sides of the basket along the broken lines with a craft knife, then stick on the grass.

Fold the sides backwards along the scored lines and join end to end in a ring by gluing each end tab under the opposite end of the other side. Glue the base under the base tabs. Cut a strip of pale blue cardboard for the handle measuring 30cm x 1cm (12in x ³⁄₈in). Stick the ends inside the basket.

Cut out two rabbits (see page 25) in brown cardboard. Glue a ball of cotton wool (absorbent cotton) to the rabbits as bobtails. Cut two strips of pale blue cardboard 4cm x 1cm (1¹⁄₂in x ³⁄₈in) and fold them widthwise in half to make hinges. Glue one half to the back of the rabbit matching the fold to the broken line. Glue the other half to the basket under the handles.

# LETTER RACK | FILIGREE STATIONERY

There is no excuse for mislaying letters with this smart letter rack. From thick mounting board cut a rectangle 24cm x 8cm (9¹/₂in x 3¹/₄in) for the front and 24cm x 10cm (9¹/₂in x 4in) for the back. Diagonally trim away the top corners and cover one side of each piece with giftwrap.

Cut giftwrap slightly smaller than the front and back sections and glue in position on the wrong side. Take a piece of wood 24cm (9¹/₂in) long by 3cm (1¹/₄in) wide and 1cm (³/₈in) thick. Cover the wood with coloured paper.

Cut a rectangle of mounting board 27cm x 7cm (10¹/₂in x 2³/₄in) for the base and cover with coloured paper. Use a strong glue to stick the front to one narrow edge of the wood keeping the lower edges level. Glue the back to the other side in the same way. Finish the letter rack by gluing this upper section centrally to the base.

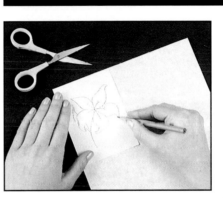

Stylish and original stationery is expensive to buy but this delicate design is cheap and easy to produce. Draw a simple motif on layout paper then retrace the design on the other side. Place your drawing on the top left-hand corner of a sheet of writing paper about 1cm (³/₈in) inside the edges. Redraw the motif to transfer it to the writing paper.

Now prick along the lines with a needle or pin. You may find it helpful to practise on a scrap of paper first to judge how far apart the pinpricks should be.

Rub out the pencil lines then trim away the corner of the paper to echo the shape of the design. Pinprick a co-ordinating motif on the matching envelope flap.

Revive the Victorian hobby of découpage and decorate a box with pretty paper pictures. Cut out suitable pictures from greeting cards or magazines or use reproductions of Victorian prints.

Arrange the pictures on the box and then stick them in place with spray glue. Smooth in place.

Make this carrier bag and you have a gift bag for your presents or go a step further and make the bag itself the present. Cut a piece of thick yellow cardboard 57.5cm x 29cm (22⅝in x 11½in). Refer to the diagram on page 25 and score along the solid and broken lines. Cut away the lower right-hand corner and cut into the base along the solid lines.

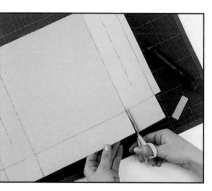

Apply a thin coat of clear gloss varnish all over the box and lid. Leave to dry and then sand lightly with fine sandpaper. Build up about six layers of varnish, sanding the box between each coat.

Fold the bag forwards along the solid lines and backwards along the broken lines. Turn the bag over and, with a pencil, lightly divide the front into quarters. Cut out a small hole at the centre for the clockwork. Cut out four pieces of red paper 1.5cm x 1cm (⅝in x ⅜in) and glue on the divisions 7cm (2¾in) from the hole.

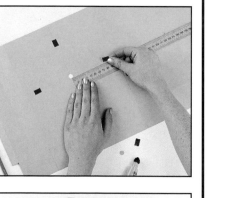

Rub out the pencil lines. Join the side seam by gluing the narrow tab under the opposite end. Fold under the small base sections then glue the long sections underneath. Cut two strips of green cardboard for handles 30cm x 1cm (12in x ⅜in). Glue the ends inside the top of the bag. Insert the clockwork rod through the hole and attach the hands.

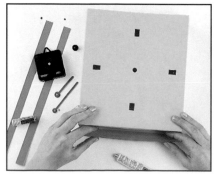

You could even decorate a simple DIY pine letter rack to match, for a lovely gift or a smart desk accessory. Sand the wood smooth and cut out two stencil sheets from the small curved rope design opposite. Tape the first stencil on to the wood and use quick-drying stencil paints, mixed up to match your decor, to stencil the first half of your design.

Match up the remainder of the design on the second stencil sheet and paint the second colour. Temporarily assemble the four walls of the letter rack with tape and stencil the large rope design (see above right) around the lower edge of the box in the same colours.

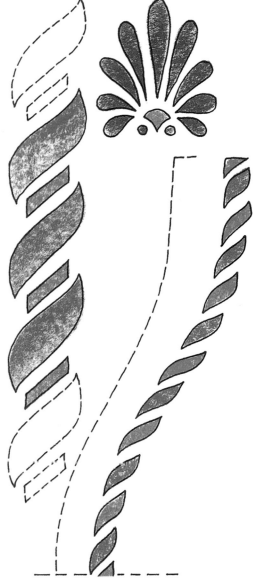

*Above: Use these patterns to cut out your stencils for the letter rack and notepaper. The curved rope pattern only shows half of the design, so trace it off marking on the straight dotted centre line. Then turn the tracing over, match up the design, and trace in the other half accurately.*

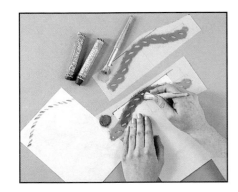

Hand painted notepaper and envelopes make a stylish and original gift. Use the stencils shown here to decorate the top of some sheets, working with oil-based stencil crayons. Rub a little crayon on to a corner of the stencil or a spare piece of acetate and then collect the colour on to a brush. Stencil the colour on to the paper using a circular movement.

Decorate envelopes to match using the stencil crayons. Use a simple design along the lower edge or just a single motif that will not get in the way of the written address. Leave the stencilling to set for a while before using the notepaper and envelopes, to avoid smudging.

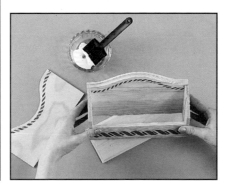

Now glue the box together using PVA wood glue. Begin with the four walls, then, when dry, glue these to the base. The centre section will then just slide into place. Glue this if you wish. Varnish the letter rack with several coats of clear polyurethane varnish to give a smooth, durable finish and to protect the stencilling.

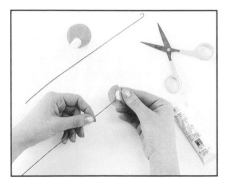

T ake a length of thick wire and
bend the end into a hook. Glue
a small ball of cotton wool
(absorbent cotton) over the hook.
Cut a 4cm (1⅝in) diameter circle of
green crepe paper. Wrap the circle
over the ball and glue the edges
around the wire. Cut two 3.5cm
(1½in) diameter circles of black
crepe paper and cut a fringe around
the edge of each circle.

Make a hole through the centre of
the black circles and insert the wire
through the holes, push the circles up
to the green ball. Use the template
on page 25 to cut out six petals in
red crepe paper with the arrow along
the grain of paper. Pull the top of the
petals between thumb and finger to
flute the edges.

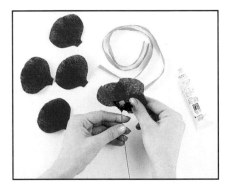

Glue the base of three petals under
the poppy centre then glue the
remaining petals in between. Bind
the wire with a thin strip of green
crepe paper and glue the ends in
place to complete.

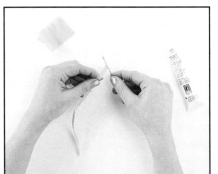

To make a daffodil, bend a 12cm
(4¾in) length of thin wire in half for
the stamen. Starting at the bent end,
bind the wire with a narrow strip of
yellow crepe paper. Secure the ends
with a dab of glue. Cut yellow crepe
paper 6cm x 4cm (2¼in x 1⅝in)
with the grain running along the
short edges. Pull one long edge
between thumb and finger to flute
the edge.

Overlap the ends of the rectangle and
glue together making the trumpet.
Place the stamen in the trumpet and
gather the lower edge tightly with
thread. Using the template on page
25 cut six petals in yellow crepe
paper with the grain running parallel
with the arrow. Stretch the petals
across their width.

Dab glue on the base of the petals
and stick to the base of the trumpet.
Place the stamen end against a length
of thick wire and bind together with
a narrow strip of green crepe paper;
glue the ends in place then bend the
flowerhead forward. Fold strips of
thick green paper in half lengthwise
for leaves and cut pointed ends.

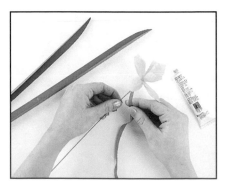

A zany idea for an unusual ornament or table centrepiece. For the apples fold a 12cm (4¾in) square of thin cardboard in half and draw half an apple shape against the fold. Cut out the apple then open out the cardboard to use as a template. Cut a total of 48 apples in light green and red tissue paper. Mix the colours and sew the pieces together along the centre.

Lift up the apple halves on one side except the bottom one. Dab glue on the bottom half close to the edge in the centre and then each side between the centre and stitching. Press down the next half and dab glue close to the edge between the first positions. Continue to the top tissue layer, alternating positions.

Glue the other half of the apple in the same way. Cut a stalk and leaf in green cardboard and glue to the top of the apple. Dab glue close to the edge in the centre and then either side between the centre and the stitching. Carefully press the two halves together and then glue the back halves together in the same way.

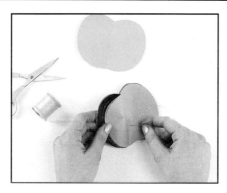

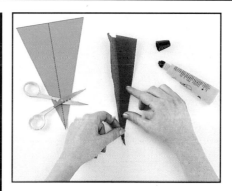

To make the carrots, draw a T shape on paper, the horizontal line 13cm (5in) long and the vertical line 20cm (8in) long. Join the lines together in a triangle. Cut out the triangle in orange crepe paper. Spread glue sparingly along one edge. Gently press the other long edge onto the glue and leave to dry.

Stuff the carrot with polyester filling, carefully pushing the filling in as far as possible with a knitting needle or skewer. Fold in the top edge for about 1cm (³⁄₈in).

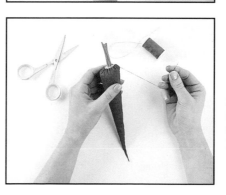

Cut two strips of green crepe paper 10cm x 3cm (4in x 1¼in), cutting the length along the grain. Roll the strips tightly lengthwise and glue along the long edges. Cut the strips in half. Hold the ends of these stalks inside the carrot and gather the folded edge tightly around the ends. Fasten the threads securely.

Stencil this attractive iris design on to thick watercolour paper for a linen texture and use wax stencil crayons for subtle colour shading. Size up the design and cut three stencils for mauve, yellow and green areas. Tape the green stencil in place and blend together two green crayons. Rub the crayons on to the acetate and then collect the colour on to the brush.

Remove the green stencil and tape the mauve one in position, lining up the vertical and horizontal marks. Blend mauve, blue and turquoise for the flowers, shading the lower petals in mauve and the upper ones in blues, and getting deeper towards the centre of each flower. Lastly, use the yellow stencil. Work the brush in a light circular motion to shade the colours throughout.

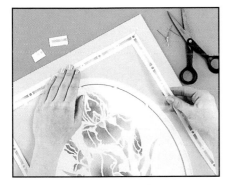

Have an oval mount cut to fit around your stencil. Cut out the border stencil from the design shown opposite and try it out on scrap paper in various colours. Cut these trial pieces into strips and lay them around your mount. Hold them in place with masking tape and then insert a pin centrally at each corner when you are happy with the position.

Carefully remove the strips and, very lightly, mark guide lines for stencilling the border using a pencil and set-square. Check the lines are exactly the right distance from the oval shape and parallel to the outer edge. The stencils at the top and sides should be equidistant from the oval and the lower stencil slightly further away to look visually correct.

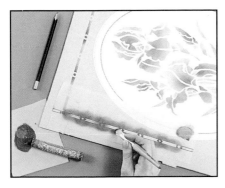

Finally, stencil the border in a single colour using stencil crayons as before. Build up the colour where the strips meet the round spots in the design to add interest. Assemble the stencil with the mount and a piece of glass in a simple frame coloured to complement your flowers and decorations.

Suggested size: One square represents 2.5cm (1in).

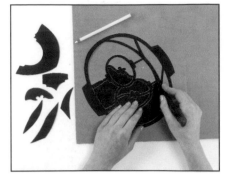

Hang this Oriental mobile at a window and watch the sun shine through the coloured tissue paper. Use the template on page 25 to cut out a pair of lanterns in black cardboard. Cut out all the sections, taking care not to cut through any of the 'bridges'.

To achieve the stained glass effect, cut out coloured tissue paper a little larger than the sections to be covered. Glue the pieces of tissue paper to the back of one lantern. Trim the edges. Glue a silky red tassel to hang from the bottom of one lantern at the centre. Now glue the two lanterns together enclosing the tissue paper. Suspend the mobile on red embroidery thread.

Here are templates and diagrams for several of the projects in the preceeding chapter. These need to be enlarged as follows: draw a grid of 3cm (1¼in) squares, then copy the design onto your grid, square by square, using the lines as a guide.

The clock is constructed from measurements. Use a ruler and set square to draw the shape onto cardboard and follow either the metric or imperial measurements but not a combination of the two.

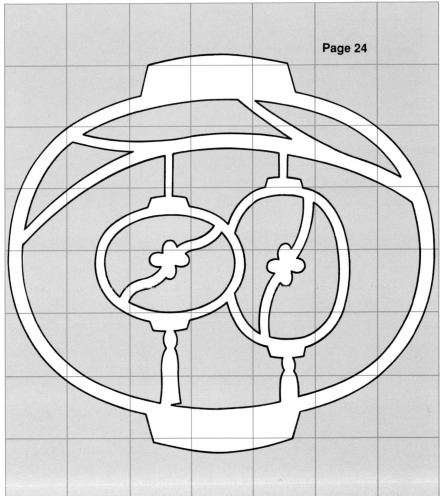

**Page 24**

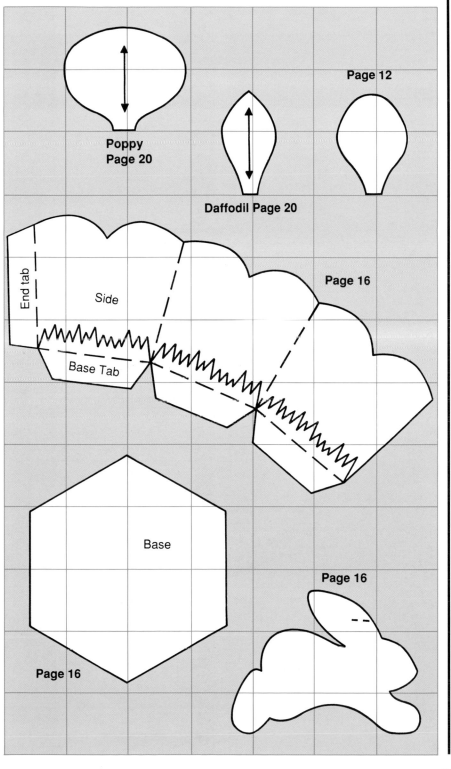

**Page 12**

**Poppy
Page 20**

**Daffodil Page 20**

**Page 16**

End tab

Side

Base Tab

Base

**Page 16**

**Page 16**

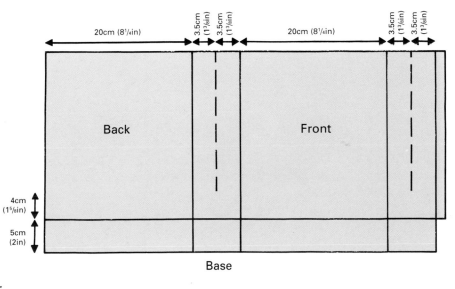

**Page 18**

20cm (8¼in)  3.5cm (1⅜in)  3.5cm (1⅜in)  20cm (8¼in)  3.5cm (1⅜in)  3.5cm (1⅜in)

Back

Front

4cm (1⅝in)

5cm (2in)

Base

# DESIGNS FOR CHILDREN

This chapter is bursting with colourful and fun designs which children can make themselves: a jolly elephant mobile, cheeky refrigerator magnets and artistic lakeside collage are all straightforward yet challenging for young minds. There is also a host of toys and ornaments to brighten up children's rooms which most adults will enjoy making themselves. All the necessary patterns have been provided on pages 38-39.

Do ensure that children are supervised if cutting out is involved. Most paper items can be successfully cut using children's safety scissors, but tougher cardboard may need to be cut by an adult with a craft knife.

Here is a mobile for animal lovers – a small herd of elephants. Cut out four elephants in co-ordinating coloured cardboard using the template on page 38. Draw eyes on both sides with a felt-tipped pen and cut slits along the broken lines with a craft knife. Make a hole with a thick needle at the top of the elephant.

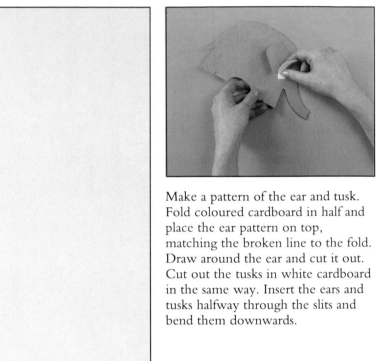

Make a pattern of the ear and tusk. Fold coloured cardboard in half and place the ear pattern on top, matching the broken line to the fold. Draw around the ear and cut it out. Cut out the tusks in white cardboard in the same way. Insert the ears and tusks halfway through the slits and bend them downwards.

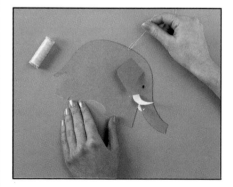

Cut four 45cm (18in) lengths of thread. Loop the threads in half and insert the ends through the hole. Pull the ends through the loop so the elephant hangs from the thread. Knot the ends together and hang on mobile wires. You could spray paint the wires to match the elephants. Hang the mobile on a length of thread.

Now you can have your very own prehistoric monster – a Stegosaurus dinosaur. Refer to the template on page 38 to make a pattern of the dinosaur body and two sets of legs on thin cardboard. Draw around the patterns onto mounting board (use a board that is six sheets thick). Cut out the sections with a craft knife.

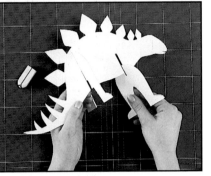

Slot the legs and body together, placing the smaller set of legs at the front, as shown.

What better way to invite friends to a party at the local hop than with this funny frog. Draw a frog with large, bulging eyes on thin green cardboard and cut it out. Cut out a narrow smiling mouth.

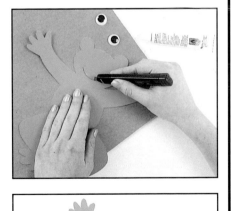

Glue on a pair of joggle eyes and write a message on the back. Now all you need is the party . . .

These funny glasses are sure to amuse all who see them. Cut a pattern using the template on page 39 and use to cut a blue cardboard front. Cut out the windows and use as a guide to cut two lenses from green transparent acetate, adding 1cm (³/₈in) to the edges all round. Glue the lenses behind the windows.

Use the template to cut out a pair of palm trees – cut the trunks in brown cardboard and leaves in green cardboard. Glue the palm trees each side of the front piece.

Cut out a pair of arms in blue cardboard using the template. Score the ends along the broken lines and bend back the tabs at right angles. Glue the tabs behind the glasses to complete.

Textured papers make an interesting collage. Cut pale blue cardboard 30cm x 24cm (12in x 9¹/₂in) for the background. Cover the lower 11cm (4¹/₄in) with clear sticky-backed plastic. Cut a strip of pale green cardboard and tear away one long edge. Glue the strip above the 'lake'. Cut pointed strips of green gummed paper and stick over the join.

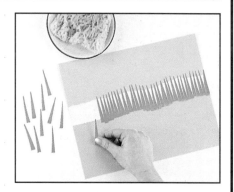

Use the template on page 39 to cut out the swan and wing in wavy textured paper. Cut the beak in orange paper and glue behind the swan. Draw the swan's eye with a black felt-tipped pen. Glue the swan to the middle of the lake and glue the wing on top.

Cut very thin strips of brown cardboard for the bullrush stems and three long leaves from green crepe paper. Glue the leaves and stems to the picture. Cut bullrushes from black flock sticky-backed plastic and glue over the top of the stems. Use the template to cut out three lily pads in green cardboard and glue to the lake.

Cast a spooky glow at a Halloween gathering with this eerie lantern. Cut a strip 50cm x 22cm (20in x 8½in) of shiny black cardboard – the sort that is white on the other side. Cut out a large and a small bat from thin cardboard and use as templates to draw three bats on the back of the strip.

When you have finished tracing the bats, carefully cut them out using a craft knife.

This jolly hippo will brighten the kitchen when stuck to the fridge door with a small magnet. Roughly cut out a design from some left-over wrapping paper. Stick the motif to a piece of thick cardboard with spray glue.

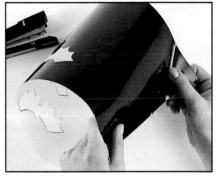

Overlap the ends of the strip and staple them together. To complete the effect, place a few nightlights inside the lantern. Do not leave the lantern unattended when it is lit.

Cut out the picture with a craft knife. Do not attempt to cut right through the board in one go, but gradually cut deeper and deeper until you reach the cutting board.

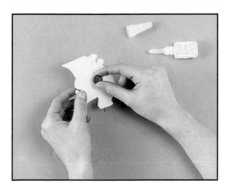

Glue a fridge magnet to the back of the character. Magnets are available at many art and craft shops.

This is a traditional kite with a difference – there is an amusing clown's face on the front. To make the frame you will need two lengths of wood dowel; one 84cm (33in) long and the other 56cm (22in). Cut two small notches 5mm (¼in) from the ends of both sticks with a craft knife.

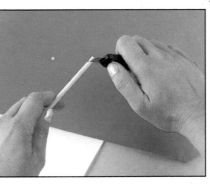

Mark the short stick at the centre and the long stick 28cm (11in) from one end. Lay the sticks across one another at right angles matching the marks, and bind tightly with fine string. Secure with a dab of glue. Tie string around the notches at one end of a stick, then wind it tightly around the other notches as shown and knot the ends of string together.

Butt the edges of a white and a green piece of paper together with the wrong sides uppermost. Lay the kite frame on top and cut around it 1.5cm (⅝in) outside the string. Cut off the corners level with the notches. Remove the frame and join the butted edges together with masking tape.

Apply double-sided tape to the edges of the kite covering on the wrong side. Place the frame on top and fold over the edges enclosing the string.

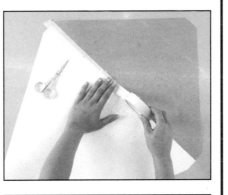

Cut a 112cm (44in) length of string and tie the ends to the top and bottom notch. Cut a 92cm (36¼in) length and tie the ends to the side notches. Balance the kite by resting the strings on a finger and fastening them together with a curtain ring where they cross over. Decorate the front with ribbons and paper shapes. Finally, tie a ball of string to the ring.

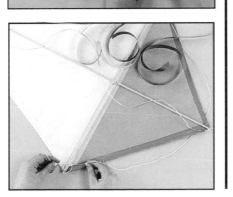

The method for making this traditional pinwheel is Origami, which is the ancient Japanese craft of paper folding. Start with a 20cm (8in) square of patterned paper. Fold the side edges to meet at the centre then fold the top and bottom edges to meet at the centre as well.

Now bring the side corners at the centre to the top and bottom edges with a diagonal fold.

Open the diagonal folds out flat then lightly hold at the centre and pull each corner of the square underneath to the outside. Turn alternate points in opposite directions to form the pinwheel. Attach the pinwheel to a painted balsa wood stick with a drawing pin.

You can peer around corners and over walls with this smart periscope. Follow the diagram on page 39 to draw the periscope onto thick cardboard. Cut out the shape with a craft knife and score along the solid lines.

Bend the periscope backwards along the scored lines so you can see how it will look when finished. Flatten out the periscope and glue a small make-up mirror on the wrong side in the middle of the base and top.

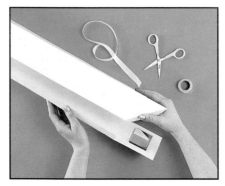

Bend the periscope back into shape and stick the long tab under the opposite long edge with double-sided tape.

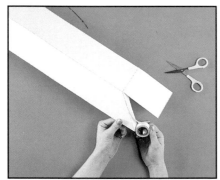

Stick the remaining tabs to the base and top with double-sided tape.

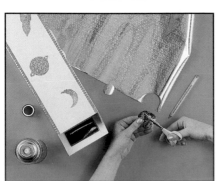

Apply decorative sticky tape over all the folds to neaten and reinforce the edges. Cut out space rockets and planets from giftwrap and stick to the periscope with spray glue.

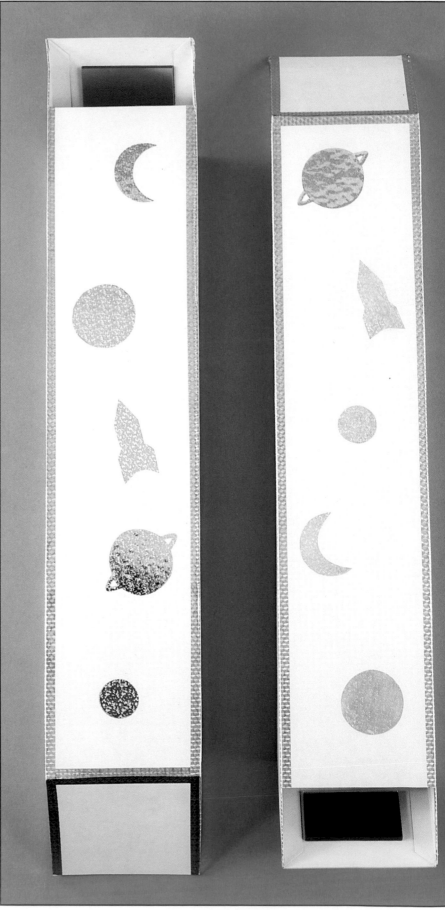

This clown is fun to make and not as difficult as he may seem. First cut a rectangle of crepe paper for the body 30cm x 24cm (12in x 9½in). Overlap the shorter edges and glue them together making a tube. Push toy filling inside and stuff the tube firmly. With a needle and thread, gather the open ends tightly, enclosing the filling.

Cut two 14cm (5½in) squares of crepe paper for the sleeves and make two tubes like the body. For the arms, cut two pink pipecleaners 16cm (6¼in) long. Insert each arm into a sleeve and glue across one end, sandwiching the arm in the middle. Gently push toy filling inside around the arm.

Bend over the end of the arms in a hook to imitate hands. Gather the sleeves tightly above the hands with a needle and thread, making a frilled edge. Glue the flat ends of the sleeves to the body.

Cut a strip of crepe paper 35cm x 6cm (14in x 2¼in), cutting the short ends parallel with the grain of the crepe paper. This will be the neck ruffle. Glue the ends together and gather one long edge. Pull up the gathers tightly like a rosette and glue the ruffle on top of the body.

Take a 7cm (2¾in) diameter cotton pulp ball and glue a red bead in the middle for a nose. Draw eyes and a mouth with felt-tipped pens. Glue curly gift wrapping ribbon each side of the face. The hat is a 14cm (5½in) diameter circle of coloured cardboard. Cut to the centre and overlap the edges making a cone. Glue the edges together and glue the hat in place.

Glue the head on top of the ruffle. Using the template on page 39, cut out the shoes in coloured cardboard. Glue the body on top of the shoes and then glue some bright pom-poms to the hat, shoes and front of the body. This clown is not for playing with but is a charming ornament for a child's room.

T his lion mask is made from
papier-mâché moulded over a
balloon. Blow up the balloon and tie
a knot in the end. Tear newspaper
into small pieces and then dilute
PVA medium with water to thin it
slightly. Spread a little of the solution
on the front of the balloon and cover
with the newspaper pieces.

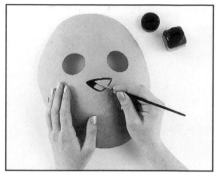

Cover one half of the balloon with
about seven layers of papier-mâché
and leave to dry overnight. Gently
pull the balloon away from the mask
and trim the edges of the mask with
a pair of scissors. Cut out two round
holes for the eyes. Paint the mask
with non-toxic ochre coloured paint
and then paint a black nose and
muzzle, as shown.

To make the mane, cut brown crepe
paper 140cm x 16cm (55in x 6¼in)
and fold lengthwise in half. Cut a
fringe along the long edges. With a
needle and long length of thread,
gather up the mane close to the fold.
Glue the mane around the lion's
face. Finally, staple a length of thin
elastic to each side of the back of the
mask, to fit.

Make this colourful head-dress and join the tribe! Cut a 4cm (1½in) wide strip of red cardboard 60cm (24in) long. Cut out simple shapes from coloured papers and glue to the strip.

Overlap the ends of the strip and glue together. Stick three coloured quill feathers upright behind the strip with sticky tape.

Although a bit more complicated to make than a cardboard mask, this mask will last much longer. The face is made from papier-mâché (see page 34 for instructions), the mould is a balloon. Blow the balloon up as big as you can without bursting it, and build up the papier-mâché over at least one half. When it is dry, gently let the air out of the balloon by piercing the knotted end.

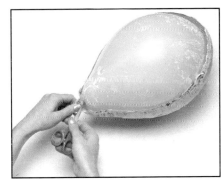

Cut six 2.5cm (1in) wide strips of black crepe paper 40cm (16in) long. Spread paper glue along one long edge and fold the strips in half. Staple three lengths together at one end and make a plait. Bind the end with embroidery thread and make another plait in the same way. Stick the plaits to each side of the head-dress with sticky tape.

Trim the mask down, cutting the pointed end into a forehead. Cut out circular eyes and a curved mouth. Now give the mould a coat of white emulsion (water-based paint), sand it down and give it another two coats to make it as smooth a surface as possible.

Around each eye paint four slightly triangular stripes. Also paint large red lips and cheeks on either side. For the nose, paint a ping pong ball red and glue it in place. For the hair, cut short lengths of yarn and attach them to strips of sticky tape; stick these to the back of the mask. Finally, take a piece of elastic, staple it to either side, and paint over the staples with a touch more emulsion.

C reate this unusual birthday table decoration, using the template on page 39 to cut a base and lid in white cardboard. Cut the end tab off the lid. Now cut a strip of mottled brown cardboard 30cm x 6cm (12in x 2¼in). Tear a thin strip of shiny red paper and glue along the middle of the 'sponge'. Score across the strip at the centre and 1.5cm (⅝in) from the ends.

Score the base and lid along the broken lines and snip the end tab to the scored line. Bend all the pieces backwards along the scored lines. Glue the 'sponge' to the side tabs on the base with the folds at the corners. Cut pale blue cardboard 12cm x 6cm (4¾in x 2¼in) and glue one long edge over the end tabs.

Cut two 12cm (4¾in) long strips of white cardboard and cut scallops along one edge. Glue to the blue end as icing. Glue one tab of the lid inside the top of the box. Cut a strip of blue cardboard for the candle. Make a 'flame' from a foil sweet (candy) wrapper and glue to one end. Fold under the other end of the candle and glue to the lid.

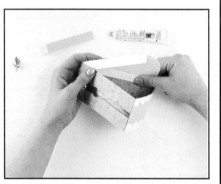

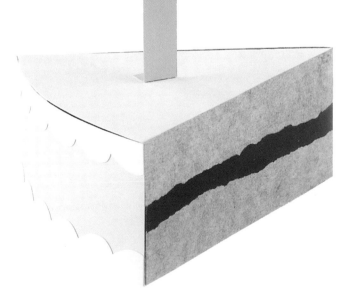

G lass paperweights such as these (available in kit form from craft shops) are ideal for making novel presents. Kids in particular will enjoy making this design. To work out a mosaic picture, draw a grid of squares about 4mm (³⁄₁₆in) apart. Trace around the paperweight template onto the grid and draw a design. Colour the picture as a guide for the finished mosaic.

Cut out tiny squares of coloured paper the same size as the grid squares. Draw a cross on a piece of paper to help keep the mosaic squares straight. Spread paper glue thinly along part of one line and press the squares in place. Nudge them into position with scissors or tweezers. Follow the grid design and glue on all the squares.

Use the paperweight template to cut the mosaic to fit the paperweight. Turn the paperweight upside down and lay the mosaic in the hollow. Peel the paper off the sticky-backed flock backing and carefully stick it over the back of the paperweight enclosing the mosaic.

These amusing finger puppets are sure to entertain your friends. Use the template on page 39 to cut out the dancer in pale pink cardboard. Cut out the dress in shiny, deep pink cardboard and glue to the puppet. Next cut an 8cm (3in) diameter circle from the centre of a white paper doily for a petticoat and glue to the dress with spray glue.

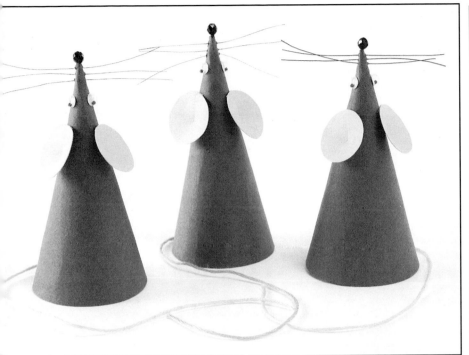

Colour the hair, draw the eyes and lightly mark the nose with a black felt-tipped pen. Draw the mouth with a red felt-tipped pen and rouge the cheeks with a red coloured pencil.

Play to the gallery with this finger puppet trio of tiny friends. Cut out a quarter-circle of thin magenta cardboard with a 9cm (3½in) radius. Pull between thumb and finger to curve the piece. Overlap the straight edges to form a cone and glue the edges together.

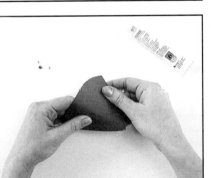

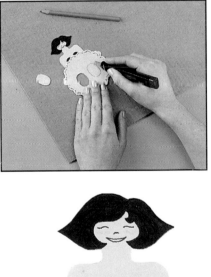

Mark the finger hole positions on the petticoat and carefully cut through all the layers with a craft knife.

Glue a small black bead to the point of the cone as a nose and then glue two small joggle eyes each side. To make the ears, cut out two small circles of thin pink cardboard. Cut to the centre and overlap the cut edges. Glue the overlapped edges together then glue the ears to the cone.

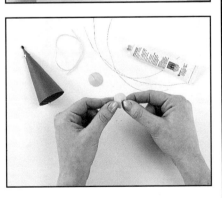

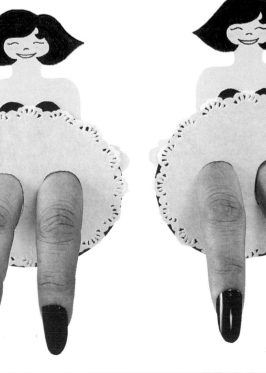

Take some toy-making whiskers and thread on a needle through the top of the cone. Drop a little glue onto the whiskers inside the cone to secure them. Trim the ends level. Thread a length of embroidery thread on a needle and attach to the base of the mouse at the back as a tail. Knot the thread inside the finger puppet.

Size up patterns as described on page 25, making each square of your grid measure 3cm (1¼in).

Papier-mâché is very durable and can be made in many ways. This traditional method uses a paste of flour and water. Tear up wallpaper lining paper into small pieces. Then grease the inside of a small bowl with Vaseline. Brush the paper pieces with paste and stick them inside the bowl, starting at the centre and working outwards.

Build up three layers of papier-mâché and leave to dry overnight. Apply at least four more layers. When the papier-mâché is completely dry, remove it from the bowl mould. Trim the top edge level with a pair of scissors. Paint the bowl with a craft paint, sanding between coats. Cut coloured tissue paper into small triangles.

Stick the triangles to the bowl with a clear varnish such as PVA medium. Once the bowl is decorated, coat it inside and out with the varnish. Line the bowl with tissue paper and fill it with pretty bathroom accessories.

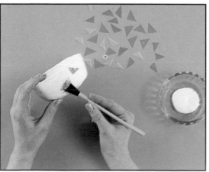

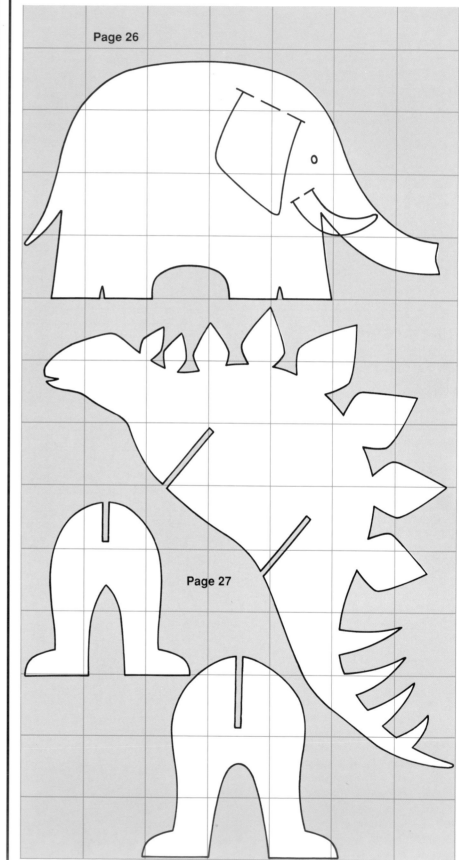

Page 26

Page 27

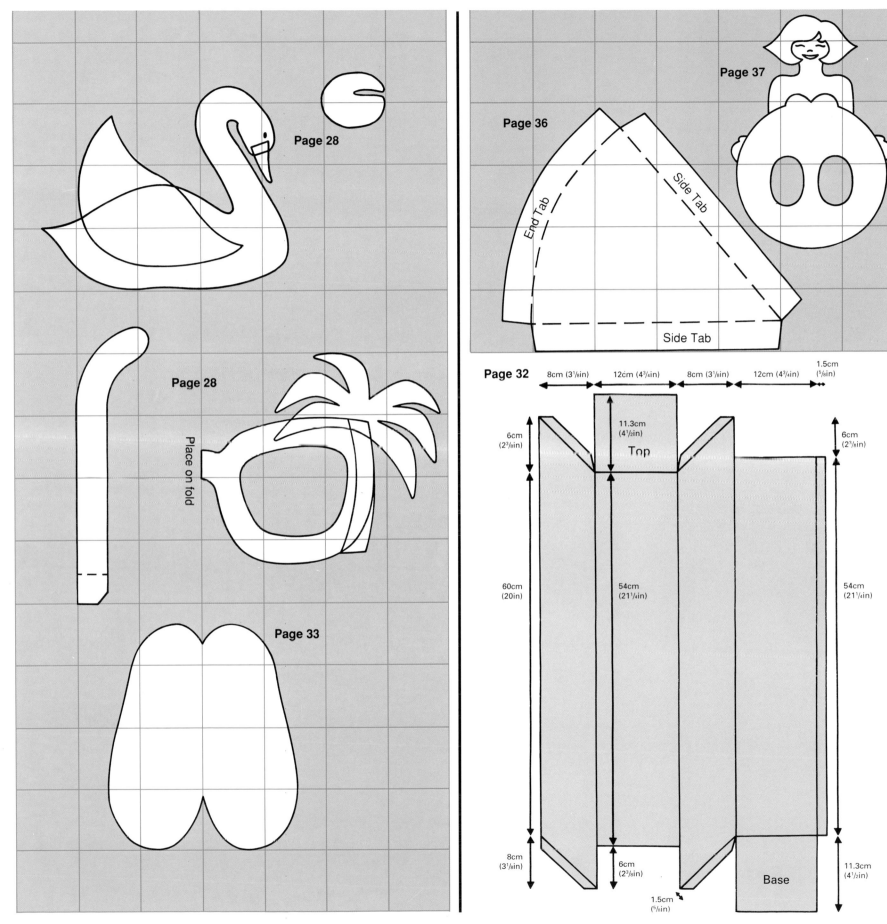

**Page 28**

**Page 28**

Place on fold

**Page 33**

**Page 36**

End Tab

Side Tab

Side Tab

**Page 37**

**Page 32**

8cm (3¹⁄₈in)    12cm (4³⁄₄in)    8cm (3¹⁄₈in)    12cm (4³⁄₄in)    1.5cm (⁵⁄₈in)

6cm (2³⁄₈in)

11.3cm (4¹⁄₂in)

Top

6cm (2³⁄₈in)

60cm (20in)

54cm (21¹⁄₄in)

54cm (21¹⁄₄in)

8cm (3¹⁄₈in)

6cm (2³⁄₈in)

1.5cm (⁵⁄₈in)

Base

11.3cm (4¹⁄₂in)

Don't spend a fortune buying party decorations, as this chapter will show you how to create a wide range of stunning effects at a low cost. From graceful paper garlands, to stylish fancy hats and jewelled masks, Christmas ornaments and festive wreaths, we include all that you might need to make your home look as festive as possible, and get everyone in the party mood. There are also designs to create your very own Advent Calendar, a pretty garland on which to hang your Christmas cards and a super winter sleigh to fill with sweets for a table centrepiece. Where possible we have included templates on page 59 to assist you.

Pull the cord and watch Santa dance. Use the template on page 59 to cut out the cardboard pieces. Cut one body and a pair of arms and legs from red cardboard. Mark the crosses on the back. Cut a pink face and glue to the head. Cut a white hat brim and beard, bobble and two cuffs. Glue the hat brim and beard over the face and the bobble to the top of the hat.

Cut out two green mittens, a black belt and two boots. Butt the straight ends of the mittens and arms together and glue cuffs over the joins. Wrap gold sticky tape around the middle of the belt and glue to the body. Glue the boot tops under the legs. Cut out a pink nose and glue on the face. Draw the eyes and mouth with felt-tipped pens.

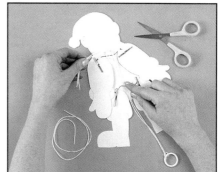

Mark dots on the limbs and attach to the body with paper fasteners at the crosses. Pull the limbs downwards on the back and tie the arms together with thread fastened through the dots. Tie the legs in the same way. Thread a small ring onto a double length of fine cord. Knot the cord around the legs' thread and then the arms' thread.

Cut a 3cm (1¼in) square of cardboard to use as a template for the doors. Draw around the square twenty-three times on the back of the tree, positioning the doors at random but leaving the trunk clear. Cut three sides of the doors, leave the right hand side 'hinged' so the door opens the right way on the other side.

On the right side of the tree, score the hinged side of each door lightly so it will open easily – but do not open the doors yet. Number the doors one to twenty-three with a silver pen.

Cut out small Christmas pictures from wrapping paper and used greeting cards. On the back of the tree, stick each picture behind a door by spreading paper glue on the tree around the doors.

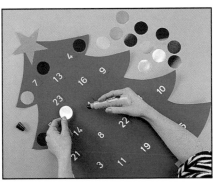

Decorate the calendar with a gold star on the top and circles of metallic cardboard between the doors.

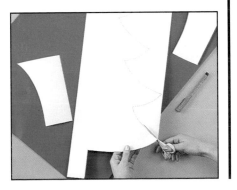

This Advent calendar can be used every year at Christmas. First make the Christmas tree pattern. Cut a piece of paper measuring about 63cm x 50cm (25in x 20in) and fold in half lengthwise. Draw half the tree with a trunk against the foldline and cut it out. Open out flat and use the pattern as a template to cut out the tree in green cardboard.

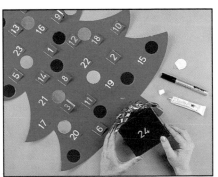

Write the number twenty-four on the front of a small red gift box with a silver pen. Stick a ribbon rosette on the top and glue the box onto the tree trunk. Fill the box with sweets. To finish, stick a picture hanger on the back of the calendar at the top.

These miniature lanterns make attractive Christmas tree ornaments. First take a piece of foil-covered paper 11cm (5½in) square. Fold it in half, and rule a line 1.5cm (¾in) from the loose edges. Now rule lines 1cm (½in) apart, from the fold up to this first line. Cut along these lines and open out the sheet of paper.

If you haven't any shiny bells for the Christmas tree, it's not difficult to make some from foil, beads and a little string. First take a saucer and mark around it onto the back of some coloured foil. Cut out the circle, then fold it in half, and cut along the fold line. Fold each half of the circle into a cone and glue it in place.

Hold the paper with the cuts running vertically, and glue the two sides together. When this is firm, set the lantern on the table and gently push the top down to make the sides poke outwards.

For the clapper, string a bead onto a length of thread — preferably waxed — and tie a knot over the bead. Lay the thread against the bell so that the clapper is at the right level, then tie a knot level with the hole in the top. This prevents the string from being pulled through the hole when threaded. Pull the string through the hole from the inside and thread on a smaller bead at the top; knot in place.

Finally, cut a strip of matching paper 13cm (5in) long and 1cm (½in) wide. Dab some glue on each end, and glue the strip onto the inside of the lantern, at the top, for a handle.

Finish each bell by dabbing a little glue around the bottom edge and sprinkling on some glitter. When you have made three bells, string them together, and attach them to a ring so that they can be hung on the tree. Wind a little tinsel wire around the string, and tie a couple of bows for that final touch of glamour.

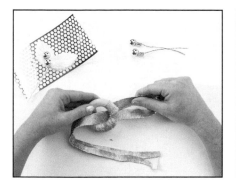

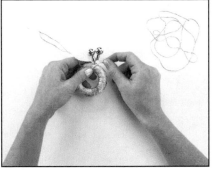

A dd a touch of regal splendour to your tree with these golden decorations. To make a miniatrue wreath, first wind the wires of two silk leaves and two small glass balls together, and bind with white florists' tape. Cut a 16cm (6½in) length from sequin waste. Next cut a long strip of gold crepe paper, fold the edges in and bind around a small wooden ring.

Tie a loop of gold thread around the ring at the paper join. Twist the leaf and ball stems around the ring over the thread, folding in the wire ends to secure.

Fold the ends of the sequin waste into the centre so that they overlap, with the selvedges at each side. Thread a long length of fine florists' wire down the middle, through all the layers. Then thread the wire back and pull up gently to make a bow shape. Twist the wires tightly to secure and bind them around the leaf wires. Arrange the leaves, bow and balls attractively over the ring.

To make a jewelled sphere, first wrap a polystyrene ball with gold crepe paper: cut a square of paper to fit generously, and pull it up tightly over the ball. Tie firmly around the gathered paper with a length of gold thread, and knot the ends of the thread to make a hanging loop. Cut a strip of crepe paper to make a bow and fold the raw edges in. Pinch the strip into a bow shape.

Run a line of clear adhesive around the ball and press a strip of beading trim into it. Repeat with a line of beading crossing in the opposite direction. Stick 'jewels' between the beads and large sequins, held in place with a pearl-headed pin. Trim the paper at the top of the sphere and attach the bow with a sequin trimmed pearl-headed pin.

**F**rom cartridge paper cut two rectangles, one 58cm x 10cm (23in x 4in), the other 58cm x 6.5cm (23in x 2½in). Mark each one into 12mm (½in) strips and draw a line 2.5cm (1in) from the long edge. Following your marks, cut out a zig-zag edge and pleat the strips. Use spray adhesive to stick gold foil to each side of the large rectangle, and silver foil to the smaller one.

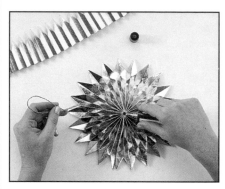

Pleat the gold strip again and fold it into a circle. Join the two ends with double-sided tape or glue and prevent the centre from popping up by smearing glue into the centre. Weight down the star with a book until it is dry. Next make a loop from gold thread from which to hang the star, and glue this to the centre of the star at the back.

Make up the silver star as before and place a double-sided adhesive pad on the centre back. Use this to attach the star to the gold star, aligning the pleats. Finally, put a little glue into the centre of the star and press a small glass ball in place.

**M**ake these delightful baskets to hang on your tree. Measure 4cm (1½in) up from the base of a yoghourt carton and cut round. Cut a 20cm (8in) diameter circle from crepe paper and cover the pot, stretching the paper up over the edges. Cover a cardboard circle with crepe paper to fit inside the base. Cut a handle 22cm (8½in) x 1.5cm (½in) from thin cardboard and cover.

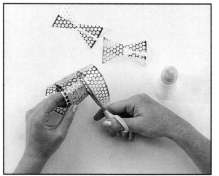

From sequin foil waste cut a strip long enough to wrap around the pot. Run a line of glue along the top and bottom of the pot and in one vertical line. Wrap the foil round, pressing into the glue, and trim, straightening the overlap along the vertical line of glue. Cut two strips 5cm (2in) wide from sequin waste, fold in half, selvedges level, and cut into bow shapes.

Staple the handle and foil bows each side of the basket. Tie bows from lengths of satin ribbon and stick over the foil bows with double-sided tape. Stick a double-sided adhesive pad in the bottom of the basket and arrange a bunch of glass balls on top.

# BLUE ANGEL

# SILVER BELLS

Cut a 10cm (4in) diameter semi-circle of silver cardboard, silver crepe paper and crinkly film. Trim the curve of the film in zig-zags and flute the crepe paper curve between your thumb and finger. Place the crepe paper on the cardboard with the film on top and glue together along the straight edges. Overlap the straight edges in a cone and glue.

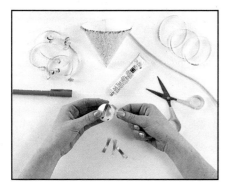

Draw eyes with a black pen on a 3.5cm (1½in) diameter cotton pulp ball. Cut short pieces of narrow giftwrap ribbon and glue to the head as a fringe. Cut longer pieces and pull the ends over a knife blade to curl them, then glue over the head. Glue ribbon around the head, then cut a slit in the base of the head and push the cone point through.

Cut silver crepe paper 11cm x 6cm (4½in x 2¼in) and flute the ends. Glue the long edges together and insert a 15cm (6in) pipecleaner for the arms through the tube and bend back the ends. Squeeze the centre and glue behind the cone, bending the arms forward. Use the template on page 59 to cut silver cardboard wings and glue them in place behind the angel.

To make these pretty silver bells cut out two bell shapes from cardboard. Peel the backing off some silver sticky-backed plastic and place the cut-outs on top, pressing firmly; then cut around them.

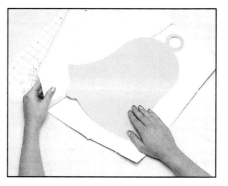

Glue the loops at the top of the bells together, spreading the bell shapes apart as shown.

Curl some gift wrap ribbon by running the blunt edge of a scissors blade along it; attach the ribbon to the bells. Finish off with a bow tied through the loops and some tiny birds cut from foil paper. The template for these is superimposed on the bell template.

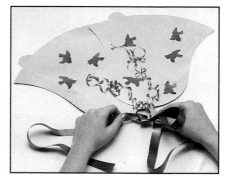

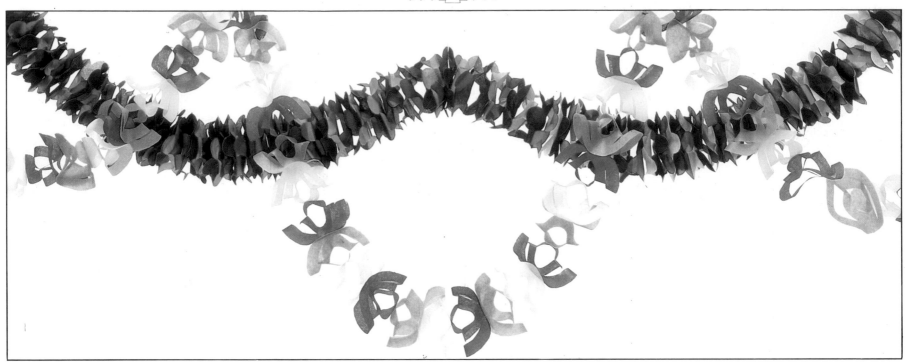

This graceful paper chain is made from circular pieces of tissue paper. First cut two circles of cardboard and lots of circles of tissue paper, all 10cm (4in) in diameter. Take about ten tissue paper circles and fold them together in four. If you use more than about ten layers, the folds won't be as good.

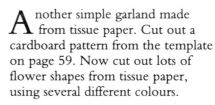

Now make two curved cuts as shown, from the single-folded edge almost to the double folds. Open out the circles. Glue the centre of the first circle to the middle of one cardboard circle.

Next, take the second tissue circle and glue it to the first at the top and bottom. Glue the third circle to the centre of the second circle. Continue in this way remembering to glue alternate circles in the same place at the top and bottom. If you alter the positioning you will spoil the effect. Finally glue the other cardboard circle to the last tissue circle to complete the garland.

Another simple garland made from tissue paper. Cut out a cardboard pattern from the template on page 59. Now cut out lots of flower shapes from tissue paper, using several different colours.

To start the garland, dab a little glue (one that won't soak through the thin paper) onto alternate petals of the first flower. Place the second flower on top and press them together.

Now on the second flower dab glue on the petals lying between those glued on the first flower. Take the third flower and press it firmly on top. Continue in this way, gluing petals in alternate positions, until the garland is long enough. Cut two extra cardboard shapes from the pattern and glue them to either end. Onto these tape a little loop of cord for hanging the garland.

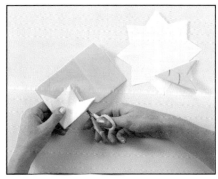

This garland is made from different coloured tissue paper stars. Refer to the template on page 59 to make the basic pattern from thin paper. Fold up to six layers of tissue paper into quarters, place a quarter of the paper pattern on top, edges level, and cut out. Fold the tissue paper in half again, (separate some of the layers if too bulky) and cut two slits in the positions marked in the photograph below. Cut a collection of different coloured tissue paper 'stars' in this way, plus two stars cut from cartridge paper for the garland ends. Glue a tissue star to each paper star using spray adhesive. Stick a small piece of double-sided tape to the centre of one tissue star and press this onto the centre of the tissue-covered paper star.

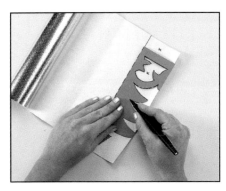

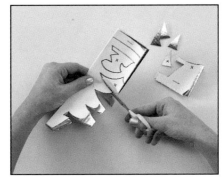

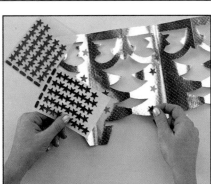

Next, place double-sided tape on four opposite points of the tissue star, and stick another star on top, aligning the points and slits. Keep repeating the sequence, pressing pieces of double-sided tape alternately to the centre, then to the four points, of each star, building up the layers until the garland is the required length. Finish by attaching the other end section.

Use this attractive frieze to decorate shelves, or to hang along a wall. From a length of foil gift wrap cut a long strip 23cm (9in) wide. Make a tree template from paper using the pattern on page 59 and line it up along one short edge of the gift wrap. Draw around the outline marking a fold line down the centre of the tree shape. Mark an X on each section to be cut out.

Fold the gift wrap concertina fashion along its length and staple the layers together above and below the pattern area to prevent the folds from slipping. Cut out through all the layers, using a craft knife to cut out the enclosed areas between the star and the bell shapes. Be careful not to cut through the folds at the edge.

Open the frieze out. The foil can be left in gentle folds, or pressed flat with a cool iron. Stick self-adhesive foil stars all over the trees. You can make the frieze to the required length simply by joining several frieze strips together, end to end, with sticky tape.

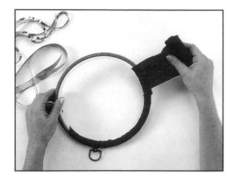

To make this festive ring, cut a long strip of crepe paper from the length of the roll, and bind a 20cm (8in) embroidery ring, securing the ends with double-sided tape near the hanging loop. Cut narrow gold ribbon about 110cm (43in) long and wind around the ring, securing with tape. Cut the same length from a gold sequin strip and wind between the ribbon.

Cut a strip of red crepe paper 1m (40in) long and 20cm (8in) wide; fold in half lengthways. Cut the same length from sequin waste and place over the crepe strip. Bind the centre with a long piece of florists' wire and trim ends into V-shape. Measure 23cm (9in) each side of the centre, bind with wire and fold the strip into a bow shape, holding it in shape with an adhesive pad.

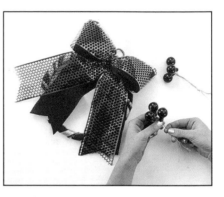

Use the trailing centre wires to secure the bow in position at the top of the ring and arrange the ribbon ends over the ring. Finally, wire three small glass balls together and wrap these around the bow centre.

# HOLLY WREATH

H ang this everlasting wreath on the door for a warm welcome to your visitors. Cut 5cm (2in) squares of green crepe paper and stick a small piece of masking tape in the centre for extra strength. Cut the point off a cocktail stick and use to make holes in a polystyrene ring. Push each square into a hole with the blunt end of the stick.

Continue pushing in squares until the ring is hidden. Take some artificial red berries on wires and push them into the wreath at random to decorate.

Tie a large bow of red satin ribbon. Bend a length of wire into a 'U' shape and thread through the back of the bow. Push the ends of the wire into the wreath.

This is a fun and simple way to hang up your Christmas cards. Simply take three long pieces of gift wrap or woven ribbon in red, green and gold, and plait them tightly together. Knot them at each end to hold them in place.

Now take some clothes pegs, lay them on several sheets of newspaper and spray them with gold paint. Turn them until all the sides have been covered and leave them to dry.

Fasten the ribbon to the wall at each end, and use the gold pegs to attach your Christmas cards to it. (If you prefer, and if you have some to spare, you could use tinsel instead of ribbon.)

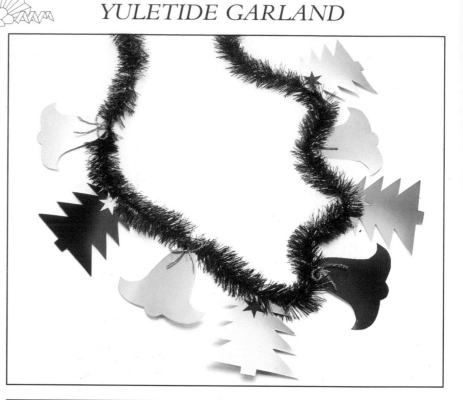

Here is a lovely sparkly garland to hang at Christmastime. If you want to make it for a birthday party instead, substitute little boxed gifts and bottles for the bells, and make trees in pastel colours. Cut the chosen shapes from foil-covered cardboard, marking them out on the wrong side. Be careful when cutting as foil cardboard tends to crinkle at the edges.

Make a tiny hole in the top of each, using a hole punch, or the tip of a skewer. Using red twine, tie each shape to a long strand of tinsel, leaving even spaces between them. At the top of each bell, fix a bow of gold-covered wire; on the trees, a little star.

Fill this sleigh with foil wrapped candies for a charming table centrepiece. Apply gold embossed paper to both sides of thick cardboard with spray glue and cut a pair of sleighs using the template on page 59. For the base, glue gold paper to both sides of a rectangle of thin cardboard 36cm x 16cm (14⅛in x 6¼in).

Mark the broken lines on the sleighs. Score along the base 1.5cm (⅝in) from each long edge. Snip away tiny triangles up to the scored lines so that the base will bend easily. Bend the snipped edge backwards at right angles.

Glue the snipped edges between the sleighs along the broken lines and lower, straight edges. Use the template to cut out two flowers in red foil paper and two leaves in green. Glue two leaves under each flower and glue three sequins in the middle. Glue a flower to each side of the sleigh and line it with scrunched up iridescent film.

For a stunning party mask, buy a ready-moulded mask from a stationer's or toy shop. The half-mask shown here is coloured with oil stencil pencils. Start with the pink; apply a little to a piece of waxed paper, then pick it up on the stencil brush. Using a circular motion, cover about half the mask. Repeat with the blue, filling in the gaps and giving the eyes a semblance of eyeliner.

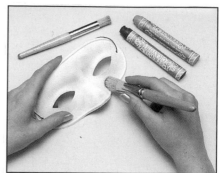

Next take a short length of lace and glue it to the back of the top half of the mask, down to where the elastic is attached. Glue some strands of curling gift wrap ribbon on either side. (Curl the ribbon by running the blunt edge of a pair of scissor along it.) Lastly, glue some large sequins over the tops of the ribbons to hide the ends, and glue another one in the centre of the forehead.

What could be simpler than these crisply-pleated paper fans, trimmed with curling ribbons? To begin, take a strip of printed wrapping paper and pleat it crosswise as shown.

For the black mask, first sew some silver tinsel wire around the edge and around the eyes. Sew on some pearl beads either side, then sew two or three grey or white feathers under the edges for an owlish look.

When you have finished the folding, hold the fan together by stapling it at one end. Cut some strips of gift wrap ribbon and run them along the edge of a ruler, or over a scissors blade, so that they curl.

Slip the ends of the ribbons between the folds of the fan and staple them in place. Finish by fixing a ribbon rosette over the stapled end.

Another beautiful mask to make; this one is lavishly jewelled. Spray glue two pieces of gold cardboard together for extra strength, then use the template on page 59 to cut out the mask. Stick double-sided tape to the top edge on the back of the mask. Cut a strip of iridescent film 50cm x 6cm (20in x 2¹⁄₄in). Scrunch up one long edge and press onto the tape.

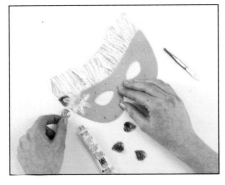

Glue an iridescent plastic flower to the left-hand corner. Glue small glass stones at random to the mask and stick one in the centre of the flower. A pair of tweezers is useful for holding tiny stones. Glue gold plastic leaves around the flower.

Spray a 30cm (12in) length of thin wood dowel gold and bind with narrow giftwrap ribbon. Glue the ends in place. Pull two lengths of giftwrap ribbon between your thumb and finger to coil them. Stick the ribbons to one end of the dowel with sticky tape and use a strong glue to stick the wooden handle behind the mask.

Here's a jaunty majorette's cap that is ideal for a fancy dress party. Cut a strip of coloured cardboard 60cm x 13cm (24in x 5in). Use the template on page 59 to cut out a peak in silver cardboard. On the wrong side, score the peak along the broken lines and make snips in the cardboard to the scored line. Bend the snipped edge upwards.

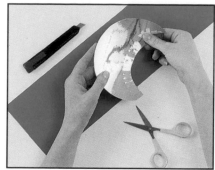

Stick an 18cm (7 in) long strip of double-sided tape in the middle of one long edge of the hat on the wrong side. Overlap the ends of the strip and lightly hold together with masking tape. Press the snipped edge of the peak onto the sticky tape. Remove the masking tape.

Wrap the hat around your head, overlapping the ends, and stick together with double-sided tape. Pleat a rectangle of foil giftwrap and bind the lower edge closed with clear sticky tape, forming a fan. Glue to the front of the hat. Finally, cut out a diamond shape from silver cardboard and glue it over the fan.

These conical hats are so easy to make that you will want to make one for each of your party guests. Cut a 30cm (12in) diameter circle of shiny cardboard for each hat and cut to the centre. Cut a slice out of the circle so that the hat is not too bulky. Overlap the cut edges and glue together.

There are many ways to decorate the hats – stick on gold stars or use glitter pens to draw a pattern. Another idea is to spread glue in moon shapes on the hat and then sprinkle on glitter, shaking off the excess.

Make a hole with the points of a pair of scissors each side of the hat and thread with hat elastic. Adjust the elastic to fit under the chin and make a knot behind the holes.

For this you need a large piece of black art paper, 38cm x 39.5cm (15in x 15½in). Mark a 1.5cm (½in) border at one end of the longer side so that you have a 38cm (15in) square. Take a compass, string and a white pencil and mark an arc between two corners. Cut along the arc, spread glue on the border, and use this to join the edges of the cone together.

Use the cone to mark a circle on some black cardboard. Draw another line around the first, about 5cm (2in) from it, then another just 2.5cm (1in) inside the first line. Cut along the inner and outer lines, then make triangular cuts on the inside of the brim. Fold them up and glue them to the inside of the cone. Decorate the hat with gold stars and moons cut from sticky-backed plastic.

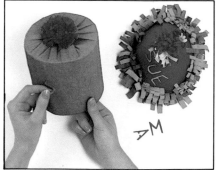

Essential wear at any children's party, these hats even bear the wearer's name. First cut the hats out of lightweight cardboard – a small circle and a rectangular piece for the fez and a semi-circular piece, about 15cm (6in) in diameter, for the conical hat. Glue the sides together to form a tube and a cone, and attach the top circle to the fez with tape. Cover the hats in crepe paper.

To make a tissue pom-pom, fold the tissue to get at least 12 layers, measuring 7cm (3in) square. Using a cup or glass, mark a circle on the paper, and cut it out. Staple the layers together at the centre. Cut strips into the centre, making them about 5mm (¼in) wide at the edge and stopping short of the staple. Fluff up the tissue paper to form a pom-pom.

Make pom-poms for both hats and attach them with glue or double-sided tape. Make a frill for the conical hat by cutting two lengths of crepe paper about 5cm (2in) deep and long enough to go around the edge of the rim. Neatly cut narrow strips about 2cm (¾in) deep on either side of the length to create a fringe. Staple the two layers of 'fringe' onto the rim of the hat.

Cut out paper letters from contrasting-coloured paper and glue names onto the front of each hat.

To make these fake neckties, first trace a pattern from a real necktie, making the top end just under 5cm (2in) across. Then draw a wide border all around this outline. Use the pattern to cut the shape from wrapping paper. Cut an inverted 'V' through the pointed end of the border up to the point of the tie. Fold the borders over, trimming off any excess paper.

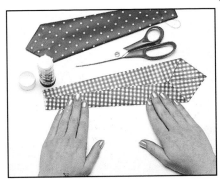

Fold under the top of the tie to hide the cut edge. Cut another piece of paper 10cm x 6cm (4in x 2½in). Fold in the long edges to meet, and wrap the band around the top of the tie. Firmly crease the folds on each side.

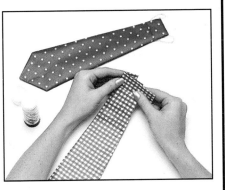

Now remove this piece and pierce a hole in the middle of each crease. Thread a piece of shirring elastic through the hole as shown; the elastic should fit comfortably around the neck. Knot the ends of the elastic, then glue the 'knot' to the tie, with the cut edges stuck down at the back.

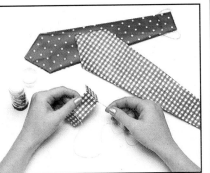

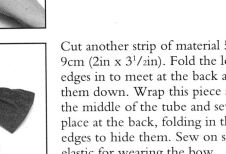

These party bow ties lend a dashing look to a costume. For the flat tie, cut a bow tie shape in thin cardboard. Simply cover the shape with foil, sticky-backed plastic or felt, and attach shirring elastic to the back.

Or make a soft fabric tie by cutting a strip of felt or other material 18cm (7in) square. Fold it in half, right sides together, and sew the long edges together to make a tube. Turn it right side out, and finish the raw edges by turning them in and slip-stitching them.

Cut another strip of material 5cm x 9cm (2in x 3½in). Fold the long edges in to meet at the back and glue them down. Wrap this piece around the middle of the tube and sew it in place at the back, folding in the raw edges to hide them. Sew on shirring elastic for wearing the bow.

If the day outside is gloomy, try brightening the outlook with some 'stained glass window' pictures. These are cut from black art paper and backed with coloured tissue. First cut pieces of art paper 38 by 30cm (15 by 12in). Mark a 3.5cm (1½in) border all the way round. Now draw your design, taking care that it is always connected in some way to the outer border.

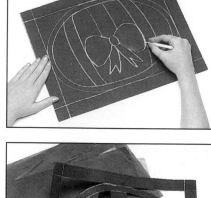

Next cut away any parts of the picture that you want to be coloured, taking care not to detach the black areas from the frame.

Now glue tissue paper to the back. For your first attempt use just one colour; then as you feel more confident, you can build up pictures using three or more different coloured tissues. When the picture is finished, affix it lightly to the windowpane, then watch what happens when the light shines through it.

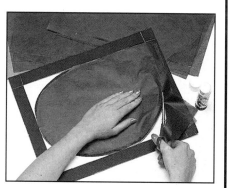

These are just as colourful as real balloons, but they won't pop, or even gently expire! Cut out balloon shapes from coloured cardboard or stiff paper, then cover them on one side with spray-on glitter.

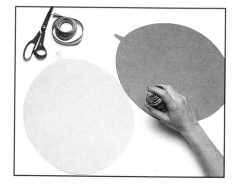

Two balloon shapes can be glued together at the edges, or they can all be strung up separately. Tape the balloons to a length of colourful striped ribbon.

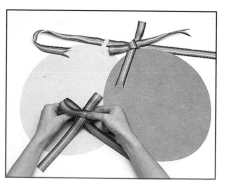

Lastly, use more of the same ribbon to make up some bows, and fix them to the balloons with some double-sided tape.

# TEMPLATES

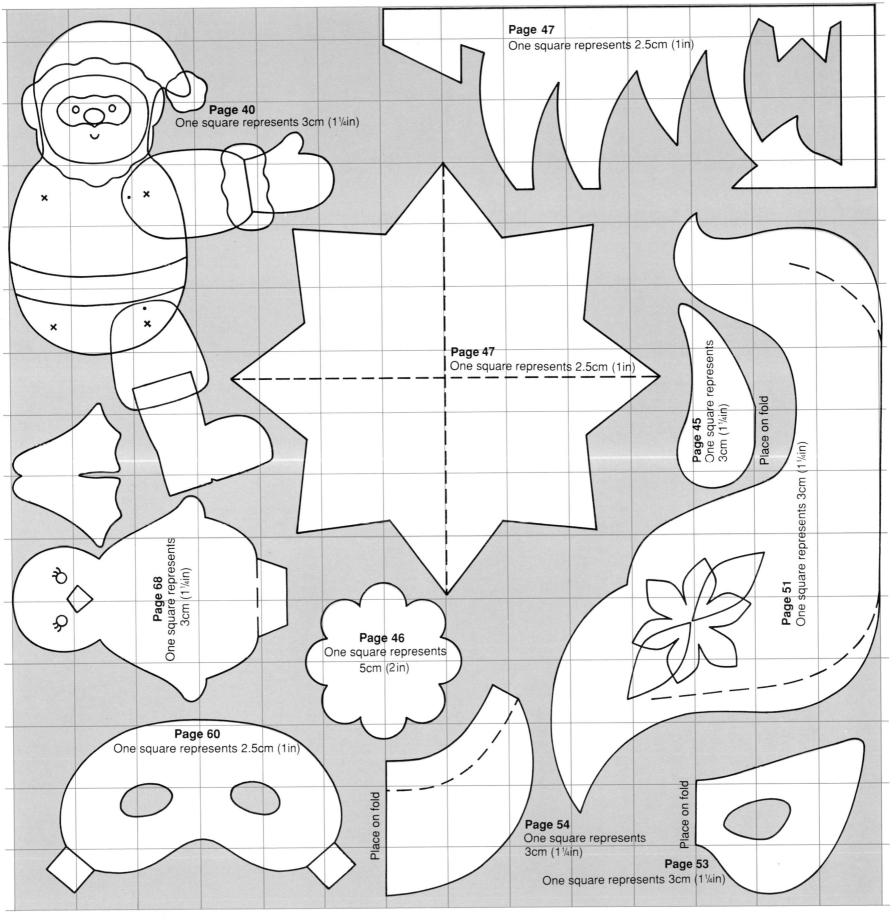

**Page 47**
One square represents 2.5cm (1in)

**Page 40**
One square represents 3cm (1¼in)

**Page 47**
One square represents 2.5cm (1in)

**Page 45**
One square represents 3cm (1¼in)

Place on fold

One square represents 3cm (1¼in)

**Page 51**
One square represents 3cm (1¼in)

**Page 68**
One square represents 3cm (1¼in)

**Page 46**
One square represents 5cm (2in)

Place on fold

**Page 60**
One square represents 2.5cm (1in)

**Page 54**
One square represents 3cm (1¼in)

Place on fold

**Page 53**
One square represents 3cm (1¼in)

Make that dinner or tea party extra special by creating table decorations in your own style, either to complement your china, the meal itself or simply the occasion. On the following pages you will find a range of ideas to transform your table. As the table centrepiece is often the most important feature we have included a number of beautiful and artistic designs. There are also clever and zany place cards to guide your guests to their seats, crackers for little take-home gifts, co-ordinating place settings as well as novel suggestions for prettying up plain napkins.

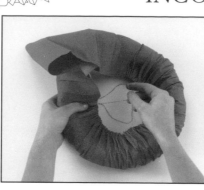

Adorn the New Year dinner table with this attractive centrepiece. Cut a length of magenta crepe paper 120cm x 20cm (48in x 8in). Stick the ends together on the wrong side with clear sticky tape. Place a 25cm (10in) diameter polystyrene ring in the middle and sew the long edges of crepe paper together with a running stitch, enclosing the polystyrene ring. Gather up the seam and fasten off.

Spray five candle holders white and push into the ring, evenly spaced apart. Then drape strings of white pearls and narrow green coiled gift wrapping ribbon around the ring, gluing the ends to the underside.

Stick two rectangles of metallic blue cardboard back to back with spray adhesive and cut out five masks using the template on page 59. Score gently along the fold line of the tabs and bend the tabs backwards. Stick each mask, by the tabs, in front of a candle. Decorate the ring with blue and green star-shaped sequins and silver stars cut from cardboard.

# MARZIPAN FRUIT PARCELS

# CONE CANDLE STAND

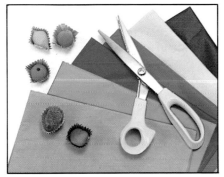

Exquisite marzipan fruits deserve special presentation. Nestling in little tissue 'parcels' and piled into a cake stand, they make a colourful centrepiece. All you need is several different colours of tissue paper and some pinking shears. Instead of marzipan fruits, you could use chocolates or marrons glacés.

Believe it or not, this arrangement is quite simple once you get the hang of folding the cones. You need two colours of foil paper. Cut out lots of boat shapes 16.5cm (6½in) along the top and 12.5 (5in) along the bottom and about 6cm (2½in) deep. Glue one colour to another, back-to-back.

From a double layer of one colour of tissue, cut a 10cm (4in) square. Pinking shears give an attractive serrated edge. From another colour of tissue, also double, cut a smaller square, measuring about 6cm (2½in).

Form each boat into a cone and glue it in place. The first few you make may not look too professional, but it doesn't matter; these can go on the outside of the stand and will be partially covered. You will soon get the hang of folding the cones. Bend the bottoms under; it helps to hold the shape and looks tidier.

Lay the smaller square on top of the larger one. Place the marzipan fruit in the centre and gather the tissue around it. Hold it in place for a few seconds and then let go; the crumpled tissue will retain its rosette shape. Place several of the parcels on a doily-lined glass or china cake stand.

When you have several cones made, start gluing them around the edge of a 20cm- (8in-) diameter silver cake board. Place another two layers inside the first, leaving room for a chunky candle in the middle.

This beautiful cracker is not designed to be pulled but to be taken home as a memento. First take a tube of cardboard and wrap white crepe paper around it. Insert short cardboard tubes into each end, leaving gaps of 5cm (2in) between the main and end sections. Cover the central and end sections on the outside with silver foil paper, and stick pink foil paper to the inside of the end sections.

Wind a length of silver sequin waste around the centre. Next take two strips of pink net and draw a piece of thread through the centre of each to gather it. Tie them at each end with a strip of curling gift wrap ribbon. (Curl the ribbon by running the blunt edge of a pair of scissors along it.)

Finish by decorating the cracker with large sequins and a pink foil heart, or with some other shape if you prefer. If you like, pop a little gift inside — a hand-made chocolate, perhaps, or even a diamond ring!

Make some spring flowers that will bloom throughout the year. For the base of each daffodil head, cut a section from an egg box and trim it down to an even edge. Use a yellow one if you can, or else paint it yellow. Next take a flexible paper or plastic straw and roll it in a strip of green tissue, gluing both long edges. Trim the ends and bend the straw without tearing the paper.

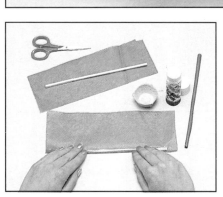

Cut out some yellow tissue petals and glue first one row, then a second, around the inside of the egg box base.

Finally, scrunch up a small piece of orange tissue paper and glue it to the centre of the flower.

# RIBBONS AND CURLS

# COLLAGE PLACE CARD

What could be prettier than this profusion of ribbons and flowers? The one shown is pink and white, but you should choose whatever matches your décor. First of all you will need a biscuit or cake tin. Cover the outside with silver foil paper, allowing a little extra at the top to turn over and glue. (This will be easier if you snip down to the tin.) Decorate it with strips of ribbon.

Take a block of florists' foam and cut it to fit inside the tin, using the extra bits to fill in the gaps around it.

Now wire up pieces of gift wrap ribbon, little baubles, strips of crepe paper and silk flowers. Curl the ribbon by running the blunt edge of a pair of scissors along it. Push the wires into the foam, arranging them until the tin is totally full. Use strips of ribbon around the outside, and let them fall over the side of the tin.

This collage place card can be made from wrapping paper and scraps of plain stiff paper. Select a gift-wrapping paper with a design that is appropriate to the theme of your party and plain paper in a harmonizing colour. Cut a rectangle of the plain paper about 14 by 9cm (5½ by 3½in) and fold it in half as shown.

Cut around the shape you have decided to use and stick this to the card with double-sided tape or glue.

Stick additional shapes onto the card as desired. Put double-sided tape onto the back of a small area of the wrapping paper, and cut thin strips with which to make up the names. Peel off the backing and attach the strips to the card to form the letters.

# HARLEQUIN PLACE CARD

Make cocktail glasses look extra smart with this chequered place card. First cut a 7.5cm (3in) square from a piece of stiff white cardboard. Use a pencil and ruler to mark off 2.5cm (1in) divisions and join these up to form a grid. Colour in alternate squares with a black felt pen to give a chequerboard pattern.

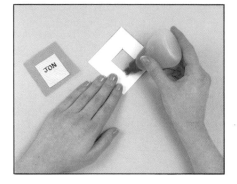

On a 5cm (2in) square of cardboard write the name. Cut out a 6cm (2½in)-square piece of pink net fabric; set it aside. Using a sharp craft knife, cut out the centre of the chequered card to leave a hole 2.5cm (1in) square. Turn the card over and apply some glue around the edges of the hole.

P!ace the piece of net over the card with the name, and hold them together in one hand while positioning the chequered card diagonally over the top. Press firmly to apply the glue to all three surfaces. Leave the card to dry for a few minutes.

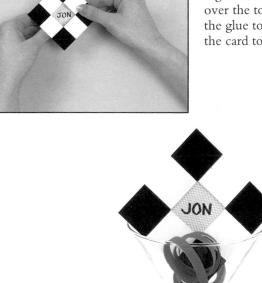

# HARLEQUIN PLACEMAT

This unusual placemat is easily made from cardboard and a wallpaper border. A black and white border has been chosen here, but you can use a colour which co-ordinates with your table setting. Cut a 30cm (12in) square from a sheet of thick cardboard, using a steel rule and craft knife to ensure precision.

Cut the border into four strips, allowing a little extra on each strip for trimming. Apply double-sided tape to the back of each strip, but do not peel off the protective backing yet. Lay two adjacent strips in place; where they meet at the corners, try to match the pattern repeat. Holding one strip on top of the other, cut diagonally across the corner.

Holding each strip in place along its inner edge, begin to peel back the protective paper from the double-sided tape, as shown. Rub a soft cloth along the border as you peel to stick it in place.

T hese unusual harlequin masks form the perfect party centre-piece, especially when co-ordinated with a black and white table setting, as shown on page 64. The masks can be bought or home-made from papier mâché. Paint each mask white.

With a pencil draw diagonal lines across the mask to create a grid. Don't worry if the squares are not exactly symmetrical. Paint alternate squares black.

Glue a length of black lace or net around the edge of the mask. Add coloured feathers and ribbons for the finishing touches. Stand the masks back to back so that one is facing each side of the table.

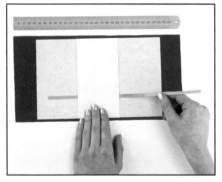

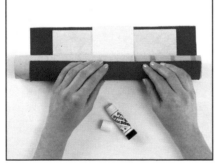

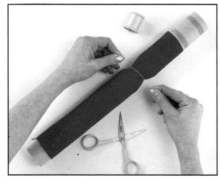

It is easy and economical to make crackers. Cut crepe paper 32cm x 16cm (12³⁄₄in x 6¹⁄₄in), keeping the grain of the paper parallel with the long sides. Lay a piece of thin writing paper 24cm x 15cm (9¹⁄₂in x 6in) centrally on top. Next cut thin cardboard 15cm x 8cm (6in x 3in) and lay it across the centre. Slip a cracker snap underneath.

Take two cardboard tubes, the sort found inside rolls of kitchen towel, and cut one in half. Lay the long tube on the lower edge of the crepe paper, with the end level with the cardboard edge. Butt a short tube against the long one and roll up tightly. Glue the overlapped edges of paper together with a low-tack adhesive.

Pull the short tube out for 5cm (2in) and tie thread tightly around the cracker between the tubes. Push the tubes together again then remove the short tube. Drop a gift, motto and paper hat inside and pull out the long tube a further 12.5cm (5in) . Tie thread tightly between the tube and cardboard inside the cracker. Untie the threads.

Cut two 25cm (10in) lengths of gold filigree lace – the kind that has a drawstring thread along one edge. Gather up the drawstring and tie the lace around the necks of the cracker. Gently stretch the ends of the cracker to flute the edge. Remove the drawstring from a length of lace and glue around the middle of the cracker. Glue a dried flower head in place to complete.

Gold and silver look stunning by candlelight and this festive arrangement will flatter any table setting. To begin, spray a vine garland with gold paint, sprinkle with gold glitter, and leave to dry.

Take three flat-based candle holders and stick florists' fixative putty under each one. Position them evenly-spaced around the garland using florists' wire to secure each holder firmly in place. To make the silver roses – four for each candle – cut strips of silver crepe paper 53cm (21in) long and 9cm (3½in) wide. Fold the strips in half lengthways and tuck the short ends in.

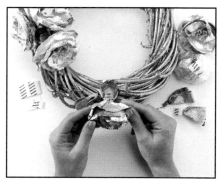

Run a strip of double-sided tape along the lower edge of a folded strip, and place a wired group of small gold balls at one end. Roll the crepe paper around the balls, removing the tape's backing paper as you go and pinching the paper tightly together at the base. When you have finished rolling, crimp the petal edges to curve outwards.

Stick a double-sided adhesive pad to the base of each rose and position four flowers around each candle holder. Cut 23cm (9in) lengths of gold ribbon and fold into double loops. Secure the ends with florists' wire and stick between the roses using adhesive pads. Tease the rose petals and gold loops into shape to hide the holders, and put candles in place.

Miniature holly sprigs give a festive touch to a place card. From thin cardboard cut a rectangle 7.5cm x 10cm (3in x 4in). Gently score across the centre, using a craft knife against a ruler, and fold the card in half. Punch a hole in the lower left side. Make a holly leaf template from thick paper and draw around the edge on to thick green paper (artist's Canson paper is ideal). Cut out.

Score lightly down the centre of each leaf and bend to shape. Bind a bunch of red flower stamens (available from craft shops) together with fine florists' wire and cut in half across the stems to create two bunches. Bind the stamens to the front of the leaves with red florists' tape.

Fold a short length of narrow curling ribbon in half, at a slight angle, and secure fold with a small piece of double-sided tape. Curl the ribbon against a scissor blade and stick to the front of the holly sprig. Write the name on the card and push the holly sprig through the punched hole, securing the stems to the back of the card with a small piece of sticky tape.

These cheerful chicks will guide guests to their seats for Easter tea. Use template on page 59 to cut out a chick in lemon coloured cardboard and a beak and feet in orange cardboard. Glue the beak to the chick and draw the eyes with a black felt-tipped pen.

Write the name of your guest with a pencil diagonally on the chick using a letter stencil. Fill in the letters with a felt-tipped pen.

Score along the broken lines on the chick and bend the tab backwards at a right angle. Glue the tab to the chick's feet.

# KITE PLACE CARDS

These colourful place cards are perfect for a children's party. For each kite you will need stiff paper in two colours. From each colour cut two rectangles, each 10 by 15cm (4 by 6in). Draw a line down the centre, then another line at right angles across it, 5cm (2in) from one end. Join up the points, then cut off the four corners; set them aside.

Use two of the corners of the red card to decorate the yellow kite, glueing them in place as shown. Similarly, use two of the leftover pieces of the yellow card to decorate the red kite. Write the name on each kite.

Cut out squares of coloured tissue, allowing three for each kite. On the back of each kite, glue a 40cm (16in) strip of thin ribbon. Pinch the squares of tissue together in the centre and tie the ribbon around them. Cut a small strip of cardboard, fold it in two and glue it to the back of the kite; use this hook to attach the kite to a glass.

# FREE-STYLE PLACE CARD

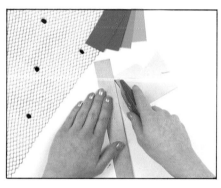

This original place card is simple to make using different colours of stiff paper and scraps of net. First cut a rectangle out of lightweight cardboard, twice the depth of the finished card; fold it in half. Using a craft knife and a steel ruler, cut sections of the card away to create an irregular edge. The cards can be any shape; in fact, it is more fun if they all look a little different.

From the coloured paper cut the letters to spell each guest's name. Don't try to cut rounded shapes, as this is more difficult. It may be easier to make some letters from two pieces. For a letter A, for example, cut a V shape, turn it upside down, and add a separate strip for the crossbar. Glue the letters in place.

Cut irregular pieces from a scrap of net, and lightly glue these in place over the name. Place each card on a plate on top of a folded napkin, as shown.

Quick and easy to make, this place mat will brighten up the supper table. Cut a wavy-edged rectangle of blue cardboard 35cm x 25cm (14in x 10in). Cut a row of wavy slits lengthwise across the mat with a craft knife.

This sparkling placemat is an obvious winner for Christmas. First draw a Christmas tree on the reverse (matt) side of a piece of shiny green cardboard. The length should be about 10cm (4in) longer than the diameter of your dinner plate and the width about 20cm (8in) wider. Cut out the mat using a craft knife and a steel ruler.

Cut wavy-edged strips 23cm (9in) long from green cardboard. Weave the first strip in and out of the slits close to one end. Weave in the remaining strips starting each alternate strip at the next slit up.

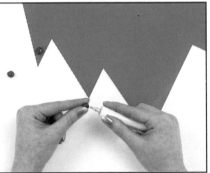

Add 'ornaments' by sticking tiny baubles to the tips of the tree using strong glue.

On the back, lift up the ends of the strips and glue to the mat. Make a matching coaster from a small wavy-edged square of cardboard.

Cut out or buy a star shape to put at the top of the tree. Finally, stick small silver stars over the mat. Or, if you prefer, just scatter the stars freely over the mat, first positioning each mat on the table.

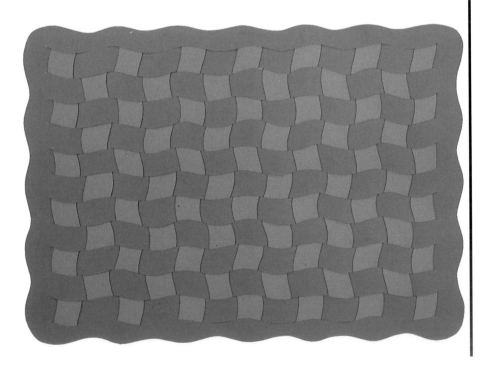

Christmas colours are woven together to make a matching table mat and napkin set. From cartridge paper cut out a

rectangle 37cm x 27cm (14½in x 10½in) and mark a 2.5cm (1in) border all round. Draw lines 12mm (½in) apart across the paper. Cut a piece of sticky-backed velour fabric a little larger all round and peel off the backing paper. Lay the rectangle centrally on top and, using a craft knife, cut through the drawn lines as shown. Fold overlapping fabric over and stick down.

Weave lengths of green and white paper rope through the cut stripes, arranging the ribbon so both ends pass under the border. Fold gold and silver crepe paper into narrow strips and weave over the green and white ribbon. Hold the strips in place with double-sided tape at both ends. Trim away the excess paper, then cut a piece of fabric to cover the back of the mat.

Cut a coaster mat from cartridge paper 17cm (6½in) square. Make a border as for the table mat, and mark, cover and cut in the same way. Weave with two lengths of each colour and cover the back with sticky-backed fabric as before.

To make the napkin ring, cut a strip from cartridge paper 17cm x 6.5cm (6½in x 2½in). Mark out a 12mm (½in) border and divide into strips 12mm (½in) apart. Cover with sticky-backed fabric, and cut strips as before. Weave green ribbon and silver or gold crepe through the slits and secure with double-sided tape. Cut a length of fabric for the backing and stick in place.

Join the two ends of the ring by overlapping them and securing with double-sided tape. Make a bow shape from white paper ribbon, binding the centre with fine florists' wire. Make a small bow shape from folded gold crepe paper and stick across the white bow with double-sided tape. Stick the completed bow across the join in the napkin ring using double-sided tape.

Here's a quick and simple way to dress up a plain napkin for afternoon tea. All you need is a square paper doily, preferably in a colour contrasting with the napkin, and a floral motif. Begin by folding the napkin into a triangle.

Here are a couple of ideas for jazzing up ordinary paper napkins. For the blue napkin, cut a star shape from a piece of cardboard — the cardboard must be slightly wider than the folded napkin. Hold the cardboard firmly in place over the napkin and spray silver or gold paint over the area. Let the paint dry for several minutes before you allow anything else to touch it.

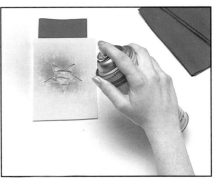

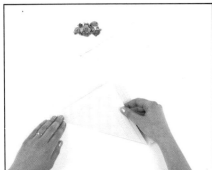

Fold the doily diagonally. To create a 'spine' to allow for the thickness of the napkin, unfold the doily and make another crease about 1cm (3/8in) from the first fold.

The white napkins have a design stencilled on them with oil-based stencil crayons. You can buy these separately or in packs, with ready-cut stencils. Choose your design, then place it over the area you want to stencil — in this case the corner of the napkin. Rub the crayon over a spare area of stencil, then take the colour up onto the brush and paint it over the stencil, in a circular motion.

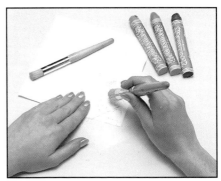

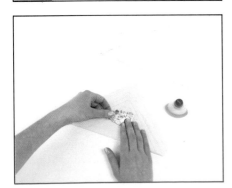

Cut out a Victorian scrap or other floral motif and glue it to the centre of the smaller (top) side of the doily. Insert the napkin.

Use the brush only over the parts you wish to show up in that colour. Now switch to the next colour. It is best to use a different brush for each colour if you want clear colour definition.

SECTION TWO

# GIFT WRAPPING & GREETING CARDS

One form of paper craft that most of us have practised
for years, probably without realizing it, is gift wrapping. Yet,
as we all know, it is so easy to run out of ideas. Well, no more. In this
section you will find over 80 imaginative ways to wrap gifts and add those all
important finishing touches. There are ideas for making your own attractive wrapping
papers, gift boxes and bags, hints on how to wrap a variety of different
shaped gifts, a wide and colourful range of pom-poms, rosettes and
unusual decorations, and some very pretty gift tags.

If you want to be really original, you can even make
your own greeting cards. The final chapter in this section
contains over 60 fun ideas for creating cards for all occassions; so
whether you wish to say 'Happy Birthday', 'Merry Christmas', 'Bon Voyage' or simply
ask someone to a party, you'll find just the card to suit you. And although
it's easy enough to make a base card out of lightweight coloured cardboard,
it's easier still to buy a 'card blank' from the
wide range now available in craft shops.

The huge selection of gift wraps on the market should give you plenty of scope for covering your presents. But you don't have to use a ready-made gift wrap — for real individuality and style, you can make your own. The following pages will give you plenty of ideas. For example, what about stencilling your own design, creating a collage, or printing a pattern with a humble potato?

And once you have your wrapping paper, there are lots of tips on how to use it properly, such as how to wrap a cylindrical gift neatly; or what to do with a spherical shape. For more, just read on.

*There's no excuse for an unimaginatively wrapped present with such a spectacular range of gift wrap available. Choose from plain, matt, shiny, pastel or bold colours, glossy or glittery designs, to make the most of your gift.*

# WRAPPING A RECTANGLE

# WRAPPING A CYLINDER

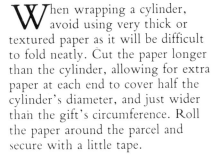

When wrapping a cylinder, avoid using very thick or textured paper as it will be difficult to fold neatly. Cut the paper longer than the cylinder, allowing for extra paper at each end to cover half the cylinder's diameter, and just wider than the gift's circumference. Roll the paper around the parcel and secure with a little tape.

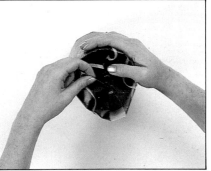

Begin folding the ends of the paper in a series of small triangles as shown here. Continue around the whole circumference, making sure that the 'triangles' are neatly folded into the centre.

Use a single piece of tape at the centre to fix all the folds in place. If the finished folds are not even, you could cheat a little by sticking a circle of matching gift wrap over each end of the cylinder.

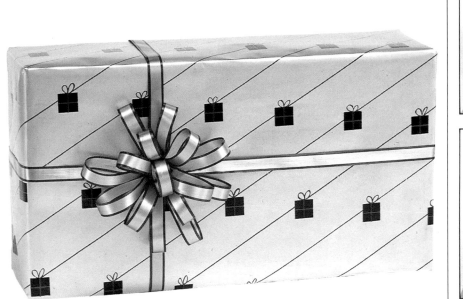

Wrapping square or rectangular presents isn't difficult — but perhaps your technique needs brushing up. Wrap the gift wrap tightly around the box. You can simply stick down the free edge with tape or, for a smarter effect, fold over the top edge of the paper and stick double-sided tape underneath it, leaving a neat fold visible at the join.

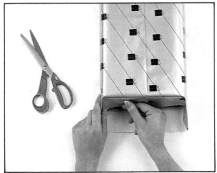

If your paper has a linear design, try to align the design so that the join is not too obvious. Fold the joined section of paper down over the end of the box to make a flap; crease the fold neatly. Trim off any excess paper so there is no unnecessary bulk.

Crease the side flaps firmly, and fold them over the ends of the gift. Smoothing your hand along the side of the box and round on to the end ensures that each flap fits tightly. Fold up the remaining triangular flap, pulling it firmly along the edge of the box, and stick down; use invisible tape (its matt surface is scarcely discernible) or double-sided for the best results.

The usual method of wrapping a sphere is to gather the paper around the gift and bunch it all together at the top. Here is a more stylish method. Put your circular gift in the centre of a square of paper, checking that the two sides of paper just meet at the top when wrapped around the gift. Cut off the corners of the square to form a circle of paper.

Bring one section of the paper to the top of the gift and begin to pleat it to fit the object as shown. The paper pleats at the top of the gift will end up at more or less the same point; hold them in place every three or four pleats with a tiny piece of sticky tape.

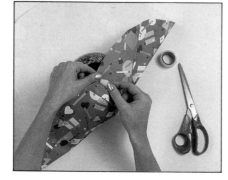

Continue pleating neatly and tightly all the way round the circle. It isn't as complicated or as time-consuming as it sounds once you've got the knack! When you have finished, the pile of pleats on top of the gift should look small and neat. Then you can either cover them with a small circle of paper stuck in place or, more attractively, add a bunch of colourful ribbons.

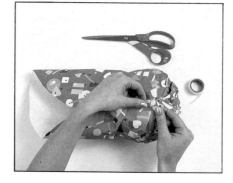

Wrapping awkwardly-shaped presents is just that — awkward. The gift wrap always looks creased and untidy around the angles of the gift. The solution is not to use paper — instead, use brightly-coloured cellophane which doesn't crumple. Cut a square of cellophane a great deal larger than your gift.

Gather the cellophane up and tie it into a bunch above the present. Fan out the excess and add some curled ribbon as a finishing touch. Alternatively, if your gift is cylindrical, roll it in cellophane somewhat longer than the parcel and gather the ends with ribbon.

Stylish, expensive-looking wrapping paper can be achieved very quickly with this method of spray stencilling. Choose some plain coloured paper for a base, and make your stencils from plain cardboard or paper. Cut the stencils into squares of two different sizes; alternatively you could use any kind of basic shape — stars, circles or whatever.

Lay some of the shapes in a random pattern across the plain paper, holding them in place with a spot of Plasticine or modelling clay. Cover the whole paper with paint spray. Use car paint or craft spray paint, but do carry it out in a well-ventilated room.

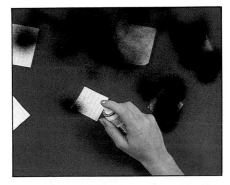

Once the paint is dry take off the sprayed squares and put a new random pattern of fresh squares across the paper. Overlap some of the original squares with the new ones to create interesting effects, then spray the entire sheet with a second colour of paint. Remove the squares and leave the wrapping paper to dry before using it.

Stencilling is great fun to do — and so easy. Design a simple motif then make a trace of it. With a soft pencil, scribble over the back of the trace and put the tracing paper face up on stencil cardboard. Draw round the design again, pressing hard so that the lines are transferred on to the cardboard beneath. Repeat the motif several times and cut out the shapes with a craft knife.

Position the cut-out stencil on plain paper, and either hold it or use masking tape to keep it in place. Mix up some poster paint, keeping the consistency quite thick. Apply the paint through the stencil, using a stiff brush. When you have finished a row of motifs, lift the stencil carefully and blot it on newspaper so that it is ready to use again. Leave the design to dry.

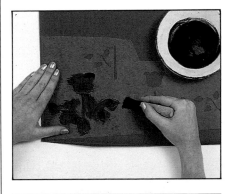

Keep repeating the process until you have covered enough paper to wrap your gift. To help you keep the spacing even between each run of motifs, add some 'markers' to the stencil. Cut half a motif at the end of the run and another one above the run to mark the position of the next row. Paint the markers along with the other motifs, then use this image for re-positioning the next row.

This method makes striking wrapping paper — with apologies to artist Jackson Pollock! Creating the pattern is great fun, but rather messy; cover your work area well with an old cloth or waste paper before you start. Begin by mixing up two or more colours in fairly runny poster paint.

All kinds of effects can be achieved with a sponge and some paint. You'll need a piece of natural sponge as man-made sponge doesn't produce the right effect. Choose some plain paper and mix up some poster paint to a fairly runny consistency. Test the paint on a spare piece of paper until you're happy with the colour.

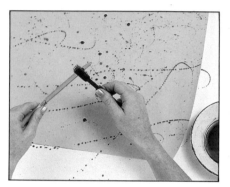

Load a paintbrush with colour, and, with a flicking movement, shake it across the sheet of paper. Repeat several times at various angles to cover the paper. Wait for the paint to dry.

Dip an old toothbrush in another colour paint, avoiding getting the brush too full of liquid. Rub the toothbrush across the blade of a knife to cause the paint to spatter over the paper. Repeat until the spattering is as dense as you like.

Dab the sponge into the paint and pat it evenly over the paper. The sponge should hold sufficient paint for about four 'dabs' before you need to dip it into the paint again. You'll need to mix up a lot of paint as the sponge absorbs a considerable amount.

Rinse the sponge out well and squeeze dry. When the paper has dried, repeat the process with another colour — you can use as many colours as you wish. Match the ribbon to one of the colours; see page 31 for instructions on how to create the ribbon trim shown here.

# -FLORAL COLLAGE-

Take a tip for decorating your gift from the Victorians, who made glorious scrapbooks and pictures using the art of collage. Collage looks best on plain paper; humble brown paper works admirably. Collect some flower catalogues and you're ready to begin.

From the illustrations of flowers, cut out as many shapes, sizes and colours as you like. Cut fairly accurately around the outline of each flower — it's fiddly, but worth it.

Lay the cut-out flowers on the wrapped parcel. Arrange the pictures in an attractive pattern, then stick them in place with glue. Finally, cut out individual flower petals to form the recipient's name. You can vary this idea by making a collage of a favourite cartoon character for a child or a current pop idol for a teenager.

# WHAT'S IN A NAME?

The ultimate in personalized gift wrapping — write the recipient's name all over it! Choose a plain wrapping paper, and three contrasting felt-tipped pens. Hold the pens together in a row and secure them with sticky tape. Before applying the tape, you must ensure the pens are level so that each pen writes with ease.

Write the recipient's name randomly across the page in a rounded, flamboyant style. You could vary the effect by grouping the pens in a cluster, rather than a row, or using four or even five pens. Another variation would be to write the name smaller in ordered columns, to give a striped effect.

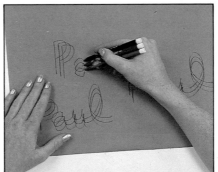

When you've finished covering the paper with the name, continue the three-tone theme of the gift by tying it up with three ribbons which match the colours of the pens. No one could mistake who this present is for!

# A GIFT IN A GIFT

# PAPER DUET

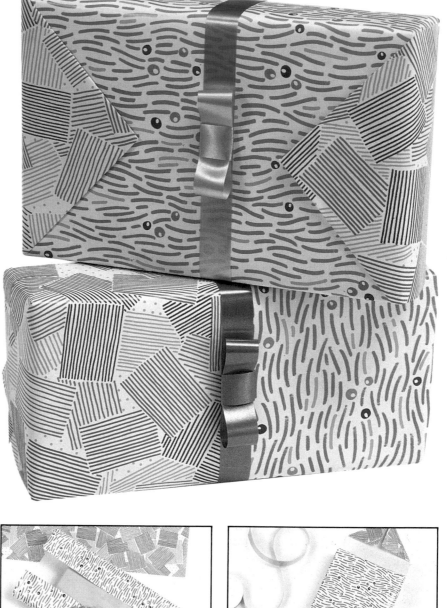

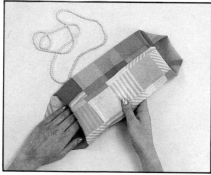

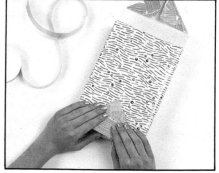

Why not wrap one gift in another? An attractive scarf makes an ideal covering. Fold the edges of the scarf over to make a conveniently-sized square and wrap the scarf around the other gift.

Tuck the top layer of each end of the scarf under the other present as shown, then fold up the end flaps. Use a ribbon or string of beads to hold the flaps in place. Alternatively, a couple of pretty handkerchiefs make a good wrapping for a small gift such as soap. Gather the hankies around the gift and secure in a bunch with a length of lace.

It is very annoying if the gift wrap you have bought is just too small to cover your present. The answer is to use two pieces of contrasting paper — the result can be very chic! Wrap your gift with one of the pieces of paper, using a strip of scrap paper to protect the gift from the tape. Fold in the ends neatly.

Cut the contrasting gift wrap into a strip the exact width of your parcel, long enough to cover the back and both ends plus two flaps. Use this strip to hide the uncovered back of the gift and fold it over the two ends. Make two flaps on the front of the parcel as shown and secure with double-sided tape. Alternatively, wrap each end of the parcel in different paper, hiding the join with a ribbon.

Employ a humble potato to create simple yet beautiful designs. Begin by cutting a large potato in half and draw a simple design on it. Use a sharp knife or craft knife to sculp the potato, leaving the design raised from the surface.

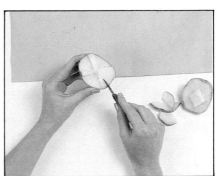

To ensure a regular print, draw a grid lightly in pencil on a sheet of plain paper. Then mix up fairly thick poster paint and apply it to the potato-cut with a paintbrush. Print the design in the middle of each square of the grid. You should be able to do two or three prints before the colour fades and needs replenishing.

Glittering wrapping paper is always glamorous, and with glitter available in such a variety of colours your creativity need know no bounds! Spread out a sheet of plain coloured paper and, using a bottle of glue with a fine nozzle, draw a series of simple patterns across it.

Cover the whole sheet with one design. Cut another design on another potato half; repeat the whole process, this time printing on the cross of the grid. When the paint is thoroughly dry, rub out the grid lines still visible and wrap up your present.

Sprinkle a line of glitter across the paper. Tip up the sheet and gently shake all the glitter from one side of the paper to the other, across the glued designs, making sure that all the patterns have been well covered. Tip the excess glitter off the page on to a sheet of newspaper; the glitter can then be used again.

Now use the glue to make more designs and coat these in glitter of a different colour. Localize the sprinkling of the glitter over the new patterns to be covered and leave to dry. Tip off the excess glitter and return it to its container.

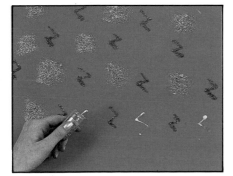

If the present you've bought is an awkward shape, why waste time and energy trying to wrap it up neatly? Make a box – or a bag – and just pop your gift inside. No more fuss or effort! And the person who receives your gift gets a bonus, since he or she can use the box or bag again afterwards.

On the following pages, there are instructions for making a number of different cardboard boxes, and two kinds of fabric bags. The patterns for the boxes can be found on pages 160–161, and by scaling them up or down you can make a box of any size you like.

*Why not try your hand at making a container from this smart selection of gift boxes and bags. They are totally professional in finish, yet remarkably straightforward to make.*

# IT'S A COVER-UP

# A LA CARTON

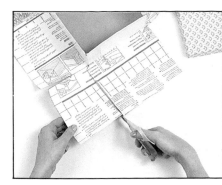

When re-covered in plastic, a shoe box makes a great container for a present. Put the box in the centre of a piece of self-adhesive plastic and draw around it. Then draw around the shape of the sides and ends of the box so you end up with a diagram of the 'exploded' box. Allow extra plastic all round for overlaps. Cut out the pattern you have just created.

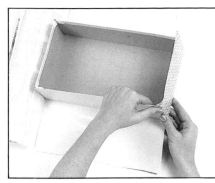

Peel the backing off the plastic and position the box carefully in the middle of the covering. Smooth the rest of the plastic up over the box, starting with the ends. Wrap the small overlap around the corners as shown.

Smooth the plastic up over the sides, trimming off the edges to make the pieces the exact size of the sides. Fold over the overlaps around the rim. Cover the lid in the same way. For complete co-ordination, you could cover the inside of the box to match. Alternatively, you could line the box with co-ordinating tissue paper or net.

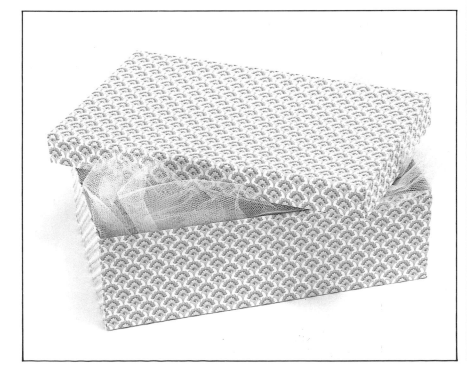

A handy gift container, ideal for home-made sweets, can be made from a well-washed juice carton. Draw V-shapes in each side of the carton. These should be inverted on two opposite sides, and pointing towards the top of the carton on the other two sides. Cut cleanly along the drawn lines with a craft knife as shown.

Cover the carton with gift wrap; adhesive in spray form achieves the best results. Make sure the join lies neatly down one corner of the box. Trim the overlap at the top of the carton so that it is even and fold the paper over the edges, taking care that the corners are neat. Punch a hole at the apex of both the pointed sides and thread ribbon through.

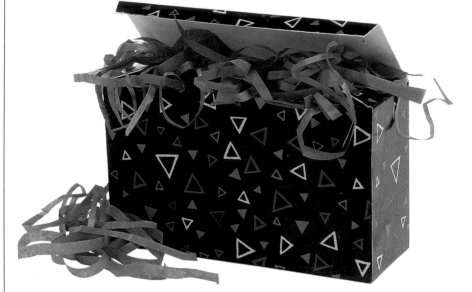

This cube-shaped box is ideal for containing any kind of gift and it can be made to any size. Measure out the shape of the box on to thin cardboard, following the template on page 160. It's very important that all the squares are exactly the same size and that all the angles are right angles. Cut out the shape, and score along the fold lines – the back of a craft knife is useful for doing this.

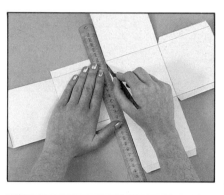

Bend the card carefully along the score lines, making a neat crease along each fold. Crease the flaps on the lid and base and fold the four sides into the shape of the box.

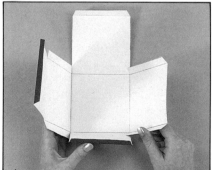

Stick the side flap to its opposite side as shown. You can glue this, or alternatively, use double-sided tape. Fold in the base flap – it should fit precisely and thus give the box rigidity. Finally close the lid flap.

Making a box from scratch can be a little complicated, so why not start with an empty cereal packet? Take your cereal packet and carefully open it out flat. Separating the joins needs care – if necessary slide a knife between the seams to part the glue, rather than tear the packet.

Draw the box you want, using the template on page 160 as a reference. Make sure the lid measures the same as the width of the side panels. Cut out the new shape with a pair of scissors, and cover it with your chosen gift wrap. Spray adhesive is best, since this gives a very smooth finish, however glue in a stick form will do. When the glue has dried, cut neatly around the cardboard shape.

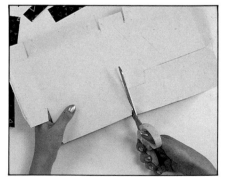

Score along the new fold lines of the box using the back of a craft knife or the blunt edge of a pair of scissors. Fold the box into shape. Stick the side flap in place as shown; you can use double-sided tape or glue. Fix the two flaps on the bottom (either glue or tape them). Put in some shredded tissue as padding, slot in your gift and tuck the lid neatly into place.

# DIAMONDS ARE FOREVER

# PUT A LID ON IT

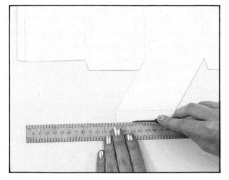

A variation on the cube gives this box an unusual diamond shape. Draw the template on page 160 on to thin coloured cardboard. Check that all the sides are the same size, and that their angles measure 90°; the angles of the lid and base should measure about 60° and 120°. Cut out the shape with a craft knife.

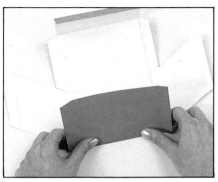

Score along the fold lines on the sides and flaps of the box with the back of a craft knife or the blunt edge of a pair of scissors. Fold the scored edges over, making sure that they are well creased for a crisp shape.

Fit the box together, sticking down the side flap with glue or double-sided tape. Fold in the base and the lid; it is the shape of these which converts the box from being an ordinary cube into the more exotic diamond shape.

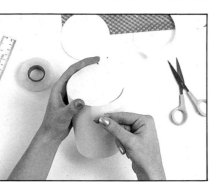

A cylindrical box looks much more difficult to make than it is. Wrap a piece of thin cardboard around the gift to determine the measurement of the box. Cut out the cardboard, roll it up and stick down the edge with a length of tape. Draw and cut out a circular base, and a slightly larger circle for the lid. Attach the base with small bits of tape.

Cut a strip of cardboard slightly longer than the circumference of the cylinder. To make the lid, stick the edge of the strip to the edge of the circle with tape. Next, spread glue on some gift wrap and roll the cylinder in it. Cut the paper to fit, allowing an overlap each end. Tuck the overlap into the open end; secure. Fold the base overlap in a series of small triangles and stick to the base.

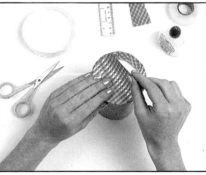

Draw a circle of gift wrap slightly smaller than the base. Cut it out and glue in position, hiding all the folds and bits of tape. Cover the lid in the same way. If you like, you can punch two holes in each side of the container and thread through short lengths of decorative braid.

S mart handles give this box style; they are also the mechanism for closing it. Use coloured cardboard for the box; if you try to cover the box pattern with gift wrap it will lift off. Copy the template on page 161, scaling it up or down if you wish. Use a compass to draw the handles. Cut out the shape with a craft knife, taking great care with the handles and their slots.

Score along all the fold lines using the back of a craft knife; crease them well. Fold the carton into shape, and stick down the side flap with double sided tape or glue. Fold the base down, pushing the flap inside the box to secure it.

Close the first two flaps of the lid, folding the handles up to fit. Pinch the handles together and fold the two top flaps of the lid over them, fitting the handles through the slots.

T his attractive and unusual bag will add prestige to any present. Draw the template featured on page 160 on to a sheet of thin cardboard with the aid of a compass and a protractor; use a pencil as some of the design will need to be erased later. Cut out the circle and score along the lines of the 'star' and the central octagon with a sharp edge – the back of a craft knife will do.

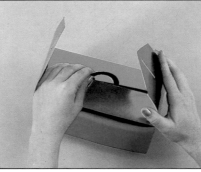

Take care not to overscore along the intersections of the lines, as the cardboard could eventually tear. Rub out any line not scored. Bend along the edges of the octagon, being careful not to crease the sides. Then fold along the arms of the 'star', to form a series of triangles (these will come together to form the container for your gift).

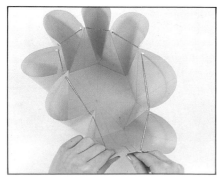

Folding the box needs patience, but it's not as complicated as it looks! When the folding is complete, punch holes either side of the top of each triangle (see the template) and thread the ribbon through the holes as shown. Arrange the curved edges so that they radiate out from the centre. You can make the bag any size you want; as a guide, though, ours had a diameter of 40cm (16in).

# TRIANGULAR TREAT

A plant is a notoriously difficult item to wrap; here's a smart solution. Measure an equilateral triangle on some coloured cardboard. The length of each side should be twice the height of the plant; use a protractor to ensure all the angles measure 60°.

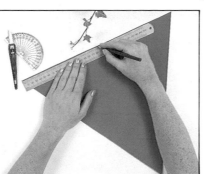

Divide each of the three sides of the triangle in half. Join all the half marks together to form an inner equilateral triangle; this will form the base. Bend the card along a ruler at each inner line as shown and bring up the sides to form a three-dimensional triangle. Punch a hole in each apex and thread ribbon through to close the parcel; double length ribbon gives a pretty finishing touch.

# SMART SACHETS

These sachets are ideal for ties, soaps, scarves, jewellery, hankies, socks and so forth. On to thin cardboard, trace the template on page 161. It's probably more interesting to cover the shape with gift wrap as shown here, but you can use plain cardboard if you wish. If using gift wrap, cut out the shape and paste it on to your chosen wrapping paper.

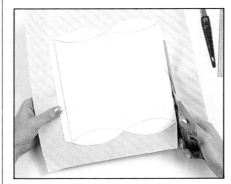

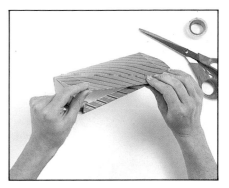

Cut out the covered shape. Then score well along the curved lines of the ellipses which will form the overlapping ends of the packet. Use the back of a craft knife or the blunt side of a pair of scissors to make the score marks.

Stick the side flaps together with either double-sided tape or glue. Fold in the ends; if you've scored the lines sufficiently they should pop in easily with just a little guidance. They can be re-opened with no difficulty but make sure the covering gift wrap doesn't begin to lift off the cardboard.

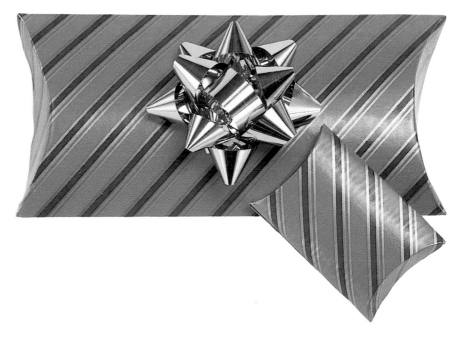

# LITTLE BOXES

# THE PYRAMIDS

T his method is best suited to a small box as the end result is not particularly strong. From thin cardboard, cut out a cross-shaped piece as shown, made up of four sides and a base, all the same size and all absolutely square. The lid will also be a square measuring 5mm (¼in) larger than the base, with sides about 2cm (¾in) deep.

Paste both shapes on to gift wrap and when dry cut off the gift wrap around the box and lid, leaving a small turning or flap around each edge. Fold in the flap on the left of each side of the box and glue it down as shown. Score along the edges of what will be the base, to form fold lines for the sides of the box.

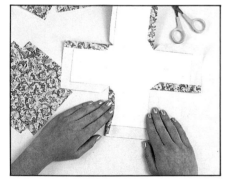

Bend the sides upwards. Put glue on the patterned side of the flaps of gift wrap left unfolded on each side; stick these flaps inside the box to the adjacent sides as illustrated. Crease down the sides firmly and leave to dry. Finally, fold in and glue the top lip. Treat the lid in exactly the same way.

T hese rigid little boxes are ideal for presenting jewellery but you can make them to fit anything you like. Choose thin cardboard, either in the colour you want the finished box to be, or white so that you can cover it later with gift wrap. Measure out the template on page 161. The size of the triangular sides doesn't matter, as long as they are all the same, and the base is a true square.

Cut out along the exterior lines with a craft knife. If you're covering the cardboard shape with gift wrap, do it at this stage, cutting the paper to fit. Score along all the fold lines carefully, using the back of the craft knife, then bend the box along the score marks creasing firmly.

Punch holes in each apex and fold the box into its pyramidal shape. Thread the ribbon in and out of the four holes and, making sure all the side-folds are tucked inside the box, tie the loose ends together with a bow.

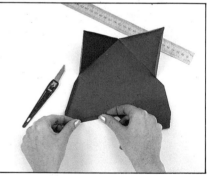

# BOXED IN

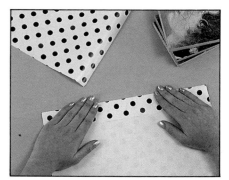

BAGS OF GOODIES

Gift bags are very useful as containers for awkwardly-shaped presents and they can be made to any size. Find something with the required dimensions of the finished bag to serve as a mould – a pile of books should suffice. Choose a good quality, strong gift wrap for making the bag. Cut a strip of gift wrap long enough to wrap round the 'mould' and fold over the top edge.

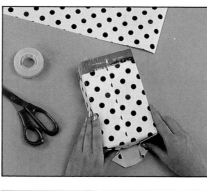

Wrap the paper round the mould; glue or use double-sided tape to join the seam at the back. Fold over the end flaps in the usual way of wrapping any parcel to make the base of the bag; be sure to attach sufficient tape to make the base strong.

This small narrow box would be ideal for giving someone a watch or a piece of jewellery – unless, of course, you make it bigger! Trace off the template on page 161 on to thin cardboard. Cut it out, and either cover it in gift wrap or, if you like the colour of the cardboard, just leave it plain.

Cut around the template with small sharp scissors to trim away the excess gift wrap; take extra care with the slots and handles. Then score along all the fold lines, using the back of the craft knife or the blunt edge of the scissors.

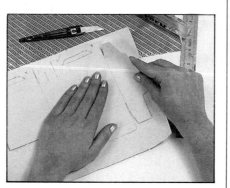

Slip the mould out. Fold in the sides of the bag, creasing them in half at the top; fold the base up over the back of the bag. Punch two holes, spaced apart, at the top of the front and back of the bag as shown. Thread through a length of cord to form a handle; knot each end inside the bag. Repeat on the other side. Alternatively, you could thread the bag with ribbons.

Crease all the folds properly. Fold the box into shape and stick the side flap to the inside of the opposite side. Close the top section, being sure to fold the lid sections upright as shown, halfway across at the point where the two handles meet. Fold over the end flaps and slot them in position to close the box. Finally close the base.

## MAKING AN ORIGAMI ENVELOPE

An origami envelope is a novel way to present a card or a gift token. You need an accurate square of any kind of paper. We cut a piece of paper 33cm (13in) square. Take your square, fold a diagonal line across and crease. Fold again in the opposite direction, do not crease but mark centre with a light press.

Open up and then fold corner up to the centre mark on your first diagonal crease. Smooth crease firmly with your fingers.

Fold again on original diagonal crease. Smooth down firmly with both hands.

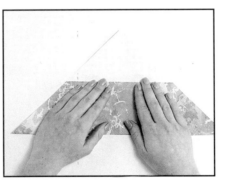

Divide this fold into three and fold right-hand point over to meet first third, and left-hand point to meet new side fold. Smooth up side creases firmly. Fold back front point so that it meets left-hand fold and crease firmly.

Open up this triangle, so that it becomes a diamond, into which the top flap will tuck to close the envelope.

Measure your folded card generously and draw out measurement onto a large piece of paper. Mark centre with a cross. Measure distance from cross to top of card and add on same again, plus 1cm (³/₈in) for overlap, to form apex of top flap. Repeat for bottom, then side flaps but exclude extra for overlap. Rule flaps in pencil.

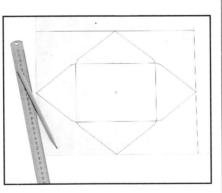

Cut out your envelope, score (if using card) and fold in side flaps. Fold in bottom flap and glue to side flaps using a glue pen. Glue down top flap when you have written your card.

# FABRIC ENVELOPE

# IT'S IN THE BAG

A flat gift can be slipped into this pretty and useful fabric envelope. Make a paper pattern measuring about 5cm (2in) wider than your gift and two and a half times its depth, cutting a shallow V shape at one end for the flap. Fold your fabric in half and position the paper pattern with the straight edge opposite the pointed end on the fold. Pin it on and cut the fabric out.

With right sides of the fabric together, pin and sew around the edges, leaving a small opening of about 7.5cm (3in); this is to enable the bag to be turned inside out. Turn the bag and press it. Then sew up the gap which was left. You can of course sew all this by hand if you prefer.

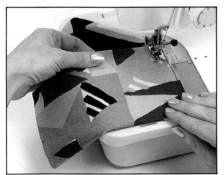

Fold the strip into an envelope shape, with the pointed flap at the top. Pin up the edges carefully and sew them in position with a double row of stitching as shown. Sew a length of ribbon on to the back of the bag with a couple of smaller stitches, pop in the present and tie the ribbon in a bow at the front.

A few pretty soaps are a doubly welcome gift when wrapped in one of these pretty fabric draw-string bags. Cut a strip of cotton fabric about 5cm (2in) wider than you want the finished bag to be, and about 10cm (4in) longer. Turn in about 5cm (2in) at the top of each edge and run a double line of stitching along it to form a channel for the draw-strings.

Pin the side seams with the right sides of the fabric together, making sure the tops of both sides match. Sew the seams, leaving a gap at each end of the draw-string channel. If you don't have a sewing machine, the sewing can be done easily by hand.

Turn the bag right side out and press it. Get some ribbon four times longer than the width of the bag and cut it in half. Attach a safety pin to the end of one half; thread it and the ribbon through the channels around the top of the bag so that both ends come out of one side. Knot the ends. Thread the other ribbon through both channels too, so the ends come from the other side; knot these too.

Usually it's easy to guess the contents of a parcel that is a recognisable shape, but not if you disguise it! In this section, a bottle turns into a pencil, a record becomes a kite, a cube is given interest as a dice and a round gift turns into a birthday cake.

The exciting ideas on the following pages are good not only for covering awkward shapes or disguising 'obvious' presents, such as bottles, books and records; they also provide novel ideas for wrapping presents for children. Gift wrapping for special occasions, such as Valentine's Day and Christmas, calls for extra inspiration; try the ideas on pages 97 and 99 to start you off.

*Whether your present is for Christmas, Valentine's Day or a christening, you can have great fun wrapping it to match the occasion. Or how about disguising it as a birthday cake or a domino? No one will ever guess what's inside.*

A romantic padded heart containing a little gift is perfect to give on Valentine's Day! Cut out two heart shapes from cardboard, one about 4cm (1½in) larger all round than the other. From red lining fabric, cut out a heart shape a little bigger than the larger heart. Take a gift box, wrap it in cotton wool (absorbent cotton) and place it on top of the smaller heart.

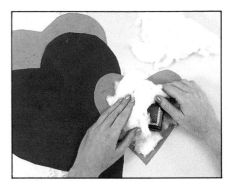

When there's enough padding, cover the heart in the red lining, stretching it over the heart shape and sticking it firmly in position on the back with plenty of tape. You'll need to snip the fabric around the inverted point of the heart so that the fabric can open out to fit properly.

Cover the larger heart in white tissue paper, otherwise the brown surface may show through the lacey doily. Cut off a frill of about 5cm (2in) from the edge of four or five doilies, and pleat them up around the edge of the large heart, fixing them with tape as shown. When the whole heart has been edged like this, apply some strong glue to the middle and place the padded heart in position.

Cube-shaped presents will look more interesting disguised as dice — and it's fun if a small, flat gift becomes a domino. For the dice, make sure the gift is a perfect cube by measuring it; the idea won't work well unless it is. Cover the gift with black paper. Then draw several circles on white paper; an easy way of doing this is by tracing the outline of a suitably sized coin.

Cut out the circles carefully and lay them on the box; glue them in place. Look at a real dice to get the juxtaposition of the sides correct. The domino can be treated in the same way.

This heart of woven paper can hold a Valentine's Day gift. Lightweight paper in contrasting colours gives the best effect. Cut a strip of paper 25cm by 10cm (10in by 4in) and draw the template on page 161 on to it. Cut the shape out and fold it in half. Then cut the two slits as indicated on the template. Repeat with another strip of paper in a different colour.

Hold a section of the heart in each hand, as shown, with the strips pointing upwards. Weave the two sections together, starting with the two inner strips. You need to open out each strip to slot the other strip through it, as illustrated.

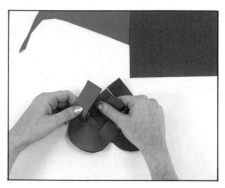

Continue doing this until all the strips are interwoven. It is fairly fiddly but does work; it's clear at this stage why you need lightweight but strong paper! The finished item will open out like a basket, so that it can hold small gifts. The basket would also be very pretty made in felt.

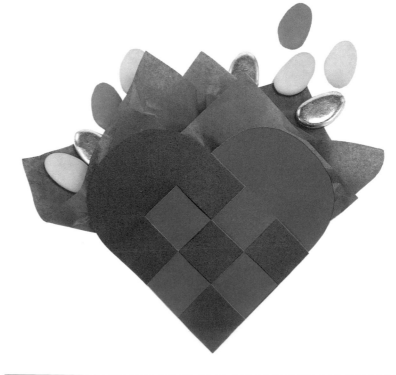

Disguise a bottle as a pencil and keep the recipient guessing! Make a cylinder, about 5cm (2in) shorter than the bottle, from light cardboard, join the sides with tape. Draw a third section of a circle – about 7.5cm (3in) radius – on pale cardboard and cut it out. Roll it in to a cone shape, running the flat edge of a pair of scissors along it to help it curl. Tape in place.

Make a small cone for the lead of the pencil and glue it on to the larger cone. Attach several lengths of sticky tape to the inside edge of the cone and, putting your arm inside the cylinder, stick the tape down to hold the cone in position. Fit the pencil over the bottle and secure with two strips of tape across the bottom.

W hat fun for a child to see Frosty and know that the snowman's hiding a gift! Wrap up a cylindrical gift in paper to form the body of the snowman. Crush newspaper into a shape for the head and stick it on top of the gift. Cover the body with cotton wool (absorbent cotton), sticking it on with dabs of glue. Create a face from bits of paper and stick in place.

For the hat you need a strip of cardboard, plus a circle big enough to make the brim. Draw an inner circle in the brim, the diameter of Frosty's head; cut it out to form the 'lid' of the hat. Roll the strip of cardboard up to form the crown of the hat; stick it in place with tape.

Stick on the top of the hat, then attach the brim, putting strips of tape inside the crown. Paint the hat with black poster paint; it'll need two or three coats. Wrap around the red ribbon to form a cheery hat-band and put it on Frosty's head. Fray the ends of some patterned ribbon to form a scarf and tie it firmly in place.

B righten up a dull-looking, flat gift by turning it into a playing card. Wrap the present in plain white paper. Make a template for the spade by folding a piece of paper in half and drawing half the outline against the fold; this way the design will be symmetrical. Trace around the template on to black paper and cut the shape out. Stick the spade in the centre of the 'card'.

Cut two small spades for the corner designs. Then, using a ruler, draw an 'A' in two of the corners, being careful to make them both the same. Glue the small spades underneath. Cut a piece of patterned paper – smaller than the card – and stick it on the back. You could vary the idea by making the King or Queen of Hearts for your husband or wife, or the ten of clubs for a ten-year-old.

**M**ake a small present look that extra bit special — and that extra bit bigger! Wrap the gift into a ball shape, then cut a strip of paper about three times the width of the gift and long enough to form loops on each side of it. Fold the edges over. Gather small pleats at each end, securing them with sticky tape. Pinch-pleat four gathers in the middle of the strip and secure.

For the trailing sections of the bow, cut a five-sided piece of paper as shown. Fold over the edges in to the centre at the back and secure with tape. Gather pinch pleats at one end and secure. At the other end cut out a V-shaped section to form a nicely-shaped tail. Repeat the procedure a second time.

Turn the pleated ends of the long strip to the middle to form the loops, and secure with double-sided tape. Stick the tails under the bow with more tape. Finally, put double-sided tape over the join on top of the bow and stick the gift in position. Puff out the loops so they look nice and full.

**J**ust the disguise if you're giving a cylinder-shaped gift to a child — the famous British red pillar-box (mailbox). You could of course adapt the idea and make a rocket, for example. Cut a strip of thin red cardboard to fit around your gift; secure it around the gift with sticky tape. Draw a circle for the lid, larger than the diameter of the cylinder; cut a line to its centre as shown.

Overlap the cut edges slightly to form a shallow cone, then fix with sticky tape on the wrong side. Wrap one end of the post-box with black paper, folding it over to prevent the present from falling out. Put double-sided tape around the inside of the lid and stick in position. Add a narrow black rectangle for the posting slit and a white rectangle for the notice of collection times.

Here's another clever idea for disguising a record. Get two large squares of cardboard; the side of a box will do. Position the record in one corner as shown and draw a line from the bottom right corner of the record to the top right corner of the cardboard. Draw a second rule from the top left corner of the record to complete the kite shape. Repeat for the other square.

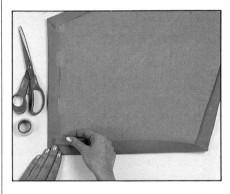

Cut out the shapes and sandwich the record between them. Cover one side in coloured paper, folding over the edges and fixing them with sticky tape on the reverse. Cut another piece of paper slightly smaller than the cardboard shape; glue it in position on the back of the kite.

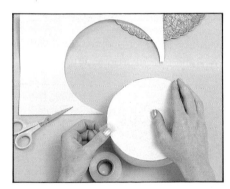

A cake, plus candle, is just the right disguise for a birthday present! First, make a drum-shaped frame for the cake; cut a strip of thin cardboard just wider than your present, curl it in a circle big enough to cover your gift and stick it in place with sticky tape. Cut a circle to fit as a lid; attach it with strips of tape.

Draw two lines joining the four corners of the kite, and put contrasting tape along them; take care not to stretch the tape as it will pucker the paper. Cut out as many paper bow shapes as you want for the kite's tail. Attach the bows with double-sided tape or glue to a length of ribbon and stick the tail in position behind the longest point of the kite.

Cut a strip of white paper to cover the sides of the drum and glue it in position. Tuck one edge of the paper under the open end of the drum and trim the other edge close to the top of the drum to leave a small turning. Cut a series of small nicks in the turning and fold the flaps over, taping them to the lid. Cut a circle slightly smaller than the circumference of the drum and glue it in place.

Place the present inside the cake and put it on a cake stand. Cut two lengths of cord to fit round the circumference of the cake and glue the ends to prevent them from unravelling. Glue one piece to the top of the cake to form 'icing', and the second piece around the bottom, to fix the cake to the stand. Finally, put the candle in the holder and pierce through the centre of the cake.

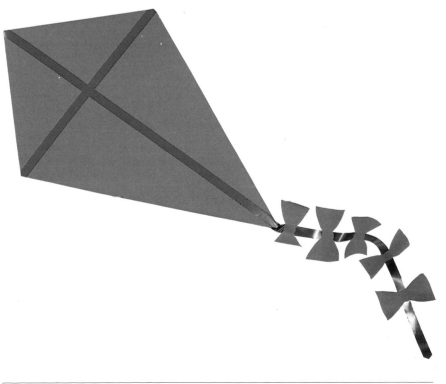

The decorative details on a gift can make all the difference to the finished article. The gift wrap might be bright and jolly, but if the present has no decoration it can look very dull. Even a pretty bow can provide the finishing touch, turning a plain parcel into a chic gift.

Buying ribbon pom-poms can make gift wrapping very expensive. Instead, try making your own decorations. In this section you'll find instructions for different types of decoration, using ribbon, tassels, foil, paper, flowers, and even pot pourri, tights (pantyhose) and sweets! Looking for a special finishing touch for a Christmas or Easter gift? Try the novel designs on pages 110 and 111.

*Reels of gift ribbon can be turned into a vast array of different decorations; from stunning rosettes that you couldn't distinguish from shop-bought versions to individual and original pom-poms. Braid, cord, tissues and even candy can be used to decorate your gifts and make parcels that extra bit special.*

A pom-pom bow adds a cheerful touch to a present of any shape or size. Use the kind of ribbon which will stick to itself when moistened. Cut seven strips; four measuring about 30cm (12in), the other three about 23cm (9in). You'll also need a small piece of ribbon about 5cm (2in), for the central loop.

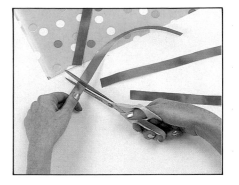

Overlap the ends of each of the long strips and moisten them; stick them together to form a loop. Moisten the centre of each loop and stick it together as shown. Cross two of the looped strips, joining them at the central point. Repeat with the other two loops. Join both crosses together so the loops are evenly spaced apart.

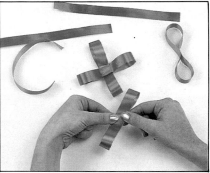

Loop the three shorter lengths, and cross them over each other, fixing them together at the centre. Stick the resulting star in the middle of the large rosette. Fill in the centre with the tiny loop. Obviously, the length and width of ribbon can be varied, according to the size you want the finished pom-pom to be.

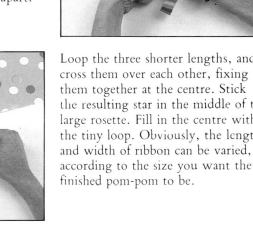

Here is an easy way to achieve a very pretty effect. Choose three colours of narrow ribbon which co-ordinate with your gift wrap. Using one ribbon, tie it around your parcel in the usual way, crossing it underneath the parcel and knotting it tightly on top; leave long ends. Tie a length of different coloured ribbon to the centre point, then do the same with a third colour.

Continue tying on lengths of ribbon so that you end up with two lengths, (that is, four ends) of each colour. Tie the central knots tightly to keep them as small as possible. Pull a ribbon length gently along the open blade of a pair of scissors; this will cause it to curl into ringlets. Repeat with each length until they are as curly as you want.

An alternative is to use wide gift ribbon. Tie it round the parcel once, making sure that the knot is as neat as possible and leaving long ends. Cut two small nicks in the ribbon, dividing it evenly into three; pull it to split the ribbon up to the knot. Run each of these lengths along the blade of a pair of scissors until they form ringlets.

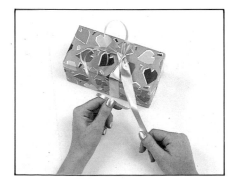

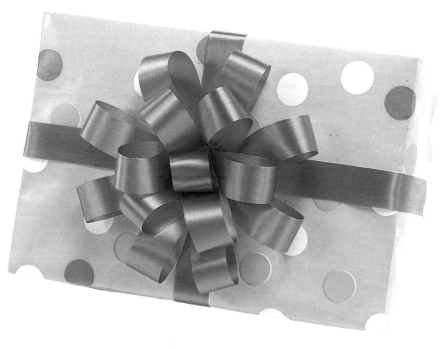

# TWISTED TRIM

This trimming can be made to match or contrast with the wrapping. You will need the type of ribbon which sticks to itself when dampened; choose whatever colours you like. The smallest strip of ribbon measures about 20cm (8in); cut it out and twist it into the shape of a figure '8'.

Twist the ribbon shape to form a point at each end as shown, then secure it in position by dampening the tape. Cut the next strip, about 7.5cm (3in) bigger; repeat the process. Put the smaller shape on top and in the centre of the new shape; fix it in place.

Make four other figures-of-eight, cutting each one about 7.5cm (3in) longer than the last. Pile them all up and fix them together in the centre. Put the decoration on your gift and attach it by wrapping ribbon round it and the parcel. Finally, arrange it so that each loop is raised above the others and not overlapping as they're inclined to do!

# A POINT TO REMEMBER

You couldn't distinguish this pointed pom-pom from a shop-bought version — yet it's a fraction of the price! Use ribbon which sticks to itself when moistened. Make a small loop by wrapping the ribbon round your thumb; moisten the ribbon and fix it in place. Now twist the ribbon back on itself to form a pointed loop, as shown; stick it in position.

Go on looping the ribbon in twists, spacing them evenly as you go. It is fairly fiddly but keep trying — you'll soon master the technique. You'll probably need to wait a minute between each fixing for the ribbon's glue to dry before turning the next loop.

Continue winding outwards in a circle until the bow is as big as you want; cut off the ribbon, leaving a small tail just visible. Attach the pom-pom to the present with double-sided tape.

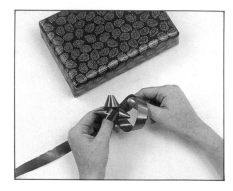

# ELIZABETHAN BOW

# FLOPPY BOW

The scrolled shapes of this decoration are reminiscent of the curlicues embellishing Queen Elizabeth I's signature. Wrap up your present, and choose some gift wrapping ribbon to match or contrast with the colours of the gift wrap. Hold the end of the ribbon in one hand, and form a loop as shown, leaving a small tail.

Make a corresponding loop below, forming a figure-of-eight shape. This will be the size of the finished product; adjust the proportion of the loops at this stage if you want a bigger or smaller bow. Continue folding loops of the same size until you have as many as you want — seven at each end is usually enough.

Check that all the loops are the same size, and pinch them all together by wrapping a piece of sticky tape around the middle. You can then hide this by wrapping a small piece of matching ribbon over it. Attach it to the present with double-sided tape.

This bow, with its floppy loops, gives a soft, casual effect. You'll need about 2m (6ft) of acetate or craft ribbon, 2.5cm (1in) wide. Cut off about 30cm (12in) ribbon; wind the rest round your fingers. Holding the ribbon firmly, make a notch in both edges with a pair of scissors as shown, cutting through all the layers of ribbon.

Take the ribbon off your hand and notch the edges of the opposite side of the loops. Flatten the loops so that the notches match in the centre and loops are formed either side. Take the 30cm (12in) length of ribbon and tie it tightly around the notches as shown.

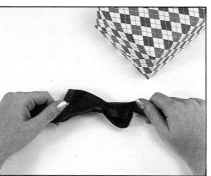

Starting with the innermost loop on one side of the folded bow, gently pull each loop away from the other loops and into the centre of the bow. You'll end up with each loop being visible, thus forming the shape of the finished rosette.

It's hard to believe that these pretty flowers and the butterfly are made from tights (pantyhose) and fuse wire. Cut up a pair of discarded tights or stockings. Cut some 15 amp fuse wire into lengths, some shorter than others, suitable for making petals. Make a circular shape out of each length and twist the ends together.

Put a piece of stocking material over a wire circle and pull it tight, making sure that the whole circle is covered. Fix it in position by firmly winding matching cotton around the twisted stem of the wire. Cut off the excess fabric.

Take seven petals, smaller ones in the centre, and bind them all tightly with thread. Bend the petals around until you're happy with the look of the flower. Tie up your parcel with ribbon and attach the flower with double-sided tape. The butterfly is made in just the same way: two pairs of 'petals' are bound together with thread, then bent into the shape of wings.

How to give a tall thin present even more presence! Take a spool of gift ribbon — the sort that sticks to itself when moistened. Roll a length round your thumb to form a small circle; moisten and stick in position.

Make another ring, larger than the first; stick that down too. Make another circle, and another, ensuring that their increase in size is in the same proportion each time. Four circles is about the maximum the ribbon can take before flopping slightly and thus losing the crispness of the decoration.

This decoration looks best on a rectangular gift. Take 66cm (26in) of woven ribbon; lay it flat. Measure 13cm (5in) from one end of the ribbon and mark both edges. Then mark along the ribbon's length a further 10cm (4in), 7.5cm (3in), 5cm (2in), 7.5cm (3in), 10cm (4in). Using one piece of thread, pick up tiny stitches at each mark along one edge.

Run a similar gathering thread up the other edge of ribbon, making sure that the stitches are exactly level on both sides. Gather up the loops as shown; it's easiest to knot the two threads together at one end of the gathers and ease the loops along.

Pull the thread tight to make properly-formed loops; sew the joins in place and cut off the excess thread. Tie the ribbon around the gift and use double-sided tape to attach the loops in the centre of the long side of the gift. Snip a diagonal cut at the ends of the ribbon tails.

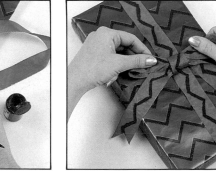

It is quite easy to paint wide ribbon to co-ordinate with your wrapping paper. And the results are stunning! Choose a gift wrap with a simple design. Decide whether you want the ribbon to be a positive version of the paper's design, like the blue example shown here, or a negative one, like the black and white suggestions. Experiment with poster paint on your chosen ribbon.

Keep the design very simple and stylized. When you're happy with your pattern, paint enough ribbon to wrap up the gift, allowing sufficient for a fairly large bow. Leave the ribbon to dry thoroughly before tying it around the parcel. If the paint does crack a little when tying up the ribbon, simply touch it up and leave it to dry again.

## CREPE PAPER RUFFLE

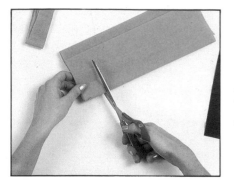

Crepe paper is the ideal material to make a stylish ruffle. There's such a range of colours to choose from, too. For each ruffle, cut two strips of crepe paper, one a little wider than the other. They should both be half as long again as the circumference of the parcel.

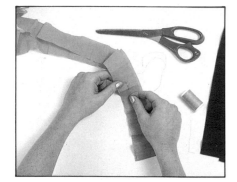

Lay the two strips flat, with the narrower one on top. Sew them both together with matching thread, running a gathering thread down the centre. Gather the strips slightly.

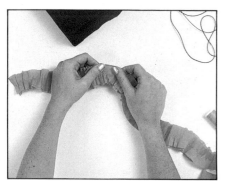

Gently stretch the crepe between both hands along the entire length of the strip; this will create a more ruffled effect. Do each strip separately, then make another ruffle. Wrap the ruffles around the gift, sticking the ends with tape. Tie narrow cord in the middle of the strips to hide the gathering stitches; fluff up the crepe ruffles either side.

## RIBBON ROSETTES

A winning idea for any gift! Cut a length of fairly wide ribbon; you'll need about 30cm (12in) for each rosette. Fold it in half with the right sides of the ribbon together; sew up the two ends to form a seam.

Using tiny stitches, gather up one edge of the ribbon. Pull the gathering thread tight, arranging the rosette into a neat circle as you do so. Finish it off by sewing across the base. Make as many rosettes as you need and attach them to your parcel with double-sided tape.

# ROSEBUDS

# IT'S IN THE NEWS

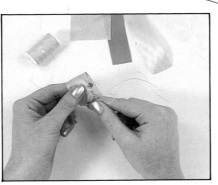

A small posy of pretty rosebuds is always acceptable — make as many as you like! Cut a small length of ribbon — about 6-9cm (2-3½in), depending on the width of ribbon you've chosen. Fold the ribbon in half, right sides together, and join the two ends with a small seam. Run a gathering thread around one edge.

Pull the gathering thread tight to form the rosebud; sew it firmly across the base. Make another two or three buds and sew them all together at the base; you may need to add the occasional supporting stitch at the top edges to hold the buds close together.

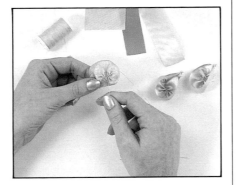

The leaves add an attractive contrast. They are made from a strip of green ribbon, two corners of which have been folded over to form a point. Fix with double-sided tape since glue can leave a mark on ribbon. The illustration below shows the rosebuds grouped on a length of ribbon twice the width of the flowers, set off with narrow green ribbon.

W hat do you do when you haven't any gift wrap and the shops are shut? You use newspaper! The flower on top gives the parcel a stunning and stylish finish. To create the flower cut several lengths of newspaper, some about 15cm (6in) wide, some a little narrower. Fold one strip in half lengthways, and make a series of cuts along its folded edge as shown here.

When you've cut along the whole length, roll up the resulting looped fringe. Secure it at the base by winding a piece of sticky tape round it. Fluff out the 'petals' of the flower.

Use up all the strips of paper in the same way. Gather the sections together, smaller ones on the outside. Join them all with tape; leave the ends unstuck and use them to attach the flower to the gift. You can even match the paper to the recipient; use a financial newspaper for a businessman, a comic for a child, a glossy magazine for a lady of leisure.

# POINTED STAR

# SWEETS FOR MY SWEET

Craft foil is the perfect material for creating this decoration. Use a compass to draw four circles; the ones shown here measure 8cm (3in), 6.5cm (2½in) 5cm (2in) and 4cm (1½in) in diameter. Draw an inner ring of 2cm (¾in) in the centre of each circle. Rule lines to divide the circles evenly into eighths; cut along the lines to the inner circle to make eight segments.

A sweet treat for children of all ages! Boiled sweets (hard candies) with plain cellophane wrappers look best because of their clear colours, but you can use alternatives such as toffees or peppermints. Select five or six of the chosen sweets, and hold them in a bunch by one end of their wrappers.

Roll each segment of the circle into a cone; use a dab of glue to secure it. Make sure that each cone shape has a good sharp point by rolling it fairly tightly. The process is a bit fiddly; you may find it easier to roll each cone around the point of a stencil to give it shape. Repeat with the other circles.

Take a narrow piece of ribbon and tie all the sweets together tightly; if the wrappers are a little short it may help to bind them first with sewing thread. Leave a reasonably long piece of ribbon on each side of the bunch of sweets so that you can attach it easily to the parcel.

Starting with the largest star shape, glue all the stars inside each other, positioning the points of each star between those of the preceding ones. When the glue is dry, gently bend each cone of the middle two stars towards the centre, to fill in the central space, so forming a semi-circular three-dimensional star.

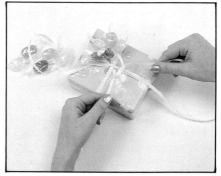

Tie the same ribbon around the parcel, leaving the ends long, then tie the sweets to the centre point as shown. Curl up each ribbon end by pulling it gently along the open blade of a pair of scissors. Try to co-ordinate your gift wrap with the chosen confectionery — black and white paper with humbugs, for example, would look very attractive.

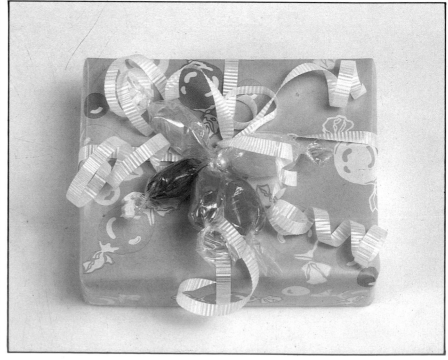

# BUTTERFLIES AND BOWS      TISSUE TWISTS

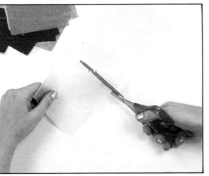

You can make these decorations in a single colour, but they look more effective if you choose several. For each twist, you need three squares of tissue for the outer colour, two for the middle colour and two for the inner (most visible) section. The squares needed for the inner section are smaller than those for the outside; the middle leaves must be of a size in between.

Pick up the squares in order, putting one on top of the other; outer colour first, then the middle, then the inner squares. Position them so that the corners of each square are at a different angle, as shown. Put a couple of stitches through the centre point to secure all the squares together and leave some thread hanging.

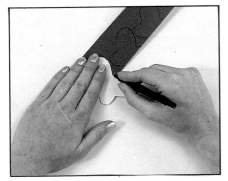

An interesting effect is achieved by attaching three-dimensional decorations all over your parcel. Wrap your gift in plain coloured paper. For the butterflies, take a strip of contrasting plain paper and fold it in half. Draw a butterfly shape on thin cardboard; cut it out and trace round half of it as shown on to the coloured paper. Draw as many as you want to cover the gift.

Cut out the butterfly shapes and fold them on both sides of the half-way fold, to give them bodies. Use glue or thin strips of double-sided tape to attach them in a random pattern to the parcel. Alternatively, tie lots of little bows of the same size using contrasting ribbon; scatter them over your gift using double-sided tape.

Fold the whole thing in half and half again, twisting the folded point at the base to form the shape of the 'flower'. Pull the thread out at the point, and wind it tightly around the twisted base to secure it; 'fluff' out the finished decoration. Make several 'flowers' and group them together on your present.

A pretty arrangement of dried flowers is a lovely idea for somebody with an autumn or winter birthday. You can pick grasses and seedheads in the country or you can dry flowers from your own garden; it's fun and quite easy. Or you can buy them, though of course it's more expensive that way! Cut the dried plants all the same length.

Bunch the flowers together; when you're happy with them, wrap sticky tape around the stalks. Hide the tape by winding ribbon over it. Tie ribbon round the parcel, finish off with a knot, and attach the little bouquet by tying its trailing ribbons over the knot; trim the ends of the bouquet ribbon away. Using the ends of the other ribbon, finish off by making a pretty bow over the bouquet.

An added bonus on this gift is the sweet-smelling pouch of pot-pourri. Select some fabric which will tone with your gift wrapping paper. The fabric should be fine, but not loosely woven; the scent of the pot-pourri can then easily diffuse through the material, but the petals and dust can't. Cut out a piece of fabric measuring about 15-20cm (6-8in) square.

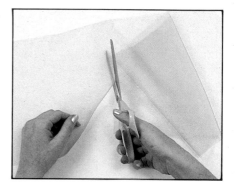

Put enough pot-pourri in the centre of the fabric to make a generous sachet — a good handful should be just right. If you can, choose a perfume which will match your present — rose pot-pourri would be ideal for a rose bowl, lavender for lavender-scented soaps. You could even use dried herbs to create a bouquet garni for a cookery book!

Pick up the four corners of the fabric to form a bundle. Wind sewing thread tightly around the neck of the bundle, and knot the thread securely. Tie the pot-pourri bunch very firmly in case the recipient uses the bag later in her wardrobe. Hide the thread by tying a piece of ribbon around it to match the ribbon on the parcel. Tie the pot-pourri to the gift using a little more matching ribbon.

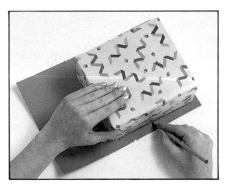

**P**aste the recipient's age in a great big number on the side of their present so that *everybody* knows how old they are! Draw around the present, so that you know exactly what size the numbers must be to fill the side of the gift and make a big impact.

Draw the appropriate number using a ruler and measure carefully. Choose thin cardboard or plain paper in a contrasting colour to the wrapping paper.

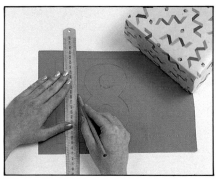

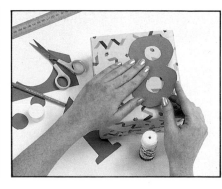

**W**hat a lovely bonus to receive with a gift — a beautiful fresh flower. This works most effectively with a long, thin present, showing off a single bloom to perfection. First choose your flower. Trim off any excess leaves and, in the case of roses, thorns. You should end up with just one sprig of leaves.

To prevent the flower from staining the gift wrap or making it damp, wrap the end of the stalk with cling film (plastic wrap). Then cut a narrow strip of matching gift wrap; wrap it around the length of the stalk, fixing it at the back with tape. Cut a small 'V' shape at the top of the paper tube, and attach the bloom to the parcel with double-sided tape.

Cut the numbers out and stick them in position on your gift. You could make a numerical tag to match. This idea could be adapted for use with gifts celebrating wedding anniversaries — 25, 50 and so on.

Holly leaves are an attractive shape and perfect for decorating a festive gift. Measure the length of the diagonal across the top of your parcel. On a sheet of plain paper, draw a large holly leaf, the 'vein' of which measures slightly more than half the length of the diagonal.

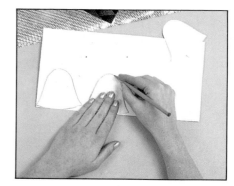

These Christmas bells ring out gaily from your present. Make two paper templates, both bell-shaped, with one showing the outline of the clapper from the bottom edge. From thin cardboard, cut out two of each shape.

Trace four holly leaves on to some green cardboard, using the template you have just created. Cut the leaves out and bend them in the middle; creasing them slightly where the central vein would be.

Cover all the cardboard shapes with gold paper (or any colour which would co-ordinate with your wrapping paper). Cover both sides, and trim away all the excess paper. On the bell shapes with the clapper, cut a slit from the curved top of the bell to the centre of the bell. On the others (the plain ones) cut a slit from the middle of the bottom edge, also to the centre.

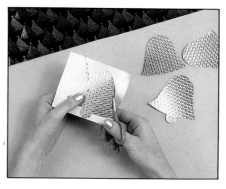

Make the berries from a ball of cotton wool (known as absorbent cotton in the United States) wrapped in two squares of red tissue paper. Put a dab of glue inside and twist up the tissue tightly at the base. When the glue is dry, cut off as much excess of the twist as possible. Group the leaves and berries on the parcel; attach with glue or double-sided tape.

Pierce a hole in the top of the plain bell shapes and thread them with a length of ribbon. Then slot the pairs of bell shapes together (i.e. the plain one, and the one with the clapper) so that they form three-dimensional shapes, as shown here. Tie a group of as many bells as you like on to your gift. This idea can also be used for decorating a wedding gift.

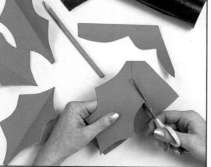

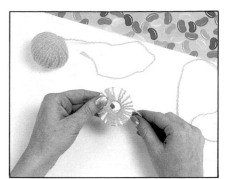

This cheery chick will brighten up any Easter gift. Cut two cardboard circles the same size, then cut a small circle from the centre of each to create two wide rings. Put both rings together and wind yellow yarn around them, passing the yarn through the centre. Continue doing this until the rings are well covered and the inner circle is almost full of yarn.

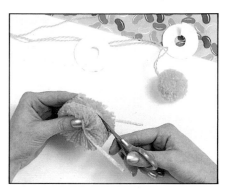

Snip through all the yarn along the outer edge of the cardboard rings. Pass a length of yarn between the two rings, wind it tightly around all the strands of yarn and tie it firmly, leaving long ends. Cut off the cardboard circles and fluff out the ball. Make a bigger ball for the body from two larger rings, and before cutting, pass a pipe cleaner through the rings to form the legs.

Tie the two balls together firmly. Bend the 'legs' up at the ends and wind a section of pipe cleaner around each foot leaving a V-shape on either side so that each foot now has three 'claws'; paint the feet and legs red. Make eyes and a beak out of felt and glue into position. This would work just as well with a Christmas robin decoration, using red and brown yarn.

A heavenly messenger bears the greetings on this Christmas present. Cut a quarter section of a circle from light cardboard to form a narrow cone for the body. On a folded piece of paper draw one arm and one wing against the edge of the fold as shown, so that when they are cut out you will have a pair of each.

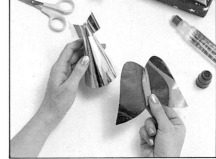

Make the cone and cover it with silver paper (aluminium foil would do). Trace the arm and wings on to silver paper; cut them out and glue them in their relevant positions on the body.

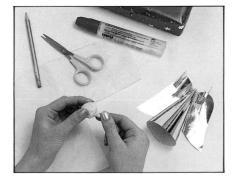

Make the head by rolling up some white tissue paper into a firm ball, twisting the ends of the tissue tightly to form a 'neck'. Glue the head into the top of the cone. Tie a scrap of tinsel into a loose knot and stick it on the head as a halo. Make a scroll from white paper, write on your message and stick it between the angel's hands. Attach the angel to the gift with double-side tape.

It's important that your gift is labelled clearly so that the right present goes to the right person — and that that person knows who the present is from! But there's no need to deface the wrapping paper on your gift by scrawling your message all over it.

Any well-wrapped gift needs a proper tag. It's easy to make one to go with your gift wrap; five methods are suggested in this section. Or perhaps you could tailor-make a tag especially designed for the person receiving the gift. And what a novelty to be able to *eat* the tag afterwards — well, here you will find two kinds of edible tags.

*Personal and original gift tags really do make a difference to the finished parcel, as this selection demonstrates. And with a little flair and imagination you can create a wide range of attractive designs.*

If you have a long message for the recipient of your gift, this fold-out tag allows lots of room. Select a gift wrap design that has a fairly large repeat. One motif must have sufficient space around it so that it can be cut out without including any others. Draw a rectangle around the motif, ensuring that all the corners are right angles.

Cut the rectangle out with a craft knife. Next, cut out a piece of thin cardboard the same height as the chosen motif and exactly three times its width. Fold the cardboard in three widthways, creasing the folds well, then fold the top two sections back on themselves, as shown. Mark the folds in pencil first to be sure they are straight.

Cut the motif from the gift wrap precisely in half. Glue each half on to the top two sections of the folded card. They should fit exactly, but if necessary trim the top and bottom to form a straight edge. Try matching the colours of the lining cardboard with the gift wrap; in the example shown here, red or even black cardboard could have been used, instead of white, for a different effect.

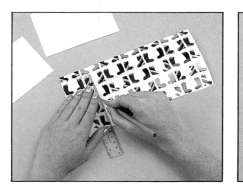

Give your presents a co-ordinated appearance by creating matching tags. For simple fold-over tags you need to select wrapping paper which has a small design. Take a piece of gift wrap and rule a rectangle on it, twice the width of the required tag. (Outline a section of the design where the motif is visible when isolated.) Ensure the corners are perfect right angles, then cut the tag out.

Paste the tag on to thin cardboard; choose a colour which picks up a shade in the gift wrap. When the glue is dry, cut around the piece of gift wrap. Fold the card in half and punch a hole in the corner. Thread a ribbon through the hole and tie it on to the gift. Alternatively, you can cut out a single image, stick it on to cardboard and cut around the outline, as with the panda tag.

Incorporate a motif from the design of your gift wrap to make a fun three-page tag. It will work with any design involving a trailing string — balloons, kites, balls of yarn and so on. The motif is stuck on the sloping top edge of the middle 'page' of the card. Cut out the motif from gift wrap. Then experiment with a sheet of white paper to get the best shape for your card.

The slanting angle of the top edge is achieved by cutting a truncated triangular shape. Having worked out the shape you want, trace around your experimental tag on to thin coloured cardboard. Don't forget to leave a bit of card protruding from the top slanting edge in the shape of the motif, as shown. Cut out the tag.

Score the two fold lines of the tag using the back of a craft knife and crease them firmly. Glue the motif in position on the middle page and draw a long string trailing down. Close the card and draw another string on the front, making sure it is continuous with the string on page two. Write the recipient's name as if it were part of that string.

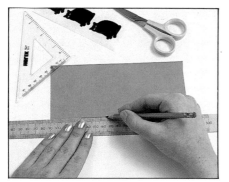

There is such a variety of stickers on the market that you're sure to find one which will make an ideal label for your gift. Take a piece of thin coloured cardboard; this will form the background for the sticker. Draw a rectangle on to the cardboard, twice the width you wish the finished tag to be.

Cut out the rectangle with a craft knife and score down the centre to form the fold; crease well. Remove the sticker from its backing and place it in position on the front of the tag. Punch a hole in the back 'page' of the tag, near the fold. Write your message inside and hang the tag on the gift.

There can be no doubt who these presents are for! It's fun to make a tag out of the initial or — even better — the whole name of the recipient. First draw the shape of the letters you want on to a piece of tracing paper. Make sure that the letters in a name interlock sufficiently.

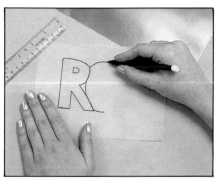

When you're happy with the result, trace the letters (or single initial) on to coloured cardboard, pressing hard to make a clear outline. Use a ruler where there are straight sections to a letter.

Create a stylish effect by matching the tag to the ribbon. Plain ribbon with a strongly patterned paper is attractive but a tartan ribbon with plain paper can look stunning. And if you don't have any ribbon, even a strip of fabric cut out with pinking shears will suffice! Glue a length of ribbon or fabric on to thin cardboard to make it rigid.

Trim away any excess cardboard. Fold the stiffened ribbon over and cut it to the length you want the finished tag to be. Punch a hole through your newly-created tag and thread a piece of contrasting narrow ribbon through the hole to tie it to the parcel. Trim the edges of the tag to match the ends of the bow.

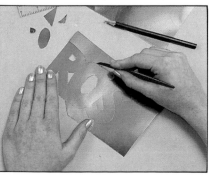

Next, cut out the shape using a craft knife, carefully following the traced lines. Punch a hole in a position where the weight of the tag will make it hang well on the gift.

# TAGS TO TUCK INTO!

One way to eat your words — or at least your name! Shortbread is the basis for these edible labels. Sift together 100g (4oz, ½ cup) of caster (fine granulated) sugar and 150g (6oz, 1½ cups) of plain flour into a bowl. Rub in 100g (4oz, ½ cup) of butter till the mixture resembles fine breadcrumbs. Add water to make a stiff dough, knead well and roll it out on a floured board.

Cut out various shapes for the tags, using either pastry cutters or paper templates. Don't forget to make the holes for threading the ribbon later. Bake at 200°C, 400°F or gas mark 6 for 15-20 minutes or until golden brown; leave to cool. Then write the name on, using icing in a piping bag, or simply with a paintbrush dipped in food colouring. This recipe will make 15-20 labels.

# CANDY TAGS

Children will enjoy eating these gift tags made of royal icing. Separate an egg and sift 225g (approximately ½lb, 1¼ cups) of icing (confectioner's) sugar into a bowl. Gradually add a little egg white to make a stiff dough. Knead well, then divide the mixture in two and add food colouring to one half. Knead the icing thoroughly to distribute the colouring.

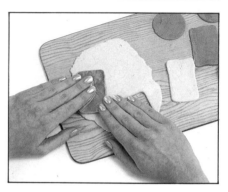

Roll out the icing to about 5mm (¼in). Cut out shapes using small pastry cutters. Colour the other portion of icing if required and repeat. Make a hole in the shapes for a ribbon, then prick out the name with a toothpick or, when the tags have dried, write the name on with a paintbrush dipped in food colouring. Leave the tags to dry out for a week. This makes about 20 tags.

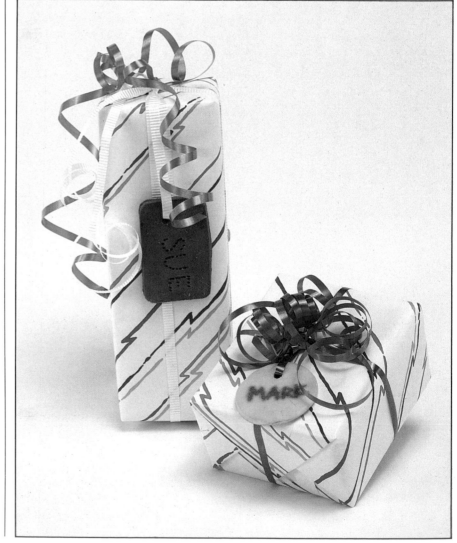

# LAZY DAISY

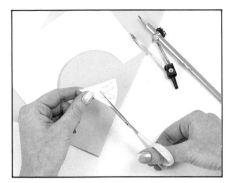

Sometimes the name tag can form the entire decoration for the gift! Wrap your gift in green paper to make a leafy-coloured background for this floral tag. Using a compass, draw a circle that will fit comfortably on top of your present. Fold it in eight and draw four daisy-shaped petals on a segment. With the circle still folded, cut the petals out. This is your template.

Draw two circles of the same diameter as the template, and trace the daisy pattern on to them; cut them out. Repeat the process with a smaller circle, to provide two inner layers for the daisy. Pile the daisies on top of each other, arranging them so that none of the petals overlaps, then stick them together in the centre with glue or double-sided tape.

Cut out a circle from yellow paper, write the recipient's name on it and fix it in the centre of the flower. Gently bend up the petals around the yellow centre. You could adapt the idea in mauves to make a Michaelmas daisy, or autumn colours for a chrysanthemum.

# CAMEO

Victorian ladies created beautiful pictures using pressed flowers. Why not make a miniature version for a pretty gift tag? Pick up a selection of flowers and leaves and lay them face down on blotting paper. Press another layer of blotting paper on top, keeping the flowers as flat as possible. Place the flowers between the pages of a heavy book and leave them for at least a week.

Take out the flowers. Make a template for a perfect oval by folding a small sheet of paper in half and half again; draw a curve across the corner as shown and cut it out. Trace round the unfolded shape on white cardboard, and make a slightly larger oval from coloured cardboard to match the gift wrap.

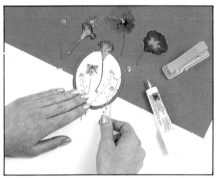

Stick the two ovals together, so that the larger one forms a frame for the tag. Arrange the pressed flowers on the white oval to your satisfaction. Glue the flowers in position, using a tube with a very fine nozzle; leave the arrangement to dry thoroughly. Punch a hole in the top of the tag, write the message on the back and tie it to the gift.

With so many presents being exchanged at this time of the year, tags become even more important. What about some special seasonal ones? Draw any festive shape you like on to thin cardboard; this one is a Christmas stocking. Cut out the shape and cover it with bright paper; try to co-ordinate the colours with those in the gift wrap you use for your present.

If your wrapping paper has a particular theme in its design make a tag to echo it. To ensure that your design is symmetrical, fold a piece of paper in half and draw on half the design against the fold. Cut around the outline through both layers of paper; open out and use this as a template for the design. Cover a piece of light cardboard with gift wrap and trace around the template.

This dotty Christmas cracker can be traced from template 47 and transferred to brightly-coloured card. Cut out, fold down centre and score. Use pinking shears to trim ends of cracker. Cut three strips of florist's ribbon to fit across cracker. Pink edges, spray glue and attach to cracker. Trim excess ribbon.

Cut around the outline and punch a hole at the top of the tag. Write your message and tie the tag on to the parcel. You could cheat a little when designing the shape of your tag by tracing an illustration from a magazine or by using the outline of a pastry cutter.

Tie two pieces of gift-wrap ribbon around 'ends' of cracker, as shown. Split ribbon down centre and curl each length.

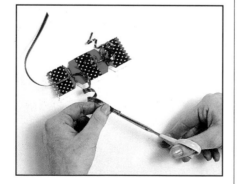

Cut a card 15 by 7.5cm (6 by 3in), score and fold 7.5cm (3in). Cut a piece of sequin waste to fit and attach to card with spray glue. Colour in circles with felt-tipped pens. Many different patterns can be made. Punch a hole in back and thread with ribbon, if desired.

# EASTER BUNNY

# AHOY THERE!

Knowing who this parcel is for is plain sailing! Fold a strip of thin cardboard in half and draw a stylized boat on to it. Cut it out and stick the ends together with tape, making a three-dimensional boat. Make two creases in the 'bottom' of the boat, along its length, to give it stability.

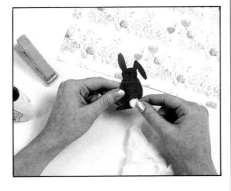

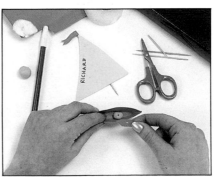

This cute rabbit tag tells the kids who their Easter present is from. Draw the shape of a rabbit on to white cardboard; if you're not good at drawing, you could cheat by tracing the outline of a rabbit from a magazine or book illustration. When you're happy with your design, cut it out.

Either paint the bunny shape, or cover it with brown paper (or whatever colour suits your gift wrap; a red or even green rabbit would be fun). Next take a piece of cotton wool (absorbent cotton) and roll it into a ball for the tail; stick it in position with a dab of glue. Make a hole in the rabbit's head for some ribbon, write your message and tie the tag to the gift.

Cut out a paper sail. For the mast, join two cocktail sticks or toothpicks with tape; break off half of one of them. Stick the mast on to the sail with more tape, leaving the pointed end of the mast at the bottom.

Add a flying pennant to the top of the mast with paper, and write the recipient's name on the sail. Attach the mast by putting some Plasticine or modelling clay in the bottom of the boat; dig the mast into it. Hide the Plasticine with a small piece of cardboard to match the boat. The finishing touch is the wave made of cotton wool (known as absorbent cotton in the United States).

Personalized cards made with care and affection are always a delight to receive and many of the designs on the following pages are special enough to frame and keep on permanent display.

Over 20 attractive, multi-purpose greeting cards, including invitations and quick cards (pages 136–139), are followed by lots of ideas for cards to celebrate calendar events – Christmas, New Year, Valentine's Day, Easter, Mother's Day, Father's Day and Thanksgiving – and other special occasions, such as birthdays, new home, engagement, new baby, wedding anniversary and retirement. You will find templates for the cards on pages 162–167.

*Card comes in a variety of finishes: cloud effect, metallic, parchment style, textured, glossy and matt. The cards on the following pages use tissue, brown, origami, marbled, wall and wrapping paper, as well as foil and cellophane, to create different effects and textures. As an alternative to making your own base cards, card 'blanks', complete with front windows, are readily available from craft shops and good department stores.*

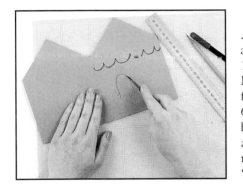

A detachable finger puppet of a jolly circus clown will delight a child. Cut card 18 by 25cm (7 by 10in). Score and fold 12.5cm (5in). Mark 5.5cm (2¼in) down sides of folded card. Measure across the top 6cm (2½in) and mark. Cut through both thicknesses of card to form apex of 'marquee'. Draw roof of marquee with felt-tipped pen. Cut a 'stand' for puppet on front of card.

The card is a ready-made 3-fold with window. Cut out circle in left-hand section to match window. Trace out template 43. Put masking tape in each corner to hold tracing still, then place silk over tracing, holding it firm with masking tape. Trace through onto silk using a soft pencil.

Trace out templates 7, 8 and 9 and transfer onto thin card to make your own templates. Cut out two balloons from card and satin ribbon strings. Using turquoise felt, cut two hats, two hands and a bow-tie. Cut two heads from white felt; two circles, one for his nose and one for his hat, from pink felt. Cut eyes from narrow black satin ribbon.

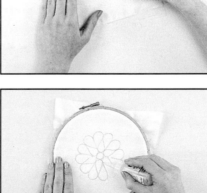

Place silk in an embroidery frame and draw over lines of design with gutta. This will stop the silk paints from running into each other. Leave to dry thoroughly — it may take an hour. A hairdryer will speed up the process.

Glue balloons and ribbons in place. Sandwich the clown's hands between the two pieces of felt for the head, holding in place with a dab of glue. Sew, with a running stitch, round the clown's head. Glue on hat, bobble, eyes, nose and bow-tie. Place clown on stand and he will appear to be holding the balloons.

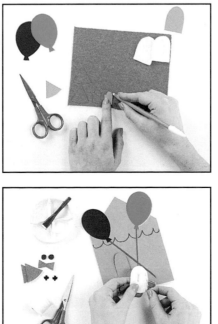

Shake or stir fabric paints and using a clean damp brush flood each petal area with paint in one swift stroke. When paint is dry place a piece of fabric under silk and iron on wrong side for two minutes to set paint. Wash out gutta from silk and dry if you wish. Trim to just larger than window, stick down fabric and left-hand card section with double-sided tape.

Beautiful paper bags, too pretty to throw away, can be turned into greeting cards. Here, delicately-patterned wallpaper is used to advantage as a background. Cut card 20 by 30cm (8 by 12in). Score 15cm (6in) across and fold. With small scissors carefully cut out your favourite flowers and some leaves.

Cut card 15 by 25cm (6 by 10in). Score and fold 12.5cm (5in) across. On inside of card rule four sets of double lines and one single at each end, the depth of weaving strip. Use an even number of slits to start and finish on the inside. Vary depth for second line of slits. Rule two lines, one with 14 dots 9mm ($^3/_8$in) apart, second with 10 dots 16mm ($^5/_8$in) apart.

Cut wallpaper background, leaving small border of card showing. Mark a small dot at each corner with a sharp pencil, so you will easily be able to line up the background.

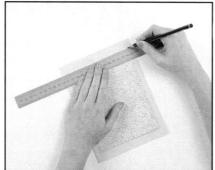

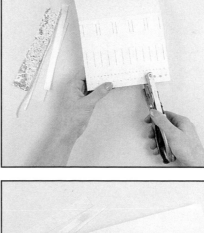

Any unusual papers can be used for weaving through the slits, particularly paper you have marbled yourself. Cut paper strips, ribbon and cord slightly longer than width of card, and carefully cut slits and punch holes.

Spray glue on to background wallpaper and stick down on to card using pencil dots as a guide. Spray backs of roses and arrange. If you lay a clean sheet of paper over the card and smooth over the freshly-glued pieces, the edges will not catch on your hands.

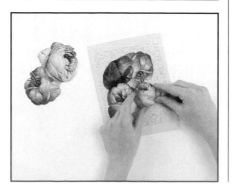

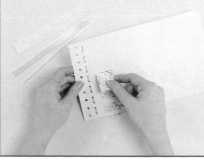

Still working from the inside weave paper, ribbon and cord and finish with a dab of glue. Trim any overhanging ends. On the front of card, glue a strip of ribbon between the two lines of woven paper.

# WOVEN SILK

# NEEDLEPOINT IN LILAC

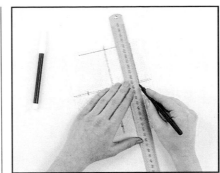

Use mono thread 'lockweave' needlepoint canvas 8 holes to 2cm or 10 holes to 1in, cut 18 by 14cm (7 by 5½in). Find centre of canvas and mark centre hole on four sides. Draw two crosses in different colours either side of centre and side holes. Without counting centre hole, count 29 holes either side lengthways and 18 widthways. Rule a border line.

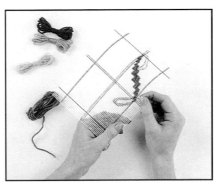

You will find a chart to follow on page 167. Thread a tapestry needle with either double-knitting wool or tapestry wool and counting holes, work long stitch in the pale lilac colour first.

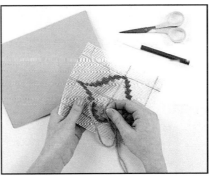

Continue working towards centre, finishing four corners last. Cut a 3-fold card 45 by 20cm (18 by 8in), score and fold at 15cm (6in) intervals. Measure finished piece and cut a slightly smaller window in centre panel of card. Trim canvas to 6mm (¼in) all round and mount using double-sided tape. Close card and stick down.

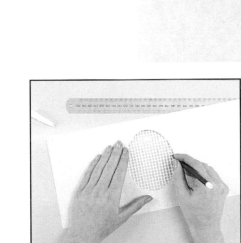

Offcuts of shot silk or other fabrics are woven into a landscape of green fields, hedges, yellow corn, blue sky and pink evening sunset. A ready-cut, 3-fold card was used. Mark top left-hand corner inside card with cross. Cut canvas about 10cm (4in) square. Lay card with oval aperture over canvas and mark edges lightly. Rule a square just outside these marks.

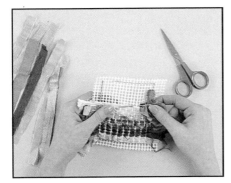

Cut stips of fabric approximately 1cm (½in) wide and 12.5cm (5in) long. Do not worry if they fray as this adds to the charm. Thread large tapestry needle and starting from the bottom weave green strips. Continue with yellow fields, hedges and sky.

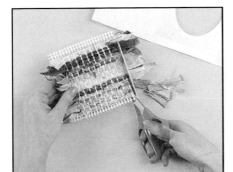

Attach double-sided tape around oval window and along three sides of panel, as shown. Trim canvas 6mm (¼in) outside the ruled square and peel off backing from double-sided tape. Stick canvas in place and close card — the left side with the cross is the side to fold in. Smooth from folded edge to outside so that card stays flat.

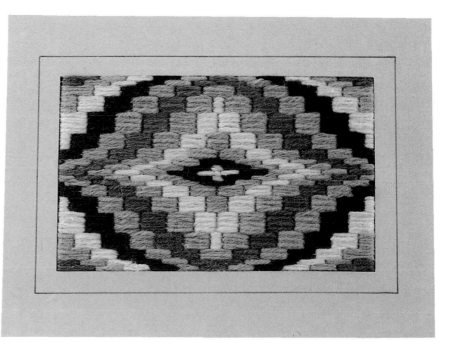

Cut card 30 by 13cm (12 by 5in), score and fold 15cm (6in). With fold on top find centre and mark with pencil dot. Measure down 6cm (2½in) on each side. Rule a line from each side point to middle mark to form roof. Stick down ribbon forming a mitre at apex of roof. Cut two pieces of medium weight wrapping paper 20 by 7.5cm (8 by 3in).

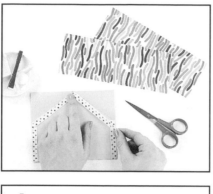

Trace out templates *11* and *12*. Fold length of wrapping paper in half then in half twice more. Draw on half boy or girl making sure hands are on folds. Cut out. When you draw the second child, check folds are in the opposite direction, so that when they are opened they are left and right of card. Open out boys and girls and refold alternate ways.

On green and pink paper cut a boy and girl. Glue them to the blank side of the folded figures. Glue the last girl and boy to the card so that their feet are on the bottom edge. Fold figures flat to fit in an envelope.

The attraction of this card lies in combining circles cut from a variety of materials of a single colour. The feather adds a final touch of frivolity. Cut card 23 by 18cm (9 by 7in), score and fold 11.5cm (4½in). Find sequins of different sizes but similar colours, then paper, sequin waste, satin paper and foil. Sequin waste can be marked with dividers.

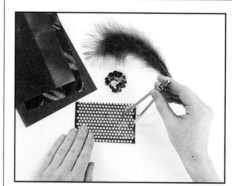

Draw circles of different sizes on your chosen materials. Any round objects can be used for this, or use a pair of compasses. Cut out.

Position circles and sequins to make an interesting arrangement and glue in place. Finally glue on a feather of matching colour.

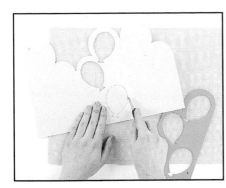

Cut yellow card 22 by 33cm (8½ by 12¾in). Score and fold 11cm (4¼in) and 22cm (8½in). Trace out template *10*, transfer to thin card to make template. Place over folded card, mark with sharp pencil around balloon outline at top and cut with sharp knife through all three thicknesses. Open out card and trace out balloon shapes onto centre panel and cut out.

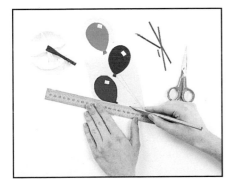

Place double-sided tape in small pieces around the balloon holes on inside centre of card. Cut small pieces of narrow ribbon and stick across neck of balloons. Using balloon template, cut three satin balloons slightly larger. Remove double-sided backing and stick them in place. Stick down left side of the 3-fold card using double-sided tape.

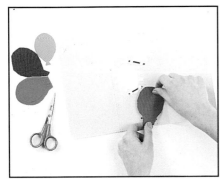

Cut three 'reflection' squares out of white or silver fabric and glue on to the three balloons. Cut four lengths of narrow ribbon, one shorter, so that it will appear to pass behind the red balloon. Using a sharp pencil, rule guide lines for where the ribbons will be placed. Glue them down, leave for a minute or two for glue to dry and then trim ends.

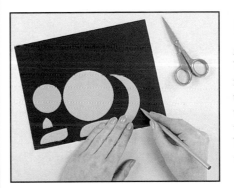

Our mischievous black cat seems not to have noticed the little mouse! Cut card 23 by 18cm (9 by 7in), score 11.5cm (4½in) across and fold along top of card. Trace out cat templates *16-21* and transfer on to thin card to make your own templates. Draw around pieces on to black paper or card. Keep paws and tail the right way round.

Cut out black cat, a tree shape from tissue-paper or card and two green eyes. Mark with a sharp pencil where the pieces will fit on card and stick on in order using spray glue: the tree, body, paws, tail, ears and eyes.

Use stationers' self-adhesive dots for cat's nose and pupils. Finish by drawing whiskers using white chinagraph pencil. Draw around limbs and ears with a soft pencil to make cat stand out.

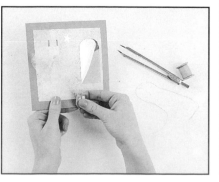

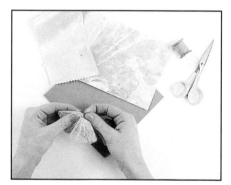

J ust the card to please a young girl who dreams of becoming a ballet dancer. Cut card 30 by 15cm (12 by 6in), score and fold 15cm (6in). Cut skirt from a piece of net 30 by 7.5cm (12 by 3in). Fold in half down its length and press with warm iron. Sew, with small running stitches, along this fold. Make a double stitch to start, gather tightly and finish with a double stitch.

Marbled paper is used for the background. Cut 13cm (5in) square. Cut mirror from silver paper or foil. Details of how to draw a curve are given on page 61. Cut bodice from satin and straps from satin ribbon.

Centre background paper and attach with spray glue. Then glue bodice and mirror. The straps will be easier to put on with rubber-based glue. Mark where skirt is to be attached and pierce two holes each side with dividers. Sew from back of card, tie knot and dab with glue. Make two more holes in the same way for the ballet shoes brooch. Finish with a silver star for a hopeful star.

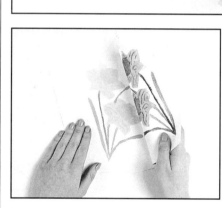

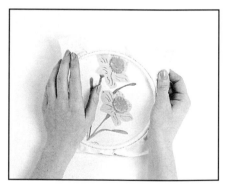

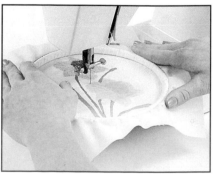

C ut card 22cm (8½in) square, score and fold 11cm (4¼in). Cut out a window 9 by 16.5cm (3½ by 6½in). Trace daffodils from a catalogue or book and transfer onto cartridge paper. Paint with transfer paints. When dry, place over square of polyester or poly-cotton fabric and press with a hot dry iron for two minutes. Carefully lift off paper.

Place print in an embroidery frame the opposite way from hand embroidery and pull until taut. To machine embroider, use same thread on top and bobbin. Take off presser foot and drop 'feed dog' so that teeth will not hold work and you will be able to move it freely. Place embroidery ring under needle and drop pressure leaver.

Moving machine wheel by hand, draw up bobbin thread to top and hold to start. Move ring, keeping your fingers on edge of frame and slowly paint with your needle. Experiment with stitches — length 0 and zig-zag are good. Sew outline first then colour in. Press on reverse, mount with double-sided tape and back with white paper.

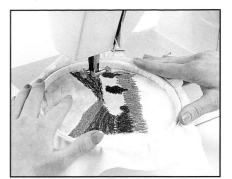

On good quality cartridge paper, draw a 12cm (4¾in) square. Using a postcard or photograph as a guide, roughly draw in mountains, lakes, trees and grass. Colour in with transfer paint, applied sparingly. The colours will not be true to the end product since they will change according to fibre content of material on which you print.

When paint is dry, place paper over poly-cotton and press for two minutes with a hot dry iron. Try not to move paper. You can make several prints from one painting. Mount the picture in an embroidery ring as shown. Follow your sewing machine's instructions for free machine embroidery. Using a selection of threads, fill in areas using satin stitch and straight stitch.

Cut card 30 by 20cm (12 by 8in), score and fold 15cm (6in) across. Trace out templates 19-22. Transfer designs onto thin card to make your own templates. Cut out from thin card two arms, two legs, head and body. From brown felt cut out same pieces but slightly larger. Glue felt to card — make a left and right leg. When glue is dry trim edges.

Tie ends of satin stitch on back when finished and press. Cut card 14 by 28cm (5½ by 11in). Cut a window 11.5cm (4½) square. Attach finished picture behind window using double-sided tape, then cut a piece of white backing paper and attach to back of your work. Trim excess paper.

Tear green tissue-paper to resemble hills and hedges and cut gingham tablecloth. Glue them to card and position 'stick-on' flowers. Glue on Teddy's head and punch holes in body, arms and legs. Mark shoulder holes on card, since Teddy will be attached through them. Punch or cut out with a cross, so that brass paper-clips will pass through.

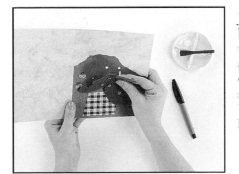

Join Teddy's legs to his body with brass paper-clips. Pass paper-clips through holes at top of Teddy's arms, body and card and open out on back to secure him. Glue on small black beads for eyes and nose. With a fine felt-tipped pen, draw in his snout and mouth.

# BLACK AND WHITE SPOTS

# PATCHWORK PARCELS

Diagonal lines of spotted ribbon and self-adhesive labels give this card a 'dotty' air. Cut a piece of black card 25 by 16cm (10 by 6¼in). Score and fold 12.5cm (5in). On inside top left-hand corner measure 4cm (1½in) along top of card and down side edge, mark with dots and score. Fold corner back to outside of card.

Rule a diagonal line across front of card from top left to bottom right. Measure and cut ribbons to fit either side of this line. Cut them slightly longer, to be trimmed later. Cut a triangle of ribbon to fit behind turned-down corner. Spray backs of ribbon with glue in spray booth. Place in position, smooth down and trim edges.

On front bottom left-hand corner of card, stick on self-adhesive dots and also on folded-over, top right-hand corner.

Cut nine heaps of lurex, silk and satin. Cut two pieces of acetate film 10cm (4in) and 9.5cm (3¾in). Draw a 7.5cm (3in) grid of 2.5cm (1in) squares with a chinagraph pencil. Use polyester thread and machine two centre horizontal lines and left-hand vertical. Stuff centre square. Machine right vertical to close centre square. Stuff squares on left; top and bottom centre.

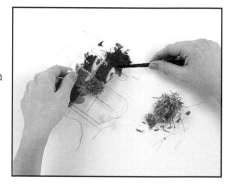

Machine left-hand edge, and then top and bottom edges to close squares. Stuff three right-hand squares and machine right-hand edge to close. Pull threads to back and knot. Trim and put a dot of glue on each knot to hold it.

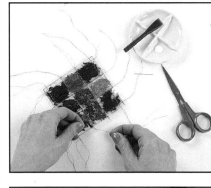

Make or buy a 3-fold card and cut a double window mount. Mark inside top left-hand corner with cross. Put double-sided tape around centre window of card and edges. Pull off backing of tape and place patchwork parcels in window. Close card and add cord and tassel.

# PUFFINS

# MATISSE INSPIRED

Colourful puffins, cut from a sheet of wrapping paper, keep a lookout from their perch. Cut card 28 by 13cm (18 by 5¼in). The card is blue on the inside and white on the outside. On the outside, from the left, score 9cm (3½in) and 19cm (7½in) across and fold. Turn card over and on the inside, from the left, score and fold 20cm (8in) across.

Cut out three puffins and spray glue the first on outside of far right-hand panel of card, facing right. Cut round him with a craft knife leaving him attached by his tail. The score line on the outside will allow him to stand forward.

Glue the other two puffins in place on the inside. Any wrapping paper with a distinct animal motif can be used in this way to make a striking card.

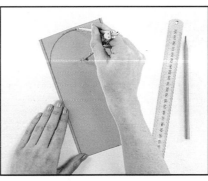

Cut card 22 by 22cm (8½ by 8½in), score and fold 11cm (4¼in) across. Centre your compass point horizontally 5.5cm (2in) from top of card. Draw an arc so that it touches the sides and top edge of card, then cut through both thicknesses. You could make a template of this shape if you wanted to make several cards.

Brightly coloured origami paper is perfect for this exuberant card. Either draw on back of paper or cut freehand a collection of shapes and colours.

Arrange paper shapes in order of gluing and stick them onto card. Tweezers will help you to apply glue to the tiny star shapes, not your fingers!

A theme card to give to a musical friend. The treble clefs are buttons. Cut red glossy card 22 by 15cm (8½ by 6in). Score and fold 11cm (4¼in). Draw a square 5.5 by 7.5cm (2¼ by 3in) on white paper. Rule two staves — groups of five lines 3mm (¹/₈in) apart — using a fine black felt-tipped pen. Cut out the square.

Centre the square of music paper on card so that you have an equal margin on three sides. Visually, it is better to have a larger margin at base of card. Mark corners of music lightly on card and stick down using spray glue. Place opened card on a piece of felt and pierce two holes for the two buttons using dividers or a thick needle.

From the back sew on buttons through the holes you have pierced, then knot the thread and trim. Finish knots with a dab of glue.

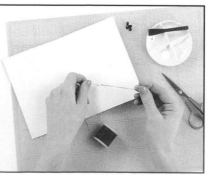

Windows open to reveal flowers cut from wrapping paper which could also wrap a gift. Cut glossy green card 22 by 15cm (8½ by 6in). Score and fold 11cm (4¼in). Cut a 4cm (1½in) equilateral triangle template. Open card flat and on the inside front draw four triangles. With steel ruler and craft knife cut two sides of triangles and score third.

Cut a piece of white paper the same size as the closed card and lay it under the card front. Open up windows and draw the triangles through the windows. These will be your guides for sticking on the pieces of flowered paper. Mark top left-hand corner of inside of card and paper with a cross. Cut out four triangles of flowers.

Glue flower triangles on paper where marked in pencil. Place a line of glue along all four edges on front of paper and attach face down on inside front of card. Open up the windows and you will see peeping flowers.

Cut blue card 23 by 16.5cm (9 by 6½in). Score and fold 11.5cm (4½in). Trace templates *2* and *3* for sail and windsurfer. Rub soft pencil over back of tracing of windsurfer, draw over outline again onto grey tissue-paper to transfer image and cut out. Make a template of the sail and draw round onto a piece of mid-blue card.

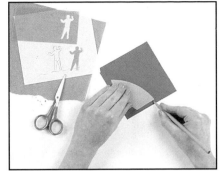

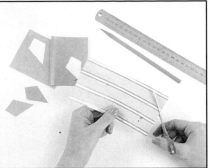

Kites flying in a high spring sky are always a cheerful sight and these three are made from wrapping paper and narrow satin ribbon. Cut pale blue card 22 by 15cm (8½ by 6in). Score and fold 11cm (4¼in). Cut out kites in three different sizes and papers using a ruler. Arrange and stick on card using spray glue.

Draw and cut a surf-board from a piece of white card 10 by 1cm (4 by ½in) and curve ends. Cut out sail, and two coloured strips of card to fit diagonally over sail. Tear waves from two pieces of blue tissue-paper — one deep blue, the other a lighter blue. Glue coloured strips on to sail.

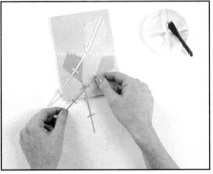

Cut narrow satin ribbons slightly longer than card so they will hang below bottom of card. Cut short lengths of ribbon for bows.

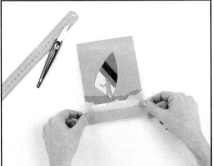

Arrange pieces on the main card and mark where they fit with sharp pencil dots. Place all components in spray booth right-side down and spray backs with glue. Place on card in order: dark waves then surf-board, sail, man and pale waves. Place a piece of clean paper over card and smooth pieces flat with your hand. Trim off any excess with craft knife.

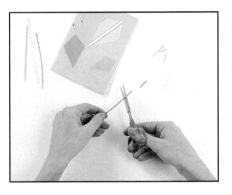

Glue and hold in place for a moment since satin ribbon tends to resist glue at first. Some of the bows can be a 'V' of twisted ribbon.

This small piece of quilting is from a ready-printed panel. It will shrink a little when it has been quilted, so measure and cut window from card *after* you have finished the piece. You will need very thin wadding (batting) to back the cotton panel. Cut a piece of card 45 by 15cm (18 by 6in) and score two folds 15cm (6in) apart. Pin panel to a slightly larger square of wadding.

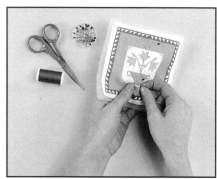

On a larger piece of work, muslin would be used as a backing fabric, but in this instance it has been left out so that there is less bulk inside the card. Working from the centre, tack (baste) the two layers together, making sure the picture covers the wadding.

Cotton thread gives best results in hand quilting. Starting from the centre, with a knot on the back, sew with tiny running stitches. Finish thread with a double back stitch. Take out tacking stitches. Do not press or you will lose quilted effect. Measure finished piece and cut window from centre of 3-fold card. With double-sided tape, stick down quilted panel and back flap of card.

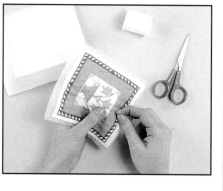

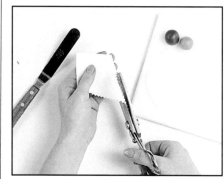

Cut card 22 by 15cm (8½ by 6in), score and fold 11cm (4¼in). Draw border around card, first in pencil then pink felt-tipped pen. Roll out a piece of white Fimo modelling material until thin and cut a kite shape. Cut edges again with pinking shears.

Roll out lots of tiny pink balls for flowers and some long green sausages to be cut for stems. Roll out some flat lengths of pink clay to make bow.

Fashion wrapping paper shape from 'kite' and place on piece of baking foil. Slip green stems inside and press on flower balls with cocktail stick. Make bow by folding pink lengths and shaping. Lay on foil and bake for 15-20 minutes on 130°C (275°F/Gas mark 1) to harden (check manufacturer's instructions). Leave to cool, glue to card and attach bow.

Cut out card 25 by 14cm (10 by 5½in). Score and fold 12.5cm (5in) across. Trace out fish (4, 5 and 6) on to the smooth side of bonding web. Cut out fish just outside pencil outline and place rough side of web on to back of your fabric. Press with a warm iron to melt the glue. Cut out on outline. Peel off backing and position on card. Press with a dry iron.

A window-box full of spring flowers is sure to bring cheer. We have used a ready-cut, 3-fold card with window. Fold under left-hand side of card (looking from the inside), marked with a cross in our second picture. With a sharp pencil, draw through window outline and cut out second window using a craft knife and steel ruler.

Draw in eyes and details of fish with felt-tipped pens. Alternatively, you can use sequins for the eyes. Cut rocks and stick down in place with spray glue.

Place 1cm (½in) of double-sided sticky tape around centre window and edges of card. Cut piece of broderie anglaise or lace to fit half the window and a piece of tracing paper cut slightly larger than aperture. Peel off tape backing and stick down curtain, then tracing paper. Peel off tape backing on edges of card and close left-hand side over. Light will filter through.

Cut sea and sand from organza and put on to card with spray glue. Trim edges with a craft knife and use offcuts to make sea ripples and waves. **Note**: Be sure to use card of at least 240gsm (160lb/sq in) or the heat of the iron will distort it.

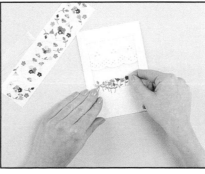

Apply 'stick-on' flowers (purchased on a strip) in a line half on the card and half on the tracing paper, then finish with a strip of satin ribbon or paper for the window box. Add a couple more flowers to the top of the window if you wish.

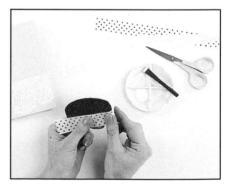

The mask is double, so that a couple could wear one each, perhaps decorating the plain one themselves. Trace out template *46* and cut a piece of black card 43 by 10cm (17 by 4in), score and fold 21.5cm (8½in). Transfer mask design onto black card and cut out with sharp craft knife through both thicknesses. Mark punch holes.

Cut pink glossy card 15 by 22cm (6 by 8½in), score and fold 11cm (4¼in). Draw out cake shape onto thin card and cut out to make template. Warm a ball of Fimo modelling material in your hands and roll out until thin. Place template on clay and cut round with a knife. Make a little dent in top centre where candle will fix.

Collect together sequins, beads and feathers. Stick them in place with rubber-based glue. Each mask could be different. If you have bought a bag of 'sweepings' you will have a variety of sequin shapes to use. You could also add silver or gold pen designs, scraps of foil, glitter, ribbon cut into shapes — have fun!

Carefully transfer to baking foil with a spatula or knife. Bake cake according to manufacturer's instructions. Cake may stretch, but you can trim with scissors after baking. Glue doiley tablecloth on card. Cut spotted ribbon and fold around base of cake. Attach with double-sided tape or glue and add second ribbon trim.

Punch holes at either side and thread ribbon through front mask. The ribbon should be long and curled by running over scissor blades. It can be re-curled if it flattens in the post. Write your invitation message in gold or silver pen to show up on black card.

Wipe back of cake with lighter fuel to remove any grease. Dab rubber-based glue on back of cake and wait until tacky before fixing to card. Spread a fine line of glue along candle and apply to card. Hold in place for a minute or two until glue dries.

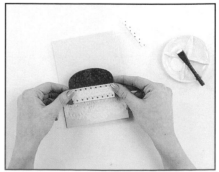

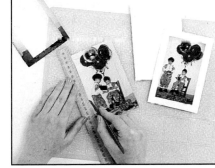

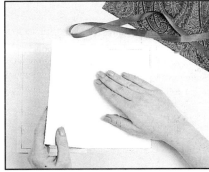

Capture the hosts of the party on a roll of film to make personal invitation cards, each one a little different. The children were delighted to be involved, especially when they opened the 'presents', even though these were empty boxes! Set up props before children come into room. Work fast before they lose concentration. A few small sweets help keep them going.

Make a mask to fit the 'sunken plate' area of the card mount and mark corners of photographs with a compass or sharp pencil point. Cut photograph with a sharp craft knife and ruler and use spray glue to affix.

Beautiful wrapping paper lasts a little longer made into a quick and effective card. Cut card, score and fold. Cut wrapping paper a little larger. Glue wrong side of wrapping paper and lay it flat. Position first half of card on paper and smooth. Bring up wrapping paper to adhere to other half of card but leave room for fold. Smooth down.

Trim edges with a sharp knife. Affix ribbon on four sides on inside of card with a little piece of double-sided tape. Tie ribbon in a bow.

Invitations can be hand-made by children too — a great way to keep them happy and involved in party planning. This rabbit is for an Easter football party given by a nine year-old boy. He drew the picture, then photocopied it a number of times. Each invitation can be hand-coloured before being glued to cards.

Photographs of flowers can be mounted on cards and sent to friends during winter months. Make a collection over the summer. Make a mask of the right size so that you may frame the most effective image. Mark four corners with a compass or sharp pencil point. Cut off excess with ruler and craft knife. Spray glue to mount.

Wonderful abstract patterns can be produced by sprinkling salt on freshly painted silk. Cut a piece of fine white silk lining and place in an embroidery frame, pulling taut. Select colours of silk paints you wish to use, shake and carefully open jars. Wet brush in water jar. Apply paint fairly swiftly and immediately sprinkle on salt. Fill frame with designs.

Leave to dry, then brush off salt. The silk will yield a variety of effects, so place different ready-cut window cards over the most attractive patterns. Mark area to be framed in window, then cut out slightly larger. The smaller the window, the more designs you can make. You could also add embroidery, beads and sequins to designs.

Mount silk in centre window of 3-fold card, using double-sided tape. Stick down left-hand portion of card over back of silk.

This magical, ever-rolling landscape is all in the imagination. It is made from layers of torn tissue-paper and plastic iridescent film. Cut pieces of card 16 by 25cm (6¼ by 10in). Score and fold 12.5cm (5in). Roughly tear several strips of tissue-paper and cut iridescent film.

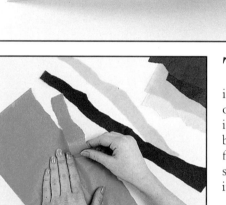

Arrange them on a sheet of A4 (21 by 30cm/8 by 12in) typing paper so that colours overlap and shade. When you are happy with your arrangement, turn strips over and spray glue. You will find one side of tissue-paper has more shine than the other. If there are gaps, you could fill them in with silver pen.

Divide sheet of paper into six or more pieces and cut with a sharp craft knife. Each landscape can now be positioned on a card and glued.

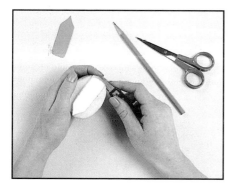

Potato cuts make quick but 'impressionistic' prints. Choose a medium-sized potato to fit comfortably into your hand. Cut in half and lay on it a motif cut from a piece of paper. Cut along edge of image, then slice potato away all round shape so that image is raised. Dry on a paper towel.

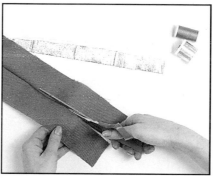

To make these quick cards even speedier to achieve, we used ready-cut 3-folds, and stickers and buttons to decorate. Cut three strips of fabric in suitable colours: here, blue glitter-spotted material for sky, silver lamé for frozen landscape and white towelling for snow.

A water-based, poster or even fabric paint can be used. Apply paint to potato image, turn over and press gently but firmly onto card. Clean off paint with tissue when you want to change colour and continue, making sure overlapping colours are dry.

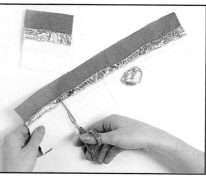

Machine the strips together with a wide satin stitch. Machine over twice if you want a thicker line. Measure size of aperture of ready-cut 3-fold cards and mark cutting lines on fabric. Machine trees with lines of stitch, or cut circles of lamé and make ponds. Let your imagination dream up a different idea for each card.

Some cards will be better than others, but this is part of their charm. Finish off candle card with gold pen flame and 'surround'. We have also made some cards using eraser lips and hearts — appropriate for a Valentine party.

Cut up sections and sew buttons in place or attach stickers. Using double-sided tape, mount pieces and close cards. Extra sequins can be added to borders for moon or stars.

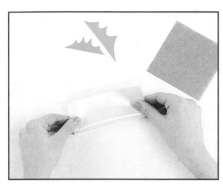

Cut silver card 30 by 15cm (12 by 6in), score and fold 15cm (6in). Trace templates *23* and *24* and transfer onto thin card. Cut 13cm (5in) square of green satin paper and 10cm (4in) square of dark green tissue-paper. Fold these two squares in half twice, then diagonally across to make a triangle.

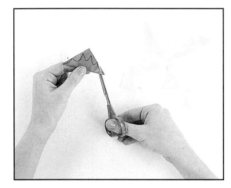

Cut out larger holly from satin paper and unfold, then dark green holly. Hold holly templates in place on paper triangles with paper clips when cutting out. You can draw round the templates first if you find it easier.

Spray glue onto backs of holly leaves. Position the larger, pale green leaves first, then the dark green on top, between the pale green leaves. Stationers' self-adhesive spots make red berries. Put on five or so.

The snowman at the window invites us to come outside to play in the snow. Cut off left-hand side of this 3-fold card so that light will shine through window. Cut a piece of film slightly smaller than folded card. Draw snowman and trees on to paper to fit between window bars. Place paper under film and on right side draw outline of snowman and trees with silver pen.

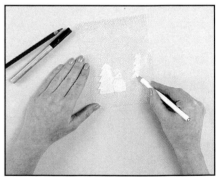

Turn over film and colour in trees and snowman using a white chinagraph pencil.

Turn back film onto right side and draw in scarf and nose with a red chinagraph pencil. Add face details in silver. Attach film to inside of card with double-sided tape and place a silver star where it can be seen shining through window.

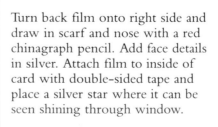

Cut glossy red card 18 by 23cm (7 by 9in), score and fold 11.5cm (4½in) across. Cut on bias four strips of Christmas fabrics 2.5 by 30cm (1 by 12in) long. Fold strips lengthways, machine 3mm (⅛in) seam allowance. Leave length of thread at end, thread with bodkin and knot. Thread bodkin back through tube with damp fingers.

Cut card 23 by 18cm (9 by 7in), score 11.5cm (4½in) and fold along top. Trace out template *41* and transfer onto thin card to make template. Place on polystyrene wallpaper and draw round with a soft pencil. Cut out with craft knife. Cut out ice caps and ground from iridescent plastic or silver paper.

Thread length of double wool through each tube. Pin ends of tubes to a firm surface. Plait by laying four strands over left hand, take left strand over two middle strands and right strand over one. Continue to end. Ease into a circle, cross over ends and sew through to secure. Trim and finish with a bow.

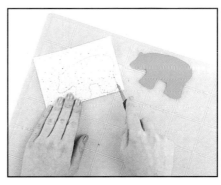

Glue down mountains, ground and polar bear, placing the latter in front of peaks. Glue on silver sequin stars.

Bind trimmed ends with embroidery cotton, tie a knot and trim. Draw an arched border (see page 61) using a gold pen. Centre finished wreath and pierce through card with a thick needle or point of dividers. Sew through from back of card, knot thread, trim and finish with dot of glue to hold firm.

With a silver pen, draw in polar bear's features: legs, paws and ears. The polar bear could also be made from white felt.

Cut card 18 by 23cm (7 by 9in). Score and fold 11.5cm (4½in). Draw border in silver pen around card. Trace off template *26* and transfer onto thin card. Draw round template onto red felt using a water-soluble pen. It is not easy to mark sequin waste so hold template in place and cut round it.

Sew sequin waste to felt by hand or machine, then trim both layers neatly.

Glue stocking to card, then add the little pony eraser or another small gift that can be glued on. Draw holly and berries using felt-tipped pens. You could also add beads and sequins if you wish.

Cut card 15 by 22cm (6 by 8½in), score and fold 11cm (4¼in) along top. Mark centre top of the card with pencil dot. Cut triangle from sequin waste, place on card and mark two sides at bottom of tree. Glue along edges of tree and hold in place on card until glue dries. Any residue glue can be rubbed away when it is dry.

Cut a base for the tree from a piece of card or paper. Curl over scissors a number of narrow pieces of ribbon cut about 9.5cm (3¾in) long.

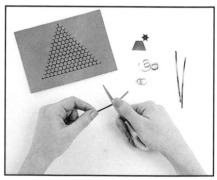

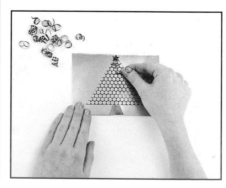

Glue on base and add sequin star to top of tree. Slip curled ribbons through every other hole in sequin waste and every other row, starting at top of tree. No need to tie them; they will stay in place. You will need to deliver this card by hand or use a box.

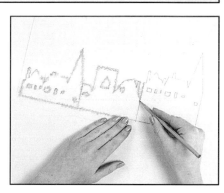

On red fabric draw in pencil four 9cm (3½in) squares and cut out. Fold in 6mm (¼in) seam allowance and press. Find centre of square by folding diagonally each way and mark with tip of iron. Fold down one corner to this mark and pin. Continue with other corners to make a square. Catch centre points with a small stitch. Fold in again and sew. Complete all four squares.

Cut four 2cm (¾in) squares from fir-tree fabric. Place two red squares right sides together and sew down one side to make a double square. Pin fir-tree patch diagonally over seam on right side and curl back folded edges surrounding patch. Slip stitch to hold in place. Repeat to make another double square.

This card could be used for the New Year or Christmas. You will see from template 28 that only two sides of the 3-sided card are shown. The left-hand portion is a repeat of the right but with 7cm (2¾in) added to the bottom, so it stands taller. Trace out template adding extra section to make left-hand part of card. Rub soft pencil over back of tracing.

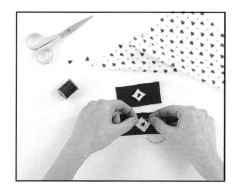

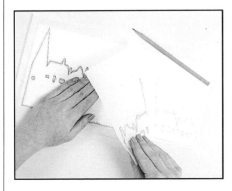

Cut a piece of white card 33 by 15cm (13 by 6in), lay tracing over right side up, lining up lower edges, hold in place with masking tape and draw over outline to transfer drawing.

Sew double squares together and place third and fourth fir-tree patches over seams. Sew tiny beads in corners of 'windows'. Cut card 25 by 18cm (10 by 7in), score and fold 12.5cm (5in). Mark top centre and sides 6cm (2½in) down with pencil. Cut through card to form a point. Glue finished square centred horizontally onto card. Add gold border.

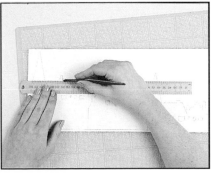

Use a ruler to help keep lines straight and cut out. Score and fold into sections. Trim lower edge and 1mm (¹/₁₆ in) from one side of card so that it will fold flat. You will need an extra piece of card in the envelope to protect the points.

# A CHRISTMAS FIR

# CANDLELIT CHRISTMAS TREE

**C**ut card 15 by 20cm (6 by 8in) and score down centre. Trace template *33*, transfer onto thin card and draw round on green card. Cut out using craft knife. Set your sewing machine to a fairly wide satin stitch. Sew moving card from side to side to form garlands. Pull threads through to back, tie off with knot and finish with dab of glue.

Stick on self-adhesive spots to resemble Christmas tree balls. Cut narrow satin ribbon into 14 1cm (½in) pieces.

**A** simple, easily-made card in unusual colours for Christmas. Cut card 11 by 20cm (4¼ by 8in), score and fold 10cm (4in). The fold is at the top of card. Cut a strip of green plastic from an old shopping bag. Tear four strips of tissue in shades of orange and yellow. The fir-tree is from a strip of self-adhesive 'stickers'.

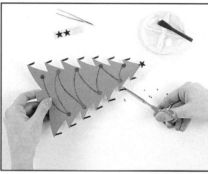

Glue them in place at end of branches on back of card. Tweezers will help you to hold them steady. Leave until glue dries. Cut tops diagonally to look like candles. Add the finishing touch — a red star on top of tree.

Arrange strips so that colours overlap and produce new colours and tones. Stick down tree. Spray glue onto back of strips and stick down.

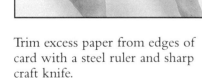

Trim excess paper from edges of card with a steel ruler and sharp craft knife.

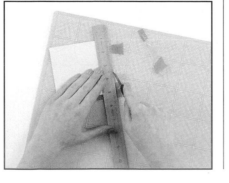

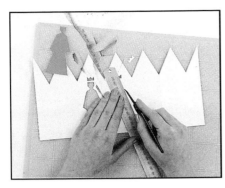

Cut gold card 30 by 15cm (12 by 6in) and score twice 7.5cm (3in) in from each side. Trace out template *25* and carefully work out where the points will fall. Mark design on back of gold card and cut out using a sharp craft knife and ruler for straight edges.

Burnish edges of gold card with the back of your thumbnail if they have lifted. Cut kings' clothes from three pieces of brocade, slightly larger than apertures. Place small pieces of double-sided tape around kings on inside of card and stick brocade in place.

Cut kings' gifts from gold card and glue in place. Attach sequins to points of their crowns. Stick on white card to cover back of centre panel. To protect the points, slip a further piece of card into the envelope. The three kings which have been cut out could be used for a further card, gift tag, or stencil.

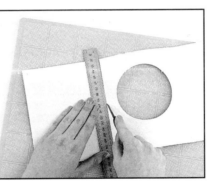

New Year celebrations are particularly associated with Scotland. So here, in traditional Scottish style, we have tartan and golden bells for our New Year greeting. A ready-cut window card was used. Remove left-hand section of 3-fold card with a sharp craft knife and ruler. Use this spare card to make two bells.

Cut a piece of tartan fabric or paper to fit inside back of card, attach with spray glue and trim edges. Trace template *27* and transfer on to spare gold card. Cut out and back with tartan using spray glue. Trim with small scissors. Punch holes in bells.

Make a bow from narrow satin ribbon and cut a length for the bells to hang from. Thread first bell and hold in place with a dab of glue. Thread second bell. Sew through bow and ends of the bell's ribbon to hold in place, glue at top of circular window, so that bells hang free.

A dove of peace for New Year. It is made from a paper doiley with calendar dates falling from its beak. Cut deep blue card 30 by 20cm (12 by 8in), score 15cm (6in) and fold. Draw freehand two curves at top of card to represent clouds and cut with craft knife.

We used a mould from a cake decorating shop and filled it with tiny cake sweets. Cut a 3-fold card 42 by 19cm (16½ by 7½in), score and fold 14cm (5½in). Tape heart to back of tracing paper. Turn over and rub along edge of heart with soft pencil to make template. Line up heart tracing in centre of middle section of card and transfer outline. Cut out with craft knife.

Trace dove template 42 and transfer to thin card to make your own template. Trace out dove onto white paper doiley and cut out, together with dates 1 and 31 from an old calendar. Add a strip of transluscent film waved along upper edge to resemble hills.

Place double-sided tape round heart aperture and around edges of left-hand portion of card, marked with a cross. Remove backing from tape around heart and place mould in position. Press to stick firmly. Put narrow line of double sided-tape around edge of heart.

Spray glue all pieces and place on card together with four star sequins. Using a silver pen, draw line along edge of cloud curves.

Pour sweets into heart until full and pack out with a piece of wadding (batting) cut to heart shape. Take off backing from tape around heart and from left-hand portion of card, fold over card and press down. A pretty pink bow is the finishing touch.

# PETAL VALENTINE

# FABERGÉ EGG

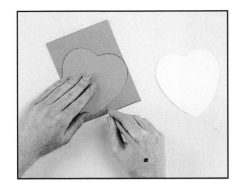

Cut card 22 by 15cm (8½ by 6in) score and fold 11cm (4¼in). Trace out heart 38 and transfer to a thin piece of card to make your own template. Cut out a heart in thin white card. Place template on front of card at a slight angle and draw round in pencil. Cut round pencil line leaving enough uncut at bottom to enable card to stand.

Glue dried flower petals on to white heart working in rows from outside to centre. Use a rubber-based glue; tweezers will help to hold petals steady. Finish with a whole flower in centre.

Cut border from a paper doiley. Spread a thin line of glue on outside of main card heart. Pleat doiley border onto glue all round heart. Stick petal heart over pleated doiley, cover with a piece of clean paper and smooth down. Hold for a minute until glue dries. Lastly stick on Victorian angel motif on top right-hand corner of card.

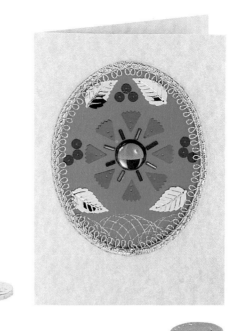

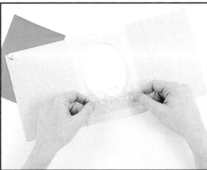

Use a ready-made 3-fold card with oval, egg-shaped window. Place double-sided tape around oval window and edges of inside of card. Peel off backing and attach strip of gold lace to bottom of oval. Cut piece of sumptuous satin slightly larger than aperture, and stick down so that the satin side will show through window.

Glue large, jewel-like bead in centre of 'egg'. Arrange beads, sequin leaves and petals, then glue in position. Tweezers will make it easier to place them accurately.

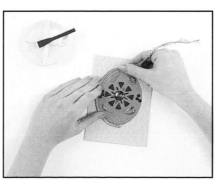

Finish with smear of rubber-based glue around edge of egg on outside of card. Leave for a moment to become tacky, then press down gold braid. Neatly trim end of braid.

A doll's straw bonnet forms the basis of this card and is decorated with spring-coloured ribbons, flowers and a butterfly. Cut card 15 by 22cm (6 by 8½in), score and fold 11cm (4¼in). Cut length of yellow ribbon and cut inverted 'V' shape at ends. Hold in place around hat and sew leaving tails at centre back. Repeat with a length of slightly narrower ribbon.

Trim stems of small fabric flowers and pin in place on ribbon at regular intervals around hat.

Sew flowers in place using double thread. Finish with butterfly at front. Centre bonnet on card and attach by sewing through brim of hat and knotting threads on inside of card. A dab of glue will make knots secure. Arrange ribbons prettily.

A lace sachet of pot pourri could be detached and used later to perfume a drawer. Pot pourri can be bought in a variety of colours and perfumes. Cut card 23 by 18cm (9 by 7in), score and fold 11.5cm (4½in). Cut out two lace flowers, pin together and oversew leaving a gap to fill with pot pourri.

Make a funnel from a piece of paper and fill lace sachet with pot pourri. Oversew to close. Make a bow from narrow satin ribbon and curl ends over scissors.

Cut three tissue paper leaves and glue onto card. Sew bow on to sachet. Using a point of dividers or a thick sharp needle, make two holes at either side of card, for positioning sachet. Sew through and knot on back, securing with a dab of glue.

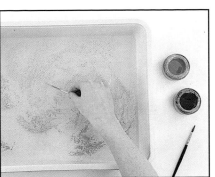

Cut card 22 by 19cm (8½ by 7½in), score and fold 11cm (4¼in) for top. Into a plastic tray put two pints of cold water, mixed with 14g (½oz) of wallpaper paste. Leave for 15 minutes. In a small jar mix 2.5cm (1in) of oil paint from a tube and a little turpentine substitute. Apply drops of the mixed paint onto the surface of the water. Disperse with an orange stick.

Place piece of paper larger than card gently on top of water and remove again fairly quickly, as soon as the paint has taken to surface of paper. Leave to dry on a sheet of newspaper. Press flat, if necessary, when dry. Cut to fit card and glue down.

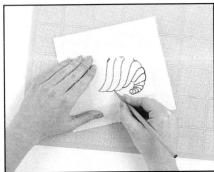

The flowers we used are Victorian scrap or motifs. You could also cut flowers from magazines or old birthday cards. Cut card 25 by 19cm (10 by 7½in), score and fold 12.5cm (5in) for top of card. Trace out template 42. Place tracing over gold card and draw again using a sharp pencil which will indent soft gold card.

Trace out car from a magazine or postcard and transfer to glossy white paper. Cut out and glue down. Trace 'chrome' details on to silver paper or card, cut out and glue in place. Add details with silver pen.

Measure a border around edges of card and mark in pencil. Go over border again in gold pen.

Glue the cornucopia onto the card, then the flowers and fruit tumbling out. Add a white dove.

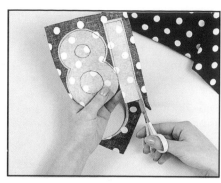

Trace out template *90* onto paper side of bonding web. Cut out just outside pencil outline. Iron onto wrong side of red polka dot fabric and cut out on pencil outline.

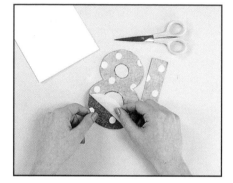

Peel off paper backing to reveal web of glue. Cut a piece of white card 14 by 24cm (5½ by 9½in). Score and fold 12cm (4¾in). Dry iron '18' onto front of card, making sure the '1' is on fold of card. The glue will melt with the heat of the iron. As long as card is not too light, ie, at least 240 gsm (160lb/sq in), the card will not curl.

Open out card and cut round edge of '18' leaving a tiny piece of card to hold together '1' and '8'. When drawing or cutting curves, it is always easier to work towards the body following curve of your hand.

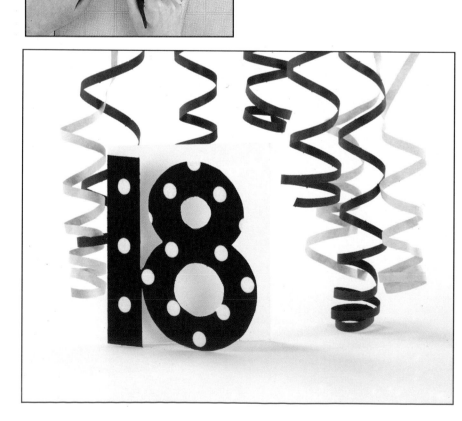

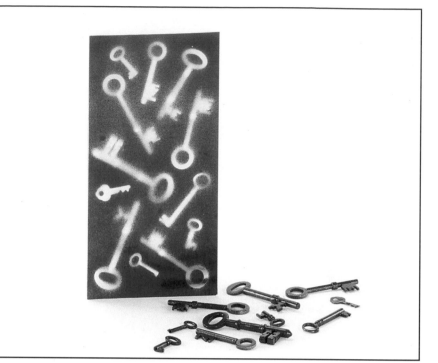

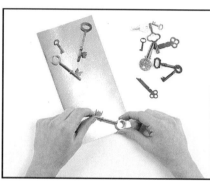

An unusual way to mark a 21st birthday and the traditional receipt of the key of the door. Cut a piece of bright silver card 22 by 22cm (8½ by 8½in) and score fold down the centre. Collect together some interesting shaped keys. Place folded silver card inside and lay keys on card in a pleasing arrangement.

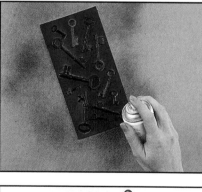

Use spray car paint, holding the can 20-25cm (8-10in) away from card, and spray in a few short bursts to cover the whole card. Allow the first coat to dry for a few minutes and then spray a second coat. To ensure even distribution you should carefully turn the card between coats. You may wish to spray a third coat. Use in a well-ventilated room.

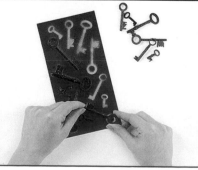

When completely dry, remove keys. You will not be able to get the cellulose paint off the keys easily, so be sure to use keys you no longer need. Other objects, such as old clock and watch parts, can also be used to make theme cards.

ut grey marble-effect card 28 by 19cm (11 by 7½in), score and fold 14cm (5½in). Trace out template 30. Cut piece of silver card to fit, turn over and hold down with masking tape. Place tracing over card and attach with masking tape. Trace through onto card with a sharp pencil. Trace base onto a piece of black card.

With a sharp craft knife, cut out cup and base. Burnish edges of silver card by rubbing gently with the back of your thumbnail.

Cut a circle of card 3cm (1¼in) in radius. Take approximately 1 metre (3ft 2in) of single-sided 2.5cm (1in) wide pink satin ribbon, pleat and machine sew round edge of card circle. Machine an inner circle of pleated blue ribbon. A wide zig-zag stitch will hold pleats in place. Fold ends under to finish. Keep excess lengths of ribbon.

Glue cup onto card with spray glue and draw in details with a sharp hard pencil. Finally, glue on base.

Cut a circle of pink metallic paper or card 2.2cm (⅞in) in radius. Using left-over ribbon, cut two tails, one from each colour and one longer than the other. Cut an inverted 'V' shape at ends.

Cut metallic card 23 by 18cm (9 by 7in), score and fold 11.5cm (4½in). Glue tails in place over ends of pleated ribbon. Glue circle of pink paper or card in centre of rosette. Attach rosette to card with glue.

Cut card 22 by 16cm (8½ by 6¼in), score and fold 11cm (4¼in). Trace out template *34* and transfer to thin card adding 10cm (4in) to depth, to match card. Cut out and place on folded card. Draw round church window shape at top of card and cut through both thicknesses. Draw border with felt-tipped pen using ruler for straight edges.

Place several layers of different shades of pink tissue-paper together in a pile on a cutting board. Cut round template *35* to make approximately 10 hearts.

Cut green card 22 by 15cm (8½ by 6in), score and fold 11cm (4¼in). Cut piece of traditional ledger-look marbled paper 15 by 9cm (6 by 3½in). Cut away top and bottom right-hand corners by measuring 4cm (1½in) along top and right-hand edges and bottom and right-hand edges.

Spray glue hearts and position on card so that they overlap. You could stick more hearts inside card and also leave some loose so that they scatter when card is opened.

Spray glue on back of paper and attach to card so that there is a 2cm (¾in) margin of green card on left-hand side. Punch a hole in centre along right-hand edge of front of card.

Thread a length of brown satin ribbon through hole and tie into a bow.

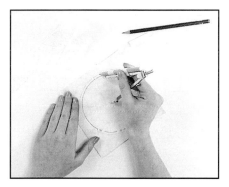

Make your own template from your dove *(37)* and cut an extra template for wing alone (see finished card). Draw round dove twice on dark blue felt so that birds face opposite directions and cut out. Cut two pieces of muslin 18 by 11.5cm (7 by 4½in), position doves between two layers and pin. Tack layers together to hold doves in place.

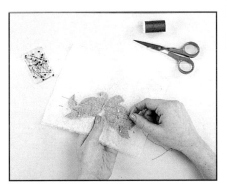

Colours can be matched to those of the bridesmaid's dresses. Cut card 15 by 30cm (6 by 12in), score and fold 15cm (6in). Bind turquoise felt-tipped pen to compass and draw a double circle on centre of card. Sew a line of running stitches along edge of strip of lace half a metre (1ft 6in) in length. Gather into a circle and sew seam.

Using two strands of embroidery thread, sew tiny running stitches around doves and stitch feet (see finished card). Place wing template over doves and lightly draw round with a sharp pencil. Quilt along these lines. When finished, take out tacking thread and lightly press.

Sew ribbon flowers onto centre of lace circle. Cut a strip of flower braid into single flowers and sew around ribbon flowers.

Purchase a 3-fold window card to fit quilted doves. Cut out matching window from left-hand section of card (see page 65). Trim muslin to about 6mm (¼in) larger than window. Check and mark top of window to avoid mounting work upside-down. Stick down using double-sided tape. Add tiny round beads for doves' eyes and pearl beads to corners of window.

Sew on a couple of strings of ribbon flowers or braid to hang from bouquet. Using a sharp needle or compass point, make several holes in card and sew on lace bouquet from back of card using double thread. Tie a knot and add a dab of glue to secure. Glue on satin bows in four corners.

Cut card 45cm by 20cm (18in by 8in). Score and fold at 15cm (6in) and 30cm (12in) to form a 3-fold card. Follow chart on page 167. You may vary the wools and use up odds and ends. Most wool is used double on 12 holes to 2.5cm (1in) canvas. Find centre point of canvas and draw on fireplace design with felt-tipped pens.

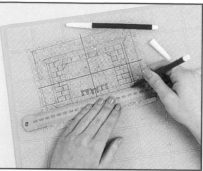

Trace out template *36* and transfer outer balloon onto blue card, inner balloon onto white card and also onto tracing paper side of bonding web. Number each segment and cut out. Mark on blue balloon where inner balloon will fit. Iron balloon segments onto wrong side of three fabrics. Cut out carefully and peel off backing.

Start in centre, working the fire in random long stitch and tent stitch, varying the colours of the flames. Next, work the fire basket in tent stitch.

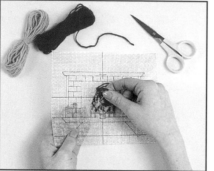

Place balloon segments onto white card balloon and press with a dry iron. Trim edges and using guide on main blue balloon, glue down. Cut a small piece of fabric for basket with pinking shears and glue in place.

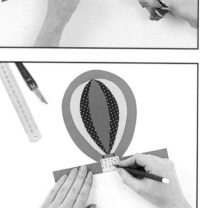

Continue with copper fireguard in slanting satin stitch, fire surround in tent stitch, brickwork in long stitch, carpet in tent stitch and walls in long stitch. For the rug, lay a cocktail stick across canvas and work stitches over stick. Cut loops to make pile. When finished, trim and cut a window in 3-fold card to fit piece. Mount with double-sided tape.

Draw in ropes then basket design on fabric using a brown felt-tipped pen. Score base of balloon where indicated on right side and fold back so that the balloon will stand. If being mailed, this card should have an extra piece of card in the envelope for protection.

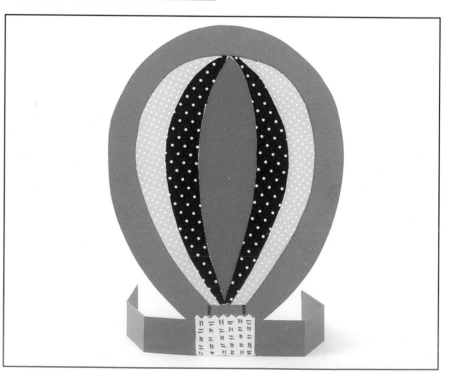

# BABY GIRL IN THE PINK

# BABY BOY BLUE

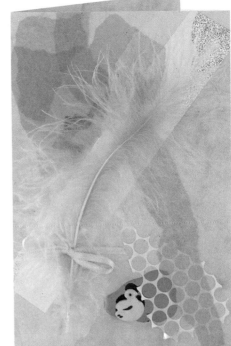

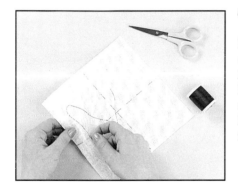

This card is worked in cross-stitch over hardanger fabric, 22 holes to 2.5cm (1in). Use six colours of stranded cotton, two strands thick. Mark centre of fabric by folding in half and running a tacking stitch along fold in both directions through holes. You will find a chart to work from on page 167.

Cut card 23 by 18cm (9 by 7in), score and fold 11.5cm (4½in). This is a spontaneous arrangement, so no two cards will look the same. Lay out a selection of blue materials: ribbon, sequin waste, buttons, feathers, tissue and silver paper. Tear tissue-paper and cut chosen papers into random shapes. When you overlay strips of tissue, more shades of blue will occur.

It is best to work one quadrant at a time, starting at the centre where guidelines cross. Work bottom diagonals of cross-stitch first, then return in opposite direction to form cross. This helps to get an even stitch since the thread tends to wear thin. Do not start with a knot but sew over ends on back as you work. Finish in same way.

Spray glue your materials and place in your favourite arrangement and trim any excess. Tie a bow from narrow satin ribbon onto base of feather and trim ends diagonally. Attach to card by sewing through.

When complete, remove guideline stitches. Press back of work using a pressing cloth and trim. Cut card to frame oval template 40, score and fold in half. Cut oval window in front. Mount work with double-sided tape and back with a piece of white paper to fit. Attach with double-sided tape.

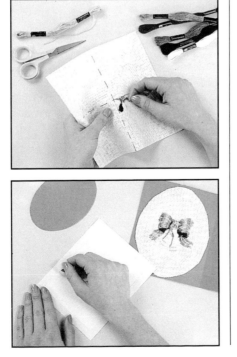

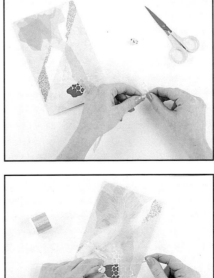

To attach duck button, make two holes with sharp needle or point of dividers, checking which way the button shank lies. Sew on duck button from back using double thread. Finish with a knot and secure with a dab of glue.

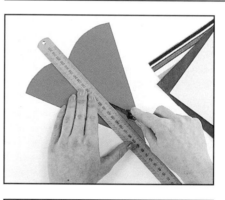

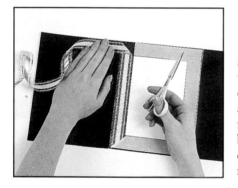

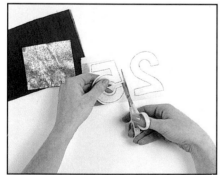

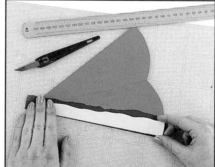

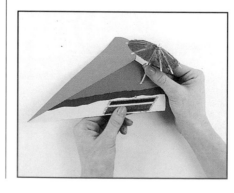

Cut a piece of blue foil card 45 by 20cm (18 by 8in). Score at 15cm (6in) and 30cm (12in) across and fold on outside. Cut out centre window 10 by 15cm (4 by 6in). On outside place double-sided tape around window. Stick down silver ribbon. Mitre corners by folding back ribbon at right-angles and cutting diagonally. Cut next piece of ribbon at same diagonal to fit.

Trace templates 44 and 45 onto paper side of bonding web, then cut out. Iron rough side onto silver lamé and when cool cut out carefully. Peel off tracing paper, turn over and iron onto a piece of silk or satin 11 by 16.5cm (4½ by 6½in), placing numbers so that they overlap.

Set machine to satin stitch and test on spare piece of fabric. Use silver thread on top and polyester thread on bobbin. Use an appliqué or buttonhole foot if you have one. If fabric puckers, place a piece of paper under fabric. When finished knot threads at back. Mount, using double-sided tape and close card.

Idyllic leisure-filled days, beach-combing in yellow sand under blue sky. Trace template 39 and transfer to blue card. Score down centre.

Tear blue tissue-paper to resemble sea. Cut a piece of yellow paper with a curved top edge to make it appear that waves are breaking. Place pieces wrong side up in a spray booth and spray glue. Fix to card and trim to fit.

Cut a piece of striped fabric or paper to make a beachtowel. Draw fringe on towel with a felt-tipped pen. Glue in place. Punch two holes and insert beach umbrella.

A bunch of golden roses to celebrate 50 golden years together. Cut card 16.5 by 25cm (6½ by 10in), score and fold 12.5cm (5in). Find horizontal centre of card and draw a circle with gold pen taped to compass. Cut three 10cm (4in) pieces of gold gift-wrap ribbon and cut ends diagonally to use as leaves.

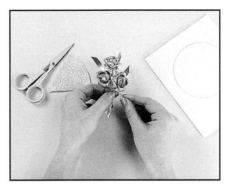

Arrange gold roses with leaves and hold in place by binding together with fine wire. Cut a piece of gold paper in a triangle shape, curving the top.

Cast on 36 stitches and knit in stocking stitch using 4-ply wools, following chart on page 167. Weave different-coloured yarns at back by laying new yarn just under-right-hand needle and looping wool for next stitch around it without making an extra stitch.

Wrap paper around flowers and glue at back to secure. You may like to put a dab of glue to hold roses in place. Apply glue to back of bunch of flowers and stick in place on card. Add golden birds and hearts and a large '50' cake decoration.

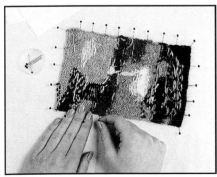

When piece is finished, block it out before pressing on wrong side into a soft surface. Pin all round edges without stretching piece. Press using a damp cloth or steam iron. Leave to settle.

Sew in beak, using yellow wool, and his eye using black wool. Cut card 45 by 20cm (18 by 8in). Score and fold at 15cm (6in) and 30cm (12in) to form 3-fold card. Measure and then cut a window in centre portion. Use double-side tape to attach knitting and close card. Make sure you mount swan the right way up.

# TEMPLATES AND CHARTS

The following templates and charts are for the various boxes described in *Boxes, Bags* and *Envelopes,* one heart–shaped gift wrapping from *Disguises,* and many of the designs from the *Greeting Cards* section. Trace outline onto tracing, greaseproof or layout paper using a sharp pencil, then reverse the paper and draw over the outline again to transfer image onto template card or paper.

Box templates are identified by design name and page number. Draw them carefully, following either the metric or jthe imperial measurements and score along the fold marks (indicated by dotted lines) on the inside of the box with the back of a craft knife or the blunt edge of a pair of scissors. Scale measurements up or down to alter the size of the box. Card templates are identified by a template number only and are given actual size for ease of use. Bold dashed lines usually indicate that only half the template is shown. Charts for four needlepoint card designs are given on page 167.

## Diamonds Are Forever (page 89)

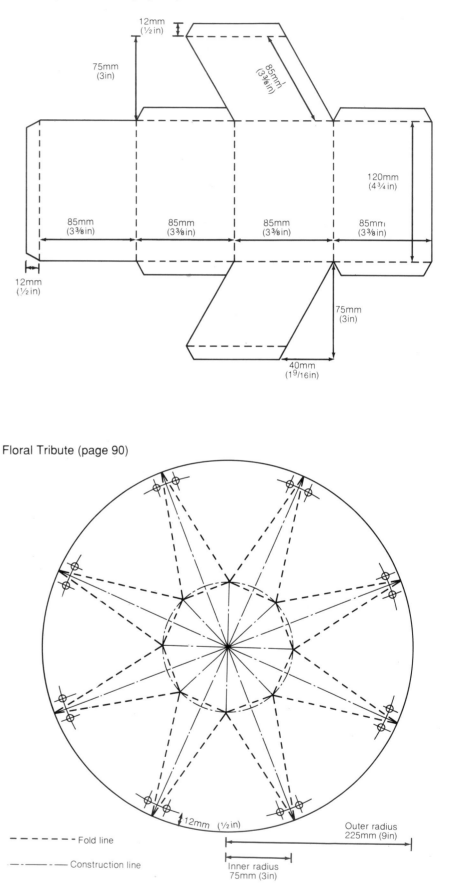

## Squared Up (page 88)

## Floral Tribute (page 90)

## Box Clever (page 88)

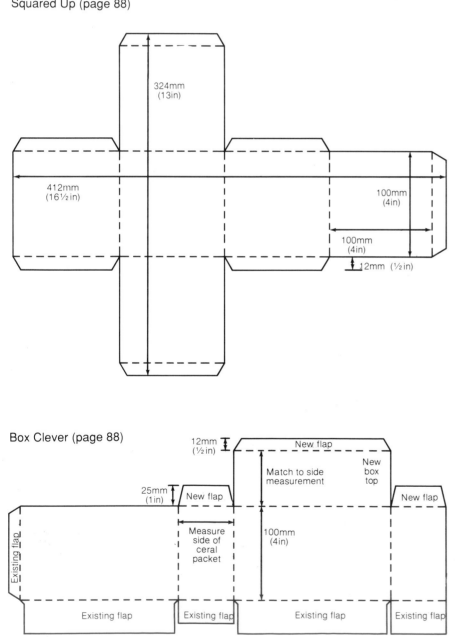

---
160

# BOX TEMPLATES

### Handle with Care (page 90)

### Smart Sachets (page 91)

### The Pyramids (page 92)

### Boxed In (page 93)

### Woven Hearts (page 98)

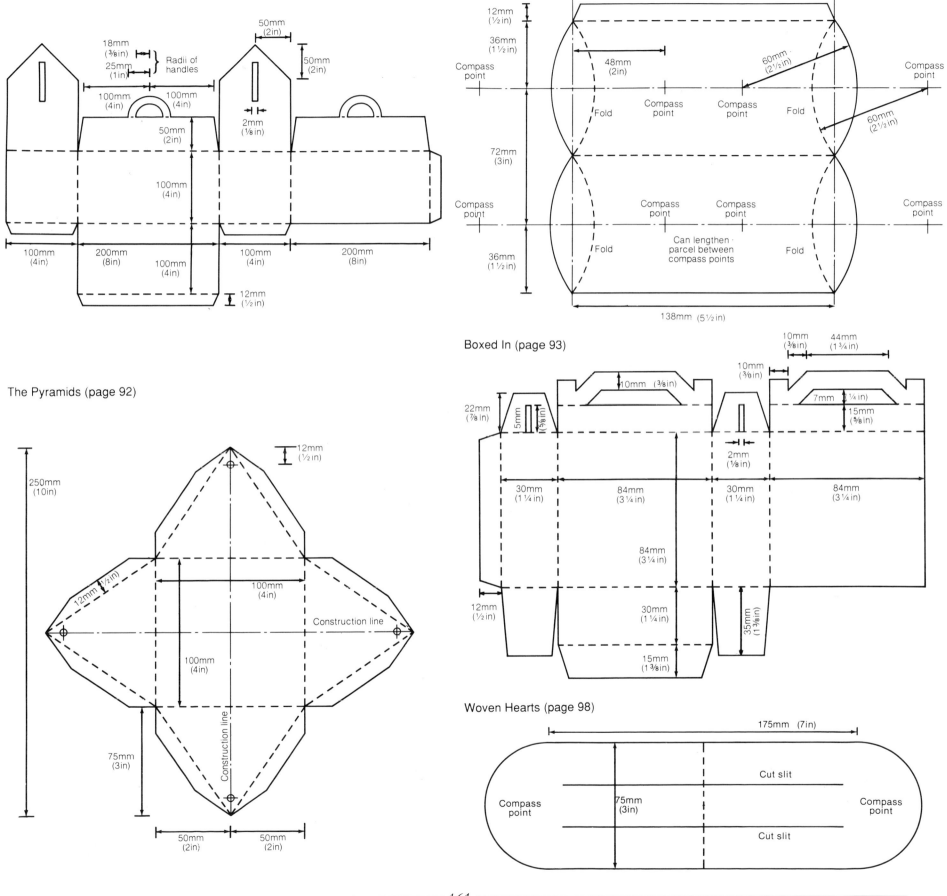

28

30

31

33

29

32

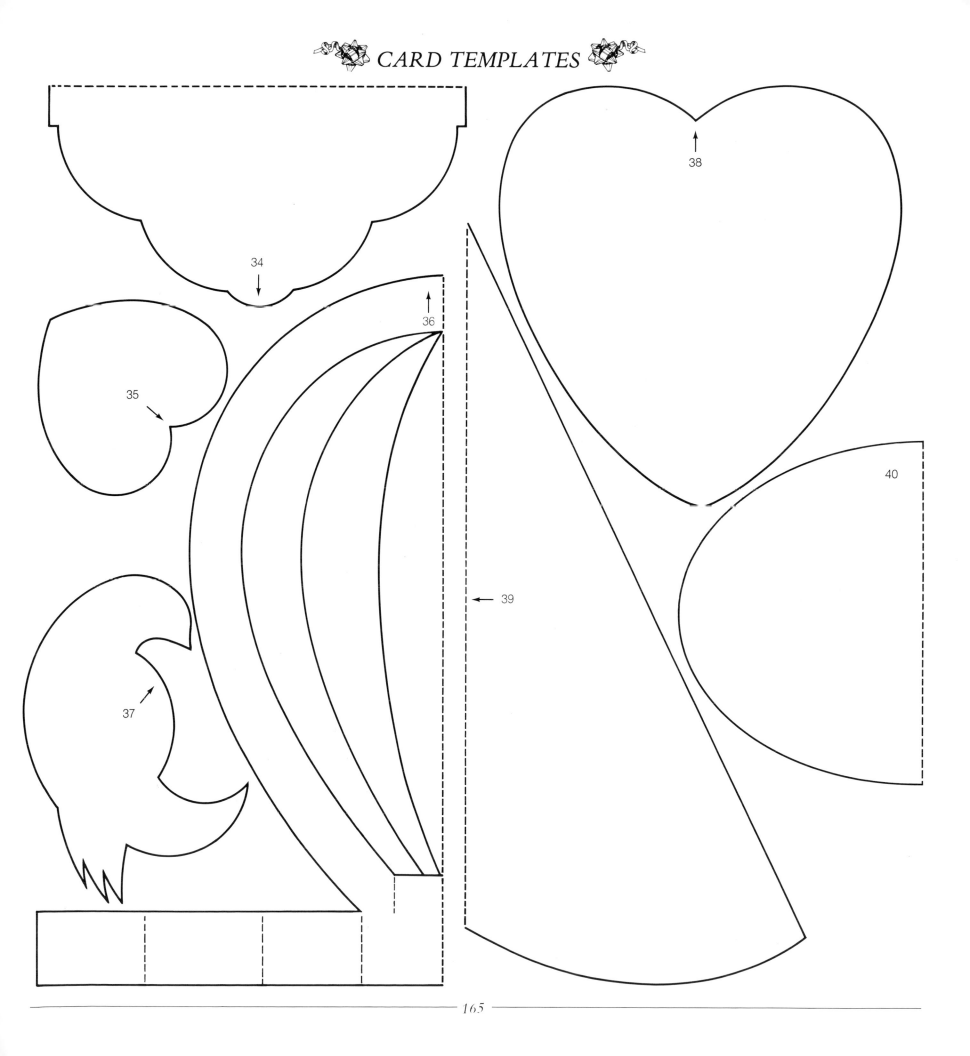

Needlepoint in Lilac (page 127)

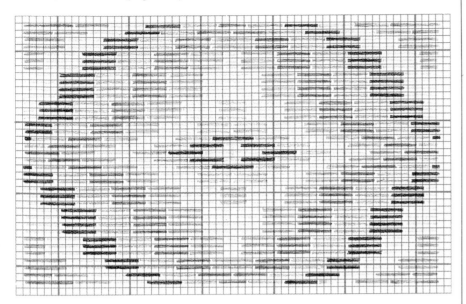

Tranquil Retirement (page 159)

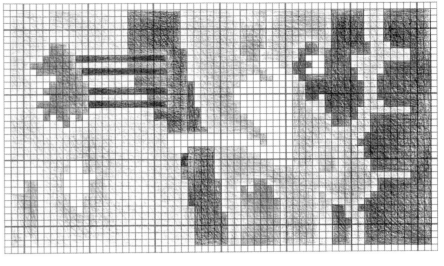

A Warm New Home Welcome (page 156)

Baby Girl in the Pink (page 157)

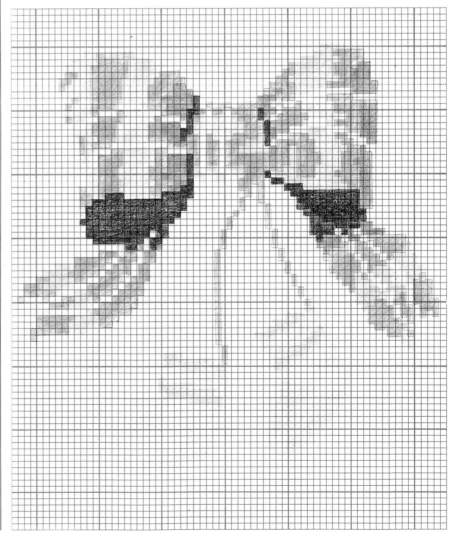

# INDEX